APPLIED DEVELOPMENTAL SCIENCE: GRADUATE TRAINING FOR DIVERSE DISCIPLINES AND EDUCATIONAL SETTINGS

Advances in Applied Developmental Psychology

Irving E. Sigel, Series Editor

Vol. 1 Advances in Applied Developmental Psychology, edited by Irving E. Sigel

Vol. 2 Continuity and Discontinuity of Experience in Child Care, edited by Donald Peters and Susan Kontos

Vol. 3 Parent Education as Early Childhood Intervention: Emerging Directions in Theory, Research and Practice, edited by Douglas R. Powell

Vol. 4 Ethics in Applied Developmental Psychology: Emerging Issues in an Emerging Field, edited by Celia B. Fisher and Warren W. Tryon

Vol. 5 Parent–Child Socialization in Diverse Cultures, edited by Jaipaul L. Roopnarine and D. Bruce Carter

Vol. 6 The Psychological Development of Low Birthweight Children, edited by Sarah L. Friedman and Marian D. Sigman

Vol. 7 Coming Home to Preschool: The Sociocultural Context of Early Education, edited by Richard N. Roberts

Vol. 8 Child Abuse, Child Development, and Social Policy, edited by Dante Cicchetti and Sheree L. Toth

Vol. 9 Two-Generation Programs for Families in Poverty: A New Intervention Strategy, edited by Sheila Smith

Vol. 10 Sibling Relationships: Their Causes and Consequences, edited by Gene H. Brody

Vol. 11 Interacting with Video, edited by Patricia Greenfield and Rodney R. Cocking

Vol. 12 Mastery Motivation: Origins, Conceptualizations, and Applications, edited by Robert H. MacTurk and George A. Morgan

Vol. 13 Applied Developmental Science: Graduate Training for Diverse Disciplines and Educational Settings, edited by Celia B. Fisher, John P. Murray, and Irving E. Sigel

In preparation:

Vol. 14 Caribbean Families: Diversity Among Ethnic Groups, edited by Jaipaul Roopnarine and Janet Brown

APPLIED DEVELOPMENTAL SCIENCE: GRADUATE TRAINING FOR DIVERSE DISCIPLINES AND EDUCATIONAL SETTINGS

ADVANCES IN APPLIED DEVELOPMENTAL PSYCHOLOGY, VOL. 13

Volume Editors:

Celia B. Fisher
Fordham University

John P. Murray
Kansas State University

Irving E. Sigel
Educational Testing Service

Series Editor:

Irving E. Sigel

ABLEX PUBLISHING CORPORATION
NORWOOD, NEW JERSEY

Copyright © 1996 by Ablex Publishing Corporation

All rights reserved. No part of this publication may be reproduced, stored in a retrieval system, or transmitted, in any form or by any means, electronic, mechanical, photocopying, microfilming, recording, or otherwise, without permission of the publisher.

Printed in the United States of America.

ISSN: 0748-8572

Ablex Publishing Corporation
355 Chestnut Street
Norwood, New Jersey 07648

CONTENTS

Preface   vii
   Irving E. Sigel

About the Contributors   xiii

Part I: From Emerging Discipline to Established Discipline

1   Applied Developmental Science Comes of Age   1
   Celia B. Fisher and John P. Murray

2   Applied Developmental Science in Colleges of Human Ecology and Family and Consumer Sciences   23
   John P. Murray

3   Graduate Education in the Applied Developmental Sciences: History and Background   41
   John W. Hagen

Part II: Models of Graduate Education in Applied Developmental Science: Psychology Programs

4   Doctoral Training in Applied Developmental Psychology: Matching Graduate Education, Student Needs, and Career Opportunities   53
   Tara L. Kuther

5   Applied Developmental Science and Training in Pediatric Psychology   75
   Thomas J. Kenny and Donna Chmielewski

6   Integrating Applied Developmental Science and Clinical Child Psychology   91
   Felicisima C. Serafica and Charles Wenar

Part III: Models of Graduate Education in Applied Developmental Science: Multidisciplinary Programs

7   Doctoral Education in Applied Child Development   121
   Donald L. Wertlieb and David Henry Feldman

8 Graduate and Postgraduate Education in the Applications of Development Science to Adult Development and Aging 143
Michael A. Smyer

9 Training Applied Developmental Scientists for Community Outreach: The Michigan State University Model of Integrating Science and Outreach for Children, Youth, and Families 163
Richard M. Lerner, Charles W. Ostrom, Julia R. Miller, James C. Vortruba, Alexander von Eye, Leah Cox Hoopfer, Patterson A. Terry, Carl S. Taylor, Francisco A. Villarruel, and Marvin H. McKinney

Part IV: Special Issues in Applied Developmental Science Education

10 Applied Developmental Science Training Should Be Grounded in a Social–Cultural Framework 189
Irving E. Sigel

11 Field Experiences in Applied Developmental Science 221
George W. Rebok and Anita Miller Sostek

12 Building Successful University–Community Human Service Agency Collaborations 237
Christina J. Groark and Robert B. McCall

13 Birds of a Feather: Administrative Choices and Issues in Creating a Specialized Applied, Multidisciplinary, Developmental Unit 253
Robert B. McCall

Author Index 273

Subject Index 281

PREFACE

Irving E. Sigel

This volume is a first for those interested in graduate education in Applied Developmental Science. The contributors to this volume explore the complexities involved in creating and/or maintaining a graduate program that meets the multilevel goals of understanding social and behavioral science research and discuss how to interpret the research findings in order to use such knowledge to deliver service in a number of different ways.

The challenges for those interested in developing graduate training must begin with a definition of the field of applied developmental science. There are three concepts that need clarification: application, development, and science. This is the first step if we are to achieve a coherent perspective of what is meant by applied developmental science.

The concept of application of research to practice, which at first glance appears to be obvious, is, in fact, not so for the following reasons: (a) the social and behavioral sciences encompass a vast corpus of information collected in different ways, from different places, and from different participants, and (b) investigators address similar problems within the context of differences. For example, a frequently studied problem has to do with intelligence, yet if one were to seek a coherent body of research with minimal equivocation, it would be difficult to find a definitive set of theory and research findings that could be used without careful interpretation. What the practitioner needs to know is how to interpret the findings and, given that, how to devise techniques for application.

Perhaps an example will illustrate the research-interpretation-application sequence. A practitioner (a parent educator) is developing a program for parents to participate in the educational process of their children. There is a body of research literature that shows that parents' reading stories to children has a positive effect on children's intellectual growth and development, which in turn influences school performance. The task for the parent consultant is a complex one because it involves more than just telling the parents what the research shows. So, the first task is to inform the parent of these findings in a comprehensive and enticiing way. If the parents resist, then what? Resistance is not an unreasonable response because the parents may claim they are too busy, or they do not know what books to get, or they have reading problems. The first level of intervention is the introductory level to create a partnership with parents. How this is done is beyond the scope of this preface, except to show how such a seemingly simple task is, in fact, not that simple. This example is one that may or may not be a sensitive one for the parent. The upshot of this discussion is that the generalization obtained from a research study or studies cannot be instantiated by just telling about the finding and letting the parent use that information in any way he or she chooses. This could lead to misinterpretation. Nevertheless, this approach is what professionals often do—give the parents the information and leave the rest up to them. Rather, the practitioners should ask themselves the following types of questions, if the question, for example, is how to stimulate children's cognitive growth: How are the findings to be implemented? How should the parents decide what books to get? How should they read to the child? Does reading to the child require teaching the child to read? Are there any special techniques parents should use while reading to children? Unless applied developmental scientists can deal with practical questions accompanying any recommendations or interventions, chances are the parents will be at a loss as to what to do and how to do it. Or they may know what they want to do but not know how to go about it. The point is, there are techniques that can be used that are research-based to approximate the results; otherwise, dispensing the information cannot be effective. The cardinal principle is that abstractions must go and concrete intervention strategies must be in place to handle the various practical contingencies.

This issue will be addressed throughout the volume as various authors struggle to come to terms with the research practitioner relationship.

Now we come to a more contentious issue—what is development? Again the views are diverse depending on the theoretical position of the researcher. Definitions of development vary greatly from the classical Freudian or Eriksonian perspective, where development is conceptualized in terms of states of object relations or emotional levels, to the linear, accumulative learning models à la Skinner. The Piagetian developmental model is structural, focusing on stages of intellectual development. There are others in the cognitive domain that emphasize skills development. Then there are those like Werner who advocate spiral transformations which move dynamically from the perceptual, concrete way of viewing the world to the conceptual approach.

Since applied psychology in the broadest sense is by no means a novel idea, including developmental science in the family of applied fields follows a tradition long established in the field. However, it may be the case that applied developmental science is unique because of the ubiquitous nature of the term *developmental* as applied to science.

Definition and boundaries of the science of development are a hoary task because the phrase "developmental science" poses a unique juxtaposition of ambiguous terms. Does the fact that "developmental" modifies "science" imply that the interest is in the science of development? The organization of this volume reflects that only in reference to psychology. If it is the case that this science addresses developmental issues, it should in principle cover fields such as genetics, embryology, and neural sciences, because these fields influence child-clinical psychology, behavioral pediatrics, and inheritability of intelligence. From the social sciences, knowledge is derived, for example, from family sociology and anthropology; each is crucial to understanding how social and cultural forces influence the growing child and his or her family. Knowledge from the behavioral fields such as psychology and topics such as emotion, motivation, and learning provide a statement of the psychological process influencing the individual's growth and development. The knowledge to be used in the service of human development (the apparent target of applied developmental science) can be from the biological, social, and behavioral sciences.

Finally, one of the major challenges in programs such as those described in this volume is the translation of research into practice. Here is where the dialogue between researchers and practitioners (in this case, the applied professional) is of vital concern. Each has to understand the workings of the other. How to use research findings in the "real world" is the challenge. It is more than giving information; it is thinking through ways of implementing in concrete, practical terms the translation of an abstract idea into an action.

The use of the term "applied developmental science" obviously creates such a breadth that boundaries need to be set so decisions can be made as to just what particular target of development will be the point of entry into the human development field.

It seems that the focus of this volume is not one of applied developmental science in general, but rather, applied development psychology. A review of the Table of Contents makes this point quite obvious. Even the chapter on "Pediatrics" is pediatric psychology.

We are hopeful that the conception of the application of the knowledge based on the science of development signifies an auspicious beginning awareness that the scientific study of human development can be viewed either from a multidisciplinary perspective (as described above) or from an interdisciplinary perspective. The latter has a long history of efforts with limited success, since the integration of the sciences is at present an ideal, rather than a reality. Perhaps we should be content with a multidisciplinary approach where graduate programs are selective and focus on usable information. Why should a professional applied daycare worker or policy advocate concern himself with the neuroanatomy of brain injury? On the other hand, why should a clinically oriented psychologist concern herself with a family policy on parent involvement in education?

My purpose is to raise some of the issues the reader will encounter in the course of reading this book. The authors have each addressed aspects of the whole. The reader will need to construct the whole in order to carry out the mission of professional training for applied science of development.

In conclusion, the essays in this volume bring together, for the first time, a comprehensive discussion of the field of applied developmental psychology. In the long term it will hopefully evolve as an integrated applied science of development.

The reason to strive for a mutually agreed upon definition of the program is to achieve a good approximation of transnational comparability of the content and the skills the prospective professionals will need. It is a major step for setting up national standards, if, in fact, the long-term aid is to develop a professional discipline. Naive as this may sound, I still believe that in order for the Applied Developmental field to achieve an identity that would distinguish it from other fields of practice, some basic conceptualization is necessary. Since this discipline was initiated by psychologists, there is a pronounced psychological emphasis as evidenced by the chapters in this volume. For a true applied developmental science to evolve, it is necessary for psychologists to give up their pronounced provincialism and be open to a restructuring of their thinking so that they become more inclusive. If this re-thinking could be accomplished, it would generate common levels of discourse that would characterize all professional graduate programs in terms of substantive knowledge, understanding, and interpretation of research and research skills accompanying the interpretation of substantive knowledge. The variations among programs should be due to differences in specialities in the applied field. But, before that time arises, the students should all have a common background in the basic disciplines pertinent to their chosen specialities. Many of the current graduate programs do have a comparable setup where a proseminar is used as the common intellectual base for the student in preparation for a specialization. Achieving a common framework for the field is a challenge because there is little consensus of what boundaries distinguish applied developmental science from any other applied field in the sciences. Applied psychology has had a long and distinguished history and it has been institutionalized in a number of divisions of the American Psychological Association—for example, Industrial and Organizational Psychology, Consumer Psychology, and Engineering. In fact, a *Journal of Applied Developmental Psychology* already exists, and the interest of the American Psychology Association in issues of application had been addressed in the volume, *Exploring Applied Psychology: Origins and Critical Analyses* (Fagan & VandenBos, 1993). The authors represent the five fields of psychology testing, education, industrial organization, psychotherapy, and experimental psychology. Applied Developmental Science or Applied Developmental Psychology is now becoming another distinct field. This volume will help in this process.

ABOUT THE CONTRIBUTORS

Donna Chmielewski, Fellow, Pediatric Psychology, University of Maryland, School of Medicine, Department of Pediatrics, Baltimore, MD 21201

David Henry Feldman, Professor, Eliot-Pearson Department of Child Studies, Tufts University, Medford, MA 02155

Celia B. Fisher, Professor & Director, Doctoral Specialization in Applied Developmental Psychology, Department of Psychology, Dealy Hall, Fordham University, Bronx, NY 10458

Christina Groark, Director, University Center for Social and Urban Research, Office of Child Development, University of Pittsburgh, 121 University Plaza, Pittsburgh, PA 15260

John W. Hagen, Executive Officer, Society for Research in Child Development, Professor and Chair, Developmental Psychology Program, University of Michigan, 10th Level-300N, Ingalls Bldg., Ann Arbor, MI 48109-0406

Leah Cox Hoopfer, Assistant Vice Provost and Program Director, MSU Extension, Michigan State University, East Lansing, MI 48824

Thomas J. Kenny, Professor Emeritus, Department of Pediatrics, University of Maryland, School of Medicine, Baltimore, MD 21201

Tara L. Kuther, Doctoral Candidate, Specialization in Applied Developmental Psychology, Fordham University, Department of Psychology, Dealy Hall, Bronx, NY 10458

Richard M. Lerner, Director, Institute for Children, Youth, & Families, Michigan State University, East Lansing, MI 48824

About the Contributors

Robert B. McCall, Director, University Center for Social and Urban Research, Office of Child Development, University of Pittsburgh, 121 University Plaza, Pittsburgh, PA 15260

Marvin H. McKinney, Visiting Scholar, Institute for Children, Youth, & Families, Program Director of Youth Programs, W.K. Kellogg Foundation, 1 East Michigan Avenue, Battle Creek, MI 49017

Julia R. Miller, Dean, College of Human Ecology, Michigan State University, East Lansing, MI 48824

John P. Murray, Professor and Director, School of Family Studies and Human Services, Kansas State University, Justin Hall, Rm. 303, Manhattan, KS 66506-1403

Charles W. Ostrom, Director for Survey Research Division, Institute for Public Policy & Social Science Research, Michigan State University, East Lansing, MI 48824

George W. Rebok, Associate Professor, Johns Hopkins University, Department of Mental Hygiene, 624 N. Broadway, Baltimore, MD 21205

Felicisima C. Serafica, Associate Professor, Department of Psychology, Ohio State University, 137 Townshend Hall, 1885 Neil Ave. Mall, Columbus, OH 43210-1222

Irving E. Sigel, Senior Scientist, Educational Testing Service, Princeton, NJ 08541

Michael A. Smyer, Dean, Graduate School & Vice President for Research, Boston College, Chestnut Hill, MA 02167

Anita Miller Sostek, Coordinator, Heath Science Administration, NIH, Westwood Bldg., Room 319C, Bethesda, MD 20892

Carl S. Taylor, Director of Community Youth & Development Program, Professor of Family and Child Ecology, Michigan State University, East Lansing, MI 48824

Patterson A. Terry, Community Evaluation Initiative, Michigan State University, East Lansing, MI 48824

Francisco A. Villarruel, Assistant Professor of Family and Child Ecology, Michigan State University, East Lansing, MI 48824

About the Contributors xv

Alexander von Eye, Professor of Psychology, Michigan State University, East Lansing, MI 48824

James C. Vortruba, Vice Provost for University Outreach, Michigan State University, East Lansing, MI 48824

Charles Wenar, Professor Emeritus, Department of Psychology, Ohio State University, 137 Townshend Hall, 1885 Neil Ave. Mall, Columbus, OH 43210-1222

Donald L. Wertlieb, Associate Professor, Eliot-Pearson Department of Child Studies, Tufts University, Medford, MA 02155

PART I
FROM EMERGING DISCIPLINE TO ESTABLISHED DISCIPLINE

1
Applied Developmental Science Comes of Age

Celia B. Fisher
John P. Murray

INTRODUCTION

The past 15 years have seen a sea change in the way developmental scientists view their roles and responsibilities. Economic, social, political, and disciplinary factors have converged to foster increased attention to the social and applied relevance of the developmental empirical database. Scholars engaged in research on developmental processes have begun to shift the focus of their work to applied issues to response to societal demands for greater knowledge about, and techniques for, stemming the tide of psychological risk associated with the poverty, violence, and despair that is increasingly haunting many of our nation's young and old.

Developmental scientists are being called upon to offer practical solutions to many of the societal problems posing risks to the development of adaptive and productive life skills. These problems include increases in the number of: families living in poverty; infants born at developmental risk; adolescents exposed to or engaged in violence, substance abuse, and high-risk sexual activities; adults caring for aged parents; and elders coping with loss of health and social networks.

Growing government fiscal constraints and the public's increased skepticism about the efficiency of federal, state, and community social services have also lead to demands for scientist-professionals who can evaluate the human and economic costs and benefits of social programs. As a consequence, policymakers are increasingly relying on scientists who can design and evaluate institutional and educational programs that will most efficiently and effectively help individuals and families (Fisher & Lerner, 1994; Fisher, Murray, et al., 1993).

Contributions of Applied Developmental Science

The contributions that applied developmental scientists can make to enhance development and prevent developmental problems span a continuum of activities from knowledge-generation to knowledge application (Fisher & Lerner, 1994; Fisher, Murray, et al., 1993; Fisher & Tryon, 1990; Morrison, Lord, & Keating, 1984; Sigel & Cocking, 1980; Zigler & Finn, 1984). On one end of the continuum are scientists who study the applicability of developmental theory to growth and development in natural contexts, or study the causes and consequences of developmental strengths and vulnerabilities of interest to parents, educators, mental health professionals, and policymakers. These applied developmental scientists generate knowledge about the cognitive and social developmental sequelae of social phenomena, such as low infant birthweight, child maltreatment, adolescent health compromising behaviors, and sensory impairment in old age. Contextually relevant research conducted by applied developmental scientists can also lead to modifications in health, education, and government policies. For example, social and health policy can be influenced through the study of phenomena relevant to the cognitive correlates of common illnesses of infancy, children's competence to provide court testimony, the impact of dual worker families on adolescent school achievement, or compensatory skills developed in later life.

A second broad set of applied developmental activities is aimed at assessing and enhancing developmental processes. For example, a developmental perspective on the construction, implementation, and interpretation of assessment instruments can contribute to the appropriate placement and treatment of individuals by providing data on a person's performance with respect to normative developmental levels as well as the continuity and/or predictability of specific abilities over time. Among other areas of societal concern, the developmental perspective on assessment is critical for the evaluation of the needs and abilities of developmentally disabled infants, the understanding of adolescent–parent communication patterns, and for the accurate evaluation of the everyday cognitive abilities of older adults. Applied developmental activities are also relevant to change within social programs servicing individuals living under risk-filled conditions. The design, implementation, and evaluation of interventions aimed at preventing developmental problems can be aimed at teaching parenting skills to adolescent mothers and fathers, helping children avoid crime and confrontations in violent neighborhoods, providing adolescents with knowledge and social skills that can reduce their risk of abusing alcohol or drugs, and helping nursing homes create conditions that increase staff job satisfaction and patient care.

Past and Current Trends in Applied Developmental Science

The current trend toward developmental science applications is in some sense both a return to the social activists roots of child psychology (Rheingold, 1986; Sears, 1975; Siegel & White, 1982; Smuts, 1986; see also Chapters 2 and 3, this volume) and traditions developed in the home economics movement at the turn of the century (Lake Placid Conference on Home Economics, 1901). These early child study and intervention movements arose from two rather different wellsprings of support, but they shared a common source of concern. In the first instance, the child study movement (Chapter 3, this volume), the support and encouragement was provided by private foundations (e.g., Laura Spellman Rockfeller) and government agencies (e.g., the National Research Council of the National Academy of Sciences). In the second instance, the home economics movement (Chapter 2, this volume), the support was largely provided by state universities (e.g., Kansas, Michigan, Iowa) and a different set of government agencies (e.g., the Department of Agriculture, through its state-based Agricultural Experiment Stations and Extension Services). These two movements coalesced in, and were nurtured by, a public sentiment that was expressed in the "child-saving" movement that began in the late 1800s and flowered in the first third of the 20th century (Platt, 1969). For example, it was the child-saving spirit that resulted in the establishment of the first juvenile court, Chicago's Cook County Juvenile Court, in 1899 and the subsequent wave of legislation to control "wayward" children (Murray, 1983).

Nevertheless, these movements parted company when the child study movement turned to more laboratory-based investigations. At the turn of the century, some developmental scholars withdrew from the mission-oriented goals of the child-saving movement out of a concern that applied studies based on this model were too closely aligned with moral issues or assumptions about religious or racial and ethnic values. In an effort to replace religious and racially biased approaches, they embraced more culturally "neutral" or "objective" methods (Youniss, 1990).

By the late 1970s, societal interest in 20th-century laboratory-based information on how individuals change and develop across the lifespan gave rise to renewed interest in the relationship of basic developmental theory and methodology to real-world contexts and problems (Fisher & Brennan, 1992). Developmental scientists began to explore the importance of ecological contexts in human development (e.g., Baltes, Reese, & Lipsitt, 1980; Bronfenbrenner, 1977; Lerner, 1984), to consider social issues as points of departure for developmental theory and research design (Montada & Schmitt, 1982; Scholnick, 1983), to realize the limited application of nondevelopmental pathology conceptualizations to the treatment of children with mental disorders (Cicchetti, 1984; Kendall, Lerner, & Craighead, 1984; Maddux, Roberts, Sledden, & Wright, 1986; Wertlieb, 1983), and to recognize the limited generalizability of developmental theory constructed from research conducted with insufficient numbers of members from low-income or culturally diverse populations (Fisher, 1993; Fisher & Brennan, 1992; Fisher & Tryon, 1990).

In the 1980s, these converging forces culminated in the appearance of edited volumes and training programs bearing the descriptive title of applied developmental psychology or applied human development (Morrison, Lord, & Keating, 1984; Shantz, 1987; Sigel, 1985), and the launching of the *Journal of Applied Developmental Psychology* (Sigel & Cocking, 1980). A decade later, concerns about the application of developmental knowledge to real world problems spawned guidelines for the training and ethical responsibilities of applied developmental scientists (Fisher, 1993; Fisher & Brennan, 1992; Fisher & Koocher, 1990; Fisher & Lerner, 1994; Fisher, Murray, et al., 1993; Fisher & Tryon, 1990).

The process of moving from basic developmental science to applied developmental science posed new challenges for graduate education. The traditional model of doctoral education in the sciences did not provide students with the skills to solve practical problems, nor did it address the complexity of ethical issues that emerge when developmental scientists conduct research or intervene in the lives of vulnerable individuals and their families (Fisher, 1993, in press; Fisher & Brennan, 1992; Fisher & Tryon, 1990). In addition, laboratory-based training did not prepare students in developmental programs for the employment challenges they would face on graduation. For example, starting in the 1970s, societal concerns with the problems of development were paralleled by an increasing shift from the funding of basic science to applied science within federal agencies. At the same time, employment shifts into nonacademic settings were driven by declining college enrollments and the shrinking academic job market (Bevan, 1979, 1980; Boll, 1985; Kiesler, 1979; Klatsky, Alluisi, Cook, Forehand, & Howell, 1985). This meant that the new generation of developmental scientists would need formalized training in skills designed to apply their knowledge to societal problems in nonacademic settings. However, a survey of applied developmental graduate programs in the United States and Canada conducted by Division 7 (Developmental Psychology) of the American

Psychological Association (APA) in the mid-1980s indicated great variability in the extent of applied skills, field experiences, and nonacademic career preparation offered graduate students (Shantz, 1987). At the same time, there were major changes underway in many human science fields that would ultimately force a return to the applied roots of the child study and home economics movements. Chief among these changes was the full flowering of the "lifespan" approach to studying human development. Begun in the 1960s with pioneers such as Paul Baltes, K. Warner Schaie, and Hayne Reese (Baltes, 1968; Baltes, Reese, & Lipsitt, 1980; Baltes, & Schaie, 1973), this approach moved the field beyond childhood and adolescence into an appreciation of the panoply of changes that occur throughout adulthood. Similarly, there was an expanded interest in developmental processes in infancy stimulated, in part, by the work on infant visual perception undertaken by Robert Fantz (1961). This expansion of the traditional child focus to encompass conception to death forced developmental scientists to confront a myriad of issues that had practical significance for daily living. As individual developmental scientists and their academic institutions began to address the concerns of persons at various stages in the lifespan, academics began to restructure the content of the courses taught and the nature of practicum and internship experiences offered to graduate students. It was this changing nature of academic institutions and their developmental science programs that stimulated scientific and professional societies to take a renewed interest in the structure of applied training experiences offered to graduate students.

In 1990, representatives from national organizations[1] concerned with the interface between developmental science and societal needs met to initiate plans to forge a national consensus on issues relevant to graduate education in the applications of developmental science to social problems facing individuals at all points along the life course (Fisher, Murray, et al., 1993). The representatives agreed that the first step toward such a consensus was to bring together leading scientists and professionals to develop and

---

[1] The final consortium of sponsor organizations for the National Task Force on Applied Developmental Science included: the American Psychological Association's [APA] divisions of Developmental Psychology (Division 7), Adult Development and Aging (Division 20), and Child, Youth, and Family Services (Division 37); the Gerontological Society of America; the International Society for Infant Studies; the National Black Child Development Institute; the National Council on Family Relations; the Society for Research on Adolescence; and the Society for Research in Child Development. Major financial support for the conference was provided by the Foundation for Child Development and the William T. Grant Foundation. Generous contributions were also received from the APA Science Directorate, the Jennifer Corn Carter Family Philanthropic Fund, the A.L. Mailman Foundation, Ablex Publishing Corporation, Lawrence Erlbaum Associates, McGraw-Hill College Division, the Psychological Corporation, and Fordham University.

disseminate educational guidelines for graduate programs seeking to educate a new generation of scientist-professionals skilled in the knowledge base and techniques of applied developmental science. The National Task Force on Applied Developmental Science, chaired by Celia Fisher and John Murray, was formed to organize the first national conference on graduate education in applied developmental science, as well as to guide future endeavors in the field. The National Conference on Graduate Education in the Applications of Developmental Science Across the Life Span was convened at Fordham University on October 10–12. The aim of the conference was to create a living document that would outline the curriculum and field experiences necessary to provide students with competencies to conduct applied developmental science activities.

THE NATIONAL CONFERENCE ON GRADUATE EDUCATION IN THE APPLICATIONS OF DEVELOPMENTAL SCIENCE ACROSS THE LIFE SPAN (FISHER, MURRAY, ET AL., 1993)[2]

The Scope of Applied Developmental Science

The first task for conference participants was to define the theoretical and practical framework underlying the applied developmental science perspective. The orientation that emerged from conference discussions emphasized three conjoint aspects of applied developmental science:

- The applied aspect stresses the fact that applied developmental science activities have direct implications for what individuals, families, practitioners, and policymakers do. The goal of applied developmental science is to synthesize knowledge from research and applications to describe, explain, intervene, and provide preventive and enhancing uses of knowledge about human development.
- The developmental aspect of applied developmental science emphasizes a focus on systematic and successive changes within human systems that occur across the life span. This perspective includes the view that individual and family functioning is an interactive product of biological, physical, and social influences continuously evolving and changing over time.

---

[2]This section summarizes the conference proceedings reported in Fisher, C.B. Murray, J.P., Dill, J.R., Hagen, J.W., Hogan, M.J., Lerner, R.M., Rebok, G.W., Sigel, I.E., Sostek, A.M., Smyer, M.A., Spencer, M.B., & Wilcox, B. (1993). The National Conference on Graduate Education in the Applications of Developmental Science Across the Life Span. *Journal of Applied Developmental Psychology, 14,* 1–10.

- The science aspect of applied developmental science stresses the need to utilize a range of research methods to collect reliable and objective information in a systematic manner, to test the validity of theory and application.

The convergence of these three aspects leads to a fostering of the reciprocal relationship between theory and application as a cornerstone of applied developmental science, wherein empirically based theory not only guides intervention strategies, but is influenced by the outcome of these interventions. Of related import is the assumption that valid applications of the developmental science base depend on recognition of the reciprocal nature of person-environment interactions and the influence of individual and cultural diversity on development. This assumption stresses the importance of understanding normative and atypical processes as they emerge within different developmental periods and across diverse physical and cultural settings. Furthermore, it calls for a multidisciplinary perspective aimed at integrating information and skills drawn from relevant biological, social, and behavioral science disciplines.

The Goals of Applied Developmental Science Training

The curriculum that emerged from this perspective was designed to provide students with the competencies to engage in the full spectrum of applied developmental science activities. Applied developmental scientists should be educated to:

- test the validity of developmental theories and professional practices in real world contexts
- investigate the developmental causes, consequences, and correlates of societal problems
- construct, administer, and interpret developmentally and culturally sensitive assessment instruments which can identify protective factors and vulnerabilities of individuals at developmental risk
- design, implement, and evaluate developmental interventions
- disseminate knowledge about developmental processes to professionals and organizations who impact the development of individuals and families at different points along the lifespan.

The Applied Developmental Science Curriculum

To ensure student competencies in these activities, conference participants recommended education in four broad domains:

> *Developmental Theory and Content:* This first domain provides students with substantive expertise in developmental theory and con-

tent, including mechanisms of change and stability in normative and atypical biological, physical, and social processes.

Research Methods: This second domain provides students with the quantitative and qualitative research techniques necessary to evaluate change over time (for both single and multiple units of analysis) and to construct psychometrically sound developmental assessment instruments.

Application Strategies: The third curriculum domain provides students with expertise in application strategies that can directly enhance human development including: individual and family assessments; communication, consultation, and human relation skills; and the ability to design, implement, and evaluate developmental interventions.

Professional Issues: The last domain sensitizes students to the ethical, legal, and professional dimensions necessary to conduct applied research and helps them to understand and assist organizations serving individuals and families from diverse backgrounds with diverse needs, strengths, and vulnerabilities.

Field Experiences

Conferees saw field experiences as an essential core element distinguishing graduate training, with an applied developmental science emphasis, from traditional training in developmental psychology or human development. The field experiential component of applied developmental science education should be designed to provide students with a supervised opportunity to extend their curriculum based knowledge and skills to social problem solving in real-world contexts. Field experiences should provide the opportunity for participation in research, evaluation, service delivery, policy development, or management decision making across a diverse array of settings including schools, departments of human services, correctional facilities, senior centers, health facilities, the media, policymaking units, governmental agencies, and private corporations. As discussed in Chapters 4 and 11, a primary goal of applied developmental science field placements is to enable the student to integrate his or her scientific expertise (e.g., research, test construction, and/or program evaluation skills) into the everyday activities of the field site. Examples of how this may be accomplished include conducting a needs analysis with family members and staff of a nursing home, constructing a test to measure parent–child communication in abusive families in a women's shelter, and/or evaluating the efficacy of an ongoing social service program.

Because field experiences will be conducted outside the university setting, the conferees emphasized the importance of establishing a clear working plan, carefully delineating the roles and relationship between the on-site supervisor and supervising faculty member, and explicitly defining and communicating the nature of the student evaluation procedures to be used. Chapter 11 discusses the unique challenges for programs offering applied developmental science field experiences, including questions concerning the administrative status, disciplinary affiliation, and research expertise of on-site supervisors.

STRUCTURAL ISSUES IN APPLIED DEVELOPMENTAL SCIENCE

University–Community Collaborations

As we move into the 21st century, applied developmental scientists will be addressing issues intimately tied to the hopes and dreams for the future that individuals hold for themselves and for the growth and development of their children. The developmental impact of social policies aimed at the delivery of health care services, environmental quality, social security benefits, education, and employment opportunities, are just some of the critical issues which will require applied developmental science expertise in the decades to come. The nature and the solutions to these problems will vary across geographically, economically, and culturally diverse communities (Lerner & Fisher, 1994). To help communities meet these challenges, applied developmental scientists will have to seek the collaboration of community members in understanding the forces that shape their development and their particular developmental goals. Applied developmental science programs must, therefore, train their graduates to become members of "community coalitions," teams of scientists and citizens collaborating to address problems faced by individuals of varying ages, economic levels, and racial, cultural and religious backgrounds as they are expressed in particular community settings (Lerner & Fisher, 1994).

Establishing university–community collaborations requires the development of a shared understanding of the differing, yet interconnected, missions of universities and community settings. For universities, the mission is to provide training experiences that will equip the next generation of professionals to address the developmental needs of society. For community organizations, the mission is to provide the services that are needed for today, not tomorrow, or in the next generation. These are not minor definitions in mission; they can have major negative implications for the collaboration if they are not clearly understood at the outset.

However, having highlighted the obvious differences in the missions of universities and community organizations where students can obtain practical field experiences, it should be noted that there are many points of convergence. As noted in Chapter 12, planning and forethought about the nature of the collaboration will yield dividends in a smooth collaboration. It is important that the university faculty and students demonstrate respect for the skills of agency staff and select a mutually beneficial project that will provide the agency with valuable information addressed to their goals and needs. In addition, successful collaborations require focused communication handled by a thoughtful, designated liaison person who is proactive in addressing issues and avoiding conflicts. To the extent that the liaison can help identify the common purpose for both parties, providing leadership and consistent monitoring of the project, collaboration will be effective and likely renewable.

In experiences at universities and in programs that have a tradition of field placements at both graduate and undergraduate levels (see Chapters 2 and 11, this volume), it is clear that field experience is a defining feature of applied programs. Students often remember this experience as the most significant aspect of their program. Indeed, the field placement should be the most memorable experience, as it is the vehicle for applying theories of research reviewed in more didactic settings. Also, we have found (Chapters 2 and 4, this volume) that the field experience should include both on-site supervision at the agency and a professional seminar at the university. The professional seminar allows students to share their experiences at various field sites and begin to understand some of the organizational dynamics of various agencies and the strategies for delivery of professional services that are common across sites.

Multicultural Aspects of Applied Developmental Science Training

One of the special advantages of the proposed restructuring of graduate education in the human sciences to establish an interdisciplinary focus on applied developmental science is the possibility that such programs may be more attractive to students drawn from underrepresented groups in the social and behavioral sciences (APA, 1995). Although it is not certain that this change in educational structure will lead to increased minority representation, at least the possibility exists because applied developmental science focuses upon the improvement of well-being and, as such, it addresses many of the issues of concern to members of underrepresented groups in higher education.

So too applied developmental science may be more hospitable to diverse populations of students because it has more "authentic" connections to such groups. For example, as noted in Chapter 10, the labels applied to the poor and underclass have "shifted from culturally deprived to culturally disadvantaged to minorities—each change attempting to eliminate terms deemed to be derogatory. However, to my knowledge none of these labels has come from the groups themselves, but rather are a reaction to the White establishment's designations" (Sigel, Chapter 10, this volume). As noted in recent surveys of graduate students in psychology (APA, 1995), although there is an increase in ethnic minority undergraduates, a comparable increase in psychology graduate students has not been seen. Nevertheless, the goal remains clear: Greater representation of minorities must be achieved if we are to address the broad issues of human well-being in a diverse society.

DISCIPLINARY AND MULTIDISCIPLINARY EMPHASES IN APPLIED DEVELOPMENTAL SCIENCE TRAINING

The applied developmental emphasis on person–environment interactions implies that graduate education in applied developmental science will be conducted across a variety of disciplines and subdisciplines (e.g., psychology, human development, gerontology, pediatrics) and educational settings (e.g., psychology departments, schools of education, child development centers, schools of human ecology). Programs may train students to understand and intervene in developmental processes by targeting different levels of human systems analysis, for example, biological, individual, small group, organizational, or community development. They may also vary in the human–environment contexts targeted for investigation and intervention, for example, physical-ecological, cultural, economic, political-legal, or historical levels of analysis (Fisher, Murray et al., 1993). Accordingly, program curricula will differ in how the five core educational areas proposed by the National Conference (Fisher, Murray et al., 1993) are translated into an understanding of human development in context. To insure that graduate training can produce students competent to function scientifically and professionally within their chosen career path, programs must clearly identify the disciplinary or multidisciplinary model and goals of training, along with the abilities and skills required to meet these goals.

Chapters 4 through 9 provide examples of how six different programs have incorporated an applied developmental science perspective into their curricula. In planning an ADS curriculum, faculty must consider the program, departmental, university, and community resources available to provide adequate didactic and experiential training, the range of applied developmental activities for which students will be trained, and how these resources can meet student career goals and opportunities (Fisher, Rau, & Colapietro, 1993). How this is accomplished will vary among applied developmental science programs as a function of a program's disciplinary affiliation, faculty expertise, university support, and available field settings. Programs described in Chapters 4, 5, and 6 are housed in psychology departments and face special challenges with respect to their relationship to traditional fields and specializations in psychology. Programs described in Chapters 7, 8, and 9, as well as the broad program description in Chapter 2, represent departments, schools, or free-standing units that involve faculty drawn from a wide range of disciplines. In the next section we review some of the issues facing psychology and multidisciplinary programs.

Applied Developmental Science Education within Departments of Psychology

Applied developmental science programs housed in departments of psychology may label themselves as applied developmental psychology (ADP) programs to identify their affiliation with the field of developmental psychology and the discipline of psychology. Faculty forming ADP programs encounter several issues related to their identification with the discipline of psychology: (a) the relationship of ADP to traditional developmental psychology, (b) the distinction between ADP and other applied psychology specializations, (c) and the relationship of ADP to the discipline and professional practice of psychology (Fisher, Rau, & Colapietro, 1993).

ADP and traditional developmental psychology

As illustrated in several chapters in this and previous volumes in the *Advances in Applied Developmental Psychology* series (Youniss, 1990; Chapters 2, 3, 7, this volume), the relationship of developmental psychology to application has a long and tumultuous history. Although the activities of basic and applied developmental psychologists fall on a continuum of contributions to knowledge generation and knowledge application (Fisher & Brennan, 1992; Fisher & Tryon, 1990; Morrison, Lord, & Keating, 1984), adherence to a false dichotomy between basic and action research has, over the years, contributed to faulty application of either acontextual laboratory based data or empirically unsubstantiated culturally value-laden assumptions to real-world developmental problems. The dangers of this false basic-applied dichotomy were succinctly identified by Urie Bronfenbrenner (1979) when he lamented on developmental psychology's positioning itself between a rock and a soft place. The goal of applied developmental psychology programs is to integrate elements of experimental control with elements of social concern to provide empirically based solutions to social problems.

Applied developmental psychologists recognize that their contribution to addressing social problems rests, in part, on their expertise in the theories, procedures, and knowledge base of traditional developmental psychology, with emphasis on the centrality of person–environment interactions in shaping developmental phenomena (Fisher & Brennan, 1992; Fisher & Tryon, 1990; Morrison et al., 1984). Traditional developmental psychology has made important contributions to enhancing our knowledge and demystifying the process of development as it emerges over the lifespan. The theory and methodology of traditional developmental psychology thus provides a critical foundation upon which applied developmental psychology must be built. At the same time, the traditional laboratory approach does not prepare students for the complexity of scientific, practical, and sociopolitical challenges that emerge when developmental theory and methodology are applied to real-world problems in arenas outside the laboratory, nor does a strictly theory orientation have any significant utility in the service arena (Chapter 5, this volume).

In creating training programs for applied developmental psychologists, faculty must address whether ADP is an independent or subspecialty of traditional developmental psychology. In many ADP programs, like that offered at Fordham University (Chapter 4, this volume; Fisher, Rau, & Colapietro, 1993), there is a desire to preserve and build on the contributions of basic developmental science theory and methods, as well as to provide students with their historic identities as developmental psychologists. Accordingly, these programs offer applied developmental psychology as a specialization in developmental psychology programs.

These programs recognize that although traditional developmental programs can include a formal focus on contextually relevant factors, such as ecological research and cultural diversity, the signature of applied developmental education is training in specific techniques (e.g., developmental assessment, program evaluation, consultation) and professional issues outside the scope of basic developmental science education. Thus, in addition to training students in basic developmental theory, content, and methodology, applied developmental specialization programs prepare students through both course work and field experiences to: (a) test the validity of developmental theory in real-world contexts; (b) understand the nature of sociocultural institutions that impact the lives of individuals and families; (c) recognize individual and cultural variation in developmental patterns and in response to research protocols and planned interventions; (d) construct, administer, and interpret developmentally and culturally sensitive instruments for evaluating the strengths, vulnerabilities, and protective factors within individuals and families; (e) design, implement, and evaluate interventions aimed at enhancing development across different points along the life course; (f) disseminate knowledge about developmental processes to parents, practitioners, and policymakers; and (g) respond to the unique ethical issues encountered when one applies the developmental science base to social problems (Fisher, Rau, Colapietro, 1993, p. 292).

ADP and other psychology specializations

Unlike their human development program counterparts, applied developmental psychology programs grant degrees in a discipline historically characterized by turf battles between various applied specialties. In the most positive sense, these battles focus on providing students with competencies that will protect the public from services rendered by incompetent professionals; in its least attractive aspects, such territoriality focuses on marketplace competition and can deprive the public of a diverse array of theoretical and methodological approaches to promoting and enhancing psychological adaptation, impeding innovation and the emergence of new and important fields (Fisher & Koocher, 1990; Chapters 4, 5, and 6, this volume).

ADP shares with other applied psychologies the goal of optimizing human functioning and adaptation. However, just as traditional developmental psychologists are unprepared in the skills needed for assessment and intervention, traditional clinical, counseling, and school psychology are unprepared to deal with developmental challenges facing normative and at-risk populations. Applied developmental psychology thus differs from, and complements, these other psychology models in its combined emphasis on: (a) developmental processes; (b) the interactive and continuously changing influences of biology, physical, and social environments on individual and family functioning; (c) a concentration on differences within, as well as between, individuals as they evolve over time; (d) an understanding of adaptive and maladaptive behaviors based on normative, rather than deviant, developmental patterns; and (e) a focus on scientifically based enhancing and preventing intervention for low and high-risk populations, rather than direct delivery of remediative interventions for impaired populations (Fisher, Rau, & Colapietro, 1993; Chapters 4, 5, and 6, this volume). It is important that ADP programs stress these differences so that students can maintain an identity and maintain boundaries of competence.

As described in Chapters 5 and 6, in some pediatric and child clinical programs, such as those offered at the Baltimore campus of the University of Maryland and at Ohio State University, respectively, there will be a blending of ADP with more traditional applied psychology. Students trained in this perspective focus on contributions from developmental science that can improve their ability to diagnose and provide remediative interventions to infants and children suffering from psychologically impairing developmental disorders. However, as indicated in these chapters, pediatric and child clinical psychologists continue to struggle to achieve acceptance and incorporation of applied developmental training in their programs. Because ADP programs can vary in their clinical versus preventive focus, it is important that programs label their offerings accurately so that students are knowledgeable about the type of approach and techniques that they will be trained and qualified to offer following graduation.

ADP and the professional practice of psychology?

In addition to understanding their roots in traditional developmental psychology and their separate identities from other applied psychology specializations, applied developmental psychologists also need to identify with their parent discipline of psychology. This means that in addition to basic and applied developmental knowledge and methodologies, applied developmental psychology students need to be trained in the core knowledge base of psychology. This core includes didactic training in: the history and systems of psychology; biological, cognitive-affective, and social bases of behavior; psychological research design; individual differences; psychological measurement; and ethical principles and professional standards of the American Psychological Association. Although some of this information will be covered in developmentally oriented coursework, students in ADP programs need to have a greater breadth in general psychology than students in traditional developmental research programs. Such breadth will enhance their ability to understand and intervene in problems relevant to psychological development and to forge partnerships with professionals from other applied psychology specializations.

Another important issue for faculty offering applied developmental psychology programs is the eligibility of their students for state licensure and credentialing as psychologists (see Fisher & Koocher, 1990, for an extended discussion of licensure and accreditation in applied developmental psychology). The purpose of licensure is twofold: (a) to ensure the public that psychologists who offer services that directly impact their lives have demonstrated competence in the knowledge base and techniques of the profession; and (b) that these individuals are subject to state codes of conduct and disciplinary procedures if these codes are violated.

Licensure in psychology is important for applied developmental psychologists whose activities may directly affect the lives of individual children, adolescents, older adults and/or their families (Fisher & Koocher, 1990; Fisher, Rau, & Colapietro, 1993; Koocher, 1990; Scarr, 1990). For example, some applied developmental psychologists provide developmental assessments of infants, children, adolescents, or older adults for institutional placement. Graduates of applied developmental psychology programs may be called upon to evaluate parenting skills or provide preventive interventions that impact the lives of individuals and their families, for example, social skills training for institutionalized elderly, programs to prevent the development of health comprising behaviors in adolescents, and parenting skills for mothers and fathers of developmentally disabled children. In such circumstances, professional licensure in psychology is appropriate because it has a direct impact on members of the public. In addition, in many nonacademic settings in which applied developmental psychologists work (e.g., hospitals, social service agencies), credentialing in psychology is an important aspect of salaries and promotional opportunities. Some faculty, like that at Fordham University, strongly feel that if a program is committed to training students to solve real-world problems it should be equally committed to providing students with the opportunity to conduct their work as equals in the applied psychology marketplace (Fisher & Koocher, 1990; Fisher, Rau, & Colapietro, 1993; Chapter 4, this volume). Program commitment to licensure eligibility for students requires faculty to become knowledgeable about their state licensing requirements as they pertain to curriculum content, practica, and predoctoral and postdoctoral supervised experience. In some states, licensure is restricted to graduates of clinical, counseling, and school psychology programs, and in these states applied developmental psychology students may be ineligible for licensure in the state which granted their degree. It is of utmost importance that programs clarify for students at the time of admission, the range of applied developmental activities that might require licensure, whether the program curriculum meets the educational requirements for state licensure, and the feasibility and availability of supervised postdoctoral experiences which will meet state licensure requirements.

Applied Developmental Science Education within Multidisciplinary Programs

The origins of multidisciplinary programs in child and family development can be found in the home economics movement, which began as part of the land-grant university system in the late 1800s. The first such university, Kansas State University, was established in 1863. The precursor of home economics, "The Women's Course" or domestic science, was established at Kansas State University in 1873. Similar domestic science or domestic arts courses were established at many land-grant universities in the late 1800s these courses raised concern about the establishment of a cohesive field of scientific and professional inquiry by the turn of the century. The organizing principle and the principal organizer resided in a charismatic leader, Ellen S. Richards, a professor at the Massachusetts Institute of Technology. Dr. Richards was interested in water quality and the transmission of disease in humans, and was greatly touched by the plight of Irish immigrants who settled in the slums of Boston in the late 1800s. From this very focused concern about disease in very poor families, Dr. Richards evolved a broad concept of an integrated, holistic science of the home. It was Dr. Richards who convened the program of conferences that helped to define the field of home economics, "The Lake Placid Conferences on Home Economics."

The Lake Placid Conferences began in 1899 and continued annually for 10 years. During that period of time, the number of universities offering programs in home economics or domestic science expanded exponentially.

These were largely land-grant universities that were founded as the "people's university" under legislation signed by President Abraham Lincoln in 1862. This charter provided a grant of free land to any state or territory that would set aside funds to build a university to promote practical education of the industrial classes by teaching agriculture and the mechanic arts without excluding other scientific and classical studies (Rasmussen, 1989).

These land-grant universities, which began with what is now Kansas State University in 1863, followed by Michigan State University in 1965, have now grown to a collection of over 80 state universities throughout the United States. In addition to what became known as the "1860s" universities, about 20 "1890s" universities, which were historically Black colleges, were added. In 1994, Congress added the "1990s" universities, consisting of Native American Colleges and Tribal Institutions.

Each of the land-grant programs has a mandate to foster teaching, research, and outreach in the service of the communities in which they reside. Therefore, the programs developed in these institutions are designed to be responsive to the needs of the citizens who support the university through their taxes. This means that land-grant universities have a special relationship with their communities, and the programs housed at these universities should be particularly receptive to the concepts of applied developmental science.

In Chapters 2, 7, 8, and 9, there are detailed descriptions of exemplary programs that have their origins in multidisciplinary approaches to the human sciences. Three of these four programs are housed in land-grant universities: Kansas State (Chapter 2), Pennsylvania State (Chapter 8), and Michigan State (Chapter 9). The remaining program is housed at Tufts University and represents the other tradition that led to the establishment of multidisciplinary units, the "child-saving" movement that was popular in America at the turn of the century (Platt, 1969).

As indicated in the program descriptions detailed in Chapters 7, 8, and 9, the continuing impetus for multidisciplinary teaching, research, and service programs resides in the mood of a society that demands accountability and responsiveness from the institutions of higher education which the society supports. This was true of the land grant university movement in the 1860s, the child-saving movement of the 1900s, and the worried society of the 1990s.

CONCLUSION

Applied developmental science is a recent response to a long-standing plea for more relevant research addressed to the pressing needs of society. The needs and concerns that gave rise to 19th-century developmental science did not disappear, but have emerged in a call for a more coordinated approach to the study of human development and human well-being. This more coordinated and more effective approach requires the establishment of effective university–community partnerships. Teams of researcher–community professionals should be able to address aspects of the multidimensional issues confronting those who would optimize human development. Both Derek Bok (1990), former president of Harvard, and David Hamburg (1992), president of the Carnegie Corporation, have lamented America's universities, and the human science professionals who emerge from these institutions, for their failure to address human needs and enhance human potential. Providing education in applied developmental science is one way the nation's academies can address this need.

Applied developmental science (ADS) is not a movement. ADS is consensual validation of the principle that no specialization is "sufficient" unto itself. To adequately meet the complex needs of society, developmental science students must be trained to collaborate with professionals from a variety of disciplines and community organizations. The spirit of ADS training leads to an open and mutually respectful learning environment in which tomorrow's professionals can impact the lives of individuals in both the communities of today and tomorrow. Just as the lifespan reconception of development shifted our narrow focus on children or the elderly to developmental processes across the life course, ADS will shift our narrow disciplinary and university-based biases to a more encompassing and holistic understanding of ways to study and enhance human development.

This revised approach to graduate education for human science professionals requires a revised understanding of teaching, research, and service by those who provide and evaluate graduate education. The applied developmental science approach to graduate education, in its integration of science and application, represents a significant improvement in the traditional vision of the academic enterprise (Boyer, 1990, 1994). Applied developmental science, with its rich educational heritage, is not so much a "new" approach to the education of human science professionals as it is a "newly urgent" approach. Applied developmental science education is a university enterprise that will produce research professionals who are creative, caring, and competent in the service of human development.

REFERENCES

American Psychological Association. (1995). *Graduate studies in psychology*. Washington, DC: American Psychological Association.
Baltes, P.B. (1968). Longitudinal and cross-sectional sequences in the study of age and generation effects. *Human Development, 11,* 145–171.

Baltes, P., Reese, H., & Lipsitt, L. (1980). Life-span developmental psychology. *Annual Review of Psychology, 31,* 65–110.
Baltes, P.B., & Shaie, K.W. (1973). *Life-span developmental psychology, personality, and socialization.* New York: Academic Press.
Benjamin, L.T. (1992). Wundt's American doctoral students. *American Psychologist, 47*(2), 123–131.
Bevan, W. (1979). Graduate education for the earthquake generation. *Human Development, 23,* 126–136.
Bevan, W. (1980). On getting in bed with a lion. *American Psychologist, 40,* 1029–1030.
Bok, D. (1990). *Universities and the future of America.* Durham, NC: Duke University Press.
Boll, T.J. (1985). Graduate education in psychology: Time for a change? *American Psychologist, 40*(9), 1029–1030.
Boyer, E.L. (1990). *Scholarship reconsidered: Priorities of the professoriate.* Princeton, NJ: The Carnegie Foundation for the Advancement of Teaching.
Boyer, E.L. (1994, January 28). *Scholarship assessed.* Paper presented at the American Association for Higher Education, New Orleans.
Bronfenbrenner, U. (1977). Toward an experimental ecology of human development. *American Psychologist, 32,* 513–531.
Bronfenbrenner, U. (1979). *The ecology of human development.* Cambridge, MA: Harvard University Press.
Cicchetti, D. (1984). The emergence of developmental psychopathology. *Child Development, 55*(1), 1–7.
Fagan, T.K. (1992). Compulsory schooling, child study, clinical psychology, and special education. *American Psychologist, 47*(2), 236–243.
Fantz, R.L. (1961). The origin of form perception. *Scientific American, 204,* 66–72.
Fisher, C.B. (1993). Integrating science and ethics in research with high-risk children and youth. *"SRCD" Social Policy Report, 7,* 1–27.
Fisher, C.B., Hoagwood, K., & Jensen, P. (in press). Casebook on ethical issues in research with children and adolescents with mental disorders. In K. Hoagwood, P. Jensen, & C. B. Fisher (Eds.), *Ethical issues in research with children and adolescents with mental disorders.* Hillsdale, NJ: Lawrence Erlbaum Associates.
Fisher, C.B., & Brennan, M. (1992). Application and ethics in developmental psychology. In D. Featherman, R.M. Lerner, & M. Perlmutter (Eds.), *Life-span development and behavior* (Vol. 11, pp. 189–219). Hillsdale, NJ: Lawrence Erlbaum Associates.
Fisher, C.B., & Koocher, G. (1990). To be or not to be? Accreditation and credentialing in applied developmental psychology. *Journal of Applied Developmental Psychology, 11,* 381–394.
Fisher, C.B., & Lerner, R.M. (1994). Foundations of applied developmental psychology. In C.B. Fisher & R.M. Lerner (Eds.), *Applied Developmental Psychology* (pp. 3–10). New York: McGraw-Hill.
Fisher, C.B., Murray, J.P., Dill, J.R., Hagen, J.W., Hogan, M.J., Lerner, R.M., Rebok, G.W., Sigel, I.E., Sostek, A.M., Smyer, M.A., Spencer, M.B., & Wilcox, B. (1993). The national conference on graduate education in the

applications of developmental science across the lifespan. *Journal of Applied Developmental Psychology, 14,* 1–10.

Fisher, C.B., Rau, J.B., & Colapietro, E. (1993). The Fordham University Doctoral Specialization in Applied Developmental Psychology. *Journal of Applied Developmental Psychology, 14,* 289–302.

Fisher, C.B., & Tryon, W.W. (1990). Emerging ethical issues in an emerging field. In C.B. Fisher & W.W. Tryon (Eds.), *Ethics in applied developmental psychology: Emerging issues in an emerging field* (pp. 1–14). Norwood, NJ: Ablex.

Hamburg, D.A. (1992). *Today's children: Creating a future for a generation in crisis.* New York: Times Books.

Kendall, P.C., Lerner, R.M., & Craighead, W.E. (1984). Human development intervention in childhood psychopathology. *Child Development, 55,* 71–82.

Kiesler, S.B. (1979). Federal policies for research on children. *American Psychologist, 34*(10), 1009–1016.

Klatsky, R.L., Alluisi, E.A., Cook, W.A., Forehand, G.A., & Howell, W.G. (1985). Experimental psychology in industry. *American Psychologist, 40,* 1031–1037.

Koocher, G.P. (1990). Practicing applied developmental psychology: Playing the game you can't win. In C.B. Fisher & W.W. Tryon (Eds.), *Ethics in applied developmental psychology: Emerging issues in an emerging field* (pp. 215–226). Norwood, NJ: Ablex Publishing Corporation.

Lerner, R.M. (1984). *On the nature of human plasticity.* New York: Cambridge University Press.

Lerner, R.M., & Fisher, C.B. (1994). From applied developmental psychology to applied developmental science: Community coalitions and collaborative careers. In C.B. Fisher & R.M. Lerner (Eds.), *Applied developmental psychology* (pp. 505–522). New York: McGraw-Hill.

Maddux, J.E., Roberts, M.C., Sledden, E.A., & Wright, L. (1986). Developmental issues in child health psychology. *American Psychologist, 41*(1), 25–34.

Montada, L., & Schmitt, M. (1982). Issues in applied developmental psychology: A life-span perspective. In P.B. Baltes & O.G. Brim, Jr. (Eds.), *Life-span development and behavior* (Vol. 4). New York: Academic Press.

Morrison, F.J., Lord, C., & Keating, D.P. (1984). Applied developmental psychology. In F.J. Morrison, C. Lord, & D.P. Keating (Eds.), *Applied Developmental Psychology* (Vol. 1, pp. 4–20). New York: Academic Press.

Murray, J.P. (1983). *Status offenders: A sourcebook.* Boys Town, NE: The Boys Town Center.

Platt. (1969). *The child savers: The invention of delinquency.* Chicago: The University of Chicago Press.

Rasmussen, W.D. (1989). *Taking the university to the people: Seventy-five years of Cooperative Extension.* Ames, IA: Iowa State University Press.

Rheingold, H.L. (1986). The first twenty-five years of the Society for Research in Child Development. In A.B. Smuts & J.W. Hagen (Eds.), *History and research in child development* (Vol. 50). Monographs of the Society for Research in Child Development.

Scarr, S. (1990). Ethical dilemmas in recent research: A personal saga. In C.B. Fisher & W.W. Tryon (Eds.), *Ethics in applied developmental psychology:*

Emerging issues in an emerging field (Vol. 4, pp. 29–42). Norwood, NJ: Ablex Publishing Corporation.

Scholnick, E.K. (1983). Scrutinizing application: An agenda for applied developmental psychology. *Journal of Applied Developmental Psychology, 4,* 329–39.

Sears, R.R. (1975). Your ancients revisited: A history of child development. In E.M. Hetherington (Ed.), *Review of child development research* (Vol. 5, pp. 1–74). Chicago, IL: University of Chicago Press.

Shantz, C. (1987, Spring). Report on applied developmental psychology programs. *American Psychological Association Division of Developmental Psychology Newsletter,* pp. 1–13.

Siegel, A.W., & White, S.H. (1982). The child study movement: Early growth and development of the symbolized child. In H.W. Reese (Ed.), *Advances in child development and behavior* (pp. 233–285). New York: Academic Press.

Sigel, I.E. (1985). *Parental belief systems: The psychological consequences for children.* Hillsdale, NJ: Lawrence Erlbaum Associates, Inc.

Sigel, I., & Cocking, R.R. (1980). Editors' message. *Journal of Applied Developmental Psychology, 1,* i–iii.

Smuts, A.B. (1986). The National Research Council Committee on Child Development and the founding of the Society for Research in Child Development, 1925–33. In A.B. Smuts & J.W. Hagen (Eds.), *History and research in child development* (Vol. 50). (Monographs for the Society for Research in Child Development.)

Wertlieb, D. (1983). Some foundations and directions for applied developmental psychology. *Journal of Applied Developmental Psychology, 4,* 349–58.

Youniss, J. (1990). Cultural forces leading to scientific developmental psychology. In C.B. Fisher & W.W. Tryon (Eds.), *Ethics in applied developmental psychology: Emerging issues in an emerging field* (pp. 285–302). Norwood, NJ: Ablex Publishing Corporation.

Zigler, E., & Finn, M. (1984). Applied Developmental Psychology. In M.H. Bornstein & M.E. Lamb (Eds.), *Developmental psychology: An advanced textbook* (pp. 451–492). Hillsdale, NJ: Lawrence Erlbaum Associates, Inc.

2

Applied Developmental Science in Colleges of Human Ecology and Family and Consumer Sciences

John P. Murray

School of Family Studies and Human Services
College of Human Ecology
Kansas State University

Applied Developmental Science (ADS) is a relatively new approach to long-standing concern about the integration of human sciences and the application of scientific findings to the solution of pressing social problems. Indeed, ADS began to take shape in the early 1990s and established its "birthdate" with the New York conference at Fordham University in October 1991 (Fisher et al., 1993).

This first ADS conference was the result of several years of informal discussion involving representatives of diverse scientific and professional organizations in the human sciences. The attention of these organizations was focused on the need to enhance the application of research results in the developmental sciences in order to achieve an enhancement of professional practice. Also, it was felt that the application of research findings would be more effective if the original research had been conducted from a multidisciplinary or an interdisciplinary perspective. In this way, the research would transcend the narrow focus that characterizes some research undertaken within the boundaries of a particular discipline.

In furthering the goals espoused by the ADS conference participants, it became clear that we needed a new approach to graduate education and professional training. Only by encouraging a new generation of interdisciplinary developmental scientists, would we be able to establish the research and professional program base needed to address the multifaceted problems confronting society.

This concern about the practical application of research findings is not a new concern, but it is newly urgent. Also, the attempt to employ multidisciplinary approaches in research has a long history and traditions in several academic and professional areas. Foremost among these traditions, is the establishment of the land-grant university system and, in a related development, the rise of the field of home economics. Both of these traditions date from the mid to late-1800s and have had a profound impact on American society.

LAND-GRANT UNIVERSITIES

The concept of the land-grant university is rooted in the notion that some portion of higher education should be focused on the training of educated persons who would devote their time and talents to the solution of practical problems confronting society. This notion sparked the development of a federal program to encourage the establishment of institutions of higher learning that would address these concerns. This plan was inaugurated by the passage of the Morrill Land Grant College Act of 1862, which was signed into law by Abraham Lincoln.

The Morrill Act provided a grant of free land to any state or territory that would use this land to build or establish what became known as "people's universities." The act established schools that were designed to: "promote the liberal and practical education of the industrial classes in the several pursuits and professions in life by teaching such branches of learning as are related to agriculture and the mechanic arts, without excluding other scientific and classical studies" (Rasmussen, 1989, p. 240).

One practical result of the 1862 Morrill Act was the establishment of state universities or "land-grant Universities" in virtually every state and some territories of the United States. For example, Kansas State University—founded in 1863 as the Kansas State Agricultural College on the

Applied Developmental Science in Colleges of Human Ecology 25

facilities that were transferred to the state of Kansas from a defunct private school, BlueMont Central College, that was founded in 1858—became the first land-grant university. Kansas State was followed in rapid succession by the establishment of what is now Michigan State University (1865) and Pennsylvania State University (1866). All of these land grant schools had an agricultural core, but were also concerned with related aspects of human life and human development (Carey, 1977; Hoeflin, 1988).

In addition to the establishment of these early land-grant schools, the second Morrill Land Grant College Act of 1890 provided federal land for the establishment of similar institutions and programs in historically black colleges. Furthermore, the new Land-Grant College Act of 1994 has designated Native American colleges and tribal institutions as land grant universities. Thus, the shorthand notation for about 80 land-grant universities has become the 1860s, 1890s, and 1990s institutions.

Beyond the establishment of educational institutions, the spirit of the Morrill Act led to the development of federal funding for research and demonstration programs at these land-grant universities. In 1887, Congress passed the Hatch Experiment Station Act that established agricultural field research programs attached to the land grant colleges. And, in 1914, Congress passed the Smith–Lever Act that established the Cooperative Extension Service, which would provide demonstrations and informal educational programs for citizens based upon the research and teaching at land-grant colleges.

All of these developments—from the Morrill Act of 1862 and its extensions in 1890 and 1994, as well as the Hatch Act in 1887 and the Smith–Lever Act in 1914—set the stage for an institutional structure throughout the United States that is dedicated to the application of research findings to the solution of societal problems.

HOME ECONOMICS TO HUMAN ECOLOGY

The field of home economics had its origins in the domestic science programs of the land-grant colleges. For example, Kansas State University, established in 1863, began "The Woman's Course" in 1873, with the appointment of Mrs. Hattie C. Chesildine as Superintendent of Sewing. The Woman's Course later differentiated into the departments of domestic science and domestic art at the turn of the century and became the Division of Home Economics in 1912. The division became a School of Home Economics in 1942, a College of Home Economics in 1963, and was renamed the College of Human Ecology in 1985 (Carey, 1977; Hoeflin, 1988).

The development of the field of home economics was shaped by a charismatic leader, Ellen S. Richards. Dr. Richards, a researcher and professor at

Massachusetts Institute of Technology, was interested in water quality and disease transmission in humans and espoused an holistic approach to studying human well-being. She was instrumental in developing a series of conferences on defining the field of home economics. The first conference was held at Lake Placid, NY on September 19–23, 1899 and continued through ten meetings culminating in a conference in Chautauqua, NY on July 6–10, 1908. Known collectively as the Lake Placid Conferences, this series of meetings outlined the purpose and scope of a field that would integrate the study of diverse aspects of human well-being. Indeed, the *Proceedings of the Tenth Annual Conference* contained the following statement of objectives: "The conference is for scientific and sociologic study of the home. Home economics includes the whole home environment; standards, ideals, health, recreation and development for an efficient life," (Lake Placid Conference on Home Economics, 1908, p. 3).

The holistic principles enunciated at the Lake Placid meetings at the turn of the century have continued to guide the nature and functions of colleges of human ecology, home economics, and family and consumer science to the present date. Similarly, family and child programs within these home economics colleges have espoused holistic and interdisciplinary approaches to the study of human well-being. Over the past hundred years, both these colleges and their constituent programs or departments have changed in a dramatic manner.

At Kansas State University, for example, the College of Human Ecology evolved from The Woman's Course, to the Department of Sewing and Household Economy and Hygiene in the 1870s, the departments of Domestic Science and Domestic Art in 1898, and then to a Division of Home Economics in 1912. It further evolved to the School of Home Economics in 1942, College of Home Economics in 1963, and finally the College of Human Ecology in 1985 (Hoeflin, 1988). In a similar manner, the program that is focused on family and child development changed its structure and function by evolving out of the Domestic Science Department into the Department of Child Welfare and Euthenics in 1928, then changing to the Department of Family and Child Development in 1955. It then grew to the Department of Human Development and Family Studies in 1985, and became the School of Family Studies and Human Services in 1995. Each of the changes at the college and department level implies significant modifications of the scope or emphasis of the teaching, research and service functions in the new organization.

There is continuity in the development of these academic programs when viewed from the perspective of an integrated scientific and professional approach to the study of human well-being. This integrated perspective includes the communication of knowledge to the general public and the application of research findings to the resolution of pressing social problems.

Applied Developmental Science in Colleges of Human Ecology 27

The photographs in Figures 2.1 to 2.4, drawn from the archives of Kansas State University, provide a glimpse of the early days of these programs. At first glance, they appear to be quaint and perhaps unrelated to the concerns of present day. But, on reflection, these scenes provide a sense of history for our consideration of applied developmental science.

The panoply of early activities and facilities displayed in these photos includes a lithograph of the original building of BlueMont Central College in 1860 (Figure 2.1) followed by a picture of the quad of Kansas State Agricultural College on "Ag Day" in 1902 (Figure 2.2). The two additional photographs show a Cooperative Extension Service vehicle loaded for a field trip around 1920 (Figure 2.3) and a Food Science Laboratory in the 1890s (Figure 2.4). Collectively, these photographs address the central functions of a College of Human Ecology, albeit in somewhat time-bound fashion. These continuing central functions are the pursuit of knowledge, the communication of knowledge to relevant publics, and the application of this knowledge derived from research and professional experience to issues of concern for human well-being. For example, the photograph of the "Ag Day" ceremony reflects the attempt to bring agricultural workers into contact with research and "best practice" activities that were demonstrated on the college campus on this particular "open house" day. Such festivals served to remove the barriers between farmers and ranchers, as well as the academic teachers and researchers. So too, Figure 2.3 represents the outreach function of 4-H instructors working on youth development projects, in this case clothing and consumer issues. The nature of the issues has

FIGURE 2.1. BlueMont Central College (1860), the foundation for the first Land Grant University, Kansas State Agricultural College (1863). Source: University Archives, Kansas State University.

FIGURE 2.2. The quad of Kansas State Agricultural College on "Ag Day" in 1902. Source: University Archives, Kansas State University.

changed over time, as have the particular methods, equipment and approaches used in conducting research. However, what has remained constant is the need for solid research, "best practice" professional standards, and a willingness to translate these scientific and professional findings into programs that benefit society. This is what applied developmental science

FIGURE 2.3 A Cooperative Extension Service vehicle packed for a field demonstration for 4-H youth members, circa 1920. Source: University Archives, Kansas State University.

FIGURE 2.4. A food science laboratory in the Domestic Science Department, circa 1885. Source: University Archives, Kansas State University.

strives to offer colleagues in the human sciences. We can learn much from this heritage.

FROM HERITAGE TO HEURISTICS

So, what do we know about the ways in which the programs in Colleges of Human Ecology or Family and Consumer Science may relate to the notion of applied developmental science? To start at the beginning, the concept of research applied to practical needs was given legitimacy in the Lake Placid Conferences. These conferences ultimately led to the establishment of a professional society known as the American Home Economics Association (in 1994, the name was changed to the American Association for Family and Consumer Sciences). Although there have been many changes in the program's focus over the past 100 years, a sample of the topics discussed at the first Lake Placid conference in September, 1899 gives a sense of the beginnings:

1. A classification of household economics as a working basis.
3. Provision for the higher education of some selected young women who shall be fitted by the best training for a higher leadership.
4. A compilation of the results of experience in teaching domestic economy in schools in this country and in Europe.
5. The preparation of a series of papers or brochures in domestic science, which the government may publish and distribute as it now does the bulletins on food and nutrition through the department of agriculture.
6. The founding of state schools or chairs of household economics in our state universities.
7. The training of teachers of domestic science.
8. What name best interprets this work? . . .
10. Some method of cooperation between experiment stations and schools of domestic science. . . .
15. Standards of living as affected by sanitary science. (Lake Placid Conference on Home Economics, 1901, pp. 3–4)

The ambitious goals previously outlined, enunciated at the first conference in 1899, are reflected in some of the concerns about establishing programs in applied developmental science. And yet, there are some clear differences in that ADS is focused on a more circumscribed—although still quite large—range of developmental sciences.

The range of disciplines covered in Colleges of Human Ecology or Family and Consumer Sciences include specialists in food science, industrial/organizational management, textile chemistry, and interior design—in addition to family and child development specialists. For example, at Kansas State University there are four departments/schools: the three departments of Clothing, Textiles and Interior Design (CTID), Foods and Nutrition (F&N), and Hotel, Restaurant, Institution Management and Dietetics (HRIMD), and the School of Family Studies and Human Services (FSHS). The primary program in which applied developmental science would be found is the School of Family Studies and Human Services. However, related interests can be found in each of the other departments. For example, dietetics and nutritional programs for the elderly can be found in HRIMD; nutrition and exercise science programs, along with special programs on infant and child nutrition, can be found in F&N. Housing design for the elderly or physically challenged and expertise in special institution design, such as Alzheimer's Care Units, can be found in CTID. These are but a few examples of overlap between departments outside of the traditional program area of FSHS.

Within the School of Family Studies and Human Services at Kansas State, the 40+ faculty are organized into six units or programs: Communication Sciences and Disorders, Early Childhood Education, Family and Consumer Economics, Family Life Education, Life Span Human Development, and Marriage and Family Therapy. Collectively, the school is composed of a diverse set of specialists in sociology and psychology, family therapy and family studies, education and economics, speech pathology and social work. These specialists address scientific and professional issues in family life education, early childhood education, gerontology, family communication and relationships, infant to adult development, language development and interventions throughout the life span, and a host of related developmental concerns.

Clearly, at Kansas State University, the School of Family Studies and Human Services is a home for applied developmental science, but it is not the only home. We are joined by colleagues in other programs in the College of Human Ecology, in departments ranging from Psychology to Sociology, Anthropology and Social Work, as well as various programs in the College of Education and other, perhaps less obvious, sites such as the departments of Agricultural Economics and Architecture and Regional Planning.

How does the structure at Kansas State University compare to other Colleges of Human Ecology and Family and Consumer Sciences at other land-grant universities around the country? The structure described earlier parallels the structure of the College of Human Ecology at Cornell University and the College of Family and Consumer Sciences at the University of Georgia. The structure at Kansas State University is quite similar to the structures at the University of California at Davis, Iowa State University, University of Missouri, Michigan State University, University of Minnesota, University of Nebraska, Oklahoma State University, University of Vermont, and the University of Wisconsin, to name a few of the sister institutions. Indeed, this structure is relatively similar at all of the 1860 and many of the 1890 land-grant universities throughout the country. The colleges that are the more recent additions to the land-grant university system, the 1994 tribal colleges and universities, have somewhat different structures, since many of these colleges and universities are undergraduate institutions.

So, to move from heritage to heuristics, how do we use these structures of human ecology programs to discover strategies for implementing applied developmental science in graduate education at both public and private universities throughout North America? It would seem that the land-grant system would be a fertile field for nurturing the seedlings of ADS (to borrow an agricultural metaphor). Indeed, the heritage of departments and programs in family and child development, human development and family studies, or family studies and human services represent the best match with the ideals and goals of ADS. These programs could become the models for

ADS graduate education. Such an initiative could provide a rationale for extending collaboration across the campus of each land grant university and could serve as a model for education in the developmental human sciences at all universities.

RATIONALE AND REFLECTIONS

Why ADS, why land-grant university models, and why now? Is there something new about ADS that is different from the heritage described in the earlier section? And, how would the concept of ADS extend beyond land-grant programs to encompass graduate education in human sciences offered at diverse public and private universities? Is there a failure on the part of all universities to fully engage students in applying research to pressing human needs? The answer to this question is decidedly, yes. Derek Bok (1990), in his book *Universities and the Future of America*, pointed to some of these failures:

> In short, we lead most industrial democracies in ignorance and in many of the pathologies of modern civilization while lagging behind in the rate of economic progress. . . . These grim statistics should be profoundly troubling to those who devote their lives to higher education. . . . One might have thought that the graduates of our outstanding professional schools, armed with the research of our social scientists, could have done more to help our government agencies and community organizations to reduce the incidence of poverty, illiteracy, and stunted opportunity. Since these results have not occurred, it is fair to ask whether our universities are doing all that they can and should to help America surmount the obstacles that threaten to sap our economic strength and blight the lives of millions of our people. (p. 6)

It would seem that one of the reasons for this failure is the lack of a concerted effort by graduate programs in the human sciences and human services to encourage interdisciplinary or multidisciplinary research and intervention programs as part of the training for students. Too often, we suggest that the price of graduate education includes the development of expertise in a very narrow range of scientific and professional practice. Although it is important to develop skills in a special field, it is equally important to learn to apply these skills in multiple settings and in combination with a wide variety of professionals.

There needs to be a greater appreciation of a more holistic approach to addressing the issues confronting individuals and society. Universities are beginning to contemplate the need for holistic solutions to social problems as they begin to review the structure and function of both undergraduate and graduate education. Some have argued that the antidote for the fragmentation of higher education into increasingly isolated specializations is to reintroduce a broad liberal general education component at the undergraduate level (Hardison, 1989). Indeed, Harvard University has offered one model for these undergraduate reforms, the Harvard "core" program, which was eloquently defended by Rosovsky (1990). However, although these undergraduate reforms are useful in establishing a broad experience base for graduate education, it remains important to ensure that students in graduate human science programs learn to work in an interdisciplinary environment and apply their research to important issues.

Much can be learned from the history of programs in human ecology/home economics. We have seen the expressed need to integrate teaching, research and professional application functions in the human sciences since the 1860s yet, almost one and a half centuries later, we are still working on the problem. Despite the slow pace and many detours, the foundations of applied developmental science exist and are well built in colleges of human ecology. Now, we need to add a few wings and furnish the new rooms.

Will this "remodeling" of the basic structure of a multidisciplinary program lead to productive interdisciplinary applied developmental science programs? The answer to this question depends on the success of some broad reforms that are underway in academe. In the first instance, there is a general appreciation of the need to develop interdisciplinary programs in the developmental sciences that predates and/or is independent of the ADS movement. For example, in the areas of clinical and developmental psychology, there is a growing interest in expanding the base of professional skills as a way to address human diversity (Allison et al., 1994; Kellam & Rebok, 1992; Rolf & Read, 1984). These changes will continue because they are seen as beneficial to the professionals, their clients, and the programs in which they operate.

In addition, there are renewed calls for rethinking and restructuring academic programs to enhance integration of knowledge (Keller, 1983). For example, Ernest Boyer (1990, 1994) has been influential in urging universities to rethink the ways in which they value the varieties of scholarship that professors display. In particular, we need to move beyond the "scholarship of discovery" or the "scholarship of teaching" that are the traditional anchor points of research and instruction. In Boyer's view, we need to add a reward structure that values the "scholarship of integration" and the "scholarship of application" if we are to have a university faculty that is willing to address important issues in society.

By "integration" Boyer (1990) means, "making connections across the disciplines, placing specialties in larger context, illuminating data in a revealing way, often educating nonspecialists, too" (p. 18). As for the scholarship of application, Boyer suggests, "the *application* of knowledge moves toward engagement as the scholar asks, 'How can knowledge be responsibly applied to consequential problems? How can it be helpful to individuals as well as institutions?' and further, 'Can social problems *themselves* define an agenda for scholarly investigation?'" (p. 21).

These forms of scholarship, integration and application, have been central concerns of land-grant universities and have defined the work of selected faculty in Colleges of Human Ecology or Home Economics. As noted earlier, the traditional functions of the Cooperative Extension Service and the Agricultural Experiment Station relate directly to the scholarship of application and could be enhanced by the scholarship of integration. The publications of the Cooperative Extension Services, in the form of bulletins that are disseminated throughout each state or across the country by local extension agents, are good examples of the application of knowledge to issues of public concern (e.g., Murray & Lonnborg, 1995). So too, there are many public and private organizations that participate in the application of knowledge derived from research and professional practice (Huston et al., 1992; Murray, 1983).

If we are to capitalize on interest in the scholarship of application and the scholarship of integration, we must ensure that there are institutional structures that provide opportunity for these activities. Appendix A contains an example of a proposal to develop a national program that draws on the expertise of land-grant university faculty and their traditions of applied research. This proposal, developed in 1995 by the Association of Administrators in Home Economics (AAHE), the Board on Human Sciences (BOHS), and others in the National Association of State Universities and Land-Grant Colleges (NASULGC), will provide a working model for the integration of research and policy. The Human Sciences Institute (HSI) will provide an opportunity for faculty to participate in multidisciplinary and interdisciplinary research applied to national needs. In particular, the HSI will draw on the expertise of over 2,000 faculty members in more than 80 land-grant universities across the country to conduct research and policy initiatives addressed to the needs of children, youth and families. The HSI can be operational at short notice because there is a tradition of applied research in colleges of human ecology across the country. The special advantage of this HSI program for ADS is that it will provide one model for construction and funding of interdisciplinary teams. Naturally, other models are needed in other areas of ADS.

Finally, it seems clear that these calls for enhanced integration and application of research need to be sustained by a revamped system of rewards within the academic community. Boyer's posthumously published monograph on *Scholarship Assessed*, which was foreshadowed in a recent paper (Boyer, 1994), provides an outline for changing the reward structure in our universities. Again, much can be learned from the history of land grant universities and the ways in which the application of research to pressing public needs has been evaluated and nurtured. Applied developmental science will provide a rallying point for a discussion of ways to enhance the tradition of applied research in human ecology and ways to export that tradition to other programs and disciplines.

REFERENCES

Allison, K.W., Crawford, I., Echemendia, R., Robinson, L., & Knepp, D. (1994). Human diversity and professional competence: Training in clinical and counseling psychology revisited. *American Psychologist, 49*(9). 792–796.

Bok, D. (1990). *Universities and the future of America.* Durham, NC: Duke University Press.

Boyer, E.L. (1990). *Scholarship reconsidered: Priorities of the professoriate.* Princeton, NJ: The Carnegie Foundation for the Advancement of Teaching.

Boyer, E.L. (1994, January 28). *Scholarship assessed.* Paper presented at the American Association for Higher Education, New Orleans.

Carey, J.C. (1977). *Kansas State University—The quest for identity.* Lawrence, KS: University of Kansas Press.

Fisher, C.B., Murray, J.P., Dill, J.R., Hagen, J.W., Hogan, M.J., Lerner, R.M., Rebok, G.W., Sigel, I., Sostek, A.M., Smyer, M.A., Spencer, M.B., & Wilcox, B. (1993). The national conference on graduate education in the applications of developmental science across the life span. *Journal of Applied Developmental Psychology, 14,* 1–10.

Hardison, O.B. (1989). *Disappearing through the skylight: Culture and technology in the twentieth century.* New York: Viking.

Hoeflin, R. (1988). *History of a college: From woman's course to home economics to human ecology—1873–1988 Kansas State University.* Manhattan, KS: Ag Press.

Huston, A.C., Donnerstein, E., Fairchild, H., Feshbach, N.D., Katz, P.A., Murray, J.P., Rubinstein, E.A., Wilcox, B.L., & Zuckerman, D.M. (1992). *Big world, small screen: The role of television in American society.* Lincoln, NE: University of Nebraska Press.

Kellam, S.G., & Rebok, G.W. (1992). Building developmental and etiological theory through epidemiologically based preventive intervention trials. In J. McCord & R.E. Tremblay (Eds.), *Preventing antisocial behavior: Interventions from birth through adolescence* (pp. 162–195). New York: Guilford Press.

Lake Placid Conference on Home Economics. (1901). *Proceedings of the first, second and third conferences.* Lake Placid, NY: Lake Placid Club.

Lake Placid Conference on Home Economics. (1908). *Proceedings of the tenth annual conference.* Essex County, NY: Lake Placid Club.

Murray, J.P. (1983). *Status offenders: A sourcebook.* Boys Town, NE: The Boys Town Center.

Murray, J.P., & Lonnborg, B. (1995). *Children and television—using TV sensibly* (Extension Bulletin L-790, Revised March, 1995). Manhattan, KS: Kansas Cooperative Extension Service.

Rasmussen, W.D. (1989). *Taking the university to the people: Seventy-five years of Cooperative Extension.* Ames, IA: Iowa State University Press.

Rolf, J., & Read, P.B. (1984). Programs advancing developmental psychopathology. *Child Development, 55,* 8–16.

Rosovsky, H. (1990). *The university: An owner's manual.* New York: W.W. Norton.

Appendix

Human Sciences Institute Washington, DC Board on Human Sciences, NASULGC

RATIONALE

The many challenges facing our youth, families, and communities include concerns about violence on our streets and in our homes, transgenerational poverty and welfare systems, disproportionate access to food and shelter, poor nutritional status, and projections of limited job and employment opportunities.

These concerns are not new, but they are newly urgent as American society struggles to address the multiple roles of government, private enterprise, and personal responsibility in the maintenance of human well-being in the late 1990s.

The Human Sciences Institute (HSI) provides a mechanism for addressing these concerns and evaluating policy options through careful and impartial research and strategic policy reports. The strength of the HSI lies in its ability to:

- provide rapid response to social policy questions by developing interdisciplinary research teams from HSI Fellows and Associates, both in Washington and in over 80 Land Grant universities and across America;
- employ the talents of approximately 2,000 faculty who have expertise in the development of programs addressed to the solution of practical issues in the human sciences;
- build on the skills in research and program development of the Cooperative State Research, Education and Extension Service (CSREES) in the evaluation and dissemination of effective solutions to critical human issues;
- extend the evaluation and dissemination skills of Land Grant university faculty to address the policy and programmatic emphases of federal agencies such as the National Institutes of Health, National Institute of Mental Health, Substance Abuse and Mental Health Services Administration, Department of Labor, Department of Health and Human Services, and related human sciences programs.

We contend that one of the reasons that the most pressing problems confronting American society have remained resistant to solution is that much of the research and policy discussion has been developed within disciplinary groups. The HSI will allow researchers and policy specialists to cross these boundaries and develop new approaches in collaboration with colleagues in diverse disciplines and universities within the land-grant system. This diversity will bring new insights and new solutions to the seemingly intractable challenges in the human sciences. The HSI will provide practical research and policy reports for Congress, government agencies, private and public institutions, and concerned citizens.

STRUCTURE

This proposed Human Sciences Institute has been initiated by the Association of Administrators in Home Economics (AAHE) and the Board on Human Sciences (BOHS). We anticipate the participation of a diverse set of professional organizations in the establishment of the HSI Advisory Board. The structure of the HSI will be open and flexible and will be constituted as outlined in Figure 2A.1. The functional heart of the HSI is the Issue Focus Groups (IFG). Each of these groups will

FIGURE 2A.1. Structure of the Human Sciences Institute.

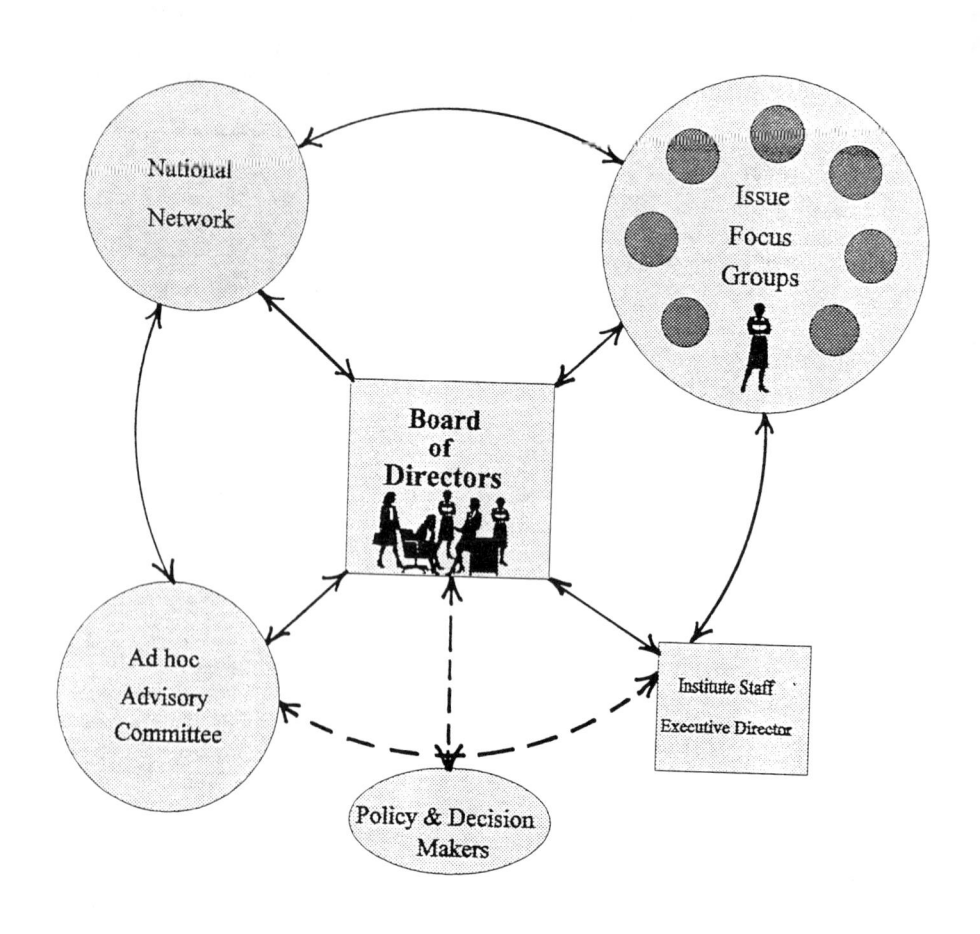

study and analyze a critical issue and articulate public policy implications, drawing on the larger network with which the members naturally relate in their scientific activities. The IFG Chairs serve on the HSI Board of Directors. The Board of Directors will set policy and provide leadership directing the institute staff. An Ad Hoc Advisory Committee, with membership drawn from congressional and private and public agency sectors, will provide advice to the board and its staff on pertinent issues. The program operation will include the following special characteristics:

- easily accessible to policymakers and programmers in Washington and other locations throughout country;

Human Sciences Institute 39

- operate under a board of directors drawn from the national association representing land-grant universities (NASULGC) and related human sciences professional organizations;
- employ HSI Fellows and Associates to develop working papers and policy reports on issues identified by Congress and public/private agencies;
- ensure timely review of all reports through special boards of scientific advisers drawn from diverse, but relevant, disciplines in the cross-section of land-grant Universities.

IMPLEMENTATION

Funding for the operation of HSI will be drawn from a consortium of public and private agencies. We anticipate support for HSI from the following sources:

- private foundations will provide the establishment or start-up support;
- project support will be provided by grants and contracts from federal agencies, state governments, public and private agencies, and other appropriate sources.

The HSI will begin operation as soon as foundation support is established and would be available for directed programming through grants and contracts. We anticipate that the initial research and policy will be focused on crucial issues confronting children, youth and families.

3

Graduate Education in the Applied Developmental Sciences:
History and Background

John W. Hagen

University of Michigan[1]

Graduate education in the United States began in the latter part of the 19th century. The first doctoral program was established at Johns Hopkins University in 1876 (Bowen & Rudenstine, 1992). When the Association of American Universities was founded in 1900, fewer than 400 doctorates were conferred. By 1920, the average number of doctoral degrees awarded was about 600 per year. From that time until the 1970s, there was a steady growth (with the exception of a decrease during World War II) with an average annual rate of increase of about 7% a year. The number of different disciplines or fields offering doctoral training also expanded greatly in the post World War II period. The basic sciences, followed by the arts, led the way in implementing graduate training.

---

[1] The author acknowledges the work of A. Chip Conley and Joseph Pleban on the gathering and preparation of materials for this chapter.

The growth of programs for graduate training in the developmental sciences in the United States can be traced to events in the 1920s, a time of rapid expansion of services by the government as well as private sources. The National Research Council, a division of the National Academy of Sciences, founded the Committee on Child Development (CCD) in 1924. The reasons for this action were at least threefold (Smuts & Hagen, 1985). Early in the century, several private foundations with very large assets had been established, and most were rethinking their commitments to provide aid to the poor and underprivileged. These foundations' new commitment was to the *prevention* of social ills, and the achievement of this goal was to be based on the new behavioral and social sciences (e.g., Bremner, 1960; Coben, 1979). Research and education in these areas was predicted to transform social practices, in much the same way that the physical sciences and technology transformed the physical environment and industry (Smuts & Hagen, 1985).

The 1920s were characterized by support coming mainly from philanthropy, not the federal government, and the emphasis on prevention naturally turned the focus from adult programs to child programs (Coffman, 1936). The child welfare movement gained great momentum following World War I. The aim was to improve the lives of all children. The problems of society, according to the prevailing view, could best be solved by beginning with children.

It soon became apparent that the practices and programs recommended by professionals went well beyond the existing base of knowledge. Organized efforts of research were few and far between at the time. Early in the century, G. Stanley Hall tried to develop a child research organization, but was unsuccessful. In 1918, Harold Jones conducted a survey and found only three psychologists and two psychiatrists whose main interest was children. Data available on children and the problems of children were very meager at best.

John D. Rockefeller had established the Laura Spelman Rockefeller Memorial Fund (LSRM), in memory of his wife, in 1918 with $74 million. Its goal was to continue her charitable work to "further the welfare of women and children." In 1923, the board of the foundation decided to modify this goal to include the "application of the social sciences for the purpose of reform" (Fosdick, 1952, pp. 192–93). Lawrence K. Frank, the program officer of LSRM, viewed research on child development as "the most effective method for dealing with our social difficulties" (Smuts, 1985, p. 111).

The first child-focused research institute in the United States, the Iowa Child Welfare Research Station had recently been established by the state's legislature. In 1924, LSRM established its first Child Development Institute at Teachers' College, Columbia University, and further provided money to the Iowa Institute to expand its programs. Three new institutes soon followed: The University of Minnesota; University of California, Berkeley; and University of Toronto. CCD was created at this critical time to try to insure that research on child development would succeed and expand. There were great expectations for its promise and eagerness for the findings of the research endeavors.

The first chair of the parent committee of the CCD was Robert S. Woodworth, a major figure in psychology at that time and a professor at Columbia. Throughout the tenure of the committee, the emphasis was to keep the focus on research. A conference convened of 30 researchers in 1925 wholeheartedly endorsed the goals and purposes of the committee and argued that its focus must be "to demonstrate that child development research was both possible and necessary" (Smuts & Hagen, 1985, p. 112). Conferences were held regularly by the committee in the late 1920s and its first serial publication, beginning in 1927, was *Child Development Abstracts and Bibliography*. A directory of researchers was compiled listing 477 investigators. A fellowship program was also established to attract strong investigators into the field. It should be noted that training of young scholars was not the main focus. Rather, the attempt was to attract persons already established in these disciplines to focus their interest on issues of child development.

We see in these initial statements many of the issues and concerns that we still deal with today. Perhaps some of the major issues still relevant are "how to achieve an integrated science of child development and to work out the proper relationship between research and practice" (Smuts & Hagen, p. 113). Lawrence Frank recognized the potential problem if one discipline were to dominate. He stated emphatically, "child development was not a new term for child psychology, but an interdisciplinary endeavor" (Smuts & Hagen, 1995, p. 113). The argument was that children should be studied by each of the relevant disciplines, with the goal being an integration of findings across all disciplines in order to better understand children. As the CCD proceeded with its work, there was much effort expended to get as many disciplines involved as possible. Included were physical growth, nutrition, medicine, psychology, and mental hygiene (the precursor to child psychiatry).

The second major concern was the relationship between research and practice. Woodworth was adamant in his argument that basic research was essential to the child welfare movement. However, he recognized that application would have to continue while new knowledge was being pursued. Furthermore, he argued that the two often must work hand in hand and facilitate each other. "Our inevitable blunders will be valuable and even necessary as clues to the investigation. Research and practice will react each upon the other" (CCD conference proceedings, 1925, p. 3).

In the early 1930s, there were new forces in society that negatively affected the fledgling child research movement. The stock market crash of 1929, and the depression that followed, led to a dampening of the optimism concerning social reform through relevant research. Funding also became very difficult. The LSRM was dissolved in 1929, causing many of its programs to suffer. It merged with the much larger Rockefeller Foundation, which did, however, provide support for some of the programs. In 1930, the White House Conference on Children was held with 3,200 persons in attendance. It prescribed a very ambitious agenda for the future and specifically set up task forces to pursue basic research. Ironically, the success of the White House Conference interfered with the work of the CCD. The committee's funding was in jeopardy and internal politics seriously threatened its continuation (see Smuts, 1985, for a detailed description of the events).

In 1932, the CCD met and drew up a plan for an independent society of researchers concerned with child development with 1933 as the date targeted for its establishment. A meeting of almost 100 scholars was held in Chicago in June 1933. The newly established organization was named the Society for Research in Child Development (SRCD). Funding in the amount of $12,600 was obtained from the Rockefeller Foundation for a two-year period. Thus, SRCD was formally founded as an independent association of researchers from all relevant disciplines. In spite of the adversities cited earlier, the 1930's saw a great expansion of work in child development and child welfare, with increasing numbers of researchers and professionals whose major focus was on children.

It is important to recognize that SRCD still adheres to the original purpose and goals of the CCD. The constitution for SRCD, ratified in 1934, states that their vision is to stimulate and support research and to encourage cooperation among researchers in many fields. Furthermore, the service function was clarified in the society committed to the support of efforts towards successful *application* of research findings. It should also be acknowledged that a critical role was played by Robert Woodworth, first in the nurturing and protecting of the CCD, and then in aiding in the transition from the CCD to SRCD. He truly shaped the course of research in child development for the decades that followed (Smuts, 1985).

The key role played by private philanthropy during this period is illustrated by the work of the William T. Grant Foundation. In its 60-year history, the W.T. Grant Foundation has had a consistency of purpose: to further understanding of human behavior through research (Cahan, 1986). Founded by William T. Grant, the entrepreneur and philanthropist who made a fortune with the W.T. Grant chain of stores, the initial commitment of the foundation was to conduct research on normal development in children. Feeling that research had been focused too much on disease, Mr. Grant and his officers decided that information was needed about "the kinds of people who are well and do well" (Cahan, 1986). Over the years, The Grant Foundation has aimed to achieve a balance between support of research that leads to understanding, application of research through demonstration and service, and social policy and advocacy. The importance of the contributions made by private foundations dedicated to the concerns of the nation's children cannot be overstated. These foundations have provided not only dollars but leadership as well. Researchers, policymakers and practitioners in child development owe a great amount of gratitude to the individuals who have established and maintained the commitments of these foundations.

The SRCD has been committed to the accomplishment of two broad goals: research from the many relevant disciplines striving to bring understanding to the whole child, and the translation of findings of basic research to application to society's problems. These goals have been reaffirmed again and again since the founding of the society. However, the difficulties encountered in actualizing these goals have also been acknowledged. For example, in 1941, Woodworth sated, "fostering the integration of the different scientific approaches to child development has not yet been fully solved" (NRC Report, 1941). In his presidential address to the society in 1949, Alfred Washburn argued that the society must be "so happy and so fruitful a common meeting point that it may serve to foster constant cross-fertilizing between many different disciplines (p. 63). In 1953, in an address at the biennial meeting in Yellow Springs, Oh., Dale Harris spoke in favor of the interdisciplinary commitment, but he acknowledged that this goal was difficult to achieve. Harriet Rhinegold (1985) acknowledged that the dilemma continued to frustrate the society and the field of child development: "The capturing of the Society by any one discipline, and specifically by psychology, was recognized very early as a threat to its original design, and as we know, the recognition still continues" (p. 131).

The second theme, that of application of research in order to be useful to children and society in general, has also continued, but not without difficulty. At the meetings in 1946, it was reaffirmed that SRCD had a responsibility to the translation of knowledge into professional practice. As editor of *Child Development,* Richards, in 1949, issued a statement of policy concerning publications. He reaffirmed the interdisciplinary nature of the journal and then said, "It is the function of publications to bring research out of the laboratory and ivory tower . . . to reach not only scientists, but also the larger public which needs to know . . . the continuous contribution of research" (Richards, 1949, p. 3).

Following World War II, the fields that comprise child development underwent remarkable changes. Until this time, theoretical orientations and methodologies were diverse and not necessarily used in rigorous ways. The domination of psychology as a discipline began to be recognized in the early 1950s. Following experimental psychology, there was a great increase of interest in pursuing research that was theoretically driven and rigorous from a methodological standpoint (Morrison, Lord, & Keating, 1984). Laboratory-based experiments quickly became the norm for many researchers in child development.

The number of graduate training programs in developmental psychology and human development also increased significantly in the 1960s. At this time, federal funds were established and earmarked for doctoral training in the sciences. The majority of these funds in the developmental sciences were in the National Institute of Mental Health (NIMH) and the National Institute of Child Health and Human Development (NICHD). Other mission-oriented research and training funds were made available as well, such as the Mental Retardation Branch of NICHD which, at one time, funded 12 major centers located at universities and about 25 university-affiliated facilities. Many programs required that all trainees conduct at least some of their research with laboratory animals as well as children, as subjects. The earlier concerns of the field, that is a multidisciplinary focus with applied issues, were deemphasized, and in some cases, lost completely. There was clearly a concern that the newly trained scientists should be seen as competent by those in the specialty fields viewed as the most "scientifically rigorous." The conduct of research in real-world settings and in obtaining practical hands-on experience often were not included. The new generation of developmental scientists were, for the most part, rather narrow specialists with great strengths in technique and methodology (Morrison et al., 1984).

This new emphasis on training researchers and the great increase in research, per se, has had many very positive outcomes. An unprecedented increase in our knowledge and understanding of many aspects of child development resulted from these developments. Much of what was written in the earlier texts simply was proven wrong and became obsolete. There are numerous examples of this occurrence. Among the many are the methodological breakthroughs and careful, painstaking work in the laboratory brought about a genuine rethinking of the capabilities of the human infant. Also, a theoretical shift of paradigms, followed by innovative studies with very small sample sizes, redefined our understanding of early language development. However, concerns began to be expressed by many that the pendulum had swung too far in the direction of scientific rigor. The focus on the whole child too often seemed to be lost.

In the 1980s, the belief that laboratory research produced findings about development that were, in some sense, more universal, as well as more basic, than results obtained from other methods (Morrison et al., 1985, p. 9) began to be questioned. Many in the field have come to recognize the complex issues we study require that serious consideration be given to real-world aspects of development and to context (e.g., Rogoff, 1981). Thus, there has been a return to the consideration of using a variety of methodologies and multidisciplinary perspectives. Furthermore, the distinction between "basic" and "applied" research has been called into question. As Woodworth acknowledged 50 years ago, one should and often does, facilitate the progress of the other.

At present, applied developmental psychology has taken on a particular set of meanings. There is acknowledgment of an underlying dimension, with basic research at the one end of this dimension and evaluation or assessment at the other (Morrison et al., 1985). The more one is working at the latter end, the more critical is the consideration of context and disciplines beyond one's own. There are also profound implications for training; these are considered in the other chapters in this volume.

An article based on a symposium organized by Frank Kessel for the 1979 biennial meetings of the society in San Francisco appeared in the *Newsletter* (Fall 1980) of SRCD. Titled "Developmental Psychology's applied and Interdisciplinary Dimensions: The Issue of Training," the four authors present views, sometimes complementary and at other times contradictory, concerning the various aspects of what constitutes appropriate graduate training. As the only nondevelopmentalist of the group, William Began presents a pessimistic view of what will become of Ph.D's if their training is not broadened. The two words he stresses are *broad* and *diversify*.

> For the behavioral sciences, breadth of experience means embedding our sciences in the real world . . . Scholarship is not debased by being directed toward the concerns of ordinary life, for at its best it offers a deeper and, hopefully, more coherent vision of the human condition. To tie scholarship to the real world means to base our theories on practice. (p. 5).

Bevan closes by expressing concern that if we become too concerned with formalisms, we lose sight of the ultimate object, that is human nature in society.

In the commentary by Willard Hartup, the importance of interdisciplinary perspectives is acknowledged. But, he argues strongly that *predoctoral* training must be anchored within a specific discipline. The training must include: "solid grounding in a discipline, solid grounding and rigorous standards in the philosophy and rules of evidence acceptable to the discipline, and experience with the technologies peculiar to the discipline" (p. 6). However, Hartup acknowledges that there should be broadened training in addition to the core training. Students must be encouraged to take advantage of the other departments containing developmental scientists on their campuses.

Presenting a somewhat different view, Sheldon H. White points to the broadening of both graduate training and of the students' interests. He argues that the history of developmental psychology is different from the history of general psychology. Within American universities, developmental psychology has become a program in psychology departments only during, roughly, the past 25 years. The emphasis on cross-disciplines and applied activities brought developmental psychology out of the psychology mainstream. Recognition has come about that the laboratory of all psychology must be broadened. Research focused on everyday settings and activities has become accepted, and the distinction between *basic* and *applied* has been blurred. Thus, it could be argued that psychology finally recognized what developmental psychology had known all along. However, we must keep in mind that when child psychology moved into psychology departments, it was greatly influenced by the prevailing theories, methods and values. Thus, the influence obviously has been bidirectional, and, for the most part, this has been positive.

In the final presentation of this symposium, Herbert Zimiles offered specific recommendations for changes to be made in our training. First, he felt the role of experimental method should be deemphasized. His second recommendation is to place more emphasis on theory. A conceptual framework that describes the child as a functioning being is missing in much of our current training. Finally, Zimiles believes that a closer working relationship with practitioners is needed. Teachers, social workers, and others know children at a level that developmental researchers often do not. If the two groups really worked together, the issues to be studied would be different, broader on the whole, and would recognize the importance of integrated functioning.

Perhaps the major lesson to be learned from this symposium is that our graduate models of training have come from a variety of sources that are diverse along several dimensions. Furthermore, they are continually changing and evolving. The context is in place for training programs that include an emphasis in applied child/human development.

Training programs in developmental psychology and in child and human development are faced with many challenges in the 1990s (Fisher & Koocher, 1990; Fisher, Rau & Colapietro, 1993; Chapters 4–7). Prospects for good employment for the graduates, especially in academic areas, have not improved despite predictions to the contrary. The graduate applicants with the strongest credentials are too often applying to other fields or programs. The faculty in these programs are often not trained in, or committed to, training in applied research and intervention. Many are questioning whether we even know how to train specialists in applied human development who will be able to work in the public and private sectors and bring about the changes that are so sorely needed to improve the lives of children and families.

In a presentation at the National Center for Poverty (1990), Lisbeth Schorr made the argument that we now know what makes certain programs for intervention effective and how these programs can reach larger numbers of those in need. However, in practice, too often we are not using what we know. She argued that "successful programs have common theoretical foundations that emphasize prevention, client outcomes, and long-term change and development" (p. 6). However, we know considerably less about what makes for good, supportive institutions and change.

Schorr then argues for the need for new training models. She feels we need to train those who are not conventional professionals, but who are able to build creative, collaborative relationships, work flexibly across disciplinary boundaries, and address a complex interplay of programs as well as utilize distinctive managerial skills. In her view, we have the knowledge to deal with most of the developmental issues, but we do not have the "new pool of talented, eager, committed individuals" (p. 12) to bring about the implementation of the knowledge. Thus, she poses a major challenge for the new training programs.

The challenge for those who are planning or already directing programs in applied human development is to establish reasonable goals that are consonant with the program's purpose, as well as and with the directives from the central administration. Then, one must obtain relevant knowledge in order to make choices about the many different aspects of training that have to be included. The chapters in this volume address policy issues as well as the issues of knowledge and procedures concerning training in applied human development. From the historical perspective, there are three important lessons to keep in mind. First, the field of which we are members grew out of a perceived need to solve societal problems through research and education. Second, it was recognized early on that no one discipline should dominate the others. In fact, in the early years, those studying physical and biological growth were as much a part of the child development movement as were those in psychology and child welfare. Third, the focus on *all* children and youth, and the belief that prevention was the best approach, set the stage for a commitment to both basic and applied issues.

Although the field of child development, as well as the fate of children and families in our country, has experienced many ups and downs since the 1930s, it is important not to lose sight of the remarkable progress that has been achieved over the past 60 to 70 years. The despair we may currently feel about diminishing resources and the resurgence of problems we thought were on the way to being conquered should be tempered by keeping the overall progress in mind. We must focus again on the plight of children and families. We are now armed with a tremendous base of knowledge—knowledge that was only dreamed of by G. Stanley Hall, Lawrence Frank, and Robert Woodworth. Their tireless efforts were rewarded, and it is up to us to carry forward with their mission. It is very reassuring that so many departments and colleges within universities are devoting new efforts and resources to programs in applied human development.

REFERENCES

Bowen, W.G. and Rudenstine, N.L. (1992). *In pursuit of the Ph.D.* Princeton, N.J.: Princeton University Press.

Bremner, R.H. (1960). *American philanthropy.* Chicago: University of Chicago Press.

Cahan, E. (1986). *A history of the W.T. Grant Foundation.* New York: W.T. Grant Foundation.

Coben, S. (1979). American foundations as patrons of science: The commitment to individual research. In N. Reingold (Ed.), *The sciences in the American context: New perspectives* (pp. 229–248). Washington, DC: Smithsonian Institute Press.

Coffman, H.C. (1936). *American foundations: A study of their role in the child welfare movement.* New York: Russell Sage.

Committee on Child Development. (1925). Conference proceedings (unpublished). Washington, D.C.: National Academy of Science Archives.

Committee on Child Development of the National Research Council. (1929b). *Quadrennial Report.* Rockefeller Archive Center, Laura Spelman Rockefeller Memorial Collection, Series III, Subseries 5, Box 30, Folder 390 p. 3.

Fisher, C.B. and Koocher, G. (1990). To be or not to be: Accreditation and credentialing in applied developmental psychology, *Journal of Applied Developmental Psychology, 11,* 381–394.

Fisher, C.B., Rau, J.B. and Colapietro, E. (1993). The Fordham University doctoral specialization in applied developmental psychology. *Journal of Applied Developmental Psychology, 14,* 289–301.

Fosdick, R.B. (1952). *The story of the Rockefeller Foundation.* New York: Harper & Row.

Frank, L.K. (1933). Childhood and youth. In President's Research Committee on Social Trends (W.C. Mitchell, Chair), *Recent social trends in the United States: Report of the President's Research Committee on Social Trends* (pp. 751–800). New York and London: McGraw-Hill.

Kessel, F. (1980). Developmental psychology's applied and interdisciplinary dimensions: The issue of training. *Newsletter of the Society for Research in Child Development,* Fall issue.

Morrison, F.J., Lord C. and Keating, D.P. (1984). *Applied developmental psychology,* Vol. 1. Orlando, FL. Academic Press.

History and Background 51

NRC Report, (1941). Committee on child development collection. Washington, D.C.: *National Academy of Sciences Archives.* Committee on Child Development Collection, p. 6.

Rheingold, H.L. (1985). The first twenty-five years of the society for research in child development. In J.W. Hagen and A.B. Smuts (Eds.) *History and research in child development* (p. 126–140). Chicago, IL: University of Chicago Press.

Rogoff, B. (1981). Schooling's influence on memory task performance. *Child Development, 52,* 260–267.

Schorr, L. (1990). Successful programs and the bureaucratic dilemma: Current deliberations. *National Center for Children in Poverty.* New York: Columbia University School of Public Health.

Smuts, A.B. (1985). The National Research Council Committee on Child Development and the Founding of the Society for Research in Child Development, 1925–1933. In J.W., Hagen and A.B. Smuts (Eds.) *History and research in child development* (p. 108–135). Chicago, IL: University of Chicago Press.

Smuts, A.B. and Hagen J.W. (1985). History and research in child development. *Monographs of the Society for Research in Child Development,* Vol. 50, 4–5.

PART II
MODELS OF GRADUATE EDUCATION IN APPLIED DEVELOPMENTAL SCIENCE: PSYCHOLOGY PROGRAMS

4

Doctoral Training in Applied Developmental Psychology: Matching Graduate Education, Student Needs, and Career Opportunities

Tara L. Kuther

Fordham University

The emerging specialization of applied developmental psychology (ADP) offers doctoral students new career opportunities and challenges. By extending graduate training beyond the confines of basic developmental theory and methodology, applied developmental psychology programs prepare students for careers ranging from academic teaching and research, to arenas of applied research and intervention, to knowledge dissemination and social policy. One challenge facing students seeking such opportunities is the current uncertainty associated with selecting a graduate program that has a clearly articulated curriculum and vision for providing applied developmental psychology students with the competencies to attain positions in academia and in nonacademic settings in which their developmental perspective will be valued.

Throughout the relatively brief history of the field of developmental psychology, the pendulum of psychological activity has swung back and forth between the poles of knowledge generation and knowledge application. For example, the turn of the century "child saving" movement drew child and adolescent researchers into theoretical and empirical paradigms aimed at buttressing social service programs designed to shape children into model citizens (Rheingold, 1986; Sears, 1975; Siegel & White, 1982; Smuts, 1986, Chapters 2 and 3, this volume). A backlash against the religious and racist biases underlying such paradigms drove developmental psychologists into the labs in an attempt to generate data which would be free of cultural values and expectations (Youniss, 1990). Only within the last two decades have developmental scientists begun to question the ecological validity of their laboratory derived data base and their responsibilities to society (Bronfenbrenner, 1977; Fisher & Brennan, 1992; Fisher & Tryon, 1990; Montada & Schmitt, 1982). However, continued tension between empirical versus practical emphases is evident in the challenges facing developmental psychology programs as they struggle to determine whether they should retain the basic research tradition, or move into the new specialization of applied developmental psychology (Shantz, 1987).

The National Conference on Graduate Education in the Applications of Developmental Science Across the Lifespan (Fisher, Murray, et al., 1993) was an exciting step towards addressing the training needs of doctoral students interested in acquiring the skills to apply the developmental database to real-world problems. These problems jeopardize the development of vulnerable individuals in today's increasingly complex and diverse society. The conference set out the scope of applied developmental science (ADS) activities and provided a curriculum blueprint designed to produce scientist–professionals who would be competent to pursue these activities. This blueprint was intended to provide a flexible educational framework for graduate education conducted across a variety of disciplines (e.g., gerontology, human development, psychology, social work, and sociology) and educational settings (e.g., psychology departments, sociology departments, institutes of child development, and medical centers). In recognition of the disciplinary breadth versus specialization characterizing various applied developmental science programs, conferees recommended that programs translate the curriculum recommendations to match their unique educational and training goals.

Programs offering specializations in applied developmental psychology must design curricula that meet not only the goals of applied developmental science, but also the standards of the discipline of psychology (Fisher, Rau, & Colapietro, 1993; Chapter 1, this volume). Accordingly, undergraduate psychology majors planning to pursue a doctoral degree in applied developmental psychology must carefully consider whether programs will provide them with the knowledge base and skills to perform competently as both applied developmental scientists and psychologists. As an undergraduate, I wanted to learn how to conduct meaningful research with the potential to assist children and adolescents in the pursuit of healthy and adaptive lives as adults. I was initially drawn to Fordham University's developmental doctoral program because I wanted a solid foundation in research methodology and developmental theory. I was intrigued by the applied developmental psychology specialization, but it was not until the initial interview with Fordham faculty and students that I realized that there was a possibility to be trained as a scientist–professional who could bring experimental rigor to practical problems facing developing individuals and their families.

FORDHAM UNIVERSITY'S SPECIALIZATION IN APPLIED DEVELOPMENTAL PSYCHOLOGY

Fordham University's specialization in Applied Developmental Psychology was first implemented in 1989, two years before the national ADS conference (Fisher, Murray et al., 1993). It was later refined to merge more closely with conference recommendations. The conference identified three conjoint emphasis of the applied developmental science perspective (Fisher et al., 1993). The *applied* aspect underlies training in knowledge generation and application techniques, which have direct implications for what individuals, families, practitioners, and policy makers do. At Fordham University, this aspect is reflected in both practica and didactic training emphasizing ecological research designs, administration of social policy and law, program design and evaluation strategies, and developmental assessment techniques. The *developmental* aspect of applied developmental science stresses the importance of understanding normative and atypical processes as they emerge within different developmental periods and across diverse physical and cultural contexts. Fordham incorporates this aspect in courses on basic cognitive and personality development, family systems, and developmental psychopathology. Fordham's program addresses the *science* aspect of applied developmental science by providing training in a variety of statistical and research methods which can collect reliable information and test the validity of theory in real world contexts. Fordham adds a fourth dimension to applied developmental science education, by training students to identify themselves as psychologists. This involves the acquisition of a core knowledge base in psychology, including history and systems of psychology; biological, cognitive, affective and social bases of behavior; research design and methodology; and professional/ethical issues (APA, 1987; Fisher, Rau & Colapietro, 1993; Chapter 1, this volume).

Although a multidisciplinary perspective is encouraged, the additional curriculum demands required to ensure that students are trained (and can be credentialed) as psychologist, means that course work in other disciplines will be limited. A multidisciplinary emphasis in applied developmental psychology programs is fostered by training students to value the expertise of other professionals and to form multidisciplinary collaborations to promote individual and family development. At Fordham, these skills are transmitted to students in coursework, research projects, and most concretely, in their third year of required field work.

The lifespan perspective (Baltes, Reese, & Lipsitt, 1980), with its focus on the reciprocity of individual and contextual factors influencing development across the life course, permeates coursework and research at Fordham. Given the continually changing demographics of the United States and the baby boom generation's progression from middle to old age, the lifespan orientation not only provides a strong theoretical base for applied research, but also translates into increased opportunities for employment. A unique aspect of Fordham's doctoral specialization in applied developmental psychology is its emphasis on ethical issues. Applications of developmental research are often more intrusive than traditional experimental lab work because of the naturalistic methods utilized and the intervention focus (Fisher, 1993, 1994; Fisher & Brennan, 1992; Fisher, Hoagwood & Jensen, in press; Fisher & Tryon, 1990). Fordham students are trained to view community participants as partners in the identification of ethical issues and the creation of innovative ethical solutions to challenges emerging in applied developmental research and intervention (Fisher & Fyrberg, 1994; Fisher, Higgins, Rau, Kuther, & Belanger, in press).

Program Development

Consistent with the national conference guidelines, Fordham University's doctoral specialization in applied developmental psychology is organized to emphasize the development of skills in four content domains: developmental theory, research methods, application strategies, and professional issues (Fisher, Murray, et al., 1993; Fisher, Rau & Colapietro, 1993). Program goals and philosophy were developed from surveys of existing curricula, student interests and employment opportunities, faculty expertise and funding options, and potential sites for predoctoral field experiences in the New York metropolitan area. The decision to create a "specialization," rather than "program," in applied developmental psychology reflected the faculty's commitment to training in basic developmental theory and research design as a foundation upon which application strategies are built. The specialization expands student expertise in basic developmental theory, content, and methodology by preparing students to: (a) test the validity of developmental theory in real-world contexts; (b) work with sociocultural institutions that impact individual and family development; (c) identify individual and cultural variation in patterns of development and in response to research and/or intervention; (d) construct, administer and interpret culturally sensitive instruments for evaluating developmental strengths and vulnerabilities; (e) design and evaluate development enhancing interventions; (f) disseminate knowledge about developmental processes to parents, practitioners, and policy makers; and (g) respond to the unique ethical issues inherent to applying the developmental data base to real-world problems (Fisher, Rau, & Colapietro, 1993).

Approximately eight new students enter Fordham's developmental program each year. Currently, all students take advantage of the applied developmental psychology specialization. The availability and talent of ancillary faculty from the psychometric and clinical faculties allow each student to receive individualized attention during the full course of doctoral training. In-depth interviews with prospective students helps to ensure that the applied developmental specialization will be compatible with entering students' career goals.

The Curriculum

Developmental theory and content

During the first two years of training, students are introduced to basic theoretical, substantive, and methodological bases of basic and applied developmental psychology. Courses in cognitive and personality development, developmental psychopathology, and foundations of developmental theory stress the importance of rigor in research design and the significance of developmental theory and methods to real-world application. Courses in neuroscience, research methodology, social science statistical techniques, and historical and ethical perspectives in psychology provide students with a foundation in the discipline of psychology.

Throughout their coursework, students are sensitized to the contributions of the lifespan (Baltes, 1987), ecological (Bronfenbrenner, 1979), and developmental contextual (Lerner, 1984, 1986) perspectives on the substantive assumptions of applied developmental psychology. These assumptions include: the temporality of change, the centrality of context, and the individual differences and within-person variables that shape developmental phenomena (Fisher & Lerner, 1994; Fisher, Rau & Colapietro, 1993; Fisher & Tryon, 1990).

For example, in my first semester at Fordham, I was introduced to developmental and methodological theory in a Developmental Psychology Foundations course. Through readings and discussion, I attempted to compose an integrative understanding of the contributions of five metatheoretical traditions in developmental psychology, those being organismic, mechanistic, psychodynamic, dialectical, and contextual. The five metatheoretical perspectives were illustrated within various content domains (i.e., language, perception, cognitive and social development) and across different applied settings (e.g., schools, medical centers, the courts, and government agencies). Characteristics of atypical development were addressed in a course entitled Developmental Psychopathology, which familiarized students with various developmental disorders, their trajectory across the lifespan, and the contribution of the developmental approach to the prevention of later psychological disorders (Cicchetti, 1989; Lewis & Miller, 1990).

A second semester course in Applied Developmental Psychology introduces methodological and ethical issues involved in the application of developmental theory and research design to real-world settings. When I took that course, we covered: the advantages and drawbacks of longitudinal and quasi–experimental designs in applied settings (Bergman & Magnussen, 1990; Bronfenbrenner, 1977); models for conducting research and interventions with culturally and economically diverse populations; the importance of developmental research as a foundation for designing and selecting appropriate outcome measures for development enhancing programs; the problem of measurement equivalence when different items and behaviors are used to measure change or the impact of an intervention across different developmental phases; and professional and ethical issues that relate to the activities of applied developmental psychologists.

Texts such as *Applied Developmental Psychology* (Fisher & Lerner, 1994), *Early Intervention: Implementing Child and Family Services for Infants and Toddlers Who Are At-Risk or Disabled* (Hanson & Lynch, 1989), and *Contemporary Families: A Handbook for School Professionals* (Procidano & Fisher, 1992) drew our attention to: (a) specific methods used to identify developmental correlates of such phenomena as infant diseases, children's eyewitness testimony, adolescent pregnancy, maternal employment, and family caregiving for older adults; (b) assessment and intervention strategies targeted for at-risk populations varying in cultural, socioeconomic, environmental, and developmental status; and (c) how to disseminate developmental knowledge and form community partnerships with practitioners and institutions serving children, youth, and older adults.

Research Methodology

The second domain of study, research methods, is emphasized throughout the four years of the Fordham program. Graduate education at Fordham emphasizes that, first and foremost, applied developmental psychologists must be proficient empiricists. We are taught that our intellectual equity as applied developmental psychologists is the methodological skills we can bring to an institution to help them conceptualize their needs and goals within a valid theoretical and methodological framework. During each year, students complete a research project that matches their increasing levels of expertise (Fisher, Rau, & Colapietro, 1993). In the first year, students participate in a research apprenticeship with a faculty mentor designed to familiarize them with the host of issues involved in conducting applied research. In their second year, students embark on a supervised, but more independent predoctoral research project. Third year students conduct research in an applied setting as part of a year-long applied developmental psychology practicum, and fourth year students begin their dissertation research.

A first year methodology course exposes students to experimental, quasi-experimental and correlational designs, including their advantages and disadvantages in terms of internal and external validity. Many students follow this with an advanced course in Developmental Research Design. Students are required to take a four course statistical sequence including introductory statistical analyses, analysis of variance, and at least two other statistics courses compatible with students' interests and needs (e.g., multivariate analysis, multiple regression, factor analysis, and structural equation modeling).

During my first year research apprenticeship, I had the opportunity to experience the difficulties of data collection with high-risk populations and attempt to apply developmental methodology to an ethical problem. The purpose of the study was to examine how urban youth judge the desirability of three reporting options available to investigators who discover that a research participant may be in jeopardy (Fisher, Higgins, Rau, Kuther, & Belanger, in press). Our goal was to provide empirical information that could assist the ethical decision making of developmental scientists working with adolescents facing a wide range of developmental risks. (This project is described in greater detail in the section entitled 'Professional Skills'). From my work on this project, I developed questions that led to my predoctoral research, the second formal research experience required at Fordham.

My predoctoral research focused on the question: How does victimization by and witnessing of community violence impact development during the middle school years? The project consisted of developing and testing a measure to gather valid and reliable information on: (a) instances and settings of community violence including physical threat, physical assault, wounding by a weapon, muggings and robberies near school, home, or shopping centers; (b) conditions under which perpetrators of community violence are adults or teenagers, strangers, someone known to the student, or a member of a gang; (c) students' immediate emotional and behavioral reactions to violent acts; (d) long term reactions and strategies for coping with exposure to violence; (e) student characteristics or behavior patterns that might be related to violence exposure, links between violence exposure patterns and child and family characteristics that might mediate the effects of exposure to violence (Kuther & Fisher, 1996).

In the spirit of university–community partnerships, prior to administering the first draft of the questionnaire, my colleagues and I met with school personnel to gain feedback on the items we thought would be relevant to their student population. We also discussed the relevance of the descriptive data derived from the survey to curriculum decisions regarding crime prevention programs and agreed to assist them with such a program during the second year of the study.

Application Strategies

Application strategies is the third domain of instruction specified by the national conference as a distinguishing characteristic of applied developmental science curricula. These application strategies and skills include (a) program development, implementation, and evaluation procedures; (b) communication and consultation strategies; (c) development-enhancing intervention techniques; (d) developmental assessment strategies; and (e) human relations skills (Fisher, Murray, et al., 1993). At Fordham, specific courses on program evaluation, social policy, and developmental psychology and law introduce students to issues such as designing and evaluating developmental interventions, staffing and administrating social programs, serving as expert witnesses, and forming partnerships with community agencies.

Students acquire assessment skills in two formal courses: Individual Mental Examination and Developmental Assessment. In these courses, students learn how to administer and evaluate the validity and reliability of standard cognitive and developmental assessment instruments including the WISC, Binet, Bayley, Brazelton, Home, and OARS. Students can also take advanced courses in personality assessment, neurological assessment, test construction, and item analysis. Students have the opportunity to use and fine-tune their application skills during the third-year applied developmental psychology practicum (This is described in the section entitled 'Field Experience'.).

Professional Skills

Professional issues are stressed throughout the program. Courses in social policy and psychology and law enhance student career development by providing real-world examples of the role of developmental psychologists in government and within the courts and judicial system. The Historical and Ethical Perspectives in Psychology seminar presents students with a solid base in ethical and professional standards and codes of conduct. The fact that both applied developmental and clinical students are required to take this course serves to broaden the perspective of both as ethical issues are presented from practice-oriented (clinical) and research/application-oriented (ADP) perspectives. Students are familiarized with the issues of informed consent, confidentiality, autonomy and privacy as they relate to: applied research and dissemination; psychological assessment; and primary, secondary, and tertiary interventions. Ethical issues associated with high-risk populations are also considered (see Fisher, 1993; Fisher, Hoagwood, & Jensen, in press for a discussion of these issues), as well as those associated with the role of psychologists in the courts (see Fisher, 1995).

An important source of input into professional roles and standards of conduct is through individual research and interactions with faculty. The most effective way to learn about professional and ethical issues is through "hands-on" practice. For example, as a first year student, I worked with my mentor on a project directly related to ethical issues in research with high-risk adolescent populations. Frequently in such research, scientists encounter information that suggests that participants are in jeopardy (e.g., they may be taking illegal drugs, considering suicide, or concerned that they have a sexually transmitted disease). Scientists have a range of alternatives available to them: they may maintain confidentiality, provide referral sources to the teenager, or report the information to an adult. Appropriate referral and reporting practices require taking participant's interests into account. In our study, urban youth were asked to rate the seriousness of various problem behaviors and state what actions researchers should take if an adolescent research participant tells them about such problems (Fisher, Higgins, Rau, Kuther & Belanger, in press).

My work on this project sensitized me to the unique balance required between a researcher's responsibility to science and the humanitarian responsibility to his or her participants. Our responsibility to produce scientifically valid results may blind us to our ethical responsibility to protect participants from harm. Maintaining confidentiality serves to protect both participant rights and the scientific validity of our results, but it may not always be the best choice, especially in applied settings. This study also illustrated to me, and the other students working on the project, the need for researchers to change their view of research participants from *subjects*, connoting passivity, to a more humanitarian and realistic view of participants as *partners* in research. Participants have an active role in research, they are dynamic beings with thoughts and attitudes that transcend their role as research "subjects." Psychologists must recognize this quality of "personhood" and consider participant attitudes when confronted with ethical dilemmas.

Field Experience

The applied developmental psychology practicum

The national conference (Fisher et al., 1993) emphasized field experiences as a crucial element of ADS education. Fordham's ADP program has translated this element into a year-long practica designed for third-year students. During this year, students gain experience working and conducting research in an institutional setting (e.g., schools, hospitals, women's shelters, nursing homes, child development centers). In most cases students conduct developmental assessments (help sites with screening and evaluation), and utilize these assessments as an empirical measure of either the characteristics of the center's population or the effectiveness of an institutional intervention. The practicum is supervised by both a Fordham faculty professor and an on–site professional. The on–site experience is accompanied by a two semester seminar conducted by a member of the faculty, focusing on issues relevant to applied work and professional development. The course is designed to present issues and to assist students in their professional development. For example, a typical homework assignment may be to describe one's theoretical orientation in lay-person's terms, as one would speak to the administrator of a clinic. Students that I have spoken to have all found the class portion of the practicum experience very valuable and rewarding in terms of providing an opportunity and outlet for professional growth.

In speaking with students that have completed the practicum experience, I have noted that nearly all were excited to work with "real" populations. Students commented that the practicum experience is most positive when they have at least one hour per week of face-to-face interaction with their on–site supervisor, providing sufficient time to ask questions and receive feedback. Like most field experiences, the quality tended to differ by individual. There are many challenges associated with field experience; however, students feel that the most important are those pertaining to the receipt of adequate on-site supervision: the need for a developmental psychologist on staff to provide supervision. Sites staffed with clinical psychologists offered novel opportunities, as well as difficulties. Challenges with the supervision of field experiences in applied developmental psychology programs are not unique to Fordham (see Chapter 11).

Difficulties with supervision by clinical psychologists may be rooted in our different philosophy. From my perspective, clinical psychology is concerned with psychological dysfunction and remediation. This differs from ADP, which is concerned with normative development, developmental risks, optimizing development, and preventing developmental problems. In most cases applied developmental psychologists also take a more contextual, rather than individualistic, perspective on protective factors and vulnerabilities. A number of students felt that supervision by a clinical psychologist was a very positive experience because it afforded them the opportunity to articulate the singularity of their ADP training and the distinct contributions an applied developmental perspective can provide.

The practicum experience is designed to bridge the gap between graduate education and professional life. It is a growth experience in which the student comes to understand, through practice, what his or her role as an applied developmental psychologist is and what the distinctive contributions of ADP are. The Fordham practicum was conceptualized to provide benefits to both student and site. This is best illustrated in the following example. A current placement is located in the neonatal clinical of a children's hospital. The student conducts follow-up developmental assessments (approximately 3, 6, or 9 months from initial evaluation) on high-risk premature infants. The student serves as part of an interdisciplinary team composed of medical doctors, nurses, psychologists and speech pathologists. For the research component of her practica, the student conducts a needs assessment with parents and staff, and designs and evaluates a parent support group. In this way, the student is an asset to her placement site at the same time she develops her applied research and evaluation skills.

Assistantships and internships

In addition to the practicum, Fordham offers other novel opportunities for field experience through assistantships and predoctoral internships; the latter often satisfies predoctoral experiential requirements for licensure. An example of the field experience opportunities unique to Fordham is its relationship with the Westchester Institute of Human Development (WIHD). The Westchester Institute for Human Development is an interdisciplinary program concerned with those who have, or are at risk for, developmental disabilities. It operates from a lifespan orientation and includes services for families of individuals with developmental disabilities. WIHD is a multidisciplinary program offering the services of audiologists, speech–language pathologists, dentists, nurses, nutritionists, occupational therapists, physical therapists, psychiatrists, psychologists, and social workers. The mission of WIHD is to maximize developmental strengths while minimizing the impact of developmental handicaps so as to optimize quality of life.

Examples of activities conducted at WIHD include parenting classes for parents of children with developmental disabilities, vocational assistance for developmentally disabled adolescents and adults, and a prevention/screening program for foster children. Many first- and second-year Fordham students hold assistantships at WIHD. First-year student assistants work at the family resource center and provide information to parents of developmentally disabled children. Students conduct research, gather information and make it available to parents in language that they can understand. Students also have the opportunity to observe screenings and assessments conducted by the facility's specialists.

An example of a second-year applied developmental assistantship involves the foster care program. WIHD provides screening/assessment and prevention services for foster children and both their biological and foster parents. Graduate students conduct parent groups, which are usually team-run. Leaders of parent groups model parenting skills, and teach parents how to be more responsive to their children and also how to set limits.

Advanced predoctoral internship activities include assessment, program development, and program evaluation. For example, WIHD provides services such as classes in parenting, financial advisement, and child care to a local homeless shelter. A current Fordham intern is conducting an evaluation to determine whether the classes and curriculum are developmentally appropriate for the parents and children. Another intern serves as part of a multidisciplinary team that evaluates (physically, educationally and psychologically) children entering foster care. She conducts in-home assessments with the foster children approximately two weeks to one month from their initial placement with a foster family. The intern evaluates the child's level of adaptive functioning, assesses the home environment and makes recommendations to both the foster mother, and to WIHD's multidisciplinary team.

Fordham University has developed many other ongoing relationships with agencies and institutions in New York and Connecticut. Formalized research and training experiences are available at the Hispanic Research Center (HRC) located at Fordham University. The HRC conducts multidisciplinary, collaborative research with anthropologists, sociologists and psychologists to study and intervene in the lives of Hispanic children, families and other adults. Through Fordham's Third Age Center, a nationally recognized multidisciplinary center for applied research and services for the elderly, students have the opportunity to work with philosophers, ethicists, psychologists and sociologists to develop and empirically examine programs for well and frail elderly and to develop survey and outreach programs for caregivers of the elderly.

In addition, Fordham University has developed relationships with many local clinics and hospital treatment centers, providing students with a variety of internship sites. For example, a current student has become an integral part of the AIDS mental health team of a local university-based hospital clinic. The program is designed to provide counseling for HIV-positive patients and their families at the location where they receive their primary medical care. The internship requires that the student conduct an evaluation of the program. This task builds upon the student's previous course work and experience as it demands that he or she be skilled in program/intervention design and evaluation, and be familiar with relevant areas of health, and social and developmental psychopathology.

FIELD REGULATION AND CREDENTIALING: ACCREDITATION & LICENSURE

At the forefront of current issues in doctoral education in applied developmental psychology are field regulation (program accreditation) and individual credentialing (professional licensure/certification) (Fisher & Koocher, 1990; Goldstein, Wilson, & Gerstein, 1983). Field regulation, in the form of accreditation, insures that graduate programs in psychology meet the current standards of the field (APA, 1986; Fisher & Koocher, 1990; Young, Chambers, Kells, & Associates, 1983). Individual credentialing, in the form of state licensure or certification as a psychologist, is intended to protect the consumer by providing assurance as to the competence of individual psychologists (Fisher & Koocher, 1990).

Accreditation and Applied Developmental Psychology

Accreditation is intended to be "a voluntary, self-regulatory process of quality assessment and enhancement among institutions and professional programs of higher education" (Fisher & Koocher, 1990, p. 383). There are four basic characteristics of accreditation. It is voluntary, self-regulatory, evaluative and focused on increasing educational quality (APA, 1986; Fisher & Koocher, 1990; Young et al., 1983). Accreditation in psychology is conducted by the American Psychological Association (APA) and, until recently, has applied only to the traditional specialty designations of clinical, counseling, school and industrial/organizational (APA, 1987, 1996).

Over the last decade, APA has debated expanding the scope of accreditation to include emerging specialties such as applied social psychology, applied cognitive psychology, and applied developmental psychology. Whether these specialties will seek accreditation now that the APA scope has broadened will depend on the degree to which faculty and students believe they will benefit professionally and economically from such recognition (Fisher & Koocher, 1990). One of the benefits of accreditation to students is the assurance that a program maintains a common standard of education and professionalism. It can also enhance opportunities for internships and recognition by state licensing boards. A disadvantage of accreditation is that it may lead applied developmental programs to offer homogenized curricula almost indistinguishable from those of the current APA specialties (Fisher & Koocher, 1990).

Accreditation criteria recently revised by the American Psychological Association

The American Psychological Association (1996) has recently accepted a new model of accreditation criteria. Whereas formerly the structural aspects of graduate education were emphasized, the *Guidelines and Principles for Accreditation of Programs in Professional Psychology* (APA, 1996) places an increased emphasis on assessing the outcomes of professional education and training. The emphasis on outcome rather than structure is intended to preserve flexibility and foster creativity in how different programs address the educational process. The ultimate goal is to produce competent graduates while preserving the unique contributions of a variety of subspecialties of professional psychology.

Accreditation is a voluntary, nongovernmental process of self-study and peer review intended to evaluate, enhance and provide public recognition of the quality of institutional programs of higher education. Its goal is to protect the interests of students and the public, and to improve the quality of teaching, research and practice. According to the *Guidelines and Principles for Accreditation of Programs in Professional Psychology*, accreditation serves an evaluative function; its objective is to judge "the degree to which a program has achieved the goals and objectives of its stated training model" (APA, 1996, p. 2).

The American psychological Association accredits programs in "professional psychology." Professional psychology is defined as "that part of the discipline in which an individual with the appropriate education and training provides services to the general public" (APA, 1996, p. 1). These services "primarily involve health and human development" (APA, 1996, p. 1). The inclusion of human development as a central aspect of "professional psychology" may motivate applied developmental psychology programs to seek accreditation. As currently conceptualized, the goal of applied developmental psychology is to enhance and optimize developmental processes while preventing and minimizing the effects of developmental handicaps (Fisher & Lerner, 1994; Fisher & Tryon, 1990). Faculty offering doctoral training in applied developmental psychology must consider whether nonparticipation in the APA accreditation process will have negative implications for students seeking professional credentials as experts in human development.

The newly proposed APA accreditation guidelines are less restrictive than earlier guidelines. Whereas accredited programs of graduate education in professional psychology must have a well-articulated philosophy and set of principles underlying their training model, the program's philosophy may be defined independent of other models, or it may be identified through a national conference of psychologists. The scope and educational guidelines set forth by the National Conference on Graduate Education in the Applications of Developmental Science Across the Life Span (Fisher, Murray et al., 1993) and recent proposals for the developmental research divisions of APA to jointly endorse a formal definition of applied developmental psychology, may make APA accreditation a more practical reality for applied developmental psychology programs wishing to apply for APA accreditation. According to the *APA Accreditation Guidelines* (APA, 1996), accreditable doctoral training programs in professional psychology should be based upon a common core of knowledge in the field of scientific psychology, as well as skills and knowledge appropriate to a particular field of practice. Graduates of accredited doctoral programs must demonstrate competence in the following areas:

- History and systems of scientific psychology and scientific and professional ethics and standards.
- Scientific, theoretical, and methodological foundations, including knowledge of research design, methodology, and statistics appropriate to that field.
- Skills in psychological assessment, intervention design, implementation, and evaluation.
- Issues of cultural and individual diversity relevant to all aspects of professional psychology including assessment, treatment, delivery of services, and conduct of research with diverse client populations.
- Discipline core areas of biological, cognitive, affective, social, and cultural aspects of behavior, as well as individual differences in behavior and dysfunctional behavior/psychopathology.

In addition to an organized curriculum plan, under the *Guidelines* (APA, 1996), accredited doctoral programs will require that students receive adequate field experiences including practica, externship and internship experiences. The program should place students in settings with appropriate and adequate professionals to supervise and provide a wide range of training through application of intervention procedures. The practicum component of the student's education should be integrated with other elements of the educational program, allowing for adequate forums for their discussion of the practicum experience.

Accredited programs will offer internship education and training in psychology with the goal of preparing students for the practice of professional psychology. An appropriate internship is sponsored by an institution whose primary function is the provision of services to a population sufficient in number and variability to provide interns with adequate training experiences over a one-year period. All interns are required to demonstrate an intermediate to advanced level of knowledge and skill in the following areas relevant to professional psychology:

- Professional interpersonal conduct, supervision and management skills
- Assessment, consultation, intervention, and evaluation
- Issues of cultural and individual diversity
- Strategies of scholarly inquiry.

The accreditation recommendations reflect the view that science and practice should not be conceptualized as opposing poles but rather as equal contributors to excellence in psychological training and basic methods. Students are to be educated to recognize "the value of science for the practice of psychology and the value of practice for the science of psychology" (APA, 1996, p. 3).

These recommendations are similar to those proposed at the National Conference on Graduate Education in the Applications of Developmental Science Across the Life Span (Fisher et al., 1993), and with the inclusion of specific courses directly related to psychology, they are consistent with the curriculum required for students specializing in Fordham University's applied developmental psychology offering.

Advantages and disadvantages of accreditation for applied developmental psychology programs

There are many benefits associated with accreditation. It can be viewed as a way of obtaining institutional funding and individual statutory recognition as a licensed professional (Fisher & Koocher, 1990; Glidden, 1983). Institutional funding improves educational opportunities and financial aid for students in the form of assistantships and fellowships. The accreditation process is also valuable as a tool to evaluate and enhance the quality of educational programs through peer review (Young, 1983). By requiring programs to clearly articulate their curriculum and program goals, students applying to applied developmental psychology programs may obtain a clearer picture of the extent to which a particular program will provide them with the competencies to fulfill the duties and responsibilities of an applied developmental psychologist.

Accreditation may increase the number of available pre and postdoctoral internship opportunities for students of ADP programs. Currently, access to internships is limited, as many students are not equipped to compete for internship placements because of a lack of training in assessment and intervention techniques (Koocher, 1990). However, even students that earn positions within internship placements may not receive adequate training; clinically-oriented internships may not be appropriate for the professional goals of applied developmental psychologists (Fisher & Brown, 1987). Fordham has addressed this issue by developing relationships with many institutions suitable for the training of applied developmental psychologists, such as multidisciplinary hospitals serving individuals and families. However, there are still few, if any, applied developmental psychologists employed at most traditional (e.g., clinically oriented) internship sites (Fisher & Koocher, 1990; Koocher, 1990; Chapter 11).

This may develop into a problematic cycle if ADP students are continually supervised by clinical psychologists or other professionals that are not trained as applied developmental scientists. Traditional clinically oriented internship settings do not encompass the full breadth of applied activities that an ADP professional must be proficient in. For example, an applied developmental psychologist must be competent in program design, evaluation, and public policy. More appropriate internship placements may include community-based settings such as schools, senior citizen centers, and day care centers. Currently, these settings do not have the funding to support year-long training experiences, so ADP students remain at an unfortunate disadvantage.

Applied developmental psychology programs must also be wary of the potential for accreditation's focus on a common core of professional training, requiring courses in assessment and therapeutic intervention to shift the focus of ADP towards tertiary preventions. This would make ADP overlap considerably with pediatric and child clinical psychology (Fisher & Koocher, 1990). ADP must be distinguishable from clinical psychology, to avoid "'back door' entry into traditional clinical roles and depiction of the applied developmental psychologist as a 'junior' clinician or 'semi-'clinician" (Goldstein, Wilson, & Gerstein, 1983, p. 352; Koocher, 1990). Programs seeking to participate in the APA accreditation process must be vigilant in their effort not to lose the focus on prevention, normative development, and contextual factors that distinguish applied developmental psychology from its sister fields.

Accreditation and licensure

While accreditation is designed to provide a standard of quality within psychology graduate programs, state licensure was developed to provide an assurance as to the competency of persons trained in such programs. State licensing provides a standard of professionalism in psychology and protects consumers from the consequences of unprofessional conduct by licensed professionals (APA, 1987; Fisher & Koocher, 1990). Licensure has both personal, professional and economic implications. It has a legitimizing and enhancing effect on any profession by providing statutory recognition (APA, 1987; Fisher & Koocher, 1990). Licensure "makes it possible to define legally who one is, or ought to be" (Fisher & Koocher, 1990, p. 384). Licensed psychologists are also reimbursable by health insurers for the provision of mental health services.

Licensure is essential to applied developmental psychologists even if their applied work is only consultative in nature (Goldstein, Wilson, & Gerstein, 1983; Fisher & Koocher, 1990; Fisher, Rau, & Colapietro, 1993; Scarr, 1990). Licensure is often thought of as a requirement only for clinicians, however, a license is required of any psychologist who offers psychological services to the public (Goldstein, Wilson, & Gerstein, 1983). The activities of applied developmental psychologists take them into the public domain. Licensure is imperative to the applied developmental psychologists' professional and economic well-being because health insurers will reimburse only licensed professionals for the provision of mental health services.

It is important to recognize that many programs within applied developmental psychology do not prepare their students for licensure (Koocher, 1990). Fordham University's specialization in applied developmental psychology is one of the few programs that provide the curriculum, field experience, and predoctoral experiential opportunities required for licensure in its state. Typically, licensure eligibility requires two years of supervised field experience with at least one year postdoctoral, as well as a formal examination, although the requirements vary from state to state.

As a student specializing in applied developmental psychology, I see licensure as important, for the aforementioned reasons as well as for professional identity purposes. Licensure is especially important in a non-therapy-oriented applied field, such as ADP, because at present it is the only avenue to public recognition that a psychologist is competent to offer services to the public. Moreover, in nonacademic settings licensure often determines employment opportunities and economic benefits.

While accreditation is a voluntary option for psychology programs, there is the potential for accreditation to become a formal requirement of licensure (Fisher & Koocher, 1990; Wilson & Hayes, 1989). For example, the Model Act for State Licensure of Psychologists (APA, 1987) has suggested that by 1995, "applicants for licensure shall have completed a doctoral program that is accredited by the American Psychological association" (p. 698). Wilson and Hayes (1989) have argued that the voluntary status of APA accreditation is merely an illusion as it is being used as the *sine qua non* of licensing. Programs offering applied developmental psychology, if they are to meet the needs of students applying for positions in nonacademic settings, must begin to seriously consider the pros and cons of program accreditation and the extent to which their students' career advancement will depend upon eligibility for state licensure.

APPLIED DEVELOPMENTAL PSYCHOLOGY: BALANCING RESEARCH AND APPLICATION

The most important boundary that ADP needs to maintain is exemption from private individual practice or psychotherapy (Goldstein, Wilson, & Gerstein, 1983). Applied developmental psychologists are not, and should not be, trained to conduct psychotherapy. Applied developmental psychology programs must be rigorous in their efforts to preserve the uniqueness of the applied developmental perspective and to foster a strong identity among their graduates. Applied developmental psychologists must maintain the delicate balance between science and application and avoid repeating the unfortunate history of clinical psychology's failure to nurture and maintain scientist–practitioners (Tryon, 1990). Students applying to Fordham University's program are carefully screened so as to encourage only those with commitment and enthusiasm for empirical scholarship. Such screening ensures that students are devoting their time and money to training that will help them meet their career goals and also preserves the integrity of the applied developmental specialization.

The balance between research and application is also threatened by the service emphasis in applied settings and the scholarly emphasis in university settings. Service settings often emphasize application strategies at the exclusion of research. It will be beneficial to social institutions and the scientific–professional development of applied developmental psychology practica students if program evaluation begins to be included as an integral part of service delivery (Tryon, 1990). The national conference emphasized that research and theory not only guide interventions, but are modified by the evaluation of interventions. A commitment to scientifically based program design and evaluation will foster the bidirectional relationship between those who generate empirically based knowledge about development and those who pursue professional practices, services, and policies affecting the well-being of members of society (Fisher, Murray, et al., 1993). Students have a role in further defining the direction of the field of applied developmental psychology through creativity in their choice of research topics, theoretical orientations, methodological styles, and career choices. Now is the time for graduate students to voice their opinions; their futures depend upon it.

REFERENCES

American Psychological Association. (1986). *Accreditation handbook*. Washington, DC: Author.

American psychological Association. (1987). Model Act for State Licensure of Psychologists. *American Psychologist, 42,* 696–703.

American Psychological Association. (1996). *Guidelines and principles for accreditation of programs in professional psychology.* Washington DC: Author.
Baltes, P.B. (1987). Theoretical propositions of lifespan developmental psychology: On the dynamics between growth and decline. *Developmental Psychology, 23,* 611–626.
Baltes, P.B., Reese, H.W., & Lipsitt, L.P. (1980). Lifespan developmental psychology. *Annual Review of Psychology, 31,* 65–110.
Bergman, L.R. & Magnussen, D. (1990). General issues about data quality in longitudinal research. In D. Magnussen & L.R. Bergman (Eds.), *Data quality in longitudinal research,* (pp. 1–31). Cambridge, MA: Cambridge University Press.
Bronfenbrenner, U. (1977). Toward an experimental ecology of human development. *American Psychologist, 32,* 513–531.
Bronfenbrenner, U. (1979). *The ecology of human development.* Cambridge, MA: Harvard University Press.
Cicchetti, D. (1989). *The emergence of a discipline: Rochester symposium on developmental psychopathology* (Vol. 1). Hillsdale, NJ: Erlbaum.
Fisher, C.B. (1993). Integrating science and ethics in research with high-risk children and youth. *Social Policy Report, 7,* 1–27.
Fisher, C.B. (1994). Reporting and referring research participants: Ethical challenges for investigators studying children and youth. *Ethics & Behavior, 4*(2), 87–98.
Fisher, C.B., Hoagwood, K., & Jensen, D.S. (in press). Casebook on ethical issues in research with children and adolescents with mental disorders. In K. Hoagwood, P. Jensen & C.B. Fisher (Eds.), *Ethical issues in research with children and adolescents with mental disorders.* Hillsdale, NJ: Erlbaum.
Fisher, C.B. (1995). The American Psychological Association's ethics code and the validation of sexual abuse in day care settings. *Psychology, Public Policy and Law. 1*(2), 461–478.
Fisher C.B., & Brennan, M. (1992). Application and ethics in developmental psychology. In D. Featherman, R.M. Lerner, & M. Perlmutter (Eds.), *Life-span development and behavior* (Vol. 11, pp. 189–219). Hillsdale, NJ: Erlbaum.
Fisher, C.B., & Brown, A. (1987, Fall). Report on applied developmental psychology. *APA Division 7 Newsletter,* pp. 12–13.
Fisher, C.B., Higgins, A., Rau, J.M., Kuther, T.L., & Belanger, S. (in press). Reporting and referring research participants at risk: Views from urban adolescents. *Child Development.*
Fisher, C.B., & Fyrberg, D. (1994). Participant partners: College students weigh the costs and benefits of deceptive research. *American Psychologist, 49*(5), 417–427.
Fisher, C.B., & Koocher, G. (1990). To be or not to be? Accreditation and credentialing in applied developmental psychology. *Journal of Applied Developmental Psychology, 11,* 381–394.
Fisher, C.B., & Lerner, R.M. (1994). Foundations of applied developmental psychology. In C.B. Fisher & R.M. Lerner (Eds.), *Applied Developmental Psychology.* New York: McGraw-Hill.
Fisher, C.B., Murray, J.P., Dill, J.R., Hagen, J.W., Hogan, M.J., Lerner, R.M.,

Rebok, G.W., Sigel, I.E., Sostek, A.M., Smyer, M.A., Spencer, M.B., & Wilcox, B. (1993). The National Conference on Graduate Education in the Applications of Developmental Science Across the Life Span. *Journal of Applied Developmental Psychology, 14,* 1–10.

Fisher, C.B., Rau, J.M., & Colapietro, E. (1993). Models of graduate education in applied developmental science: The Fordham University doctoral specialization in applied developmental psychology. *Journal of Applied Developmental Psychology, 14,* 289–301.

Fisher, C.B., & Tryon, W.W. (1990). Emerging ethical issues in an emerging field. In C.B. Fisher & W.W. Tryon (Eds.), *Ethics in applied developmental psychology: Emerging issues in an emerging field.* (pp. 1–15). Norwood, NJ: Ablex.

Glidden, R. (1983). Specialized accreditation. In K.E. Young, C.M. Chambers, H.R. Kells, & Associates (Eds.), *Understanding accreditation* (pp. 187–208). San Francisco, CA: Jossey-Bass.

Goldstein, D., Wilson, R.J., & Gerstein, A.I. (1983). Applied developmental psychology: Problems and prospects for an emerging discipline. *Journal of Applied Developmental Psychology, 4,* 341–348.

Hanson, M.J., & Lynch, E.W. (1989). *Early intervention: Implementing child and family services for infants and toddlers who are at-risk or disabled.* Austin, TX: Pro-Ed.

Koocher, G. (1990). Practicing applied developmental psychology: Playing the game you can't win. In C.B. Fisher & W.W. Tryon (Eds.), *Ethics in applied developmental psychology; Emerging issues in an emerging field* (pp. 215–226). Norwood, NJ: Ablex.

Kuther, T.L., & Fisher, C.B. (1996). *The effects of victimization in suburban adolescents.* Paper presented at the annual meeting of the American Psychological Association, Toronto, Ontario.

Lerner, R.M. (1984). *On the nature of human plasticity.* New York: Cambridge University Press.

Lerner, R.M. (1986). *Concepts and theories of human development,* (2nd ed.). New York: Random House.

Lewis, M., & Miller, S.M. (1990). *Handbook of developmental psychopathology.* New York: Plenum Press.

Montada, L., & Schmitt, M. (1982). Issues in applied developmental psychology: A life-span perspective. In P.B. Baltes & O.G. Brim, Jr. (Eds.), *Lifespan development and behavior* (Vol. 4). (pp. 2–34). New York: Academic Press.

Procidano, M.E., & Fisher, C.B. (1992). *Contemporary families: A handbook for school professionals.* New York: Teachers College Press.

Rheingold, H.L. (1986). The first twenty-four years of the Society for Research in Child Development. *Monographs for the Society for Research in Child Development, 50,* 108–125.

Sears, R.R. (1975). Your ancients revisited: A history of child development. In E.M. Hetherington (Ed.), *Review of child development research* (Vol. 5, pp. 1–74). Chicago, IL: University of Chicago Press.

Scarr, S. (1990). Ethical dilemmas in recent research: A personal saga. In C.B. Fisher & W.W. Tryon (Eds.), Ethics in Applied Developmental Psychology: Emerging issues in an emerging field. (pp. 29–42). Norwood, NJ: Ablex.

Shantz, C. (1987, Spring). Report on applied developmental psychology programs. *APA Division of Developmental Psychology Newsletter,* 1–13.

Siegel, A.W., & White, S.H. (1982). The child study movement: Early growth and development of the symbolized child. In H.W. Reese (Ed.), *Advances in child development and behavior* (pp. 233–285). New York: Academic Press.

Smuts, A.B. (1986). The National Research Council Committee on Child Development and the founding of the Society for Research in Child Development, 1925–33. *Monographs for the Society for Research in Child Development,* 50, 108–125.

Tryon, W.W. (1990). Predictive parallels between clinical and applied developmental psychology. In C.B. Fisher & W.W. Tryon (Eds.), *Ethics in applied developmental psychology: Emerging issues in an emerging field* (pp. 203–214). Norwood, NJ: Ablex.

Wilson, K., & Hayes, S.C. (1989). The tangled web of licensing. *APS Observer,* 2(5), 12, 13–21.

Young, K.E. (1983). Accreditation: Complex evaluative tool. In K.E. Young, C.M. Chamber, H.R. Kells, & Associates (Eds.), *Understanding accreditation* (pp. 19–36). San Francisco, CA: Jossey-Bass.

Young, K.E., Chambers, C.M., Kells, H.R., & Associates (Eds.). (1983). *Understanding accreditation* (pp. 19–36). San Francisco, CA: Jossey-Bass.

Youniss, J. (1990). Cultural forces leading to scientific developmental psychology. In C.B. Fisher and W.W. Tryon (Eds.), *Ethics in applied developmental psychology: Emerging issues in an emerging field* (pp. 285–302). Norwood, NJ: Ablex.

5

Applied Developmental Science and Training in Pediatric Psychology

Thomas J. Kenny, Ph.D.
Donna Chmielewski, Ph.D.
University of Maryland School of Medicine

Pediatric psychology is itself a relatively new discipline that seeks to extend the methods and knowledge of psychology to benefit children and adolescents in medical settings. Wright described the union of psychology and pediatrics as a blending or marriage that has potential benefits to both professions and the people served by those disciplines (Wright, 1967). The addition of applied developmental science is a natural extension of the earlier union growing from a common pathway.

Pediatrics is the branch of medicine most clearly involved in the process of development as it interfaces with physical, social, and cognitive processes. Applied developmental science (ADS) can contribute to pediatrics and can benefit significantly from sharing the interests of ADS with pediatrics. In the pediatric setting, the special knowledge of development is a mutual strength. ADS will have a laboratory to take the theoretical base of psychology and extend it to the applied setting of a medical clinic or hospital. At the same time the science of ADS will enhance the research efforts of pediatricians by expanding the emphasis on the context of the patient to include the effect of development, environment and, social issues. This chapter will begin by examining the historical background of pediatrics, pediatric psychology, and applied developmental science to focus on the potential benefits of combining these areas. Issues of training in both academic and field or clinical settings will be presented to identify potential problems and conceptualize new approaches.

In presenting models for field training, significant attention will be given to issues that could effect the implementation of appropriate training throughout the training cycle. We will attempt to offer ways of adjusting the system to maximize the potential for extending the knowledge base of psychology, as represented by pediatric psychology and applied development science, into the medical system. The issue of appropriate training for using ADS in a pediatric psychology setting will be addressed and will cover four basic areas:

1. Academic preparation and coursework including proposed core courses as well as elective courses that will most effectively prepare the student for a field training experience.
2. Practicum experiences, including types of setting, populations, and specific training that would best prepare for a pediatric psychology training.
3. An internship experience with specific training goals outlined and training experiences described.
4. The relationship between the academic institution and the field setting that is required to optimize the training experience.

After describing these general issues relating to field training, three specific types of field training experiences will be described: (a) A clinical training model, (b) A research training model, and (c) A community program model.

A HISTORY OF THREE FIELDS

The impetus for the establishment of pediatrics, pediatric psychology, and applied developmental science have fascinating similarities. All three began in spite of the adult emphasis of the established professions in medicine and psychology and because of concerns of subgroups of these professions for the special needs of children as a separate professional focus. Until the late 1930s, the field of pediatrics was a division or part of the broader entity internal medicine. Training for pediatrics was done largely by the traditional adult–oriented model. In essence, for the purpose of educating physicians, children were treated as small adults. Pediatricians were not happy with this model, but enjoyed the benefits of being a part of the powerful specialty of internal medicine. The issue that split pediatrics from internal medicine was the commitment of pediatricians to advocating the needs of children. Specifically, pediatricians split with their colleagues in internal medicine and the American Medical Association by supporting the Townsend Act provision to include children in social security benefits. The evolution of a more appropriate training model was a supplemental benefit to the advocacy issue.

Newly independent pediatrics did little to change the content or form of medical training. The focus on development was emphasized, but largely as a part of a traditional physically based, illness–oriented model. After a period referred to as the golden age of curative pediatrics in the 1920s, emphasis began to broaden, going beyond illness and cures to consider the child in a developmental context that included aspects of cognitive, behavioral, and social factors (Levine, 1960). In 1951, the American Academy of Pediatrics issued a statement declaring

"the Board does not believe that pediatricians should be less adequately trained in the care of the sick infant and child. It does believe, however, that a study of growth and development can be advantageously incorporated into such training" (American Board of pediatrics, 1951).

By the late 1960s, departments of pediatrics were establishing training in what was variously called behavioral or developmental pediatrics as part of the regular pediatric residency training curriculum. In 1976, the W.T. Grant Foundation awarded a grant to fund a training program in behavioral pediatrics at the resident and fellow level. The Grant Foundation subsequently funded over a dozen programs in departments of pediatrics across the country. The Division of Maternal and Child health of the National Institute for Child Health and Development awarded the first government grant to encourage training in behavioral and developmental pediatrics in 1986. This new field generated literature describing practice and research with the publication of a text book in 1975 and the beginning of the Journal of Behavioral and Developmental Pediatrics in 1979 (Kenny & Clemmens, 1975).

Pediatric psychology began in 1967 as a means of identifying the special needs of children, especially those with behavior and development problems that were not usually seen in psychiatric settings. The large and powerful field of clinical psychology, like the field of internal medicine, was much more concerned with adult psychopathology, and academic training largely reflected that focus. The onset of Veterans Administration internship programs provided funds for training that directed clinical psychology into a model geared to adult in-patient psychiatric populations. A psychologist interested in working with children had a difficult time finding appropriate training. Like their medical colleagues in internal medicine, clinical psychologists felt it was reasonable to train professionals in an adult model and consider children small adults. In 1980, Routh wrote an article reviewing the opportunities for academic training geared toward child or pediatric populations and concluded that the best hope lies in taking clinical courses in a program that offered electives focusing on children and supplementing this academic experience with an internship in a pediatric psychology setting (Routh, 1980). By the 1970s, internship training in pediatric psychology was becoming available in medical centers at the University of Oklahoma, Indiana University, the University of North Carolina, and the University of Maryland. In 1974, the clinical training branch of the National Institute of Mental Health awarded what may have been the first training grant to a psychology internship based totally in a department of pediatrics at the University of Maryland School of Medicine.

Research in pediatric psychology was growing, and placed emphasis on a variety of areas reflecting the interface between psychology and pediatrics. The *Journal of Pediatric Psychology* appeared in 1969 and, after overcoming some early financial problems, grew into one of the most respected journals in psychology. A body of literature dealing with pediatric psychology issues developed including: *Encyclopedia of Pediatric Psychology* (Wright, Shaefer, & Solomons, 1979), *Handbook for the Practice of Pediatric Psychology* (Tuma, 1982), and the *Handbook of Pediatric Psychology* (Routh, 1988).

The field of applied developmental science evolved within the broad framework of psychology to influence optimal development across the lifespan. The concept blends several areas of traditional psychology to focus on physical, social, and cognitive processes occurring over time within different cultural and economic contexts (Fisher & Lerner, 1994). Applied developmental science is a marriage of art and science, the theoretical and practical aspects of psychology. It extends both research and application of psychologic principals into the broadest arena of society and throughout the entire developmental spectrum. Many areas of psychology dealt with parts of the field of applied developmental science including clinical, counseling, school, and developmental psychology. The so called professional fields of psychology—clinical, counseling, and school—tended to be illness or problem oriented, circumscribed in scope and conceived in a medical, mental health, or tertiary care, model. Developmental psychology had a broader scope but was so theory oriented that it had little influence in the service area. The impetus for this new field represented a desire to move traditional psychology into new fields of endeavor that could be both theoretical and practical, proactive as well as reactive, and primary rather than tertiary. Practical forces played a major part in identifying the need for training in applied developmental science. For example, the increased sophistication of treatment for premature infants markedly altered the survival rate and led to efforts to identify infants at risk for developmental complications related to their high-risk birth. In looking to psychology for expertise in the assessment of these children, it became apparent that there was a problem. Psychologists, prepared to deal with the issues of development and research, were less well prepared in the skills needed for assessment and intervention. At the same time psychologists trained in assessment and intervention tended to have problems assessing infants and in dealing with issues of development.

As was the case with developmental pediatrics and pediatric psychology, it was necessary to create training programs that could blend the features of different fields of psychology to meet the needs of applied developmental science (Fisher, Rau & Colapietro, 1993; Fisher et al., 1993; Chapters 4, 6–9). As a result, this emerging program came from different points in psychology and had different emphasis. By 1981, there were graduate programs called "Applied Developmental Psychology", as well as programs with different names but similar goals. There was a need to define and justify the field and the resistance from the established areas of psychology. The National Conference on Graduate Education in the Application of Developmental Science was a clear and direct response to that need (Fisher, et al., 1993). Similarly, publications such as this book will enhance the knowledge base of ADS and facilitate further advances in training and research.

TRAINING ISSUES—PROBLEMS, MODELS AND SUGGESTIONS

The major challenge to ADS is to overcome obstacles to change that are pervasive throughout most systems, including psychology. Once again, the problem is similar to that faced by behavioral pediatrics and pediatric psychology. In 1984, Kenny described the problems facing pediatric psychology (Kenny, 1984):

1. The acceptance of pediatric psychology as a diverse but purposeful discipline.
2. The acceptance of psychology's role in a primary health care system as contrasted to a tertiary mental health model.
3. The need for innovation in the preparation of psychologists to work in this field.
4. The evaluation of pediatric psychology by standards in our domain rather than by adaptations of standards from other related disciplines.
5. The legitimate interdisciplinary collaboration of pediatric psychology with other professions.

Many of these issues still face pediatric psychology today in a similar form; they are the challenge to fully realizing the potential for training in applied developmental science.

The establishment in psychology has created many compartments representing special interest areas in psychology. As a consequence, this approach has drastically limited flexibility or innovation in training. The educational approach in psychology is similar to the old system in manufacturing where every worker had a specific job or task and did not cross into another worker's territory. American industry recognized the problems in this model as competition from other systems lead to the development of teams of workers training to share jobs and skills. Unfortunately, psychology has yet to take that step and change its system.

Problems with funding, staffing, accreditation, and competition have worked to impede innovation or change. In 1992, the National Institute of Mental health cosponsored a conference to address ways to expand public–academic linkages between academic psychology and the public mental health service system (Wohlford, Myers & Callan, 1993). The purpose of the meeting was to examine the psychology training system and identify problems in preparing psychologist to work in the public mental health system, as well as proposing ways to remedy the problem. Directors of clinical psychology training programs identified two major problems: there were no faculty prepared to teach courses appropriate to the goal and no room for new courses in the curriculum. If taken in the extreme, this finding suggests that if organized psychology discovered a treatment or approach that would cure all mental health problems, it might languish because we didn't have faculty to teach it or room to add the teaching in the curriculum.

The major changes required to fully develop the potential of applied developmental science are more flexibility in academic training and better communication between the graduate school program in psychology and the field training area (see Chapters 4 and 11). Until these changes evolve, the student will have an exaggerated responsibility in maneuvering through the training system in order to gain the optimal training experience.

GENERAL TRAINING

Models

We propose three training models in pediatric psychology that would take advantage of the skills associated with applied developmental science: a clinical experience, a research experience, and a community systems experience. The preparation for each will vary and, as suggested by the national conference, elements of the field experience will be different (Fisher, et al., 1993). There will be an integration of the three in all models, but with different foci, so that, all students in general, will need preparation in a) developmental theory; b) treatment or application strategies; c) research methods; and d) professional issues.

We will begin by discussing general areas of training that will prepare the ADS student for a pediatric psychology training experience and then move on to specific models of field training. The core or shared areas of academic preparation will contain these four areas with some variation dependent on the model to be pursued. A student aiming to work or train in a pediatric psychology setting should have preparation covering the theoretical conceptions of mechanisms involved in change and stability in child development. This would suggest a need for coursework in child development, including family systems. Since pediatric psychology is largely a medically based training experience, there should be courses dealing with the biological, psychological, and social influences on development. The student should have also taken coursework relating to atypical development, including both physical and behavioral exceptionality.

Application

In order to prepare for a training program in an applied or clinical setting, all students should have some degree of exposure to concepts of interviewing, assessment and intervention or treatment. Similarly, all students should have basic preparation in research, including the ability to design and assess or measure research questions.

Finally, core preparation should include coursework relating to professional issues, ethical standards, and legal issues relating to psychology. Included in the concept of professional issues would be coursework focusing on cultural diversity and ethnicity. To work effectively in a clinical field training experience, the student must be prepared to understand the patient or family in the context of the cultural and ethnic history. To be effective in a pediatric/medical setting, the student should also have some familiarity with professional issues involving patient treatment, medical confidentiality, and communication and interprofessional relations such as roles, privileges, and credentialing. Coursework covering the core areas outlined is usually a part of the curriculum of academic programs in applied areas of psychology. The student's task is to select the courses that most match his or her training goals. To work in a pediatric psychology setting, the developmental courses should focus on infants, children, and adolescents, as should the courses in assessment and intervention.

As noted earlier, coverage of professional and legal issues in a medical setting is critical to the curriculum content if students are to be able to function in a pediatric psychology training program.

The student should be trained in developmental assessment including cognitive and neuropsychologic tools. Preparation should include the ability to present diagnostic formulations and produce a meaningful report of an assessment. Training in the so called projective tests is useful, but not as central as developmental assessment skills.

Practica

Practicum experiences are another critical element in preparing for pediatric psychology training. Practicum placements should be congruent with the application of the course preparation in assessment and intervention. Potential settings should include pediatric facilities, in-patient hospital settings, out-patient clinics, or child development centers. In some cases, child psychiatry settings might be useful and there would be benefits in experiences in a school placement. The practicum experience should be child centered, but also include work with parents and/or families. An ideal placement would incorporate a multidisciplinary training experience. There are marked theoretical and attitudinal differences between training in psychology and medical training. Early exposure to these differences will facilitate adapting to the pediatric psychology training. Psychologist are trained to question their findings, to be more cautious and circumspect, and, a frequent criticism from other disciplines, not to give "answers". Physicians are seen as authority figures—decisive and action oriented. Medical training has been seen as producing experts who can do anything. There is more than a grain of truth in the characterization of medical training as "see one, do one, teach one". Psychologists have to be exposed to these differences to adapt effectively in the role of "co-expert", in order to fully share the resources of psychology with their medical colleagues. Neil Miller (1983) emphasized this need in his contribution to the National Conference on Training in Health Care Psychology. He stated:

> In a medical setting, it is futile for health psychologists to complain about lack of status or understanding; it is up to them to discover those problems that the medical specialists consider to be important and to which they can make an obvious contribution. It is up to them to communicate about possible contributions from their specialty in terminology that the physician can understand" (Miller, 1983, p. 12).

FIELD EXPERIENCE—INTERNSHIPS

Clinical training model

A field experience in pediatric psychology or an internship should clearly describe its program in order to allow the prospective trainees to determine if it will meet their career goals. A quality program should have a balance of applied experiences in assessment, intervention, and consultation, as well as with a strong supervisory and didactic program. Specific experiences can vary, but a reasonable core would consist of elements covering a broad range of ages and types of patients. All programs should have an experience involving clinical assessments. This experience should include settings or rotations that would offer opportunities to assess infants, school age children, and teens and would vary the focus of the assessment to include problems relating to physical, emotional, and cognitive development. Examples of some experiences would include assessment of premature or high risk infants, experience in a multidisciplinary program assessing problems of development or learning, and an experience in the assessment of illness related problems in special populations such as diabetic, epileptic, and HIV patients, as well as patients with other types of chronic illnesses.

The assessment experience includes training in formulating a diagnosis, preparing a professional report that interprets the results of this assessment, and presenting a set of recommendations that impact the identified problems and a diagnosis. A logical result of an assessment is a plan for intervention. The trainee should be exposed to a variety of patient problems and various techniques that address these problems. Many settings focus on specific types of problems and one form of intervention, that is, problems of behavior or adjustment that are affected by the so called behavior therapies. However, the field of pediatric psychology is involved in a wide range of problems and, as a result, a variety of intervention techniques are viable. The trainee should be presented with a training experience that provides for both short term and long term programs of interventions. They should work with populations that cover a wide range of ages and identified problems including dysfunction related to physical or developmental issues, family problems, and problems of behavior. The trainee should have the opportunity of planning and implementing interventions that include behavior therapy, parent counseling, anticipatory guidance, family therapy, and psychodynamically based interventions.

A clinical field training experience must include direct supervision of the trainee's work. This may take the form of direct observation, video or audio taping, review of the trainee's reports, and may be conducted in individual or group settings. The trainee should have a supervisor for his or her work in assessment and supervision for the intervention experiences. Guidelines for appropriate supervision would require at least four to five hours of supervision per week.

The field experience is designed to provide direct patient contact, but knowledge gained from this contact should be integrated with didactic experiences that integrate and enhance the clinical experience. A regular schedule of seminars should be a core part of the field experience. The program should include required seminars that cover topics central to the training experience, as well as elective seminars that would allow the trainee to straighten areas of specific interest or need. The didactic component of the field experience will probably comprise 15–20% of the trainee's schedule.

A typical core of seminars would include one seminar dealing with issues of assessment, one devoted to therapy/intervention, another discussing consultation/liaison, as well as a seminar covering professionals issues that would include ethics and legal issues, as well as issues of racial and cultural diversity. A seminar relating to research, or at least a journal club to help the trainee keep abreast of scientific findings in the field should also be offered.

Elective seminars would focus on specific populations or topics including coverage of special medical populations such as endocrine patients (including diabetics, and children with growth disorders, as well as other illnesses). These seminars may also focus on areas that affect specific ages, such as infant assessment or adolescent issues. Special areas of psychology like neuropsychology or family therapy are other possibilities.

Finally, the trainee should have some time allotted for elective experiences. These would include research opportunities, teaching, or special clinical experiences. The trainee should be familiar with the types of electives available in a field training experience and look for opportunities that mesh with the trainees' professional goals.

Incorporating the elements of the field training experience outlined earlier, the trainee could expect a one year program to allocate time as follows:

Assessment	20%
Intervention/therapy	20%
Didactic/teaching	20%
Supervision	10%
Consultation/liaison	10%
Electives	20%

As this is proposed as a guideline for a typical field training experience, the needs of the trainee and special programs in the field will result in adjustment in this balance and all programs will vary somewhat.

RESEARCH MODEL

A research experience in a pediatric psychology setting with an ADS focus should most likely be viewed as an experience in clinical or applied research as opposed to more theoretical research. The field experience can present a variety of research options but, by and large, the setting is problem and population oriented and the goal of research is to change, improve or avoid problems. [See Chapters 4 and 11, this volume, for more information regarding field experience in ADS]

In the model being proposed, research is the focus but, because it is conducted in a clinical setting, the experience incorporates aspects of the clinical model just described. To fully participate in the setting, the trainee should be involved in clinical aspects of the field experience, or at least have been trained to understand clinical procedures such as assessment and therapy.

Academic preparation for a research experience would incorporate the core subjects previously outlined but, in place of extended course work in assessment and therapy, there would be an increase in courses in research design and statistics. Coursework should also include exposure to practical issues of measurement involved in clinical research such as finding, evaluating, and selecting appropriate tests, questionnaires, or informal measures. Preparation in research design should include coverage of subject selection and sampling, as well as coverage of data management. The trainee should choose practicum experiences that are medically based, involve clinical research, and focus on children. However, experience can be more general for a research program than for a clinical program. A program offering a research based field experience should describe the research areas that are being covered by faculty in the program. It would also be important to describe support systems available to trainees including: space; time; data management and computing resources; financial support; and mentoring options.

The ongoing research at a field setting should allow the trainee to join in on existing activities and work with more experienced mentors. In a one year field experience, working on existing research minimizes the problem of conceiving, designing, and starting up a new project. Working on an established project also provides the opportunity to develop a spin-off project involving the same population or a modification of the process or data.

At the same time, the trainee should plan a research proposal of his or her own. The training site should provide the support the student will need to work out the plan, set up the design, and formulate the protocol. This experience is useful whether the trainee completes the projecting during the field experience or transfers it to his or her next position. Proficiency in research involves working through the process and generalizing the experience. The model proposed for a pediatric psychology setting provides the opportunity for interdisciplinary research. The trainee should be exposed to this experience in the field setting.

In addition to the trainee's research activities, the program should include clinical activities usual to the setting. The trainee should do assessment and intervention as outlined in the clinical model, but with a reduced time allocation. This requirement is both experiential and practical. The more familiar the trainee becomes with clinical problems and procedures, the more attuned he or she will become to potential research questions. In addition, the clinical activity will enhance the trainee's ability to work with his or her colleagues in the training program and break down the perception of lab research as separate from the real world.

The didactic elements of the program are identical to those listed in the clinical model, but the time spent in assessment and therapy seminars is reduced and there is an increase in the teaching of research issues. The trainee should receive supervision in clinical areas such as assessment and therapy. In addition, the trainee should be assigned a research mentor and a research supervisor. The mentor should work with the trainee on theoretical aspects of research, including helping the trainee develop his or her own research project. The research supervisor should be a member of the ongoing project selected for the trainee to work on. This person should be responsible for the practical, project oriented performance of the trainee.

The field training program should include time for elective experiences including computer use, data management, and epidemiology. While the trainee is focused on research, the elective experience should be all inclusive and not limited to research. A proposed one year program for research training would divide the experience as follows:

Research	30%
Assessment	10%
Intervention/therapy	10%
Consultation/liaison	10%
Didactics	15%
Supervision	10%
Electives	15%

COMMUNITY SYSTEMS MODEL

A field training experience in community systems may present the most challenge to the trainee seeking a community placement. This may be a lesser known area of opportunity for training. Organized psychology has divided itself between theoretical and applied areas, but these choices are usually interpreted as academic psychology or professional practice psychology. Medical training has faced this issue and developed an area of specialization that is variously called preventative medicine, epidemiology, or public health. Departments in medical schools teach students interested

Applied Developmental Science in Pediatric Psychology 87

in the field and there are schools of public health that specialize in postdoctoral training. An established career track exists that covers practice in state and local health departments, teaching in medical schools, and research.

Psychology has a less developed approach to the area of community systems, with less training and a barely recognized career track. There are programs in place that offer field experience in community systems but these tend to be few in number, small in size, and very individual in focus. The American Psychological Association has participated in a congressional fellowship that provides the trainee with a practical experience working as part of a congressional office staff. The Public Interest Directorate of the American Psychological Association has a trainee position that amounts to an internship working through the APA office on projects or programs in the public domain. While these programs are of high quality, they tend to be individualistic in nature and do not have a well defined set of preparatory requirements to aid the student. In most cases, the student develops his or her own academic program and has an interest in a particular area of public services that draws them into the field.

There are some, though not many, academic programs that describe their curriculum as "Community Psychology". A student interested in community systems may have to develop a program that crosses division of psychology and even schools. The trainee will need to take core courses in psychology, as outlined earlier in this chapter. The trainee should have basic courses in applied areas such as assessment and research tools, but the balance should be shifted to meet the needs of the student. If the student's goal is to work in community systems that lie in the service area, there should then be more coursework in assessment and intervention. On the other hand, if the student's goal is research or policy areas, less assessment/intervention course work and more courses in statistics and social theory would be necessary. In an ideal situation, the student would be able to take courses in a medical school department of epidemiology or at a school of public health. In this training model, there should be a significant emphasis on courses covering professional issues and cultural diversity.

The actual field placement could involve a program that is project related or could be based on a mentor–student relationship. In the project based model, the student would join a group working on a specific task or project, such as developing an effective program for AIDS prevention in adolescents. This project could be based in an academic institution, a medical center, a public agency, or a community program. Wherever the program is based, the trainee should be exposed to the operations of other types of facilities. That is, if the project is being carried out in a medical center, the program should rotate the trainee to public agencies, community programs, and governmental or professional settings that would network with the project.

An example of this mentor type of training experience would be the Congressional Fellowship or the APA Public Interest Directionate internship program. In this model, the trainee works in a particular setting in close relationship with a mentor who is responsible for seeing that the trainee is exposed to the processes of community systems and has experience interrelating with other settings. The main goal of this training model is to expose the trainee to systems of service and have them learn the operations of the system. Much of the activity is observational, however, the trainee should be involved in direct systems related activities. These activities could include participation in, or the development of, a specific project, or could focus on research or program development. The supervision that is part of the other models would become more of a mentoring in this model and would cover the student's project activity and organizing of the rotational exposure to other settings.

The didactics would center on a seminar that would cover the various service system sites and have presentation covering the organization, goals, and activities of the agency. Another seminar should be devoted to topics related to cultural diversity. There should be a seminar devoted to research issues. In this model, the trainees interest would lead to the selection of elective seminars that related to the specific interest.

SUMMARY

Pediatric psychology provides an exciting arena to demonstrate and utilize the professional contributions of applied developmental science. There is a multidimensional role for ADS in pediatric psychology that covers clinical service, research, and community service systems. Conceptual models have been proposed and described that would lead to an effective and productive marriage of pediatric and applied developmental psychology. The critical steps needed to facilitate the application can be achieved by a spirit of positive interaction and cooperation between the elements in the model—trainees, the graduate training programs, the field experience sites, and, most of all, the professional structure of psychology. The greatest benefits will only be reached by loosening the traditional constraints on innovation in professional training. This would allow for new combinations of elements of clinical, developmental, and social psychology to contribute to the core curriculum required to prepare an applied developmental scientist. To achieve this breakthrough, we must fulfill the recommendation of the National Conference on Graduate Education in the Application of Developmental Science across the Life Span which states "The nature of the work of applied developmental science is reciprocal in that science drives application and application drives science." (Fisher et al., 1993).

The opportunities of ADS in pediatric psychology should influence the academic preparation of future professionals. In this case, application should influence preparation and allow the trainee to bring the optimal skills into the field experience. Professional psychology must help involve the new curricula to meet new opportunities to apply our professional skills. The field needs to recognize the benefits to psychology and the community that can result from allowing psychology to recognize and support the concepts and role of applied developmental science.

REFERENCES

A statement by the American Board of Pediatrics on training requirements in growth and development. (1951). *Pediatrics 7:*430–31.

Fisher, C.B. & Lerner, R.M. (1994). Foundations of applied developmental psychology. In C.B. Fisher & R.M. Lerner (Eds.), Applied Developmental Psychology (pp. 3–10). New York: McGraw–Hill.

Fisher, C.B., Murray, J.P., and Dill, J.R., Hagen, J.W., Hogan, M.J., Lerner, R.M., Rebok, G.W., Sigel, I.E., Sostek, A.M., Smyer, M.A., Spencer, M.B., & Wilcox, B. (1993). "The National Conference on Graduate Education in the Applications of Developmental Science Across the Lifespan." *Journal of Applied Developmental Psychology, 14:*1–10.

Fisher, C.B., Rau, J.M., & Colapietro, E. (1993). Models of graduate education in applied developmental science: The Forcham University doctoral specialization in applied developmental psychology. *Journal of Applied Developmental Psychology 14*, 289–301.

Kenny, T.J. & Clemmens, R.L. (1975). *Behavioral pediatrics and child development: A clinical handbook.* Baltimore: Williams and Wilkens.

Kenny, T.J. (1984). We have met the enemy and he is us American Psychological Association 92nd Annual Meeting, Toronto.

Levine, S.Z. (1960). Pediatric education at the crossroads, presidential address to American Pediatric Society. *American Journal of Diseases of Children, 100:* 650–656.

Miller, N.E. (1983). Some main themes and highlights of the conference *Health Psychology, 2:*11–14.

Routh, D.K. (1980). Research training in pediatric psychology. *Journal of Pediatric Psychology 5:* 287–293.

Routh, D. (Ed.), (1988). *Handbook of pediatric psychology.* New York: Guilford Press.

Tuma, J. (Ed.), (1982). *Handbook for the practice of pediatric psychology.* New York: Wiley.

Wohlford, P., Myers, H.F., and Callan, J.E. (1993). *Serving the seriously mentally ill: public–academic linkages in services, research, and training.* Washington, D.C.: American Psychological Association.

Wright, L. (1967). The pediatric psychologist: A role model. *American Psychologist, 22:* 323–325.

Wright, L., Shaefer, A.B., & Solomons, G. (1979). *Encyclopedia of pediatric psychology.* Baltimore: University Park Press.

6

Integrating Applied Developmental Science and Clinical Child Psychology[1]

Felicisima C. Serafica
Charles Wenar
The Ohio State University

HISTORICAL OVERVIEW

Clinical psychology in the United States began in March 1896, with Witmer's establishment of the first psychological clinic for the purpose of helping children with psychoeducational difficulties, at the University of Pennsylvania (Fernberger, 1931). Given this origin, it can be said that clinical psychology in the United States started out as clinical child psychology. Prior to World War II, students of clinical psychology were almost exclusively interested in children and issues pertaining to their develop-

---

[1] Portions of the Historical Overview and The OSU Clinical Child Psychology Program description in this manuscript appeared initially in the following article: Serafica, F.C., & Wenar, C. (1985). A developmental perspective on training clinical child psychologists: The Ohio State University. In J. Tuma (Ed.). (1985). *Proceedings: Conference on Training Clinical Child Psychologists* (pp. 116–120). Washington, DC: Section on Clinical Child Psychology, Division of Clinical Psychology, American Psychological Association.

ment (Ross, 1972). In 1962, Sundberg and Tyler (cited in Ross, 1972) noted that almost all clinics in which psychologists worked were designed to serve the needs of children. Clinical psychology assumed an adult orientation only as a result of the action demands of World War II (Ross, 1972). However, the adult orientation became so dominant that clinical child psychology's early existence was virtually forgotten. Despite its having been around since 1896, clinical child psychology was still viewed as an emerging specialty almost a century later (Wohlford, 1979).

At its inception, clinical child psychology had a close relationship with child psychology. In an address delivered to the American Psychological Association in December 1896, Witmer proposed the training of students for a new profession—the psychological expert. He or she would be employed in the school system or in connection with the practice of medicine, and his or her primary responsibility would be the examination and treatment of mentally and morally retarded children (Witmer, 1907). Members of this new profession, using statistical and clinical methods, would also engage in the investigation of the phenomena of mental development in school children, particularly in those manifesting mental and moral retardation. A course in child psychology, which included a demonstration of its various methods, was an integral part of the curriculum for the training of this new profession.

Witmer's image of a close relation between child psychology and the theory and practice of clinical child psychology underwent a number of changes. Four of these changes will be briefly described.

The period between 1920 and 1960 was dominated by Freudian theory. The theory itself was inherently developmental, having a major impact on child psychology and clinical practice. In regard to child psychology, learning theorists such as Miller and Dollard and Sears set out to operationalize Freudian concepts and make them amenable to testing using conventional methodology. Emphasis on early child-rearing practices, the frustration—aggression hypothesis, anxiety as the anticipation of pain, the conscience as internalized parental values, and the importance of relations with same or opposite sex parent in the early years, were some of the highlights of this translation into learning theory (Dollard et al., 1939; Dollard & Miller, 1950; Miller & Dollard, 1941; Sears, Maccoby, & Levin, 1957; Sears, Rau, & Alpert, 1965). In the clinic, the emphasis was on affectively charged relationships and broad, typically unconscious, motivational systems, while the goal of treatment was mastery of unconscious conflicts. However, a number of modifications of this classical picture were made to accommodate special populations, such as delinquents and schizophrenics, and special settings such as child guidance clinics. In regard to children, the use of play in diagnosis and therapy represented a unique contribution. Thus, while Witmer's image was realized, it was in a form he never dreamed of.

During the 1960s, the psychodynamic influence began to wane. The recent modifications of the classical psychoanalytic theory, in regard to the primacy of the self and of interpersonal relations, has had little impact on academic child psychology. Only the concepts of identity in adolescence and attachment in infancy continue to be generative ones.

At the same time that psychodynamic theory was on the decline, two other movements were on the rise. The first of these was behavior therapy, that continued to expand and proliferate for the next three decades. Behavior therapy represented a conscious choice of learning theorists who formerly worked in the laboratory to engage wholeheartedly in the applied task of changing deviant behavior. Thus, a new bond was established between academic psychology and the clinic. However, when the operant model initially held sway, the theory claimed to be based on universal principles of learning which held across all ages. Hence, the role of the child's developmental status in psychopathology or treatment received less attention. Subsequently, this model was supplemented by models from social learning theory and from cognitive-behavior therapy, both of which are amenable to including the developmental dimension. However, the relation of learning theory to development tends to be a guarded one, rather than one of wholehearted acceptance (Ollendick & King, 1991).

The second movement was community mental health which, for a time, radically altered the nature of clinical psychology. The movement gained momentum in the 1960s as a response to the unrest and violence throughout the nation. It shifted attention from the clinic to society, from psychopathology to poverty and other social ills, from psychotherapy to prevention, as well as advocacy, a concern with rights, and political action. Its ambitious goal was not only to decrease psychopathology in at risk populations, but also to remedy conditions such as poor health, discrimination and prejudice that prevented people from fulfilling their potential.

At about the time that community mental health was emerging, there also began an unprecedented growth of research on cognition, language, and other aspects of development, particularly during infancy and early childhood. This growth was made possible by research funds which became available because of public concern over the American space program's ability to compete with Russia. Research in the 1960s strongly suggested the existence of a critical period (or at least the primacy of early experience) in regard to intellectual development. This evidence, in turn, was used by researchers led by Hunt (1961), Zigler (Zigler & Valentine, 1979), and others as the rationale for a variety of early intervention programs, with infant stimulation and Head Start being the most prominent of these programs. Funding for such programs became available as the civil rights and the community mental health movements heightened public awareness and willingness to deal with the consequences of poverty and other risk conditions. Applied developmental science evolved from this combination of basic and applied research on development during the early years of life. According to Fisher & Lerner (1994) as it evolved, applied developmental science was also influenced strongly by ecological systems theory (Bronfenbrenner, 1979, 1989), lifespan developmental psychology (Baltes, 1979, 1987), and the developmental–contextualism perspective (e.g., Lerner, 1992).

The final major change occurred within clinical child psychology itself. In the 1960s, research in child psychology not only increased tremendously, but also became more concerned with describing and explaining sequential changes in development, transforming the field into developmental psychology. This transformation meant that the basic task for the field was now to identify, chart, and conceptualize the major changes characterizing developmental periods. Prominent clinical child psychologists were quick to grasp the potential usefulness of the emerging body of scientific knowledge about development. Ross (1972) recommended developmental psychology as a source of principles and methods that can be applied to the clinical situation. Cass (1974) proposed that the concept of development be the core of theoretical knowledge, the common denominator in clinical child psychology and, ideally, for all clinical psychology. Both suggested that treatment and prevention of psychological disorders are more appropriately construed as problems of development. Therefore, a knowledge of how behavioral systems evolve is necessary for the proper assessment and treatment of psychological disorders and the prevention of their occurrence.

Ross (1972) and Cass (1974) were focusing essentially on knowledge of normal development as a critical building block in the training of clinical child psychologists. But another change, co-occurring within the two fields, would bring them even closer together. This was the advent of developmental psychopathology (Cicchetti, 1984, 1989; Wenar, 1982). Beginning around 1980, various research efforts to bring a developmental perspective to the description and explanation of psychopathology had increased sufficiently in number and impact to coalesce and become identified as a separate and viable area of research. Like developmental psychology, developmental psychopathology also emphasizes the importance of the variable of time. Differential diagnosis, prognosis and treatment are no longer at the heart of the enterprise as they are in traditional clinical child psychology. Rather, the task is to understand the origins and time course of a given disorder, its manifestations in development, and its developmental sequelae (Sroufe and Rutter, 1984).

Furthermore, developmental psychopathology makes the more radical claim of a symbiotic relation between normal and abnormal development. All development is one, confronting the same basic task as described earlier. The only difference is in whether one addresses the issue of understanding the normal course of development or the conditions that divert and sustain psychopathological development and, in certain instances, return it to its normal course. Such a symbiosis, in turn, means that normal development, not adult psychopathology, is the core discipline for clinical child psychology. (See Cicchetti, 1984; Garmezy, Masten, & Tellegen, 1984; Kazdin, 1989; and Wenar, 1982).

The centrality of normal development has major implications for education, training, and accreditation in clinical child psychology. Recognition of this centrality is indicated by the following resolution approved by The Conference on Training Clinical Child Psychologists: "Resolution 1. We recommend *all* APA approved programs providing professional training in clinical psychology *require* a course on the developmental bases of normal behavior (emphasizing a lifespan developmental approach)". (La Greca, 1985, p. 141). Greater appreciation for the potential contributions of developmental psychology to clinical child psychology is indicated further by the growing number of developmentally oriented clinical child psychology programs. In addition, ads in *The APA Monitor* show that the demand for clinical child psychologists with a developmental orientation is increasing.

In conclusion, current conditions favor the close relationship between child psychology and clinical child psychology that Witmer espoused. However, contemporary clinical child psychology training programs still face essentially the same question that Witmer confronted: How can theories and research on human development be incorporated in the training of clinical child psychologists? The aims of this chapter are: a) to illustrate how basic and applied developmental science can be integrated into the training of clinical child psychologists, and b) to discuss the future issues and challenges facing this endeavor.

Applied developmental science, which "involves the programmatic synthesis of research and applications to describe, explain, intervene, and provide preventive and enhancing uses of knowledge about human development" (Fisher, Murray, et al., 1993, p. 4), had not yet emerged as a distinct interdisciplinary field when the program to be described was established. Hence, described herein are efforts to integrate basic and applied developmental psychology into a clinical child psychology program. From its inception, this clinical child psychology program incorporated many of the guidelines that were adopted later at The National Conference on Graduate Education in the Applications of Developmental Science Across the Life Span (Fisher, Murray, et al., 1993). These similar guidelines, however, do not imply that a developmentally oriented clinical child psychology (and perhaps clinical child psychology programs in general) and applied developmental science are identical. The convergences and divergences between these two fields will be highlighted in a later section of this chapter.

Before describing in detail the illustrative clinical child psychology program, it is important to stress the fact that it is only one of several such programs which vary among themselves, but share a common goal. The aim of the program is to produce clinical child psychologists with a developmental orientation who are able to conceptualize psychopathology as deviations from the normal developmental pathway, conduct developmentally oriented assessments, and incorporate the developmental perspective into the treatment and prevention of psychological disorders. In addition, clinical child psychologists are scientific professionals trained to design and test the efficacy of developmental approaches to assessment, treatment, and prevention of psychological disorders in infants, children, and adolescents. A more general discussion of training developmental psychopathologists can be found in Cicchetti and Toth (1991).

THE CLINICAL CHILD PSYCHOLOGY PROGRAM AT THE OHIO STATE UNIVERSITY: 1967–1987

The Clinical Child Psychology program at The Ohio State University (OSU) was established in 1967 by Charles Wenar, a member of the Developmental Area within the Department of Psychology. From the beginning and throughout the two decades of Wenar's leadership, the program pioneered and championed the idea that clinical child psychology could not be adult clinical psychology extrapolated downward, but must be based on the tenets of a developmental psychopathology.

Program Philosophy

The OSU Clinical Child Psychology program was founded on two major premises. The first premise was that clinical child psychology is distinct from adult clinical psychology. Its distinctiveness arises from the following conditions: (a) the relatively more rapid rate of change during the pre-adult versus the postadolescence years; (b) the qualitative differences between immature and mature individuals' psychophysiological, cognitive, linguistic, social, and affective functioning; and (c) the uniquely dependent and reactive status of infants, children, and adolescents. These conditions imply that psychopathology during the pre-adult years must be conceptualized differently from adult psychopathology. They also indicate that the clinical child psychologist has to have communicative, interactive, assessment, and treatment skills which differ in important ways from those used with adults. Furthermore, these conditions underscore the necessity for viewing the client in context, that is, in relation to his or her environment, particularly the family, peer group, and school. Finally, they suggest that the clinical child psychologist is in a more effective position to engage in the prevention of psychological disorders. In sum, clinical child psychology is sufficiently distinct from adult clinical psychology so that it merits being taught programmatically in its own right.

The second major premise was that developmental psychology is the appropriate theoretical and empirical core of a clinical child psychology program. At the empirical level, a number of symptoms of child psychopathology, such as destructive rage, terror at being left alone, stubborn defiance, and bizarre ideas concerning causality, were once part of normal development. Thus, psychopathology is more a matter of when behavior occurs, rather than what behavior occurs. Next, the clinical child psychologists must be able to distinguish disturbances that are likely to be "outgrown" in the normal course of development (such as certain phobias), from those that are likely to persist (such as conduct disorders). Because of the fluid nature of development, this distinction is a shifting, complex one, and the results of longitudinal studies suggest that even the experts have sometimes been seriously mistaken in regard to prognosis. Finally, it is equally important for child clinicians to be aware of the environmental and intraorganismic factors which either facilitate or impede development so that the client may be understood in his or her totality. According to Rie (1975), "Ignorance of these issues can and does lead to grossly unsuitable interventions, failure to intervene when necessary, avoidable distress, or unwarranted hope" (p. 2).

The research challenge of a developmentally oriented clinical child psychology is to discover the conditions which divert development from its normal course and the conditions which either sustain such deviations or foster the return to normal growth. One way of conceptualizing this challenge at the most general level is to view all development as resulting from the balance between growth promoting and protective factors on the one hand, and risks and vulnerabilities on the other (Masten & Garmezy, 1985). When the former pair is dominant, normal growth can take place; when the latter pair is dominant, psychopathology results. The relative potency of the two pairs also determines whether psychopathology will be sustained or "outgrown". Thus, investigators need to discover what the four crucial factors are at different levels of development, how they interact over time, and the mechanisms through which they function (Rutter, 1990).

While advocating the centrality of developmental theory and research to clinical child psychology, the OSU Clinical Child Psychology program also took the stand that students ought to be exposed to diverse theoretical orientations and the research they have generated. Students were encouraged to judge for themselves the validity and usefulness of these theories, and determine in what way different theories overlap, complement, and differ from one another.

The program was also firmly committed to the scholar–practitioner model of training (Hoch, Ross, & Winder, 1966), that was predicated on the notion that the role of the clinical child psychologist is not limited to the delivery of psychological services. Rather, he or she has an obligation to contribute to the growth of scientific knowledge.

Finally, the program's philosophy included the view that clinical child psychology training should build on a broadly based background in psychology. The clinical child psychologist is first a psychologist and should be familiar with the history of psychology as a science and with basic research on the biological, cognitive, perceptual, affective, and social bases of behavior, as well as with learning and individual differences.

Program Goals

The overall goal of the program was to produce PhD level clinical child psychologists with a predominantly developmental perspective on diagnosis, assessment, treatment, and prevention of psychological disorders during infancy, childhood, and adolescence. More specifically, the program sought to turn out highly competent clinicians and researchers who would continue to elucidate the developmental approach to clinical child psychology through creative and critical application of clinical techniques, teaching, systematic research, theoretical essays, research reviews, case studies or all of these.

Planning Procedures and Structure

The establishment of the clinical child psychology program was preceded by discussions among representatives of the psychology department's clinical psychology and developmental psychology areas as well as its school psychology program. These discussions centered around: a) the administrative structure for the program, b) faculty, c) admissions procedures, d) status of the students, e) curriculum, f) practicum sites, g) practicum supervisors, and h) evaluation.

From these discussions, it was decided that the program would be a joint venture of the developmental and clinical psychology areas and the school psychology program. Core faculty would be drawn from the sponsoring units. Applicants for admission would be screened by representatives of the two areas, but with applicants being admitted as clinical child psychology students in one area or the other. In order to qualify for Ph.D. candidacy, clinical child psychology students would have to pass qualifying examinations in both clinical child and developmental psychology.

The proposed administrative structure was submitted to, and approved by, the two areas and the School Psychology program, then implemented.

After two years, personnel changes in the latter two resulted in the clinical child psychology program being exclusively in the developmental area with a less formal relation with clinical and school psychology. Over the years, the closest tie was with the Department of Pediatrics and the Department of Psychology in Columbus Children's Hospital, for reasons that will be presently discussed. Clinical child psychology faculty held joint appointments in both psychology and pediatrics. A close relation was also maintained with the clinical area and, to a lesser extent, with child psychiatry. In addition, students were required or encouraged to take courses in other areas of the Department of Psychology, as well as in departments throughout the university. In general the program was well received and the high calibre of students made them welcome in a variety of classes. Finally, a variety of children's mental health facilities throughout the city provided supervised practicum experiences for advanced students.

Other clinical child programs have different mixes of the developmental, adult clinical, child psychiatry, and pediatric components, depending on their philosophies, the availability of resources and congeniality of faculty. In terms of the OSU Program, the close affiliation with pediatrics was uniformly advantageous. It exposed students to a wider range of problems than those encountered in a child psychiatric setting, while offering unique opportunities for training and research. In fact, a number of students chose working in a pediatric setting as a career goal.

The Curriculum

The clinical child psychology curriculum was comprised of a scholarly component and also a component preparing students to become practitioners. The former included, among others, courses in normal development which might well be shared with a specialty in applied developmental psychology. The latter prepared students for the assessment, treatment, and prevention of psychopathological conditions and, therefore, differs from the practice component of an applied developmental psychology specialty, which emphasizes the enhancement of developmental processes and prevention of developmental handicaps (Fisher & Lerner, 1994; Fisher & Tryon, 1988, 1990). Table 1 summarizes the core curriculum or set of required courses and experiences.

Didactic courses

As a reflection of the importance attached to normal development as a basis for understanding psychopathology and clinical intervention or prevention, students were required to take six courses in developmental psychology, an unprecedented number for a clinical child psychology curricu-

TABLE 6.1
Core Curriculum of the OSU Clinical Child Psychology Program

Theoretical and Empirical Background
History & Systems of Psychology
Developmental Psychology (6 courses): Nature & Direction of Human Development, Psychoanalytic & Social Learning Theories, Structural Theories of Cognitive Development, Infancy, Child Development, Adolescence.
Personality Theories
Psychopathology (3 courses): Concepts of Childhood Psychopathology, Psychological Disturbances of Childhood, Adult Psychopathology
Assessment (2 courses): Concepts & Techniques of Assessment, Survey Course on Tests for Infants, Children, & Adolescence
Therapy (2 courses): Child Psychotherapies, Child behavior and Therapy
Neuropsychology (3 courses)
Social Psychology
Seminar on Ethical, Professional, & Legal Issues
Clinical Training
Intellectual assessment
Personality assessment
Interviewing and Behavioral Observation
Clinical methods—placement in psychology department clinic
Clinical methods—placement in a community setting
Clinical internship
Research Training
Research apprenticeship for first year students (3 quarters)
Methodological Problems in Developmental Psychology
Statistical (3 courses): Descriptive Statistics in Psychology, Analysis of Variance, Correlational Analysis.
Research for master's thesis and dissertation

lum. In each quarter of the first year, the students were introduced to theories in developmental psychology. In each quarter of the second year, they learned about theories and research on human development at a specific period, starting with infancy and ending with adolescence. As will be discussed in detail, the curriculum was also designed so that there would be a constant interplay between clinical child and developmental psychology courses, as well as between academic and applied courses.

The three first-year courses on theories of human development formed the background for the courses on psychopathology and psychotherapy, both of which were taught from a developmental perspective. The first psychopathology course addressed the issue of how child psychopathology was conceptualized. Three different approaches were presented and critically evaluated—both in their own right and in terms of how the developmental dimension was incorporated into them. The three approaches were: (a) classificatory, as exemplified by *The Diagnostic and Statistical Manual of Mental Disorders*, third edition, or DSM-III-R (American Psychiatric Association, 1987); (b) normative-dimensional, as exemplified by the Child Behavior Checklist (Achenbach, 1979; Edelbrock & Achenbach, 1981); and (c) psychodynamic. Research on specific psychopathologies was then discussed, again in its own right and in terms of its developmental orientation.

The advanced psychopathology seminar allowed for the exploration of more specialized topics. One seminar was devoted to clinical observation as a research tool, using the classical studies of Kanner (1943) on autism, Redl (Redl & Wineman, 1951), on conduct disorders, and Freud and Dann (1951), on children reared in concentration camps, along with other clinical studies as exemplars. Another seminar addressed the development and mental health needs of minority children in this country, years before this topic became a required component in clinical curricula.

Students were introduced to theories of child therapy in the autumn quarter of their second year. The developmental perspective was incorporated into this course in several ways. First, an introductory historical perspective showed how advances in the treatment of children's psychological disorders were linked not only to changing conceptions of psychopathology, but also to modifications in conceptions of attitudes toward children, some of which were brought about by the results of research on infant and child development. Second, there was a unit on cognitive–developmental approaches to treatment of psychological disorders (e.g., Chandler, 1973; Gibbs, Arnold, Ahlborn, & Cheesman, 1984; Harter, 1977, 1988). Third, developmental considerations were introduced when other theories of therapy (e.g., client-centered therapy, behavioral and cognitive–behavioral therapies) were presented. Last, a unit on factors that influence treatment included topics such as age-related differences in children's understanding of psychological disorders, help-giver preferences, knowledge of psychologists and other treatment-relevant developmental findings.

In the first year while the student was learning how to administer, score, and interpret intelligence tests, he or she also took a course on assessment, focusing on measurement theory. Similarly, the course on personality testing was complemented by an assessment course which surveyed and evaluated tests most frequently used by clinical child psychologists. Likewise, the course on interviewing and behavioral observations concurred with a course on child behavior assessment and therapy taught from a behavioral perspective. In the second year, while students were taking courses on infancy, childhood, and adolescence, the clinical practicum provided more intensive training in the assessment and treatment of psychological disorders manifested by toddlers, children, and adolescents. The clinical practicum will be discussed in greater detail in the section on field experiences.

Finally, students were required to take a course in the history of psychology in order to give them a perspective on the field and another course in ethics in order to prepare them for their functioning as professionals engaged in the delivery of psychological services.

In addition to the core, students typically took additional courses in developmental psychology, such as cognitive styles, language development, sociomoral development, adulthood, and aging. They also took courses offered by the Developmental Disabilities program on adaptive behavior, projective testing, or play therapy for the developmentally delayed. A number of courses in other departments and colleges were also popular: neurological assessment and pediatrics in Pediatrics, family relations in Family Relations and Human Development, family therapy in the College of Social Work, delinquency in Sociology, children and the law in the College of Law, and mental healing practices in nonindustrialized societies in Anthropology. This aspect of the curriculum was tailored to the individual student's style; some students liked to stay close to home, others liked to venture out.

Research training

Research training began in the first year when the student underwent a research apprenticeship, usually with his or her faculty adviser. The research apprenticeship involved working on the faculty adviser's research project. Depending on the phase of the project, the work could be assisting in the preparation of a grant proposal, data collection, data analysis, or report writing. Beyond the first year, students often continued to be involved in faculty research projects while conducting their own master's thesis or dissertation research.

In their first year, students also took a three course statistics sequence. In the second year, usually in the first academic quarter, all second-year students took the required course on research methods in developmental psychology. In the third or fourth year, students were urged to take a fourth statistics course as an elective. In general, students were encouraged to take as many statistics courses as they could while in graduate school.

All students were required to do an empirical master's thesis and doctoral dissertation, usually on a topic of the student's choosing. Students were encouraged to choose masters thesis or dissertation topics that asked research questions from a developmental perspective. Some undertook studies of development in normal populations (e.g., development of compliance in toddlers and preschoolers), or clinical populations (e.g., development of language in children with early infantile autism). Others investigated etiological factors associated with a particular disorder (e.g., information processing deficits in boys with dyslexia), while still others conducted studies on the efficacy of developmentally-based approaches to treatment (e.g., effects of children's developmental level on cognitive-behavioral therapy outcomes). As part of their professional socialization, students were encouraged to submit papers for presentation at professional meetings and to publish in research journals.

The close affiliation between the clinical child psychology program and the OSU Department of Pediatrics enhanced the students' research opportunities and training. Clinical child psychology students worked as graduate research assistants or conducted their own masters and dissertation research using a hospital population (e.g., body image development of adolescents with rheumatoid arthritis).

Professional socialization

Training and professional socialization also took place through periodic meetings of the Clinical Child Psychology Club, held for the purpose of socializing and discussing, informally, pertinent topics of local and national interest. There was a colloquium series on professional topics (ethics, legal aspects of clinical child psychology, legislation, APA accreditation, etc.) and on relevant research being conducted in the university and in the community. As members of the developmental psychology area, both faculty and students regularly attended the area's colloquium series and occasionally made presentations. Thus, clinical child psychology students were exposed not only to new research in their own field, but also to new findings from basic research in developmental psychology.

Field Experiences

Clinical practica and internship

As in any clinical child psychology program, the predoctoral clinical child practica and internship comprised the major preparations for future professional functioning.

In a three course sequence offered during their first year, students in the clinical child psychology program learned to observe, interview, and administer, as well as score and interpret, intelligence and personality tests for children. Children's Hospital was the primary site for the first-year practicum experiences, providing opportunities to work with children who were in the hospital for a routine pediatric checkup or a medical illness, but not for psychological problems.

Because so much time had to be spent on the technical aspects of test administration, scoring, and interpretation, the developmental dimension was introduced at a pragmatic level. Thus, students were asked what they would talk about with a seven year old boy, or with a 12 year old girl; how would they explain who they were and what they and the child were going to do, to a five year old, as well as to a school aged child. Such questions stimulated students to think in terms of social and cognitive development. After discussing the test findings, students were asked, "Is this child disturbed?" Answering the question required knowledge of normal development and normal developmental problems of children of different ages. It also required an evaluation of assets and resources as well as vulnerabilities and deviations. The implicit goal of all such questions was to stimulate students to "think developmentally". Theories were introduced primarily as the clinical material provided apt illustrations; for example, the W response on the Rorschach was related to Werner's orthogenetic principle of differentiation and hierarchical integration, while various TAT stories lent themselves to interpretation in terms of Freudian, Adlerian or Rogerian theories.

The second-year clinical child practicum provided students their first opportunity to work with actual clients referred for psychological problems. In contrast to the first-year practicum, the second year involved supervised experiences in the assessment, diagnosis, and treatment of psychological problems in infants, children, or adolescents. Students also worked with parents and families, drawing from the courses on parenting, adult psychopathology, and family therapy. In addition, they provided psychological consultation to health and school personnel. Case management was an integral component of the second year practicum; responsibility for planning, providing, and coordinating services for a particular client from intake to termination rested with the student to whom the case was assigned, as well as his or her supervisor.

For many years, Children's Hospital of Columbus was also the site of the second-year practicum. However, adequate clinic space at Children's Hospital became increasingly difficult to obtain so, in 1984, the practicum site was transferred to temporary quarters in the Department of Psychology. In 1985, the Department of Psychology moved into its own building which included space and facilities for a psychological clinic that would serve as a training facility for graduate students in clinical psychology, clinical child psychology, and counseling psychology. To this day, the OSU Psychological Services Center remains the primary clinical practicum site for second-year clinical child psychology students and, occasionally, for some of the more advanced students.

The second-year practicum provided both formal and informal opportunities for the integration of developmental psychology and clinical child psychology. The formal opportunities were represented by the orientation meeting which took place at the beginning of the second year, the weekly case conference, and the case study assignment. An entire day was devoted to the orientation meeting for the purpose of introducing students to the policies, procedures, and standards governing the delivery of psychological services at the Psychological Services Center and, more specifically, at its clinical child psychology unit. In presenting this information, it was always emphasized that children varying in age or developmental status would react differently, therefore clinicians would have to modify their interactions with clients in order to take into account these age-related differences. For example, a discussion of age-related differences in children's competence to consent (Weithorn & Campbell, 1982) accompanied the introduction of the consent form to students. Similarly, a review of age-related differences in children's understanding of psychological disorders was part of the discussion on intake procedures.

Another formal opportunity for integrating applied developmental science and clinical child psychology was through the weekly case conference. Although each student received individual supervision, the entire second-year practicum class, which usually consisted of four to five students, also met as a group with the supervisor once a week. These weekly meetings were devoted to a case conference and a discussion of the implications for the case of relevant theoretical and/or empirical literature. Often, these readings included pertinent reports of developmental psychology research, such as a study of the development of children's understanding of defense mechanisms (Chandler, Paget, & Koch, 1978).

The third formal opportunity was the annual term paper. At the end of the second year, students were required to submit a written case study illustrating how developmental theory and/or research could be applied to understanding and handling a particular clinical case that the student had worked with during the year. Through this assignment, the student demonstrated his or her ability to conceptualize psychopathology, assessment, and/or treatment of a psychological problem (e.g., peer relations difficulties) or psychiatric disorder (e.g., childhood depression) from a developmental perspective.

Informal opportunities to integrate basic and applied developmental psychology into the clinical practicum were identified and facilitated mainly through the individual supervisory process. In their attempts to conceptualize a case, students were encouraged to draw on knowledge they had acquired from their didactic courses about human development, developmental psychopathology, and theories of child therapies. If necessary, students were asked to reread specific sections (e.g., the development of attention) of developmental psychology textbooks. For the students, this review gave new meaning to the research findings in addition to enhancing their understanding of a child's psychological difficulties. Whenever appropriate, it was suggested that students use measures from developmental psychology research to supplement standardized psychological tests. Such measures yielded additional insights into the case. For example, a measure of sociomoral reasoning might be administered to a child referred for conduct problems. (See Gibbs, Basinger, & Fuller, 1992, for the latest revision of this measure.) Along the same lines, students were helped to incorporate developmental concepts and strategies into their treatment planning. For example, the selection of potential reinforcers for a behavior modification program was guided by empirical data regarding the potency of various reinforcers at different ages, as well as by the preferences of the client and his or her parents. Developmentally-based treatment strategies were used whenever appropriate. To facilitate the implementation of these suggestions, the clinic library included developmental psychology textbooks, professional reference books on developmental approaches to psychopathology, assessment, and treatment, and a file of developmental measures and intervention strategies.

Beyond the second year, students could obtain their practicum experiences outside of the university setting. The advanced practicum was designed to provide supervised experience in specialized techniques (e.g., neuropsychological evaluation), assessment and therapy with special populations (e.g., adolescents), or in special settings (e.g., a community mental health center, pediatric hospital, or psychiatric hospital). In these settings, they were supervised by licensed clinical child psychologists who typically held a joint or adjunct appointment in the Department of Psychology.

Field experience in applied developmental psychology: The OSU Infant Stimulation Program

The OSU Clinical Child Psychology program was established when the community mental health movement was at its peak. Outreach and preventive programs were popular and well financed at various governmental levels. The Department of Pediatrics obtained funds for, and subsequently established an infant stimulation program in collaboration with the clinical child psychology program. The psychologists, who had a joint appointment in the Department of Pediatrics, were in charge of the program. The program itself was largely implemented by clinical child graduate students. Their required course in infancy covered the theory underlying, rationale for, and research on, infant stimulation programs. Through the infant stimulation program, students during the early years of the clinical child psychology program were able to obtain a field experience in what has become one of the hallmarks of applied developmental science. This experience was uniformly both a popular and enriching one.

Postscript

During its first years, when the clinical child psychology program was administered jointly by the clinical and developmental psychology area, it was considered a part of the clinical psychology area for accreditation purposes by the American Psychological Association. However, when it became housed exclusively within the developmental psychology area, it was never evaluated for accreditation by the American Psychological Association, which does not accredit developmental psychology as a specialty.

For the first two decades, lack of accreditation presented no major problems, especially as an increasing number of graduates established themselves in leadership positions in clinical and professional settings. At that time, too, there was a movement advocating the accreditation of clinical child psychology as a specialty by the American Psychological Association (APA).

Toward the end of the 1980s, however, it became apparent that the American Psychological Association, for a variety of reasons, would not create any new specialties in the near future. This meant that the OSU Clinical Child Psychology program could not expect to win APA accreditation on its own. Furthermore, it could not expect to be accredited as long as it remained a part of the developmental psychology area, since APA does not accredit developmental psychology programs. [See Chapter 4, this volume as well as Fisher & Koocher (1990), for a discussion of issues pertaining to accreditation, credentialing, and applied developmental psychology programs.] At the same time, clinical child programs had proliferated and top applicants might well prefer other quality programs that were accredited. More importantly, there seemed to be an increasing emphasis on accreditation, not only within the profession, but among mental health agencies and organizations responsible for reimbursing mental health professionals and their clients. It appeared that lack of accreditation might have a significant impact on the program and its graduates. Therefore, the program was moved to the clinical psychology area where it retains its developmental approach, although the curriculum, of necessity, has been curtailed.

FUTURE ISSUES AND CHALLENGES

Gaining Acceptance For the Developmental Perspective in Clinical Child Psychology

Although the Conference on Training Clinical Child Psychologists strongly endorsed the importance of a course in lifespan developmental psychology, not all clinical child psychology programs are ready to give basic and applied developmental science the centrality in the curriculum that was advocated by Witmer (1907), Ross (1972), or Cass (1974). While there are more developmentally-oriented clinical child psychology programs now than existed two or three decades ago, these programs still remain a minority. More than one course in developmental psychology or developmental psychopathology is necessary in order to do justice to a developmental orientation that would lead to an integration of developmental science and clinical child psychology.

In the clinical arena, clinical psychology, as noted earlier, has been identified with adults. This means that clinical child is traditionally viewed as something to add on to a program once the basic adult courses have been mastered. The fact that clinical child psychology has a unique subject matter (since a number of psychopathologies have no counterpart in adulthood), requires unique clinical skills (such as establishing rapport with children), employs unique therapeutic techniques (such as play), as well as having an ever expanding research base that can not be crammed into a single course, has not been fully grasped in many instances. The situation is not helped by the American Psychological Association's failure to recognize clinical child psychology as an independent specialty. Thus, when clinical child psychology with a developmental orientation is a track within a clinical psychology program, the clinical child psychology students have to take the basic courses for adults in addition to clinical child psychology courses. The curriculum may provide opportunity for them to take only one developmental psychology course and even that may not be taken before they begin the clinical child practicum. Under these conditions, integrating applied developmental science in a clinical child psychology track within a clinical psychology program does not seem a realistic goal.

Extrapolating from the clinical child psychology curriculum within a clinical psychology program, there is a potential risk that a similar situation could occur within an applied developmental science program. That is, an applied developmental science program might offer only a single course in developmental psychopathology with little inherent relation to the rest of the curriculum. The lack of developmentally oriented clinical child practica further limits the students' grasp of developmental psychopathology.

Continuity in training that emphasizes the developmental perspective is yet another issue in regard to gaining acceptance for the developmental perspective in clinical child psychology. The clinical child practica and internship are critical to the integration of applied developmental science and clinical child psychology. However, once students venture beyond the university clinic to other practicum sites, they may not be encouraged to perceive and use opportunities to employ the developmental perspective. Their practicum supervisors may have other theoretical orientations. While the purpose of the advanced practicum and the predoctoral internship is to broaden the students' horizons and expose them to other perspectives, it would be mutually beneficial if the settings of these clinical experiences also evidence an appreciation for the developmental perspective and enable students to learn how it can complement other theoretical orientations. The availability of practicum and internship supervisors with a developmental orientation, or at least an appreciation of it, is an issue that has to be addressed if applied developmental science is to be successfully integrated into the training of clinical child psychologists.

Curriculum Content

Another issue is whether applied developmental science has amassed a sufficiently large body of knowledge in the domains most germane to clinical child psychology that is concerned mainly with the etiology, assessment, as well as treatment of psychopathology and to some extent, prevention. When the OSU Clinical Child Psychology program was begun in 1967, the concept of child psychopathology as normal development gone awry was a promissory note. The subsequent exponential growth in research, both in developmental psychology and developmental psychopathology, is fulfilling this promise. Insofar as developmental psychopathology is concerned, there is now an extensive conceptual and empirical literature on this topic (reviewed by Wenar, 1994), along with a handbook (Lewis & Miller, 1990), numerous books (for example, Cicchetti & Beeghly, 1990; Robins & Rutter, 1990; Rolf et al., 1990), and a journal, *Development and Psychopathology*, devoted to the topic. However, parallel significant advances have not occurred at the same growth rate in developmental approaches to assessment, treatment, or prevention of psychological disorders except, perhaps, mental retardation. The 1993 National Institute of Mental Health (NIMH) Conference on Developmental Approaches to Assessment highlighted the paucity of such methodologies. In regard to treatment, the generalizability and long-term stability of effects produced by developmentally-based approaches to treatment of psychological disorders (e.g., Gibbs, 1993; Selman et al., 1991) have yet to be demonstrated and/or replicated in several studies.

Integrating Clinically Relevant Research Into Developmental Psychology Courses

The cooperation of developmental psychology faculty is vital to the successful integration of developmental psychology into the preparation of clinical child psychologists. Such cooperation is clearly evident in those developmental psychology programs that have established specializations in applied developmental psychology, such as the program at Fordham University (Fisher, Rau, & Colapietro, 1993; Chapter 4, this volume).

The receptivity of other developmental psychology programs remains to be seen, particularly among the more traditional programs that emphasize a distinction between basic and applied research, and favor basic research on normative developmental processes. Now that clinical child psychology has embraced developmental psychology as one of its core disciplines, are these programs ready to take on the challenge of making a significant contribution to producing clinical child psychologists with a developmental orientation? Are their faculty willing to meet the unique needs of clinical child psychology students by making the content of their courses more clinically relevant? In this section, we discuss some of the issues attendant to this enterprise and the potential rewards for those who accept the challenge.

At the outset, it should be emphasized that clinical psychology students ought to be introduced to the same developmental theories and research deemed necessary for developmental psychology students. However, they also need to be exposed to clinically relevant developmental research, that is, studies of normal development that have clinical implications. It is not being suggested here that a graduate course in, for example, child development deal with developmental psychopathology or developmental approaches to assessment and treatment.

One issue is that some clinically relevant developmental studies may not be covered (e.g., development of self-monitoring, or development of children's understanding of sadness), yet they are actually important enough to both disciplines to warrant coverage. Another issue is that for those areas where one aspect might be of greater interest to clinical child psychologists, more effort could be made to accommodate that interest. Take the case of the development of the ability to give informed consent. Here, the work of Abramovitch, Freedman, Thoden, and Nikolich (1991) on children's capacity to consent to participation in research could be assigned to all students. Additionally, clinical child psychology students could be directed to the Weithorn and Campbell (1982) article on development of the ability to make informed treatment decisions. Still another issue is that some developmental psychology faculty, for a variety of reasons, may simply not wish to modify their course syllabi. Such faculty could at least give clinical child psychology students the option of devoting the required term paper to a review of normal development in a process which has important clinical implications (e.g., normal development of children's understanding of psychological disorders). Making a developmental psychology course more clinically relevant would benefit not only the clinical child psychology students, but also developmental psychology students and students from other programs such as school psychology, counseling psychology, or guidance and counseling, among others, in the class.

There are a number of reasons why developmental psychologists may not want to take on the challenge of making their courses more clinically relevant. One reason could be inertia—the tendency to continue the fruitful pursuits of traditional issues and to repeat successful lectures on traditional topics. Another reason could be a reluctance on the part of some developmental psychologists to include normative studies which they do not perceive as "mainstream" developmental research (e.g., social cognitive studies on the development of children's knowledge about psychologists, that have implications for a child's receptivity to professional help). Still another reason could be an unwillingness or, at least, ambivalence about venturing into applied areas. Yet another reason could be a concern about the impact on graduate students in developmental psychology if a course designed primarily for them were to be modified to accommodate the needs of clinical child psychology students. Finally, developmental psychologists who are receptive to the challenge may still be deterred by a feeling of unfamiliarity with clinically relevant developmental studies.

In order to secure the cooperation of developmental psychology faculty, clinical child psychology faculty will have to establish collaborative relationships and a dialogue with their developmental psychology colleagues. This bidirectional exchange could address, among other things, the concerns of the latter about making their courses more clinically relevant and the potential benefits for developmental psychology faculty who chose to do so.

Bright clinical child students who might decide to conduct developmentally based clinical research with developmental psychology faculty is one benefit. Clinical psychology and clinical child psychology programs still attract a significant proportion of the brightest students seeking careers in psychology. Increased enrollments in developmental psychology courses may be another. If school psychology and other programs also find that their students' unique needs are being addressed in developmental psychology courses, such courses could also become part of their core requirements, thereby increasing enrollments in developmental psychology courses. Perhaps the greatest reward for developmental psychology faculty may be that their own horizons would expand, and the developmental–clinical interface will lead them to new and exciting research directions that they never would have taken otherwise. Fortunately, there are a number of developmentalists (see Fisher & Lerner, 1994) who serve as models of how fruitful applied ventures can be. To cite just two examples: Ceci (Ceci & Bruck, 1993; Ceci, Toglia, & Ross, 1987), whose work on the effects of adult suggestions on recall of events in early childhood was stimulated by a concern for the validity of children's testimony in cases of sexual abuse. Also, Selman (Selman, Schultz, & Yeates, 1991), who applied his findings on levels of interpersonal problem solving in normal children to the etiology and treatment of conduct disordered groups.

Boundary Issues

At present, perhaps the greatest challenge to the integration of applied developmental science and clinical child psychology is clarifying the current state of ambiguity regarding the boundaries between them. In this section, the recommendations of the National Conference on Graduate Education in the Application of Developmental Science Across the Life Span (Fisher, et al., 1993) will be used as the defining position paper concerning the scope, goals, curriculum, field experiences, and multidisciplinary emphasis in applied developmental science. For comparative purposes, we will be concerned only with clinical child psychology programs with a developmental orientation. Because the developmental approach is not widespread, it should be emphasized that the image of clinical child psychology to be presented is not comprehensive. In the following comparison of applied developmental science and developmentally oriented clinical child psychology, areas of convergence will be described first, then areas of divergence, and finally some unresolved issues.

Convergences

For both disciplines here, there is either total agreement, or agreement on general principles with some differences in regard to specifics. Both applied developmental science and clinical child psychology take a multidetermined, interactive view of human behavior. This means that behavior is viewed as the product of the interaction among biological, intraindividual, interpersonal, group and societal factors. Both place development at the core of their specialty, and agree that this means charting and conceptualizing successive, systematic changes. The principal difference between the two is that applied developmental science covers the entire lifespan, while clinical child psychology is limited to the period from infancy to adulthood. (Developmental psychopathology, per se, has a lifespan perspective, however). Both are based on scientifically gathered information. Both emphasize the mutually enhancing nature of science and application. Thus, application is not merely a shift from controlled studies to real world setting, but a testing of the validity of such studies in a naturalistic setting. By the same token, application is not merely an attempt to find "what works," it is also a relating of lessons learned through practice to the accumulated body of findings and conceptualizations that define the science of psychology.

There are many areas of overlap in regard to curriculum. Both specialties require courses in developmental theory and content. The two main differences are in the area of content, in that applied developmental science courses cover the lifespan and normative and atypical processes, while those in clinical child psychology stop at adulthood and cover normative and psychopathological processes. Courses in research methods are identical, consisting of methods of studying change over time, designs for single and multiple units and levels of analysis, quantitative and qualitative methods, and test construction. Exemplars might differ, however, being tailored to the particular subject matter of the two specialties. For example, tests of infant cognitive development would be appropriate for applied developmental science, while checklists for psychopathology would be appropriate for clinical child psychology. While courses in professional issues and field experiences are common to both, they are sufficiently distinct to be presented in the next section.

Divergences

Before starting, it will be helpful to present a generalization that will integrate many of the specific differences to be discussed. Clinical child psychology begins with the etiology, assessment, remediation, and prevention of psychopathological conditions. It looks to normal development for leads to understanding the variables and processes involved. Applied developmental science begins with normal development and scans the social landscape for problems that might be targets for applying its knowledge. Thus, applied developmental science is based in normal development and is context seeking in regard to application; clinical child psychology is context based in psychopathology and seeks clues to understanding in normal development.

Clinical child psychology is concerned with treating and, to a lesser extent, preventing psychopathological conditions. Applied developmental science has a stronger commitment to prevention and is not concerned with psychopathology and its treatment. This discipline also addresses itself to enhancing and optimizing development, having a commitment to education and disseminating knowledge. Neither of these factors play a major role in clinical child psychology.

For applied developmental science, the "real world" is society at large while, for clinical child psychology, the "real world" is bounded by mental health settings and immediately relevant social and institutional contexts such as schools or community centers. Thus, applied developmental scientists might well be found equally in governmental agencies or private corporations, as in departments of human services or correctional institutions. Moreover, applied developmental science is more concerned than clinical child psychology with the functioning of social institutions, such as service delivery, policy development, budgetary and management decision making. This concern with a broader range of social institutions accompanies an emphasis on program development, implementation, and evaluation, all of which are treated casually or are left to small special interest groups in clinical child psychology.

The professional preparation of clinical child psychologists is more extensive than that of the applied developmental scientist because they must deal with more disturbed populations, become more intensively involved, and use techniques which require certain specialized skills. Consequently, clinical child psychology has a number of practica as part of the graduate curriculum along with a required internship, the latter corresponding to field placement in applied development science. On the other hand, it may be that consulting plays a larger role in the professional preparation of the applied developmental scientist.

Internships and field experience share the same goals of increasing student's skills while integrating the academic and applied components of their education. The importance of supervision in achieving such goals is also shared. Incidentally, quality internship programs are probably easier to locate than quality field placements because internships have been a regular part of clinical training for many years and are evaluated by the American Psychological Association. Yet, field experience differs significantly from internships by focusing on issues of societal import in diverse social settings. Internships concentrate on psychologically disturbed children in broadly defined mental health settings. In spite of overlap, then, field experience and internships prepare students for different professional functions in different real-world contexts.

A somewhat similar point concerning commonalities and differences can be made concerning courses on professional issues. Again, there is agreement as to the general goals of producing a comprehensive education in ethical and legal issues and in professional standards. However, applied developmental science adds a fourth component—the influence of social and cultural contexts and organizational systems and functions in program development and implementation—which plays little role in clinical child psychology. Moreover, it may well be that the content of the first three components may significantly diverge. The ethical and legal implications of the implicit message, "I need your help" (clinical child psychology) are different from those in the implicit message, "We need your help" (applied developmental science) from institutions or community organizations, just as the ethical and legal issues involved in assessing and treating psychopathologically disturbed children are different from those of preventing and ameliorating the noxious effects of social ills. Applied developmental scientists have shown great sensitivity to relevant ethical and legal issues and attempted to address them (Fisher, 1993; Fisher & Brennan, 1992; Fisher & Tryon, 1988, 1990).

Finally, the interdisciplinary emphasis that, of necessity, is crucial to the applied developmental science venture is also present, but not as central to the more narrowly focused clinical child psychology.

Unresolved issues

When applied developmental scientists go beyond research and actually engage in the application of their findings, they cross the border from science to practice and become scientist–professionals. Here, there is a need for greater clarity in regard to this emerging field's target populations and techniques in order to avoid confusion on the part of the public, including students considering careers in either field, and potential conflicts with practitioners of diverse disciplines, among them clinical child psychologists.

Clinical child psychology has been presented as context based on psychopathological behavior. This is an accurate, but incomplete, picture. Since the mental health movement, clinical psychology has been expanding its scope to include nonpsychopathologically disturbed populations. Current examples of such populations in clinical child psychology are physically ill children (pediatric psychology), physically and sexually abused children, and neglected children. There is even a movement afoot to include emotionally disturbed children, a wide ranging category including children living in a war zone or a deteriorated neighborhood, to those who are victims of prejudice and discrimination (Brassard, Germain, & Hart, 1987). Similarly, the Diagnostic and Statistical Manual of Mental Disorders, 4th edition (DSM-IV), also recognizes conditions that are not psychopathological, but place the children at risk. One important characteristic of these populations is that although they do not manifest psychiatric disorders, they show a significant increase in psychological problems over and beyond those encountered in normal development. Thus, they are also deemed to be in need of professional attention from clinicians.

The expanded populations described earlier sound very much like the ones that are targeted by applied developmental science. The ambiguity is created by the general and, at times, vague definition of the province of applied developmental science—namely, atypical development and normative changes. It is not clear what devils, if any, lurk in the details. Moreover, when specific conditions and populations are referred to, the ambiguity is increased rather than dispelled. For example, "health compromising behavior" might include substance abuse and anorexia nervosa, and "educational settings" might cover children with learning disabilities and mental retardation.

The situation, in regard to techniques, is not as troublesome as that concerning populations, but it too has its problems. Applied developmental scientists might wish to use standardized psychological tests in order to assess the effects of an early intervention or prevention program. In regard to treatment, one could envision a continuum of techniques with individual psychotherapy at one end (clinical child psychology), and education of groups at the other (applied developmental science). However, in between lies an area that both groups might claim. Even a clinical child psychologists doing individual therapy might well have contact with teachers, schools, and community centers and may function like an applied developmental scientist. By the same token, applied developmental scientists might find that the incorporation of certain aspects of behavioral or cognitive therapy would enhance developmentally-oriented approaches to prevention or treatment of antisocial disorders. In addition, populations do not come in two neat packages labeled developmentally atypical and psychopathological. To shift clients with overlapping problems back and forth from one specialty to another might well undermine the goal of providing help to these clients.

It would be to the advantage of the public and the disciplines themselves if these issues were to be clarified. Both clinical child psychology and applied developmental science are dynamic fields and as they evolve, both will occasionally bump into each other. But, as Piaget (1950) has shown us, cognitive conflict facilitates transitions to higher stages in development. Confronting these issues can help applied developmental science, an emerging specialty, to define its own identity, to highlight its unique characteristics, as well as how it differs from other specialties and can contribute to them. Similarly, clinical child psychology, a relatively more mature field, can redefine its identity by confronting its own limitations, recognizing that other emerging specialties might be better suited to meet some of the newly identified needs of children and families, and that it would be enriched by incorporating developmental approaches to psychopathology, assessment, and treatment.

These two fields complement one another. Applied developmental research can enrich the curricula of clinical child psychology, as was shown with the program at OSU. Thus, it is important that those responsible for graduate education in these two fields conduct an ongoing dialogue concerning which populations and techniques are specific to their discipline and which are shared. Such a dialogue would contribute to their shared goal of producing well trained, highly competent, and ethical scientist–practitioners. Because of the similarity of background between applied developmental scientists and clinical child psychologists with a developmental orientation, there is every reason to believe that these issues can be resolved on the basis of mutual understanding, respect, willingness to accommodate, and above all, concern for the welfare of children.

REFERENCES

Abramovitch, R., Freedman, J.L., Thoden, K., & Nikolich, C.C. (1991). Children's capacity to consent to participation in psychological research. *Child Development, 62,* 1100–1109.

Achenbach, T.M., & Edelbrock, C.S. (1978). The classification of child psychopathology: A review and analysis of empirical efforts. *Psychological Bulletin, 85,* 1275–1301.

American Psychiatric Association. (1994). *Diagnostic and statistical manual of mental disorders* (4th ed.). Washington, DC: Author.
Baltes, P.B. (1979). Lifespan developmental psychology: Some converging observations on history and theory. In P.B. Brim & O.B. Brim (Eds.), *Lifespan development and behavior* (Vol. 2, pp. 256–279). New York: Academic Press.
Baltes, P.B. (1987). Theoretical propositions of lifespan developmental psychology: On the dynamics between growth and decline. *Developmental Psychology, 23*, 611–626.
Brassard, M.M., Germain, R.B., & Hart, S.N. (1987). *Psychological adjustment of youth*. New York: Plenum.
Bronfenbrenner, U. (1979). The ecology of human development. *Journal of Applied Developmental Psychology, 10*, 425–445.
Bronfenbrenner, U. (1989). Ecological systems theory. In R. Vasta (Ed.), *Annals of child development*, (Vol. 6, pp. 187–251). Greenwich, CT: JAI Press.
Cass, L.K. (1974). The training of clinical child psychologists. In G.J. Williams & S. Gordon (Eds.), *Clinical child psychology* (pp. 463–482). New York: Behavioral Publications.
Ceci, S.J., Toglia, M.P., & Ross, D.F. (Eds.). (1987). *Children's eyewitness memory*. New York: Springer-Verlag.
Ceci, S.J., & Bruck, M. (1993). Suggestibility of the child witness: A historical review and synthesis. *Psychological Bulletin, 113*, 403–439.
Chandler, M.J. (1973). Egocentrism and antisocial behavior: The assessment and training of social perspective-taking skills. *Developmental Psychology, 9*, 326–332.
Chandler, M.J., Paget, K.F., & Koch, D.A. (1978). The child's demystification of psychological defense mechanisms: A structural and developmental analysis. *Developmental Psychology, 14*, 197–205.
Cicchetti, D. (1984). The emergence of developmental psychopathology. *Child Development, 55*, 1–7.
Cicchetti, D. (1989). An historical perspective on the discipline of developmental psychopathology. In J. Rolf, A. Masten, D. Cicchetti, K. Neuchterlein, & S. Weinraub (Eds.), *Risk and protective factors in the development of psychopathology* (pp. 2–28). New York: Cambridge University Press.
Cicchetti, D., & Beeghly, M. (Eds.). (1990). *Children with Down syndrome: A developmental perspective*. New York: Cambridge University Press.
Cicchetti, D., & Toth, S. (1991). The making of a clinical psychopathologist. In J.H. Cantor, C.C. Spiker, & L.P. Lipsitt (Eds.), *Child behavior and development: Training for diversity* (pp. 34–72). Norwood, NJ: Ablex.
Dollard, J., & Miller, N.E. (1950). *Personality and psychotherapy: An analysis in terms of learning, thinking and culture*. New York: McGraw-Hill.
Dollard, J., Dobb, L.W., Miller, N.E., Mowrer, O., & Sears, R.R. (1939). *Frustration and aggression*. New Haven: Yale University Press.
Edelbrock, C.S., & Achenbach, T.M. (1981). Behavioral problems and competencies reported by parents of normal and disturbed children aged four through sixteen. *Monographs of the Society for Research in Child Development, 1* (46, series no. 188).
Fernberger, S.W. (1931). The history of the psychological clinic. In R.A. Bro-

temarkle (Ed.), *Clinical psychology: Studies in honor of Lightner Witmer to commemorate the 35th anniversary of the founding of the first psychological clinic* (pp. 10–36). Philadelphia: University of Pennsylvania Press.

Fisher, C.B. (1993). Integrating science and ethics in research with high risk children and youth. *Social Policy Report, 7*(4), 1–27.

Fisher, C.B., & Brennan, M. (1992). Applications and ethics in developmental psychology. In D. Featherman, R.M. Lerner, & M. Perlmutter (Eds.), *Life-span development and behavior* (Vol. 11, pp. 189–219). Hillsdale, NJ: Erlbaum.

Fisher, C.B., & Koocher, G. (1990). To be or not to be? Accreditation and credentialing in applied developmental psychology. *Journal of Applied Developmental Psychology, 11*, 381–394.

Fisher, C.B., & Lerner, R.M. (1994). *Applied Developmental Psychology.* Boston: McGraw Hill.

Fisher, C.B., Murray, J.P., Dill, J.R., Hagen, J.W., Hogan, M.J., Lerner, R.M., Rebok, G.W., Sigel, I., Sostek, A.M., Smyer, M.A., Spencer, M.B., & Wilcox, B. (1993). The National Conference on Graduate Education in the Applications of Developmental Science Across the Lifespan. *Journal of Applied Developmental Psychology, 14*, 1–10.

Fisher, C.B., Rau, J.M. & Colapietro, E. (1993). Models of graduate education in applied developmental science: The Fordham University Doctoral Specialization in Applied Developmental Psychology. *Journal of Applied Developmental Psychology, 14*, 289–302.

Fisher, C.B., & Tryon, W.W. (1988). Ethical issues in the research and practice of applied developmental psychology. *Journal of Applied Developmental Psychology, 9*, 27–39.

Fisher, C.B., & Tryon, W.W. (1990). *Ethics in applied developmental psychology: Emerging issues in an emerging field.* Norwood, NJ: Ablex.

Freud, A., & Dann, S. (1951). An experiment in group upbringing. *Psychoanalytic study of the child, 6*, 127–168. New York: W.W. Norton.

Garmezy, N., Masten, A.S., & Tellegen, A. (1984). The study of stress and competence in children: A building block for developmental psychopathology. *Child Development, 55*, 97–111.

Gibbs, J.C. (1993). Moral–cognitive interventions. In A.P. Goldstein and C.R. Huff (Eds.), *The gang intervention handbook* (pp. 159–185). Champaign, IL: Research Press.

Gibbs, J.C., Arnold, K.D., Ahlborn, H.H., & Cheesman, F.L. (1984). Facilitation of sociomoral reasoning in delinquents. *Journal of Consulting and Clinical Psychology, 52*, 37–45.

Gibbs, J.C., Basinger, K.S., & Fuller, D. (1992). *Moral maturity: Measuring the development of sociomoral reflection.* Hillsdale, NJ: Erlbaum.

Harter, S. (1977). A cognitive–developmental approach to children's expression of conflicting feelings and a technique to facilitate such expression in play therapy. *Journal of Consulting and Clinical Psychology, 45*, 417–432.

Harter, S. (1988). Developmental and dynamic changes in the nature of the self-concept: Implications for child psychotherapy. In S.R. Shirk (Ed.), *Cognitive development and psychotherapy* (pp. 207–246). New York: Plenum.

Hoch, E.L., Ross, A.O., & Winder, C.L. (1966). Conference on professional preparation of clinical psychologists. *American Psychologist, 21,* 42–51.
Hunt, J. McV. (1961). *Intelligence and experience.* New York: Ronald Press.
Kanner, L. (1943). Autistic disturbance of affective contact. *Nervous Child, 2,* 217–250.
Kazdin, A.E. (1989). Developmental psychopathology: Current research, issues, and directions. *American Psychologist, 44,* 180–187.
La Greca, A.M. (1985). Academic training in clinical child psychology. In J.M. Tuma (Ed.), *Proceedings: Conference on training clinical child psychologists* (pp. 141–143). Washington, DC: American Psychological Association.
Lerner, R.M. (1992). *Concepts and theories of human development* (2nd ed.). New York: Random House.
Lewis, M., & Miller, S.M. (1990). *Handbook of developmental psychopathology.* New York: Plenum.
Masten, A., & Garmezy, N. (1985). Risk, vulnerability, and protective factors in developmental psychopathology. In B. Lahey & A. Kazdin (Eds.), *Advances in clinical child psychology: Vol. 8* (pp. 1–52). New York: Plenum.
Miller, E., & Dollard, J. (1941). *Social learning and imitation.* New Haven: Yale University Press.
Ollendick, T.H., & King, N.J. (1991). Developmental factors in child behavior assessment. In P.R. Martin (Ed.), *Handbook of behavior therapy and psychological science: An integrative approach* (pp. 57–72). New York: Pergamon.
Piaget, J. (1950). *The psychology of intelligence.* New York: International Universities Press.
Redl, F., & Wineman, D. (1951). *Children who hate: The disorganization and breakdown of behavior controls.* New York: Free Press.
Rie, H.E. (1975). *Clinical child psychology program accreditation.* Unpublished manuscript.
Robins, L., & Rutter, M. (Eds.). (1990). *Straight and devious pathways from childhood to adulthood.* New York: Cambridge University Press.
Rolf, J., Masten, A.S., Cicchetti, D., Nuechterlein, K.H., & Weintraub, S. (1990). *Risk and protective factors in the development of psychopathology.* New York: Cambridge University Press.
Ross, A.O. (1972). The clinical child psychologists. In B.B. Wolman (ed.), *Manual of clinical child psychology* (pp. 1287–1296). New York: McGraw-Hill.
Rutter, M. (1990). Psychosocial resilience and protective mechanisms. In J. Rolf, A.S. Masten, D. Cicchetti, K.H. Nuechterlein, & S. Weintraub (Eds.), *Risk and protective factors in the development of psychopathology* (pp. 181–214). New York: Cambridge University Press.
Sears, R.R., Maccoby, E.E., & Levin, H. (1957). *Patterns of childrearing.* Evanston, IL: Row Peterson.
Sears, R.R., Rau, L., & Alpert, R. (1965). *Identifications and child rearing.* Stanford, CA: Stanford University Press.
Selman, R.R., & Schultz, L.H. (1988). Interpersonal thought and action in the case of a troubled early adolescent. In S.R. Shirk (Ed.), *Cognitive development and psychotherapy.* (pp. 207–246). New York: Plenum.
Selman, R.I., Schultz, L.H., & Yeates, K.O. (1991). Interpersonal understanding

and action: A developmental and psychopathology perspective on research and prevention. In D. Cicchetti & S.L. Toth (Eds.), *Models and integration: Rochester symposium on developmental psychopathology Vol. 3* (pp. 289–316). Rochester, NY: University of Rochester Press.

Sroufe, L.A., & Rutter, M. (1984). The domain of developmental psychopathology. *Child Development, 55,* 17–29.

Welthorn, L.A., & Campbell, F.B. (1982). The competency of children and adolescents to make informed treatment decisions. *Child Development, 53,* 1589–1598.

Wenar, C. (1982). Developmental psychopathology: Its nature and models. *Journal of Clinical Child Psychology,* 192–201.

Wenar, C. (1994). *Developmental psychopathology from infancy through adolescence* (3rd ed.). New York: McGraw-Hill.

Witmer, L. (1907). Clinical psychology. *The Psychological Clinic, 1,* 1–9.

Wohlford, P. (1979). Clinical child psychology: The emerging specialty. *The Clinical Psychologist, 12,* 25–26.

Zigler, E., & Valentine, J. (Eds.). (1979). *Project Head Start: a legacy of the war on poverty.* New York: Free Press.

PART III
MODELS OF GRADUATE EDUCATION IN APPLIED DEVELOPMENTAL SCIENCE: MULTIDISCIPLINARY PROGRAMS

7

Doctoral Education in Applied Child Development

Donald L. Wertlieb
David Henry Feldman

Eliot-Pearson Department of Child Study
Tufts University

More than a decade ago, our faculty proposed some foundations and directions for doctoral training in applied developmental psychology (Wertlieb, 1983), and began to stake out a frontier territory for a field of inquiry we called "developmental science" (Feldman, 1982, 1986). This volume convenes some of our fellow travelers and provides a forum for describing our approach to advanced graduate training at the nation's first doctoral program in Applied Child Development. When historians chronicle the history of our field, they will see the social reform movements at the dawn of the 20th century as pivotal shifts in this society—compulsory schooling, juvenile courts, mental hygiene, and the growth of institutions serving children with an array of "child-saving" initiatives (Cohen, 1985, and Cravens, 1985 in Fagan, 1992). Well informed analysis of the field's historical progress is provided by Davidson and Benjamin (1987), Seigel and White (1982), Youniss, (1990) and Bronfenbrenner, Kessel, Kessen and White (1986). An especially influential chapter in this history can be grasped in the chronicle of the "midlife crisis" in clinical psychology (Fox,

1982; Levy, 1984; Peterson, 1991). Today's designers and implementers of graduate education programs need to be mindful of such historical perspectives as they forge a vision shaped by the contemporary milieu of a postmodern society (Bronfenbrenner, 1986; Elkind, 1994).

It is our belief that this society is once again at a turning point, and that traditional training programs in clinical, counseling, educational, and developmental psychology will have to be supplemented by interdisciplinary programs that integrate scholarship with professional practice, define new specializations, and break down barriers between basic and applied research.

If we, and colleagues who have joined us, including those in the present volume, are right in reading the many conflicting and confusing indicators of future social needs, over time, there will be an increasing number of programs like the ones described in this chapter and the rest of this volume.

A BRIEF HISTORY OF THE ELIOT–PEARSON DEPARTMENT OF CHILD STUDY

In 1922, Abigail Adams Eliot established the Ruggles Street Nursery School in Boston, importing from Europe a compelling model for the care and education of young children, supplanting extant public health orientations with a more forward thinking child development and family support orientation. It was quickly apparent to Eliot that if these new nurseries were to flourish and propagate, then a cadre of professionals would need to be trained. By the late 1920s, the Nursery Training School of Boston was established. It was a variation on the finishing and nursing schools of the day where the care and education of preschool children, in the context of the emerging child development theory, data, and the skills associated with group management and curriculum were the training foci. Young women from across the socioeconomic spectrum were among the candidates for certification, and, eventually, college degrees.

By the 1950s, the Eliot-Pearson School, an independent professional institution, flourished with the support of philanthropist Mrs. Henry Greenleaf Pearson. Eliot ran the school for young children and women while joining the national efforts to establish what is now the National Association for the Education of Young Children. She was also involved in crucial educational and child family policy initiatives in the Works Progress Administration (WPA), the Children's Bureau and related federal and regional projects. By 1959, a new director of the Eliot-Pearson School was brought in from Yale University and the laboratory of Arnold Gessell. Dr. Evelyn Pitcher built upon Dr. Eliot's efforts, emphasizing the base of the now flourishing field of child development research and institutionalizing the laboratory school as a focus for community service, professional training and research. By the mid-1960s, the Eliot-Pearson School merged with Tufts University to become the Eliot-Pearson Department of Child Study in the faculty of Arts and Sciences at that institution—one of the only named departments of this kind in the nation. Eliot's own account of these times is presented in her memoirs, *A heart of grateful trust* (Manning, 1983).

Faculty gathered that included developmental psychologists and clinical psychologists as collaborators with teacher–educators and the powerful cross-fertilization process evident in today's programs began. One culmination of this process is the doctoral program in applied child development described later. Thus, for more than 70 years, Eliot-Pearson has prepared students for a variety of careers that have as a common core a comprehensive understanding of children, their families, and their development. The initial focus was on the preparation of early childhood teachers as child development specialists. The commitment has broadened to other professions where children are a major focus and interdisciplinary integration is a key to competence and success. In all programs, however, children and their well being are a central and abiding focus of all that we do.

Philosophy

Doctoral level training in applied child development is a new and challenging undertaking for academic departments, whether traditional psychology or education faculties, or interdisciplinary hybrid faculties such as Eliot-Pearson's. We are in an age of increasing awareness, even urgency, about the need to apply theory and research about child and family development to the many problems confronting those who are concerned about the care, education and welfare of children. We are increasingly aware of the need to consider such problems as elements of our science and our social contract.

It is our belief that the preparation of applied child development professionals knowledgeable in theory and research and competent in the application of this knowledge will help fill the dangerous, costly, and frustrating gaps that exist among theoreticians, researchers, and practitioners. As propounded by John Dewey (1930), we believe "psychology can be an empirically based instrument for promoting human development and social progress in a democratic society" (in Cahan, 1992). G. Stanley Hall, founder of the American Psychological Association and leader of the child study movement, helped Dewey "recognize the need to balance this formal, theoretical interest with careful attention to the concrete, empirical and practical." (p. 205).

The newness of the applied child development orientation ought not be overemphasized—renewal is perhaps the more accurate frame. In his 1992 presidential address to the APA Division of Developmental Psychology,

Parke (1992) noted the return of developmental psychologists to "their forerunners' concern for applying science to social problems . . . and their renewed interest in interdisciplinary work also resembles early developmental psychology." Elsewhere, he notes "the applied/nonapplied distinction is an increasingly blurry and perhaps dubious one, as researchers continue to recognize the multifaceted value of social experiments such as Headstart for evaluating both basic theoretical issues and social policy concerns." (Parke, 1992, p. 987). Our forerunners were perhaps even bolder in asserting such views. When discussing the case of a "chronic bad speller" referred to his clinic, Witmer, a founder of clinical psychology, noted that "if psychology was worth anything to me or to others it should be able to assist the efforts of a teacher in a retarded case of this kind. The final test of the value of what is called science is its applicability" (1907, p. 4, cited in Fagan, 1992, p. 237).

Just what is "applied child development"? Or more pointedly, how is the notion interpreted and implemented in our specific context at Tufts and Eliot-Pearson? We see applied child development as the nexus of two sets of activities, those that are broadly encompassed under the rubric developmental science, and those we characterize as professional or applied specialties. Developmental science is a relatively new term (Feldman, 1986), intended to draw together scholarly disciplines that focus upon various issues of change, including, but not limited to, geology, physical anthropology, cosmology, developmental biology and psychology, socialization, clinical psychology, archeology, history, and systems theory. As with the label cognitive science, developmental science is intended to reflect an increasing need for disciplines to cross-fertilize, to bring disparate perspectives together to better address the most challenging issues that are their purview. For cognitive sciences, these issues include the acquisition of language, the nature of thinking, the constraints of human and machine thinking capabilities, problem-solving, hypothesis testing, and the like.

For developmental science, the core issues include the natural course of life change in human and nonhuman systems, how human and other organic life have evolved, how the earth and universe came to be, accounts of social institutions and how they change over time, cultural evolution as revealed through artifacts and fossil records, the course of historical movements, and—more directly and narrowly pertinent to our own concerns—how children and families change over time under various sets of conditions, and how bodies of knowledge and skill that children need to acquire develop and change (Feldman, 1994).

Within our own faculty, there are several scholarly disciplines and professional fields represented, occasionally found in the same individual, but more often seen in different colleagues on the staff. Among the disciplines are several specialties in developmental psychology (cognitive, socioemotional, language), clinical psychology, pediatric psychology, neuropsychology, early childhood education, and sociolinguistics. Professional specializations include teacher education, day care, curriculum assessment, early intervention, and social policy analysis.

One way our vision of applied child development is expressed is in a firm commitment to the salience, mutual influence, and balance among the scholarly/academic and applied fields. We see great benefits arising from the transactions, interactions, and linkages among the several areas of specialization. From this perspective, we see it as equally likely that basic research will be productively informed by knowledge accrued from a field of practice, as from application of a theoretical insight to an applied field. In this sense, we see application as iterative and bidirectional—practice to theory and theory to practice.

Although it is now relatively well accepted that applied issues are increasingly central to the field of developmental psychology, as discussed earlier, it is not so clear just how such issues are to be integrated into the disciplinary training that has evolved in departments of psychology, child development, human development, family studies and the like. At Eliot-Pearson, we have something of an advantage in that what is now the Department of Child Study began as a nursery school, became a professional training school and now operates as an academic department. In this respect, it makes a great deal of sense that we would have designed a Ph.D. program that has involvement in practical arenas and issues as a central feature.

Both our founding tradition, a focus on young children in nursery settings, and an intentional definition of our mission as child development rather than human development or lifespan development, distinguish our program. Our "child–centeredness" reflects both a philosophical and political value that is not necessarily in conflict with the life-span perspective, so basic to the fabric of the National Conference on Graduate Education (Fisher, et al., 1993a). Rather, we consider an emphasis upon a particular subset of life stages by a single program or subprogram to be a viable expression of the lifespan perspective. At Eliot-Pearson, our emphasis has been on the first decade of life, though faculty expertise and student interest certainly extend through adolescence. In addition, parent and teacher development involve an integration of adult development theory and research. Most recently, as a family development orientation is adopted, there is greater appreciation for adult and gerontological issues, though still mainly from the perspective of parental and generational influences upon child development. In their cogent analysis of the work of the National Commission on Children, Jacobs and Davies (1991) alert us to the costs and benefits in the child-centered versus family-centered balance. Their points about policy applications can be generalized to other applied developmental science domains. Particular political forces in our own university setting have also played a role in maintaining and elaborating our "child-centeredness." Only recently have some archaic turf and territory obstacles become surmountable. For instance, the focus of Tufts' Department of Education upon the preparation of secondary school teachers and the expertise on adolescence in Tufts' Psychology Department's social-developmental program are now considered resources rather than constraints upon applied developmental science at our university.

For us, the Ph.D. in applied child development represents the culmination of more than 70 years of involvement in the preparation of practitioners in early childhood education and related areas. We have grown to include advanced training in theory and research in disciplines such as developmental and clinical psychology by building upon our traditional strengths in teacher education and early childhood. It therefore seemed like a natural step to cultivate and integrate our various interests and commitments into a vision that characterizes our doctoral training in applied child development.

Program Structures

Inasmuch as our department is lodged in the Arts and Sciences faculty at Tufts University, it has been a constant and welcome challenge to include, even emphasize, our applied work among the valued contributions and activities of our faculty. Our university is a traditional, research-oriented setting where the value of applied research or practice is not always easily perceived or acknowledged. We maintain a commitment to rewarding practice and application as part of faculty expectation and responsibility, and, on the whole, have been successful in convincing our Arts and Science colleagues that the mix of activities and involvements we value is consistent with the central values of our university. This is not always an easy thing to accomplish and requires continuous vigilance and effort, but becomes more accepted as the context of higher education has itself shifted toward community responsibility and participation (Kennedy, 1993). As the University recognizes and accepts its obligation to serve society and be part of the solution of social problems, doctoral training in applied child development becomes a prototypical vehicle for progress. Indeed, Tufts has recently made service to the community one of its central values and explicit commitments. We would like to think that we have contributed toward this shift in emphasis in our university.

An additional philosophical cornerstone of graduate education in applied child development is its ethical imperative. From its earliest roots as an element of a movement for social justice and for strengthening democracy by enhancing our socialization entities, especially school and family, ethical concerns stay in the forefront. More recently, with "professionalization" so rapid and politicized, and the burgeoning of professional models of training, the applied child development focus provides an anchor or a reminder of an orientation that emphasizes heightened ethical concern for researchers and practitioners (Fisher, 1993). Whether in adequately protecting vulnerable research populations, asserting a scientific and rational basis for psychological intervention, or in addressing the interests and needs of an increasingly diverse society, faculty and students in applied child development integrate an ethical framework into problem formulation and solution.

Program Goals

Our program has a broad goal—the training of highly qualified child development specialists—along with considerable flexibility in its implementation. We expect students in applied developmental science to gain competence in research and scholarly inquiry and to comprehend and build theories and databases on the social, emotional, linguistic, intellectual and physiological growth of children. Students are expected to apply this theoretical and empirical knowledge in a range of practical or real world settings or situations. He or she embarks upon a career as an independent academic or professional, with the substance of that independence derived from the capacity and effectiveness of deep disciplinary training, as well as interdisciplinary translation and collaboration. The skills for such work are acquired and honed as a key part of graduate education at Eliot-Pearson. The product of the program is a "scientist-practitioner" well positioned to contribute to the advancement of the field and to the enhancement of the quality of life for children.

Our goals are consistent with those articulated by the National Conference on Graduate Education in the Applications of Developmental Science Across the Life Span (Fisher et al., 1993a). Our faculty and graduates are expected to cultivate expertise in developmental theory, research, and practice using multiple levels of analysis, for example, biological, psychological, sociocultural, or historical analysis, using appropriate scientific inquiry methods. Our graduates will design, implement, and evaluate interventions aimed at enhancing human development, including both traditional and innovative approaches in education, health and human services, and social policy. They will have command of these substantive areas of expertise as well as the skills for its dissemination, translation, and utilization.

Our goal is well articulated by Kanfer (1990): "to foster and blend the skills, perceptivity, and pragmatism of the professional along with training in methods, and exposure to the skeptic-empirical attitude of the researcher" (p. 269). This bridge between science and practice is one "in need of constant attention." Some psychologists need to be translators who a) devote systematic attention to research and dissemination of practical implications and methods derived from various domains of social science, and/or b) formulate professional problems in basic science language and collaborate with (or act as) scientists whose expertise encompasses the domain in which these researchable questions are phrased." (p. 265)

When we are successful in achieving our goal, the Ph.D. in applied child development can rise above the historical quagmires of scientism versus clinicalism (Perry, 1979), and applied versus scientific acceptability. Fagan (1992) notes that "both Hall and Litmer were popular with teacher and parent constituencies, but not always with psychologist colleagues, many of whom viewed their work as less than scientific" (p. 239).

The Faculty

In building a faculty to carry out its mission of both basic scholarship in child development as well as its applications, a guiding principle has been to recruit individuals who have manifested excellence and commitment to these goals. We expect our faculty to have training and expertise equivalent to colleagues in the various disciplines and subdisciplines that we draw from, such as education, developmental psychology, clinical psychology, and social policy, but also to have sustained applied interests and practices. We expect our colleagues to publish their scholarly work in the standard journals of their discipline and we also expect activity and leadership in arenas like policy, early intervention, education, the media, or consultation. Our commitment to "interdisciplinarity" and "transdisciplinarity" is consistent with the key recommendations of the National Conference on Graduate Education for "Multidisciplinary Emphases." (Fisher, et al., 1993a, pp. 9-10).

Our faculty are currently involved in projects such as child advocacy in the court system, consulting to foundations on the research agenda for family homelessness, improving adolescent health standards for a national commission, developing alternative assessment procedures for describing strengths of children from diverse backgrounds, enhancing the literacy skills of immigrant children, and directing large scale national studies of child welfare reform initiatives. Other projects include: rewriting national policies guiding educational programs for talented children; providing legal counsel for the United States Department of Education's Office of Civil Rights; and counseling children, parents and teachers on issues of family life, sexuality and sex education. The breadth and depth of our interests continue in projects such as developing and evaluating interventions for children and families living under extreme stress; consulting to hospitals, schools, and other human service agencies on developmental language and reading disorders; and rewriting state regulations governing child care.

Faculty members provide testimony before state and federal legislative committees, consult to corporations on child care, and make frequent appearances in the local and national print and electronic media. *Good Morning America, Oprah Winfrey, Sally Jesse Raphael Show, 20/20, National Public Radio, 48 Hours,* and the *New York Times* are frequently among the activities of our applied child development faculty.

Within the department we have established a Center for Applied Child Development (CACD) to coordinate and market our various activities and services. Many, though not all, of the projects listed above are provided through the center. Some services are provided by the center itself, especially outreach, technical assistance and consultation to school systems, and assessment and evaluation services for individual families or human service agencies. The center has its own staff and includes professional associates who are not necessarily members of the Child Study faculty, but who are affiliated with the Center for Applied Child Development to augment and enhance the range of professional services we can provide. The CACD also offers opportunities for our students to become involved in a variety of service and outreach activities.

The faculty is, of course, also actively engaged in research, carrying out traditional laboratory studies as well as field studies, using quantitative, qualitative, and ethnographic methodologies. Studies involve populations ranging from at-risk children in the public schools to patients in post-trauma rehabilitative care, families coping with divorce, victims of the Gulf War, African American children as storytellers. Several of the studies conducted by faculty or students draw heavily upon the resources of our affiliated laboratory settings. In our own building complex, we operate the Eliot-Pearson Children's School serving 110 children ages three years through second grade, as well as the Evelyn Pitcher Curriculum Resource Laboratory. Across the campus, serving 80 families with children from the ages of two years old to six years old, from both the University and local communities, is the Tufts Educational Day Care Center. The directors of these laboratory facilities serve on the Child Study faculty. The sites support not only research activity, but also a range of preservice professional training for teachers and other child development specialists. Many a first job for our graduates is employment at one of these settings.

The overall sense, then, is of a faculty actively engaged in basic research and scholarship, applied research and scholarship, and demonstration and dissemination of great variety. At the core of this work is the commitment to the elucidation and application of the processes of child development. Efforts in each arena support, refine, and inform efforts in the others. Our students become involved in the work of the faculty during several stages of their training. Celebrations for the faculty in a recent year include congratulating a junior faculty member for coauthorship of a monograph in the Society for Research in Child Development series, appreciating a colleague releasing a best-seller on family life in postmodern society, and acknowledging a faculty colleague as convener of a national conference on the roles of fathers in economic and family support policies. At Eliot-Pearson, doctoral students are socialized and trained to build careers inclusive and integrative of theory, basic research, applied research, and professional practice.

The Curriculum

Achieving these goals involves careful selection of candidates most likely to benefit from the doctoral program curriculum constructed by our faculty. Achievement is also based upon the philosophical, historical and ethical cornerstones just noted. Most candidates enter with already demonstrated capacities and early career success consistent with our orientation; over 85% already hold a masters degree and there are only a few instances of immediate matriculation after college. Several entering candidates have brought significant career achievements as part of their credentials. For example, four students were previously full time members of faculties in departments of early education, child life, and nursing. Thus, both faculty and students contribute to the intellectual and experiential resources of the community. The curriculum unfolds in both traditional and innovative renditions. Its themes play out in a rigorous course of theoretical study—in graduated experiences to cultivate the skills of translation, transfer, and collaboration noted earlier as key features of applied child development, and in a series of constructions and productions of new knowledge culminating in the doctoral dissertation.

At a general level, the curriculum is consistent with relevant basic frameworks articulated in the National Conference on Graduate Education in the Applications of Developmental Science Across the Lifespan (Fisher et al., 1993a), the Guidelines for Training Psychologists to Work with Children, Youth and Families (Roberts, Erickson, and Tuma 1985) promulgated by the American Psychological Association Division of Child, Youth, and Family Services, and the Hilton Head Conference on Training in Clinical Child Psychology (Tuma, 1985).

The course of theoretical study is most easily conveyed in terms of the sequence of coursework over the first four to six semesters. Courses provide an intensive survey of current theory and knowledge in child development with particular attention to developmental processes, continuities and changes in context and normative/nonnormative variations. The orchestration of biological, sociocultural, and psychological influences is emphasized in domain-general principles, as well as in domain-specific or application-specific principles. For instance, the practice and impact of early childhood education draws upon a range of developmental "givens" and "potentials".

These may be played out in contexts of family, school, and social policy influences or in any given classroom or teacher–learner interaction. We conceptualize a developmental science "core" with interrelated and overlapping tracks, spokes, or specializations reflecting faculty expertise and interests—educational studies, clinical studies, family studies, and policy studies. Any individual faculty member or graduate student is likely to be committed to two or more of these spokes in terms of coursework, fieldwork and/or research activity. There are a few students who have emphasized the developmental science core of the program in their course of studies.

Much of the content of the core courses is similar to what would be found in a traditional child development training program. There is a core of child development courses required of all programs at all levels of the curriculum, including undergraduate and masters programs, as well as the Ph.D. Students are expected to understand the major lines of research and theory pertaining to the intellectual, socioemotional, and linguistic development of children. These core courses differ from many traditional developmental psychology courses in that they explicitly attempt to draw implications for applied issues and integrate such issues into their content. They also tend to include research and theory topics that seem most pertinent to the areas of application that most students pursue (such as early education, clinical and counseling, special education, policy, and health).

At the masters level, programs are differentiated into three strands: teacher preparation, applied professional training, and child development research. All three programs have a common core of child development knowledge and often overlapped other areas, but students choose one of the three emphases offered. For Ph.D. programs, the expectation is that, other than the common child development core, programs will, from the outset, involve integration of practice with scholarly work. Ph.D. students also differentiate their programs into strands, but this is done more individually and over a longer period of time. All Ph.D. students begin together in a Proseminar and typically take child development core courses their first two semesters. Research apprenticeships, field experiences, and additional coursework typically mark the beginnings of differentiation into specialty areas.

There is great diversity of student interests and goals. In many courses, advanced undergraduates, masters, and doctoral students study together. An individual with several years experience in the field preparing for an educational leadership career, perhaps aiming to direct a laboratory school, participates actively in courses with a student just entering the field planning to design mental health services for children with disabilities. A third classmate is aiming to return to a career in Washington advocating for better child welfare policies. Faculty must engage and address these multiple constituencies.

There is, therefore, a strong centripetal force to the program that makes it difficult to integrate all of the Ph.D. students into a viable community of aspiring scholar/professionals. The very diversity that gives the program its distinctive character also makes it difficult to find common ground that all students can claim as their own. The main purpose of the proseminar (required for the first two years for Ph.D. students) is to help both students and the faculty find areas of common interest and concern. This is not an easy task, as the format and topical content of the proseminar are still evolving. More of a centrifugal force than the common core of child development knowledge is needed in a program such as ours, and there is continuing concern that the program tries to do too many things for too diverse a group of students. We remain committed to the ideal of a community of scholar/professionals of such great diversity, but recognize that the challenges in providing a successful program will continue to test the ingenuity and flexibility of our small faculty.

Fortunately, there is emerging literature for the field of applied developmental science itself. For instance, comprehensive reviews such as that by Zigler and Finn-Stevenson (1992), collections by Resnick (1984), the text by Fisher and Lerner (1994), or new articulations such as the "science of prevention" proposed by Coie, Watt, West, Hawkins, Asarnow, Markman, Ramey, Shure and Long (1993), have begun to comprise a new canon for applied child development. We try to use Masterpasqua's (1981) three premises to capture important facets of our philosophy and common goals and to help guide selection of materials and emphases in courses: "the drive toward competence is inherent in individuals and in social systems" (p. 782); "there is a need to study competence as it occurs in natural settings" (p. 783); and "the evaluation of real life developmental needs can lead to the advocacy of developmental rights in community settings." (p. 785)

Simultaneous with more child development content-oriented courses and the proseminar is a series of research methods courses where content is the vehicle for exposing values and techniques for scholarly inquiry. Concepts, ethics, tools, and skills emerge from a sequence of courses in statistics, quantitative methods and design, program evaluation, and qualitative methods and designs. Montada (1984) has sketched the special dimensions of the research enterprise in applied developmental psychology. His steps are useful in articulating distinctions between our program and more traditional research training.

Montada suggests "six questions or steps characterizing a plan for application for the retrieval of relevant scientific information" (p. 270). These questions also shape the production of new knowledge, a key responsibility of the applied child development professional. The first of these questions, "What is the phenomenon or the problem we have to deal with?" (p. 270), defines description and classification as a basic endeavor. The second,

"How did the phenomenon come into existence?" (p. 272), defines causal modeling as a basic endeavor. The third question, "what will be the outcome?" (p. 274), reflects research designs that describe the natural courses of developmental trajectories or processes or designs that focus on interventions to alter such trajectories. At the risk of reducing the scheme to a traditional medical model, we note that these first three steps correspond to diagnosis, including etiology and prognosis.

A fourth step, the task of goal setting, requires definitions of desired outcomes. Montada requires applied developmental science to fill the gap between what "is" and what "ought to be" (p. 276). Steps five and six ask "How can the goal be achieved?" (p. 277), and "Were the goals achieved?" (p. 279), thus bringing the tools and processes of intervention, social policy analysis, and program evaluation into the basic skills compendium of the applied developmental scientist. In our curriculum for the doctorate in applied child development, students engage and implement these research paradigms and master a relevant subset as part of their professional expertise.

The third and fourth years of the Ph.D. curriculum move toward individualization and application of a series of experiences to test and consolidate the understandings and skills nurtured in the more structured course environment. More intensive independent scholarly activity and field-based practica, as well as internship experiences are coordinated and supervised by faculty teams. The student constructs his or her unique expression of applied child development, guided by a faculty with diverse backgrounds, orientations, and shared commitments to the applied child development framework.

During the third or fourth year, in consultation with the faculty advisory team, the student embarks upon preparation of two qualifying papers. At least one of these papers is related to the dissertation topic. The two papers address separate content areas, either in terms of domains noted earlier, populations (toddlers, parents, teachers), particular integrations, or a specific applied problem. The student and advisors plan the qualifying papers to simultaneously capitalize upon synergy and insure breadth and depth. Models include reviews of the type published in *Developmental Review* or *Psychological Bulletin*, or empirical reports reflecting high quality master's thesis research, similar to recent publications in journals such as *Developmental Psychology, Child Development, Journal of Applied Developmental Psychology, Journal of Clinical Child Psychology, Journal of Pediatric Psychology, American Journal of Orthopsychiatry, Early Intervention,* or *Topics in Early Childhood Special Education*.

The doctoral dissertation is approached in a relatively traditional way. It is considered a demonstration of the student's scholarly and professional capabilities, mastery of a well defined research problem, and a contribution to existing theory, knowledge, or practice in the developmental sciences. A significant distinction between the Ph.D. in applied child development and many contemporary doctorates in clinical psychology, or in programs oriented toward the Ed.D. degree or the Psy.D. degree, is reflected in the qualities of the dissertation. Independent research is pursued often, but not always, in association with a faculty mentor's research program. A particular tradition for several faculty mentors derives from the founding principles in clinical psychology, as described by Shakow (1978). In the earliest articulation of the dissertation as a requirement for the clinical psychology Ph.D., the synergy between the internship and the dissertation was emphasized. Sequencing had the trainee carry out internship responsibilities while formulating a real and relevant clinical research problem. The trainee would return to the university after the internship and research the problem as his or her dissertation. Implementation over the recent decades has had a variety of sequences, with a divorce between the internship and the dissertation as the most common experience.

The applied developmental science Ph.D. returns to a more integrated or synergistic framework. This integration of dissertation and internship is a key element of our program, as we have described elsewhere (Wertlieb, 1983). Before turning to a description of field experiences, it is useful to view the following partial listing of our graduates' dissertation titles to indicate the diversity of topics:

"Levels of expertise in early childhood teaching: An initial field test of a diagnostic instrument" (Benjamin, 1989).

"Patterns of interaction in divorced and nondivorced families" (Brach, 1990).

"Families at dinner: Observed roles and relationships in mother-custody, father-custody, and two-parent households" (Brennan, 1991).

"Building on children's strengths: Examination of a Project Spectrum intervention program for students at risk for school failure" (Chen, 1992).

"The transition from words uttered as paired associates to words uttered as symbols" (Ely, 1990)

"Developmental influences on medical compliance in children and adolescents with cystic fibrosis" (Gudas, 1989)

"An empirical approach to defining symbolic play" (Place, 1987).

"Individual differences in adolescent attachment and its relationship to family cohesion and adaptability: an exploratory study" (Resnick, 1989).

"Automaticity, cognitive flexibility, and mathematics: A longitudinal study of children with and without learning disabilities" (Roditi, 1988).

"Temperament as a moderator of adaptation in childhood asthma" (Strzok, 1989).

Field Experiences

The National Conference on Graduate Education in Applied Developmental Science (Fisher, et al., 1993a) points to field experiences as a key distinguishing feature in contrasting "applied developmental" and "traditional developmental" programs. Further, in the tensions and anxieties that emerge when applied developmental programs are contrasted with clinical psychology programs, or when applied developmental programs are tagged as inappropriate "back doors" into clinical psychology, it is often the types and sequences of field experiences, especially practica and internships, that become the focus or foil. Our program is not intended as a clinical psychology training sequence; it stands on its own in terms of rationale and purpose. Thus, the particular rationale and practices for field experiences become key elements in our applied child development curriculum. Already emphasized earlier in describing the synergy between the internship and the dissertation, the "capstone" experiences of the doctoral program, is the notion of integrating field and lab experiences. The commitment to such integration, though in varying degrees, is evident at the earliest stages of the program as well. In addition to the integration priority, there is a breadth of settings employed for field-based training, reflecting the range of problems for the applied developmental scientist and approximating the range of faculty experiences and interests. Traditional "clinical" field experiences, where a student is trained as a mental health professional with diagnostic and psychotherapeutic skills, are a part of that range. "Normal" settings are emphasized again, in part, as a contrast to clinical psychology, but also reflective of the philosophical commitment of the program. School, child care, and community settings, including our own laboratory school (Feinburg, 1992) are common venues for practica and internships. General and pediatric hospitals provide sites for training with research activity as a focus or emphasis as likely as service or program development. Other fieldwork settings include government agencies, museums, businesses, and policy institutes.

The internship is intended to take place over a full academic year at a minimum of 20 hours per week. Students receive supervision from a member of the agency site as well as from a faculty supervisor. Team meetings involving the faculty supervisor, site supervisor, and the student are a crucial element of the supervisory structure and process. Formal evaluation of the internship is included in the student's portfolio, and is part of the cumulative record of accomplishment. The specific role and purpose of the internship in each student's program varies. For students whose primary goal is to work in a university setting, the program insures that their programs are not excessively research-oriented, but have a balance between professional and research training. About a third of our doctoral students aspire to hold university academic positions.

Other students entered the program from an applied field and intend to return to it, either in a faculty or professional role. Students have come from fields such as nursing, childlife, social policy, and early education. For these students, the internship provides an opportunity to develop professional skills, as well as work in a setting likely to foster their dissertation pursuit. Decisions critical to both the student and his or her faculty committee are whether to send the student back to a familiar setting, with altered responsibilities, or to extend the student's range by placement in an unfamiliar setting where new areas of skill may be added to their repertoire.

Because goals of students coming through our doctoral program are varied, and the overall size of the program is quite small (fewer than 20 students in the program at a given time), the internship tends to be the place where the diversity of interests and objectives is most manifest. Students have completed internships in family advocacy programs, policy institutes, early intervention programs, computer science institutes, applied research settings, hospitals, clinics, schools, and a variety of community agencies. In principle, it would be possible to construct an internship experience in legislative bodies, businesses, museums, publishing companies, court clinics, fertility centers, and any other setting where the generation and application of knowledge about child and family development is part of the process of enhancing the quality of life for children and families.

Overall, the internship is intended to be the most ambitious in a series of field experiences built into the student's program, one that provides the most intensive and challenging set of professional opportunities that the student will encounter during the years of study at Tufts. Indeed, having such a heavy emphasis on field experiences tends to lengthen the program, a problem for some of our students since they tend to come from professional settings and have often been successfully engaged in a career trajectory. These students are typically older and may have family responsibilities as well. When possible, an effort is made to provide paid internships though funding issues are complicated and growing more so. Whether paid or not however, the internship and other field experiences are central to the preparation of the scholar/professionals we train in the field of applied child development.

Future Issues and Challenges

As a pioneering program in applied developmental science, our doctoral program in applied child development must appeal to the pioneering spirit of both colleagues and applicants. Indeed, during the application and recruitment process, and at various stages of the advising process throughout training, the costs and benefits of pioneering and breaking new ground are frankly discussed. None of us, as faculty members, is a "Ph.D. in Applied Child Development," yet each of us is committed to our program and students as an applied developmental scientist. Traditional doctoral training involves a kind of cloning process whereby the same processes to which we were subjected as graduate students are provided for our students to create the next generation. We, as faculty, each come from a relatively more traditional or mainstream graduate education experience. It is in our dissatisfaction with some aspects of that experience, in our recognition of the enhanced interest and opportunity inherent in the applied child development mission noted earlier, and in our effort to maintain relevance and meaning in today's intellectual, economic, and sociocultural environment that we commit ourselves to the philosophy and program described above. In our first several years, the sense of being on our own, even isolated, was considerably greater than it is today. The other contributions to this volume, as well as the growth of other vehicles for an applied developmental science community—journals, monograph series, training conferences—help us feel part of an important and growing movement. As we send graduates out into the world, we test the viability of our vision of a new field of applied developmental science.

As a small program just twelve years in operation, we look to early career positions of our graduates as an index of the quality of our training and the receptivity of the community to our program. A few years from now, we will know better of their progress and success. To date, fourteen individuals have graduated from Tufts University with a Ph.D. in Applied Child Development. Among the positions they hold (or have held) are: assistant professor, research psychologist in a pediatric hospital, cofounder of an agency serving and researching children with learning disorders, mental health professional in a community agency, director of a university-based laboratory school, mental health professional in a residential treatment center, director of a national child and family policy center, consultant to a statewide early intervention project, research psychologist in a national school reform project, and project director for a special education technical assistance project. The range of positions is noteworthy for its inclusion of traditional, as well as innovative jobs emblematic of the applied child development mission. Simultaneously, new career paths are opening for which we expect our students to be especially well prepared, with some likely to emerge from the innovative fieldwork and internship construction described earlier (e.g., Mozdzierz, Snodgrass & De Leon, 1992). The list of positions is also suggestive of some of the key challenges that face our program, as well as other applied developmental sciences, especially in the areas of funding for training, accreditation, and credentialling. Part V of this volume addresses many of these salient and complex concerns.

Licensure and credentialling, as well as program accreditation, are controversial and problematic issues influencing students, faculty, and administrators in many ADS programs (Fisher & Koocher, 1990; Wertlieb, 1983; ch. 4, this volume). In our own case, we have had an explicit definition of our doctoral program as one not oriented, as its main priority, toward preparation for licensure examination in existing professional domains such as clinical psychology, counseling psychology, or health services delivery. Pioneering, innovating, and boundary-cutting as we established the Ph.D. in Applied Child Development over the last decade, we remained wary of the potential constraints inherent in having licensure and credentialling drive the curriculum. Labor market dynamics and guild politics figure prominently in the licensure and accreditation processes. In designing and implementing our program, scientific and pedagogical integrity were more central concerns. As our own program, as well as related ADS programs described in this volume, mature, it may become increasingly important to integrate the demands of the accreditation and licensure processes, especially in sustaining professional career viability for our graduates and especially as a potential avenue for quality control and ethical oversight. We concur with the Fisher et al. (1993b) observation that applied developmental science programs such as ours:

> will need to consider the pros and cons of recognition by an accrediting body. Although accreditation can enhance program credibility and prestige, attract students to the field, help qualify students for specialized practice, and attract potential federal training funds, it also runs the risk of diffusing field identity, restricting field development, limiting program independence, and placing financial burdens on educational institutions. (p. 301) [For further discussion of accreditation in ADS programs, see Chapter 4 this volume.]

An appreciation for the complexity and challenge of our mission grows as each new group of students enters, enlightening us about the ways in which they view rigorous training in applied developmental science as a way to meet their intellectual needs, and their need to enhance the quality of life for children and families. Especially heartening are decisions where the pioneering, risk taking spirit wins out, and a student who has been offered or is holding a slot in a traditional developmental or clinical psychology training program concurs with us that his or her interests and needs are better met here with us in applied child development. As our programs and students mature, we can anticipate growth in scientific rigor and relevance in both traditional and innovative programs, as shared and complementary objectives and priorities become better articulated and we adapt to emerging scientific and social contexts.

REFERENCES

Bronfenbrenner, U., Kessel, F., Kessen, W., & White S. (1986). Toward a critical social history of developmental psychology. *American Psychologist, 41*(11), 1218–1230.
Cahan, E.D. (1992). John Dewey and human development. *Developmental Psychology, 28*(2), 205–214.
Cohen, R.D. (1985). Child saving and progressivism, 1885–1915. In J.M. Hawes & N.R. Hiner (Eds.), *American childhood: A research guide and historical handbook* (pp. 273–309). Westport, CT: Greenwood Press.
Coie, J.D., Watt, N.F., West, S.G., Hawkins, J.D., Asarnow, J.R., Markman, H.J., Ramey, S.L., Shure, M.B., & Long, B. (1993). The science of prevention: A conceptual framework and some directions for a national research program. *American Psychologist, 48*(10), 1013–1022.
Cravens, H. (1985). Child saving in the age of professionalism, 1915–1930. In J.M. Hawes & N.R. Hiner (Eds.), *American childhood: A research guide and historical handbook* (pp. 415–488). Westport, CT: Greenwood Press.
Davidson, E.S. & Benjamin, L.T., Jr. (1987). A history of the child study movement in America. In J.A. Glover & R.R. Ronning (Eds.), *Historical foundations of educational psychology* (pp. 41–60). New York: Plenum Press.
Dewey, J. (1930). From absolutism to empiricism. In J.A. Boydston. (Ed.), *The later works of John Dewey, 1925–1953* (pp. 147–160). Carbondale, Illinois: Southern Illinois University Press.
Elkind, D. (1994). *Ties that stress: The new family imbalance.* Cambridge: Harvard University Press.
Fagan, T.K. (1992). Compulsory schooling, child study, clinical psychology, and special education. *American Psychologist, 47*(2), 236–243.
Feinburg, S. (1992). The Eliot-Pearson Children's School. In Moller, B. (Ed.), *The logics of education*, (Vol. 4, pp. 109–122). Oldenburg, Germany: Bibliotheks und Informationssytem der Universitat Oldenburg.
Feldman, D.H. (1982). Developmental science: An alternative to cognitive science. Paper presented at colloquium. Cambridge, MA: MIT.
Feldman, D.H. (1986). How development works. In I. Levin. (Ed.). *Stage and structure: Reopening the debate*, (pp. 284–386). Norwood, NJ: Ablex.
Feldman, D.H. (1994). *Beyond Universals in Cognitive Development: 2nd edition.* Norwood, NJ: Ablex.
Fisher, C.B. (1993). Joining science and application: Ethical challenges for researchers and practitioners. *Professional Psychology: Research and Practice, 24*(3), 378–381.
Fisher, C. and Koocher, G. (1990). To be or not to be? Accreditation and credentialling in applied developmental psychology. *Journal of Applied Developmental Psychology, 11,* 381–394.
Fisher, C.B., & Lerner, R.M. (Eds.). (1994). *Applied developmental psychology.* NY: McGraw-Hill.
Fisher, C.B., Murray, J.P., Dill, J.R., Hagen, J.W., Hogan, M.J., Lerner, R.M., Rebok, G.W., Sigel, I., Sostek, A.M., Smyer, M.A., Spencer, M.B., Wilcox,

B. (1993a). The National Conference on Graduate Education in the applications of developmental science across the lifespan. *Journal of Applied Developmental Psychology, 14,* 1–10.

Fisher, C., Rau, J., & Colapietro, E. (1993b). The Fordham University doctoral specialization in applied developmental psychology. *Journal of Applied Developmental Psychology, 14,* 289–302.

Fox, R.E. (1982). The need for a reorientation of clinical psychology. *American Psychologist, 37*(9), 1051–1057.

Jacobs, F. & Davies, M. (1991). Rhetoric or reality: Child and family policy in the united states. *Social Policy Report of the Society for Research in Child Development, 5, whole.*

Kanfer, F.H. (1990). The scientist–practitioner connection: A bridge in need of constant attention. *Professional Psychology: Research and Practice, 21*(4), 264–270.

Kennedy, Donald (1993). Making choices in the research university. *Daedalus, 122,* 127–156.

Levy, L.H. (1984). The metamorphosis of clinical psychology. Toward a new charter as human services psychology. *American Psychologist, 39*(5), 486–494.

Manning, M. (Ed.). (1983). *A heart of grateful trust: The memoirs of Abigail Adams Eliot.* Medford, MA: Tufts University.

Masterpasqua, F. (1981). Toward a synergism of developmental and community psychology. *American Psychologist, 36*(7), 782–786.

Montada, L. (1984). Applied developmental psychology: Tasks, problems, perspectives. *International Journal of Behavioral Development, 7,* 267–286.

Mozdzierz, G., Snodgrass, R. & DeLeon, P. (1992). A new role for psychologists: Hospital ethics committees. *Professional Psychology: Research and Practice, 23*(6) 493–499.

Parke, R.D. (1992). A final word: The passing of the editorial mantle and some reflections on the field. *Developmental Psychology, 28*(7), 782–786.

Perry, N.W., Jr. (1979). Why clinical psychology does not need alternative training models. *American Psychologist, 34*(7), 603–611.

Peterson, D.R. (1991). Connection and disconnection of research and practice in the education of professional psychologists. *American Psychologist, 46*(4), 422–429.

Resnick, L.B. (1984). Toward an applied developmental theory. In B. Gholson and T. Rosenthal, (Eds.), *Applications of cognitive developmental theory* (pp. 263–280). New York: Academic Press.

Roberts, M.C., Erickson, M.T., & Tuma, J.M. (1985). Addressing the needs: Guidelines for training psychologists to work with children, youth, and families. *Journal of Clinical Child Psychology, 14*(1), 70–79.

Shakow, D. (1978). Clinical psychology seen some 50 years later. *American Psychologist, 33,* 148–158.

Siegel, A.W. & White, S.H. (1982). The child study movement: Early growth and development of the symbolized child. In H.W. Reese (Ed.), *Advances in child development and behavior, Vol. 17,* (pp. 233–285). New York: Academic Press.

Tuma, J. (Ed.). (1985). *Proceedings: Conference on training clinical child psychologists.* Washington, DC: APA.

Wertlieb, D. (1983). Some foundations and directions for applied developmental psychology. *Journal of Applied Developmental Psychology, 4,* 349–358.

Youniss, J. (1990). Cultural forces leading to scientific developmental psychology. In C. Fisher, and W. Tryon, W. (Eds.), *Ethics in applied developmental psychology: Emerging issues in an emerging field,* (pp. 285–300). Norwood: Ablex.

Zigler, E. & Finn-Stevenson, M. (1992). Applied developmental psychology. In M.H. Bornstein, & M.E. Lamb, (Eds.), *Developmental psychology: An advanced textbook,* (pp. 677–729). Hillsdale, NJ: Erlbaum.

8

Graduate and Postgraduate Education in the Applications of Development Science to Adult Development and Aging

Michael A. Smyer[1]
Dean, Graduate School of Arts & Sciences
Boston College

INTRODUCTION

The starting points for this chapter are three questions posed by the French philosopher, Michel Philibert (1979): "Of aging, what can we know? With aging, what must we do? About aging, what may we hope to?" (p. 384). Philibert's inquiries immediately cast the study of adult development and aging as an active, interpretive, and intervention-oriented process. Implicit in the questions are concerns about the limits of knowledge,

---

[1]Michael A. Smyer was a faculty member at The Pennsylvania State University when he wrote this chapter. He has since moved to Boston College, where he is Dean of the Graduate School of Arts and Sciences and Associate Vice President for Research.

the limits of intervention, and the links between one's professional and personal encounters with aging. In short, Philibert reminds us that the substance and process of gerontology, the study of normal aging, is inherently an applied developmental science.

In this chapter, I will describe an approach to graduate and postgraduate training in adult development and aging that has been developed and implemented for more than two decades at Penn State University. During this time, several federal sources, including the National Institute on Aging, the National Institute of Mental Health, and the National Institute for Child Health and Human Development (prior to the development of the National Institute on Aging) have supported our efforts. Their support was based, in part, on the clarity of our philosophy, purpose, and structure. These elements form the basis of this chapter.

Gerontology is the study of the processes of normal aging. At Penn State, there are several mechanisms available for studying gerontology. The Gerontology Center, a university wide entity, has developed a minor in gerontology that is available to both undergraduate and graduate students. Coursework for the minor draws from faculty members and substantive offerings across the campus (e.g., biology, sociology, human development and family studies, and exercise and sports science). Students seeking to major in gerontology also have several options, depending upon their substantive interests. For example, biology students can emphasize aging issues within a standard biology major. In the social and behavioral sciences, the largest cohesive set of undergraduate and graduate course offerings are in the Department of Human Development and Family Studies (HDFS).

The faculty of HDFS emphasize the developmental plasticity of adulthood and later life (e.g., Baltes, 1983; Baltes & Baltes, 1990; Diamond, 1993). Therefore, HDFS students choosing this area focus on adult development and aging. The HDFS coursework in adult development and aging includes information regarding the description, explanation, and processes of intervention with the processes of both normal and abnormal patterns of aging. This emphasis spans the spectrum from basic descriptive information to assessing the limits of preventive and remedial interventions with older adults and their families. Thus, the offerings in HDFS are consistent with recent formulations of the purposes and activities of applied developmental science (Fisher et al., 1993; Fisher & Lerner, 1994).

These themes are exemplified in the varied research programs of the HDFS faculty. For example, in the area of changing intellectual abilities in later adulthood, Drs. Schaie and Willis have described normal, age related changes in cognitive functioning and their links to older adults' everyday competence (e.g., Schaie, 1983; Schaie, 1990; Willis, 1991; Willis & Schaie, 1994). They have also assessed the short term and long term impact of intervention strategies designed to maintain cognitive capacities (e.g., Schaie & Willis, 1986; Willis, 1987; Willis, & Schaie, in press). Similarly,

Smyer and his colleagues have described patterns of mental illness among nursing home residents (e.g., Smyer, Shea, & Streit, 1994). They have also developed preventive efforts designed to reduce mental health problems among residents by working with nursing home staff and supervisors (e.g., Smyer, Brannon, & Cohn, 1992; Smyer & Walls, 1994).

Penn State's experience illustrates basic issues encountered in the design, implementation, and evaluation of applied development science programs focused on adult development and aging. I hope that our experience may be informative for others who are considering program development in this important domain. At the very least, the Penn State case study exemplifies the role that program philosophy, faculty strengths and interests, and substantive emphases play in developing and refining applied developmental science graduate and postgraduate offerings.

In the next section, two sets of underlying philosophical assumptions will be highlighted: our starting premises regarding the nature of graduate and postgraduate education, and our assumptions regarding the nature of adult development and aging.

The following two sections of the chapter summarize our program goals and planning procedures, emphasizing the important role of faculty members as both program developers and research mentors for individual graduate students and postgraduate fellows. The theme of individual differences—in academic backgrounds of our incoming students and in their professional goals and career trajectories—has been a hallmark of our graduate and postgraduate educational efforts. This makes our faculty members' active participation in an apprentice model of graduate education essential.

The curriculum is briefly highlighted in the fifth section. Here three interrelated elements are sketched: the requirements for our graduate program as a whole; the requirements for those emphasizing adult development and aging; and the requirements for those interested in human development intervention. Although this listing may seem extensive, the curricular choices available to our students are substantial, again reflecting the theme of individual differences.

The role, nature, and timing of field experiences in our program is presented in the sixth section. Our starting point for field placements are our students' differing career goals and substantive interests. Therefore, the definition of "field experience" necessarily includes a range of settings (e.g., from NIH intramural research laboratories to congressional committees), with varying purposes. Again, these emphases are consistent with recent national discussions of the importance of field experiences in applied developmental science (e.g., Chapter 11 of this volume, and Fisher et al., 1993).

The chapter's final section focuses on emerging issues and challenges in the field of applied adult development and aging. Here, the impact of recent national developments for graduate and postgraduate education will be considered.

Program Philosophy

Graduate and postgraduate efforts in adult development and aging take, as their starting points, the underlying premises regarding graduate education and the aging process. Clarifying these initial assumptions is essential for both an integrated faculty effort and an effective process of recruitment and retention of outstanding graduate and postgraduate students. The starting assumptions of the faculty in Human Development and Family Studies (HDFS) at Penn State, described briefly here, illustrate one set of starting assumptions. They are presented here, not as the sole or even the most appropriate set of assumptions for every program. Instead, they are meant to exemplify both the process and substance of our faculty's deliberations regarding these important first principles.

Assumptions regarding graduate education

The HDFS graduate program is built upon the expertise of faculty members drawn from several disciplines (e.g., psychology, sociology, anthropology, behavior genetics, demography, history). Their areas of research range from prenatal influences on development, through issues of later life. Their investigative strategies include historical research, field work, laboratory experiments (both animal and human), and survey research. This diversity is a source of considerable heterogeneity among the faculty, as well as a source of considerable strength. It also provides a context for the initial premises of the program (HDFS, 1993 pp.1–2):

1. A lifespan perspective is useful for the analysis of human development and the improvement of intervention strategies. This strategy recognizes that most important aspects of development and types of life tasks and situations vary from the prenatal period through childhood and adolescence to maturity and old age, as well as through the life cycle of the family, and that each phase of development is a precursor to the next.
2. Human development is complex and occurs within a complex environment. Understanding this complexity is best accomplished when interdisciplinary and multiprofessional efforts and approaches are encouraged and rewarded.
3. Sustained advances in the knowledge and methods of human development are most likely to occur when rigorous methods of inquiry, and of empirical investigation, are employed.
4. The professional excellence of new members of the field is developed when it is consistently expected, sought, modeled, and rewarded.
5. Innovative and independent productivity is most likely to be achieved

within a program where (a) learning opportunities are broadly conceived to include a range of coursework, assistantships, practica, and independent learning experiences, (b) individual differences in goals, prior preparation, and learning styles are recognized and valued, and (c) standards of excellence are monitored and maintained.

These starting assumptions are consistent with earlier formulations of the lifespan perspective of human development and the current applied developmental science perspective (e.g., Baltes, 1983; Birkel, Lerner, & Smyer, 1989; Fisher & Lerner, 1994; Fisher et al., 1993; Hetherington, Lerner, & Perlmutter, 1988; Sorenson, Weinert, & Sherrod, 1986). They are also consistent with an apprentice model of graduate education which assumes that a major element of graduate and postgraduate education is the process of research apprenticeship. Through close collaboration with faculty members, students learn both the process and substance of the research enterprise. This collaborative, collegial apprenticeship is labor intensive, but offers educational benefits that are not available solely from classroom experience.

Assumptions regarding adult development and aging

Our educational efforts in adult development and aging take, as a starting point, the context of the HDFS graduate program. Thus, our efforts in gerontology share the assumptions outlined above. Our current NIMH funded training effort in research on mental health and aging (Zarit, 1992) illustrates additional, more specific assumptions regarding applied gerontology:

1. Developing and maintaining the mental health of the aging is a process which involves biological and psychological capacities, as well as social contexts.
2. Research experience and classroom work should explicate the contributions of these domains to the normal aging process and to differentiating patterns of mental illness from normal aging.
3. Attention should be given to deficits in functioning due to aging or disease, as well as to the conditions for maintaining continuity or growth of abilities.
4. Students will conduct research in a variety of clinical and nonclinical settings to expose them to a range of mental health issues encompassing prevention and promotion, as well as rehabilitation and treatment.

These assumptions are consistent with earlier discussions of the range of mental health and mental illness found among older adults (e.g., Birren, Sloane, & Cohen, 1992; Butler, Lewis, & Sunderland, 1991; Gatz & Smyer, 1992). They also underscore the importance of biological factors (e.g., Bronfenbrenner et al., 1993; Diamond, 1993; Plomin, 1989; Plomin & McClearn, 1990; Scarr, 1993), biographical factors (e.g., Cohen, 1993; Kivnick, 1993), and context (e.g., Bronfenbrenner et al., 1993; Plomin et al., 1988; Plomin & McClearn, 1990; Scarr, 1993; Schooler, 1990; Wykle & Musil, 1993) in shaping development and the experience of aging. Finally, these assumptions remind us that the concern of applied science in adult development and aging encompasses a range of functioning from severe impairment through optimal aging (e.g., Baltes & Baltes, 1990; Cohler, 1992; Rowe & Kahn, 1987; Smyer, 1995).

Program Structure and Goals

The program structure and goals of the study of adult development and aging at Penn State are designed to take advantage of the diversity of faculty disciplines represented in Human Development and Family Studies (HDFS). As noted earlier, undergraduate and graduate students can major in adult development and aging in HDFS. On the undergraduate level, adult development and aging is one of five different options in the major, all within the bachelor of science in HDFS. At the graduate level, adult development and aging is an emphasis within the graduate program and the master's, and doctorate program in HDFS.

The HDFS faculty is explicitly multidisciplinary, including colleagues from anthropology, demography, sociology, and psychology. Not surprisingly, we attract graduate students from a wide range of disciplinary and professional backgrounds. Some students come from core disciplines of psychology, sociology, anthropology, or other areas. Some have worked in a professional role before seeking graduate education; others come directly from another educational setting. Approximately half of our graduate students initially seek admission for a master's degree with the assumption that successful progress will lead to eventual admission to doctoral candidacy. The other half of our graduate students come with an advanced degree, seeking to complete the doctorate in HDFS.

The HDFS graduate program and our training efforts in applied gerontology share several goals for graduate and postgraduate education. Taken together, these provide a framework for channeling the efforts of faculty and students. A primary objective is to develop and maintain a distinguished graduate program, with particular expertise in adult development and aging. While this may seem self-evident, explicitly acknowledging this goal reminds all involved—faculty, staff, and students—that continued excellence requires continued attention to this goal. Specific attention is paid to graduate and postgraduate recruitment efforts, designed to attract students who will benefit from the intellectually stimulating and diverse context of the HDFS program.

Because of the HDFS history and tradition at Penn State, we emphasize a second goal: bringing together knowledge and methods from diverse disciplines and professions to integrate, elaborate, and apply them to substantive issues in human development (HDFS, 1993). Consistent with this interdisciplinary goal, our faculty and graduate student recruitment are not limited to members of a particular discipline. Similarly, the faculty's research methods are not limited to a single approach.

Because of the diversity of faculty and student experience, a third major goal focuses on developing the optimal match between the student's substantive interests and the faculty's expertise. This requires crafting individually tailored courses of study that blend course work, research apprenticeships, and if appropriate, field experiences to assure the student's breadth and depth of knowledge. Examples of these procedures will be provided later in this chapter.

The final goal of the HDFS program and, within it, of our applied gerontology efforts, is facilitating the early career development of our graduate and postgraduate students. If successful, the substance and process of our graduate education will enable our students to become important contributors to the process of applied developmental science. Throughout their time with us, our students will become increasingly involved in professional activities as part of their research apprenticeships. Thus, they are expected to collaborate with faculty members on presentations at national meetings, theoretical and empirical publications, and where appropriate, grant development activity. In short, by the end of their tenure with us, our students should have both a substantive expertise as well as a wealth of professional experiences to enable them to pursue an initial position in either an academic or applied research setting.

Planning Procedures

Accomplishing these goals requires planning on two related levels: institutional and individual.

Institutional planning

Programmatically, a sign of an institution's maturity is its ability to flexibly arrange and rearrange groups of faculty members to collaborate on specific substantive issues. We are fortunate that the HDFS program provides a context that supports such flexibility. For example, our faculty members are loosely affiliated with three domains of graduate education: family development, individual development, and human development intervention research. The boundaries between these groupings are fluid however, and the overlap among them is considerable.

Similarly, our applied gerontology effort is organized around four substantive areas and three crosscutting themes (Zarit, 1992). The four areas reflect our faculty members' ongoing research programs, emphasizing a variety of settings, contexts, and methodologies for studying mental health issues of older adults. The four substantive areas are: a) multidimensional assessment of individuals, families, and communities (e.g., Poon, 1986; Schaie & Hertzog, 1984); b) research on mental health interventions at the individual, family, community, or institutional level (e.g., Smyer, Zait, & Qualls, 1990; Zarit & Teri, 1991); c) mental health of families (e.g., Zarit & Reid, 1994); d) behavioral genetics and mental health (e.g., Plomin et al., 1988; Plomin, 1989; Plomin & McClearn, 1990).

Three cross cutting themes complement these substantive emphases: research methodologies for the study of aging and change (e.g., Hertzog & Nesselroade, 1987; Schaie & Hertzog, 1984; Zarit 1990); diversity issues in mental health and aging (e.g., Wykle & Musil, 1993); and the responsible conduct of research. Our assumption is that these themes are essential for all of our graduate and postgraduate students, regardless of their substantive focus.

Table 1 reflects our faculty members' grouping across these substantive themes and cross cutting issues. Note that faculty members affiliate with several themes, again reflecting their range of expertise and interests. The main lesson to be learned from our experience, however, is the importance of identifying the expertise of your faculty and providing mechanisms for that expertise to become available to graduates and postgraduates.

TABLE 8.1
Illustrative Integration of Substantive and Cross-Cutting Themes in Research Training

Substantive Themes

Multidimensional Assessment	Mental Health Intervention	Mental Health of Families	Behavioral Genetics
Lago	Burton	Booth	McClearn
Schaie	Lago	Burton	Plomin
Smyer	Rovine	Plomin	Schaie
Susman	Smyer	Smyer	Willis
Willis	Willis	Zarit	Zarit
Collins	Zarit		
Zarit			

Diversity: Burton
Research Methodology: Rovine, Schaie, Collins
Responsible Conduct of Research: Smyer, Zarit

Individual planning

The disciplinary and substantive heterogeneity of our incoming graduate and postgraduate students, when combined with the diversity of curricular options available to them, requires careful planning to assure optimal substantive expertise and professional development before they leave our department.

For our graduate students, the master's or doctoral committee is responsible for planning course selection, research apprenticeships, and field experiences. They undertake their advisory role within the graduate school's general requirements for master's and doctoral degrees. In addition, HDFS has curricular requirements (outlined in the next section), along with doctoral candidacy and comprehensive examination procedures. These requirements form a procedural framework that the student and his or her committee uses to develop the most appropriate combination of experiences to achieve his or her professional goal.

For postdoctoral fellows, the structure is much different and more appropriately individually tailored to take advantage of the advanced training that the student has already completed. The postdoctoral fellow will typically spend two years in the program. At the outset, we request each fellow to outline several elements: a primary and secondary research affiliation; desired coursework to fill in substantive or methodological gaps from previous training; and plans for publications coming from his or her own current research, typically the dissertation research.

The primary and secondary affiliations are the main research apprenticeships that the fellow will initially undertake. The expectation is that the postdoctoral fellow will work with faculty members on their ongoing projects, developing a substantive project within the context of the already existing projects.

Our typical postdoctoral fellows also take advantage of advanced statistics and developmental methodology courses. They also, from time to time, sit in on substantive courses (e.g., biology of aging). However, the major focus of the training experience is not coursework—it is the research apprenticeship.

In addition to working with faculty members, postdoctoral fellows are expected to develop publications from their earlier work. Faculty members are available as informal reviewers and advisors prior to submitting the manuscripts for publication. By the end of the first year, each fellow is expected to identify a topic for grant development during the second year. The goal is to have each fellow submit a grant proposal for external funding before the end of the second year.

For example, a postdoctoral fellow who recently completed a two year experience at Penn State had a primary research affiliation with the Penn

State Nursing Home project (Smyer et al., 1992), and a secondary affiliation with an evaluation of the effect of adult daycare on caregivers of Alzheimer's patients under the supervision of Dr. Steven Zarit. She selected methodology and statistics courses to complement her strong training in qualitative methodology. She coauthored several presentations at national meetings, coauthored one book chapter and submitted three manuscripts. Prior to taking a position in a research institute, she had drafted a grant proposal with plans to submit it from her new setting.

Once again, the procedural details of our approach are not important. What is essential is the individualized professional development plan that each graduate or postgraduate student is expected to develop. This emphasis on individual initiative emerges from the program's relatively modest curricular requirements.

The Curriculum

On the graduate level, any curriculum for those emphasizing applied adult development and aging will be a function of three interrelated elements: the general degree requirements; special requirements of the adult development and aging training grant; and special requirements for those who emphasize intervention research. Each of these elements within Penn State's HDFS program will be described briefly to illustrate the synergy among these areas.

Degree requirements

The Penn State graduate school requires a minimum of 30 graduate credits for a master's degree; there is no comparable minimum credit load requirement for the doctoral degree. The doctoral committee is the final arbiter of the student's requirements.

Within this graduate school structure, the HDFS program requires one introductory seminar of all graduate students, plus six courses in statistics and methodology for doctoral students. Four of these courses are required: Introduction to Research Design and Statistics; Statistical Models (e.g., the general linear model, analysis of variance, repeated measures analysis of variance); Measurement in HDFS; and Developmental Research and Design. In addition to these required courses, students must choose two electives. Most students take courses in addition to these electives. Typical selections might include courses such as Program Evaluation, Nonparametric Approaches, LISREL, Survival Analysis, Factor Analysis, or Applied Time Series Analysis.

This relative emphasis on developmental methods and statistics reflects two assumptions of our faculty: that methods for the study of change are an essential tool for all of our students (e.g., Rovine & von Eye, 1991; Schaie et al., 1988); and that our students will complement methodological expertise with substantive depth in their chosen area of emphasis.

Adult development and aging requirements

Our training grants assume that students will develop a background in three disciplinary perspectives on adult development and aging—the biology of aging, psychology of aging, and sociology of aging. Graduate students emphasizing the gerontology perspective take a course in each domain. In addition, the NIMH training grant requires students to participate in a weekly colloquium on research in aging, take a seminar on mental health and aging, and participate in occasional seminars on diversity issues in aging and on the responsible conduct of research.

These curricular requirements are designed to underscore the multidisciplinary nature of the field of gerontology. They are also designed to reflect the current research activities of Penn State faculty and outside visitors. Finally, the occasional seminars emphasize the heterogeneity of older adults, as well as the ethical responsibilities of research professionals (Fisher et al., 1993). The seminars also offer an opportunity to discuss a range of professional development issues that are salient in applied developmental areas (Fisher et al., 1993; Fisher & Lerner, 1994).

Intervention research

Graduate students interested in applied adult development and aging are also encouraged to complete a sequence of courses designed for those emphasizing intervention research. This sequence includes four required courses and two electives. (Two of these courses can be used as electives to meet the methodology requirement outlined earlier.) The required courses focus on intervention theory, program design and evaluation, consultation and program implementation, and developmental assessment. Students also are usually involved in a series of graded practica and internship experiences. Together with coursework, this sequence includes theoretical preparation, skills oriented coursework, and opportunities for application of skills with increasing responsibility. In short, the sequence focuses on the research expertise and application strategies necessary for applied developmental science in the latter part of the lifespan (Fisher et al., 1993).

The intent of the intervention research core is to prepare our students for a variety of research roles linked to the process of applied developmental science (Fisher et al., 1993) in general, and preventive research in particular (Coie, et al., 1993; Muehrer & Koretz, 1992). We have explicitly differentiated this career trajectory from a variety of direct service roles (e.g., clinical psychologists, social workers). Therefore, although an occasional student may qualify for state licensure by an applied profession (e.g., psychology or social work), the intent is to prepare researchers, not practitioners.

To attain this educational goal, we require that our students specialize in both intervention research and a substantive area. Commonly, coursework in developmental theory complements a concentration on one element of the lifespan (e.g., infancy and early childhood, adult development and aging, etc.), or on a unit of analysis (e.g., family development). The adult development and aging emphasis described earlier illustrates a substantive concentration that complements the intervention core.

Postgraduate curricular requirements

Our postdoctoral fellows have minimal course requirements since the assumption is that the research apprenticeship will be the major focus of the training process. They are required to attend the weekly research colloquium, occasional seminars on diversity issues and responsible conduct of science, and the seminar on aging and mental health. While not required to, postdoctoral fellows often participate in other course offerings to complement and expand upon their earlier training, particularly in the area of developmental methodology and statistics. For example, some fellows may take course work in program evaluation strategies. Others may take coursework in nonparametric approaches or perhaps a seminar in LISREL. The choices are highly idiosyncratic as a function of the fellows' previous coursework, career goals, and substantive interests.

Field Experiences

Field experiences play two important roles in the professional development of our graduate and postgraduate students. They allow our students to have access to different settings and additional sets of expertise, and sample additional professional roles without great risk to their professional development. To accomplish these goals, we use a range of field experiences that include practica based in the Penn State community, as well as extended internships in other settings.

Our faculty's underlying assumption is that the student's field experience will include increasing responsibility with increasing professional maturity in the program. For example, initial field practica may involve working under close faculty supervision in an intervention research project. Later in the student's training, field placement might include a program evaluation role in a setting that requires only sporadic direct faculty supervision. At the end of doctoral training, many of our students seek an internship expe-

Graduate and Postgraduate Education 155

rience (ranging from a few weeks to several months) in another setting chosen to complement their previous training and their substantive interests.

The internship experiences offer a student the chance to work with other faculty colleagues beyond Penn State's HDFS faculty, and to also work in different professional settings. The timing and selection of such internship experiences vary with the student's own academic program and professional goals. For example, one doctoral student sought an internship with the staff of the U.S. House Committee on Aging. This placement complemented her dual emphases of adult development and aging and public policy, since she eventually received a master's in public administration, as well as her doctorate in HDFS. Another doctoral student worked with research staff members in the General Accounting Office on health policy research. For this student, a major goal was assessing research career options in addition to the traditional academic role that was so familiar to her.

These field experiences provide an important service beyond expanding the faculty and expertise that our students work with; they also give the student a chance to sample a potential professional role without making an initial career commitment to that setting.

This low stakes lesson can be very important and influential in the subsequent professional development of the student. For example, after the internship with the House Committee on Aging, our student decided that she was much more interested in state level involvement. She subsequently worked as a research staff member for the Secretary of Aging in one of the midwestern states. Since that assignment, she has assumed a faculty role, bringing to it a range of research expertise, policy experience, and a substantive commitment to aging issues. The result, however, does not have to be a negative one. Our student who worked with the General Accounting Office found that, to her surprise, she very much enjoyed the process of policy research at the federal level. After graduation, she joined the staff of the Agency for Health Care Policy Research, subsequently playing a key role in analyzing data from the National Medical Expenditure Survey.

Each of these students used the field experience to assess the fit between their expertise and the demands of particular roles. Other students have used field experiences to work with faculty members and learn particular intervention research techniques (e.g., standardized clinical interview approaches) or to develop particular statistical techniques (e.g., advanced application of event history analysis).

In summary, we use field experiences at different points in the student's career to complement the research apprenticeships and classroom training offered by our program. Again, the nature, timing, and role of the field experience for each student is a set of individualized decisions that the student and faculty advisor will make.

Future Issues and Challenges

The current consideration of the future of applied developmental science occurs at the same time that there is a great deal of professional ferment regarding doctoral and postdoctoral training. For example, a national conference, cosponsored by the National Institute of Mental Health and the American Psychological Association, recently developed a set of recommendations for the substantive areas necessary for educating psychologists who work with, or do research on, clinical issues of older adults (Teri et al., 1992). Similarly, another national conference recently developed recommendations for postdoctoral training in professional psychology (Larsen et al., 1993). Similarly, as part of the recent Human Capital Initiative, there has been a national conference charting priority issues in research on the psychology of aging linked to applications. The conference document, *Vitality for Life* (Cavanaugh et al., 1993), has highlighted both the progress and the prospects for applications of applied developmental science to pressing issues of later life.

These developments suggest that attention to the appropriate process and substance of applied developmental science is particularly timely. Demographic trends of an aging society have also raised concerns regarding our ability to intervene appropriately with other adults and their families (e.g., Cassel et al., 1992; Schneider & Guralnik, 1990). Simultaneously, there is an ongoing debate within the gerontological research community regarding appropriate frameworks for research and application in the field of adult development and aging (e.g., Baltes & Baltes, 1990; Cohler, 1992; Cole et al., 1993; Hudson, 1993; Tornstam, 1992). For example, some have argued that the focus of adult development and aging should shift from normal or usual aging to successful aging (Baltes & Baltes, 1990; Rowe & Kahn, 1987). Others have responded that emphasizing success implies certain assumptions regarding the criteria for success, the proportion of those who can achieve it, and the realistic prospects of both growth and decline in later life (Cohler, 1992; Cole et al., 1993). As Philibert (1979) noted, the process of aging and the research on aging is, inevitably, hermeneutic and interpretive. In short, we can anticipate both an increase in attention to adult development and aging and increased scholarly activity in the developmental sciences underlying applications in gerontology.

The educational approaches outlined in this chapter represent one attempt to provide a framework for applied gerontological research. Others might emphasize different aspects of graduate education (e.g., a relatively greater emphasis on course work, with less weight given to the research apprenticeship). Similarly, others might emphasize other aspects of adult development and aging (e.g., relatively less weight given to behavioral genetics, with more attention being given to personality factors).

Regardless of the programmatic specifics, development in applied gerontology will require two types of progress—internal and external. Internally, the advancement of this area of education and research, however, requires clarity of philosophy, process, and substantive emphases. Each institution must, for its faculty and students, clarify its underlying philosophical premises, assumptions about graduate and postgraduate education, and its substantive focus. The Penn State example is offered to illustrate one attempt to make explicit these foundations of graduate and postgraduate education in applied adult development and aging.

Externally, those who are active in this area must effectively communicate with potential sources of support for our educational efforts. For example, the Penn State's program development has occurred in a setting that has received federal training grants, as well as private and federal external funding for research projects. Our model of graduate education assumes that availability of such resources. Increasingly, however, the scientific community must engage in discussions with policymakers and agency staff to highlight important areas of continued funding and priorities for research and training. The *Vitality for Life* document illustrates an effective collaboration among the scientific community, funding agencies, and private funding sources. We can anticipate other similar efforts as potential funding sources seek advice in an era of limited resources.

The contributions of our graduates will be one measure of the maturity of our internal and external development. If successful, we will have prepared them for a variety of roles. For example, among Penn State's recent graduates, some have moved into faculty roles in gerontology, adult development and aging, or psychology of aging. Others have joined research institutes (some university affiliated, some linked to the V.A. system, others in private or public research operations), focusing their efforts on applied research. Still others have assumed policy oriented roles in executive or legislative branches of the states and the federal government. In short, if we are successful, our graduates will pursue professional careers that embody Boyer's (1990) four types of scholarship: the scholarship of discovery, the scholarship of integration, the scholarship of application, and the scholarship of teaching.

In the end, we return to our starting point: Philibert's (1979) questions. This chapter has tried to illustrate what we can know of aging, what we must do to develop programs of applied adult development and aging, and what we may hope to accomplish through such programmatic developments. If successful, this chapter has illustrated both the progress and prospects of applied developmental science in adult development and aging. The next steps are important for all of us, since aging represents our collective future.

REFERENCES

Baltes, P.B. (1983). Lifespan developmental psychology: Observations on history and theory revisited. In R.M. Lerner (Ed.), *Developmental psychology: Historical and philosophical perspectives* (pp. 79–111). Hillsdale, NJ: Erlbaum.

Baltes, P.B., & Baltes, M.M. (Eds.). (1990). *Successful aging: Perspectives from the behavioral sciences*. Cambridge, England: Cambridge University Press.

Birkel, R.C., Lerner, R.M., & Smyer, M.A. (1989). Applied developmental psychology as an implementation of a lifespan view of human development. *Journal of Applied Developmental Psychology, 10*, 425–445.

Birren, J.E., Sloane, R.B., & Cohen, G.D. (Eds.). (1992). *Handbook of mental health and aging* (2nd ed.). San Diego, CA: Academic Press.

Boyer, E.L. (1990). *Scholarship reconsidered: Priorities for the professoriate*. Princeton, NJ: The Carnegie Foundation for the Advancement of Teaching.

Bronfenbrenner, U., Ceci, S., & Lenzenweger, M.F. (1993). *Nature–nurture reconceptualized in developmental perspective: Toward a new theoretical and operational model*. Unpublished manuscript. Ithaca, NY: Cornell University.

Butler, R.N., Lewis, M.I., & Sunderland, T. (1991). *Aging and mental health: Positive psychosocial and biomedical approaches* (4th ed.). NY: Macmillan Publishing Co.

Cassel, C.K., Rudberg, M.A., & Olshansky, S.J. (1992). The price of success: Health care in an aging society. *Health Affairs, 11*(2), 87–99.

Cavanaugh, J.C., Park, D.C., Smith, A.D., & Smyer, M.A. (1993). *Vitality for life: Psychological research for productive aging*. Washington, DC: The American Psychological Society.

Cohen, G. (1993). Comprehensive assessment: Capturing strengths, not just weaknesses. *Generations, XVII*(1), 47–50.

Cohler, B.J. (1992). The myth of successful aging. *Readings: A Journal of Reviews and Commentary in Mental Health*. (December), 18–22.

Coie, J.D., Watt, N.F., West, S.G., Hawkins, J.D., Asarnow, J.R., Markman, H.J., Ramey, S.L., Shure, M.B., & Long, B. (1993). The science of prevention. *American Psychologist, 48*(10), 1013–1022.

Cole, T.R., Achenbaum, W.A., Jakobi, P.L., & Kastenbaum, R. (Eds.). (1993). *Voices and vision of aging: Toward a critical gerontology*. New York: Springer.

Diamond, M.C. (1993). An optimistic view of the aging brain. *Generations, XVII*(1), 31–33.

Fisher, C.B., & Lerner, R.M. (1994). Foundations of applied developmental psychology. In C.B. Fisher & R.M. Lerner (Eds.). *Applied developmental psychology* (pp. 3–20). New York: McGraw-Hill, Inc.

Fisher, C.B., Murray, J.P., Dill, J.R., Hagen, J.W., Hogan, J.M., Lerner, R.M., Rebok, G.W., Sigel, I., Sostek, A.M., Smyer, M.A., Spencer, M.B., & Wilcox, B. (1993). The national conference on graduate education in the applications of developmental science across the lifespan. *Journal of Applied Developmental Science, 14,* 1–10.

Gatz, M., & Smyer, M.A. (1992). The mental health system and older adults in the 1990s. *American Psychologist, 47*(6), 741–751.

Hertzog, C., & Nesselroade, J.R. (1987). Beyond autoregressive models: Some implications of the trait–state distinction for structural equation modeling of developmental change. *Child Development, 58,* 93–109.

Hetherington, E.M., Lerner, R.M., & Perlmutter, M. (Eds.). (1988). *Child development in lifespan perspective.* Hillsdale, NJ: Erlbaum.

Hudson, R.B. (1993). Social contingencies, the aged and public policy. *Milbank Quarterly, 71*(2), 253–277.

Human Development & Family Studies. (1993). *A handbook to graduate study in human development and family studies.* University Park, PA: The Pennsylvania State University.

Kivnick, H.Q. (1993). Everyday mental health: A guide to assessing life strengths. *Generations, XVII*(1), 13–20.

Larsen, K.G., Belar, C.D., Bieliauskas, L.A., Klepac, R.K., Stigall, T.T., & Zimet, C.M. (1993). *Proceedings: National Conference on Postdoctoral Training in Professional Psychology.* Washington, DC: Association of Psychology Postdoctoral and Internship Centers.

Muehrer, P., & Koretz, D.S. (1992). Issues in preventive intervention research. *Current Directions in Psychological Science, 1*(3), 109–112.

Philibert, M. (1979). Philosophical approach to gerontology. In J. Hendricks & C. Davis Hendricks (Eds.), *Dimensions of aging* (pp. 379–394). Cambridge, MA: Winthrop Publishers, Inc.

Plomin, R. (1989). Environment and genes: Determinants of behavior. *American Psychologist, 44*(2), 105–111.

Plomin, R., & McClearn, G.E. (1990). Human behavioral genetics of aging. J.E. Birren & K.W. Schaie (Eds.), *Handbook of the psychology of aging* (pp. 67–78). San Diego, CA: Academic Press.

Plomin, R., McClearn, G.E., Pedersen, N.L., Nesselroade, J.R., & Bergemann, C.S. (1988). Genetic influence on childhood family environment perceived retrospectively from the last half of life. *Developmental Psychology, 21,* 391–402.

Poon, L. (Ed.). (1986). *Handbook for clinical memory assessment of older adults.* Washington, DC: American Psychological Association.

Rovine, M.J., & von Eye, A. (1991). *Applied computational Statistics in longitudinal research.* Boston: Academic Press.

Rowe, J.N., & Kahn, R.L. (1987). Human aging: Usual and successful. *Science, 237,* 143–149.

Scarr, S. (1993). Biological and cultural diversity: The legacy of Darwin for development. *Child Development, 64*(5), 1333–1353.

Schaie, K.W. (1983). The Seattle Longitudinal Study: A 21 year exploration of psychometric intelligence in adulthood. In K.W. Schaie (Ed.), *Longitudinal studies of adult psychological development* (pp. 64–135). New York: Guilford Press.

Schaie, K.W. (1990). Intellectual development in adulthood. In J.E. Birren & K.W. Schaie (Eds.), *Handbook of the psychology of aging* (3rd ed., pp. 291–309). New York: Academic Press.

Schaie, K.W., Campbell, R.T., Meredith, W., & Rawlings, S.C. (1988). *Methodological issues in aging research.* New York: Springer Publishing Co.

Schaie, K.W., & Hertzog, C.K. (1984). Measurement in the psychology of adulthood and aging. In J.E. Birren & K.W. Schaie (Eds.), *Handbook of psychology and aging* (2nd ed., pp. 61–92). New York: Van Nostrand Reinhold.

Schaie, K.W., & Willis, S.L. (1986). Can decline in adult intellectual functioning be reversed? *Developmental Psychology, 22,* 223–232.

Schneider, E.L., & Grualnik, J.M. (1990). The aging of America: Impact on health care costs. *Journal of the American Medical Association, 263*(17), 2335–2340.

Schooler, C. (1990). Psychosocial factors and effective cognitive functioning in adulthood. In J.E. Birren & K.W. Schaie (Eds.), *Handbook of the psychology of aging* (pp. 347–358). San Diego, CA: Academic Press.

Smyer, M.A. (1995). Formal support in later life: Lessons for prevention. In L.A. Bond, S.J. Cutler, & A. Grams (Eds.), *Promoting successful and productive aging* (pp. 186–202). Thousand Oaks, CA: Sage Publications.

Smyer, M.A., Brannon, D. & Cohn, M.D. (1992). Improving nursing home care through training and job redesign. *The Gerontologist, 33*(3), 327–333.

Smyer, M.A., Shea, D.G., & Streit, A. (1994). The provision and use of mental health services in nursing homes: Results from the National Medical Expenditure Survey. *American Journal of Public Health, 84*(2), 284–287.

Smyer, M.A., & Walls, C.T. (1994). Design and evaluation of interventions in nursing homes. In C.B. Fisher & R.M. Lerner (Eds.), *Applied developmental psychology* (pp. 475–501). New York: McGraw-Hill.

Smyer, M.A., Zarit, S.H., & Qualls, S.H. (1990). Psychological intervention with aging individuals. In J.E. Birren & K.W. Schaie (Eds.), *Handbook of the psychology of aging* (3rd ed., pp. 375–403). New York: Academic Press.

Sorenson, B., Weinert, E., & Sherrod, L.R. (Eds.). (1986). *Human development and the life course: Multidisciplinary perspectives.* Hillsdale, NJ: Erlbaum.

Teri, L., Storandt, M., Gatz, M., Smyer, M., & Stricker, G. (1992). *Recommendations from a national conference on clinical training in psychology: Improving psychological services for older adults.* Unpublished manuscript. Seattle, WA: University of Washington.

Tornstam, L. (1992). The quo vaide of gerontology: On the scientific paradigm of gerontology. *Gerontologist, 32*(3), 318–326.

Willis, S.L. (1987). Cognitive training and everyday competence. In K.W. Schaie (Ed.), *Annual review of gerontology and geriatrics* (Vol. 6, pp. 159–188). New York: Springer.

Willis, S.L. (1991). Cognition and everyday competence. In K.W. Schaie (Ed.), *Annual review of gerontology and geriatrics* (Vol. 11, pp. 80–109). New York: Springer.

Willis, S.L., & Schaie, K.W. (1994). Assessing everyday competence in the elderly. In C.B. Fisher & R.M. Lerner (Eds.), *Applied developmental psychology* (pp. 339–372). New York: McGraw-Hill.

Willis, S.L., & Schaie, K.W. (in press). Cognitive training in the normal elderly. In F. Boller (Ed.), *Cerebral plasticity and cognitive stimulation*. New York: Springer-Verlag.

Wykle, M.L., & Musil, C.M. (1993). Mental health of older persons: Social and cultural factors. *Generations, XVII*(1), 7–12.

Zarit, S.H. (1992). *Training in research on mental health and aging*. Unpublished grant submitted to the National Institute of Mental Health. University Park, PA: The Pennsylvania State University.

Zarit, S.H. (1990). Issues and directions in family intervention research. In E. Light & B.D. Lebowitz (Eds.), *Alzheimer's disease treatment and family stress* (pp. 458–486). New York: Hemisphere Publishing Corp.

Zarit, S.H., & Reid, J.D. (1994). Adult children and their chronically ill elderly parents. In C. Fisher & R. Lerner (Eds.), *Applied developmental psychology* (pp. 237–262). New York: McGraw-Hill.

Zarit, S.H., & Teri, L. (1991). Interventions and services for family caregivers. *Annual Review of Gerontology and Geriatrics, 11*, 287–310.

9

Training Applied Developmental Scientists for Community Outreach: The Michigan State University Model of Integrating Science and Outreach for Children, Youth, and Families[1]

Richard M. Lerner
Charles W. Ostrom
Julia R. Miller
James C. Votruba
Alexander von Eye

Leah Cox Hoopfer
Patterson A. Terry
Carl S. Taylor
Francisco A. Villarruel
Marvin H. McKinney

Michigan State University

To scholars of human development, periods of change are comparable to double edged swords, in that change brings the risk that formerly successful behavioral patterns will no longer be adequate, and periods of change may

---

[1]The preparation of this chapter was supported in part by grants from the W.K. Kellogg Foundation, the C.S. Mott Foundation, and by NICHD Grant HD23229.

involve the emergence of new competencies or the opportunity to elaborate existing ones.

For those professionals involved in the study of human development, in the application of human development knowledge, and/or in graduate education of the next generation of scholars and/or practitioners of developmental science, the 1990s will be seen as such a "double edged" period. In many ways, the risks and opportunities confronting developmental scholars and practitioners converge with the challenges that confront the universities wherein most graduate training occurs and the preponderance of developmental science is conducted.

Financial problems confronting institutions of higher education, and the communities they serve, are leading simultaneously to internal reorganizations in order to foster better fiscal health, and rearrangement of external relations in order to provide more specific accountability to funders and to community constituents (Bok, 1992; Boyer, 1990, 1994; Lynton & Elman, 1987; Votruba, 1992). Moreover, economic and societal pressures converge. Government, business, and "grass roots" constituents demand that the resources society allocates to both public and private universities be spent on activities that are relevant to the needs of the constituents, as the constituents—not the professorate—conceive of and define these needs (Boyer, 1990, 1994; Lerner, Terry, McKinney, & Abrams, 1994; Lynton & Elman, 1987).

Together, internal reorganization and external reorientation will forge a revised approach to the knowledge "functions" of the academy, that is, knowledge generation, knowledge transmission, knowledge preservation, and knowledge application (Boyer, 1990). This revision involves the use of these functions of scholarship to address key and pervasive problems confronting society—economic development, environmental quality, health care, and the quality of life of children and families—and to do so in ways that both serve society and maintain the integrity of what universities do best, that is, enact these knowledge functions with specialized skill (Votruba, 1992).

Integrative responses by universities to these human, economic, and societal pressures may be especially important at this point in our nation's history. Over the course of the last several years, we believe that the important national emphasis on geopolitical and international trade concerns has become interrelated with a focus on many social issues. Among these are homelessness among American families; teenage pregnancy and childbearing; hunger; a weakened educational system; a shortage of quality day care; and deteriorating living and economic conditions among children and families near or below the poverty line. These issues are competing for a place on the ever more crowded "front burner" of the American political agenda (Anderson, & Hula, 1989; Huston, 1992; Lerner, et al., 1994; McKinney et al., 1994).

Clearly, these are issues that a field devoted to the study of human development should be especially well suited to address. They are problems involving: How children and their parents behave; how they eat, or in fact whether they do; how they plan for and attempt to actualize their economic, social, and personal goals; how they design their environments to live enjoyable, efficient, and safe lives; how they relate to each other, both positively and negatively, in the family the community; and whether society's policies and services allow them to attain lives of quality and enrichment in order to maintain a life marked by health, spiritual well being, and financial security, developing successfully with dignity and respect.

However, these child and familial problems are not clustered in the ways that academic disciplines, professions, or services are configured. To address these problems we need to break them down into manageable elements; here disciplinary research is relevant and useful. But, in order to adequately deal with the problems as they exist in our world, scholars, policy makers, and interventionists involved in human development study and service must be committed to putting the elements of the problems together.

This integration should be a key facet of the mission of academic fields or professions aimed at advancing science and service for human development. Moreover, it may be that providing a frame for such integration is a special contribution that universities can make to society. We believe that society, the communities within which universities are embedded, demands that universities play this role in addressing human needs and, as such, is pressuring universities to enter into coalitions with the public, business, and private sectors in order to address the human issues and needs of communities (Lerner & Fisher, 1994). Accordingly, to address these concerns, academics must join in both multidisciplinary and multiprofessional collaborations and in associations that require knowledge of, and the participation by, the members of the specific communities one is attempting both to understand and to serve (Lerner & Miller, 1993; Lerner, et al., 1994; Miller & Lerner, 1994). In other words, an appreciation of the diversity of people and of variation in the settings in which they live is fundamental to successfully integrate the disciplinary, professional, and community knowledge requisite for the advancement of both scholarship and service to society.

Thus, it is arguably the case that this pressure to collaboratively link the knowledge functions of the academy with the needs of the community—an activity we label as "outreach"—is greatest within the areas of scholarship associated with the study of human behavior and development. Similarly, it may be argued that there is no arena of study better able to illustrate what may be gained by the academy and by society when scholarship and outreach are merged. On the one hand, the impetus for outreach may be most salient among scholars and practitioners of human behavior and development because, ultimately, all problems of society involve behavior and development. Individuals and social groups may be either producers of the instances of these problems and/or they may be agents of the policies and programs aimed at addressing them (Lerner, 1982). On the other hand, historical changes in the multiple disciplines involved in the fields of study dealing with human behavior and development have resulted in an emphasis on knowledge application in order to systematically enhance people's life trajectories. This emphasis on applying science to optimize human life in systematic and progressive ways is subsumed under the label of applied developmental science (Fisher et al., 1993; Fisher & Lerner, 1994).

Moreover, this emphasis has been both legitimated and extended by the articulation of a theory of human development known as "developmental contextualism" (Lerner, 1986, 1991, 1992; Lerner & Kauffman, 1985) that has become prominent in psychology and sociology over the course of the last two decades (Baltes, 1987; Featherman, 1983). This view conceptually frames what are perhaps the two major developmental perspectives of this period: The lifespan view of human development (e.g., Baltes, 1968, 1979, 1983, 1987; Baltes & Schaie, 1973; Brim & Kagan, 1980; Elder, 1979, 1980; Featherman, 1983, 1985; Featherman & Lerner, 1985; Lerner, 1984; Lerner & Busch-Rossnagel, 1981; Lerner & Spanier, 1978; Nesselroade & Baltes, 1979; Schaie, 1965), and the ecological view of human development (Bronfenbrenner, 1977, 1979; Bronfenbrenner & Crouter, 1983).

Developmental contextualism provides a view of the basic process in human development (as one of changing individual-context relations); of causality (involving configural, or field explanations) (Ford & Lerner, 1992); and of the means through which these explanations of human development may be tested through multilevel, multivariate, and change-sensitive longitudinal research; (Nesselroade & Baltes, 1979; von Eye, 1990a, 1990b). These features of developmental contextualism result in a revised (and, admittedly, perhaps even a radical) conceptualization of the relationship between basic and applied research. This notion is that intervention research is basic research in human development (Lerner, et al., 1994).

We believe that developmental contextualism provides a means for the academy and the community to collaborate around issues of scholarship and outreach pertaining to human behavior and development. This collaboration provides not only challenge to existing modes of scholarship, but an opportunity to alter graduate education and the academy in which such training occurs. Thus, if the challenge this collaboration represents is met, we may develop the means to create institutions, and the scholars to populate them, that will change both the academy and the community of the 21st century.

THE CHALLENGE FOR AMERICA'S UNIVERSITIES

How may a university contribute to usefully addressing the problems of contemporary human life, including the issues confronting the children, youth, and families of America's diverse communities? Clearly, paradigms of the past have been insufficient, at least as gauged by the burgeoning problems of America's children, youth, and families (Boyer, 1994; Huston, 1992; Lerner & Fisher, 1994; Lerner, et al., 1994; Magrath, 1993; McKinney, et al., 1994).

It is unfortunate that much of the scholarship related to children, families, and their communities that flows from university faculty does not engage the communities involved in the scholarship. This lack of integration with the needs and world views of the community will make the findings of such scholarship difficult to translate into policies and programs of meaning and value to the community. Because such scholarship will appear distant from what the community believes is important, actions predicated on such scholarship will not be "owned" by the community. Moreover, when the community does not collaborate in the formulation of scholarship, any community capacity building that may accrue from such partnership is not likely to be produced (Dryfoos, 1990; Lerner, 1993a, 1993b).

It is possible, however, to conceive of research that is integrated with community needs; of scholarship that derives from a collaboration between the university and the people involved in the scholarship; and of scholarship that is therefore linked to community-based actions and capacity building. Such research can be conceived as the type of scholarship that was intended to be associated with the American land-grant university. Although, in recent decades, the research paradigm pursued prototypically at these institutions has not been consistent with the land-grant vision (Boyer, 1994; Lerner, 1993b; Lerner, et al., 1994; Magrath, 1993; McKinney, et al., 1994; Miller & Lerner, 1994), there is a growing commitment across our nation to revitalize this traditional mission (Enarson, 1989). The reinvigoration of this community collaborative integration of research and service (or "outreach") has been championed largely by the paradigm of scholarship promoted by faculty associated with land-grant institutions' colleges of home economics (or their derivatives, such as colleges of human ecology or human development) (Miller & Lerner, 1994). It is this approach that is taken at Michigan State University to integrate research and outreach for the children, youth, and families of the diverse communities it serves. A focal point for this integration occurs through the work of the Institute for Children, Youth, and Families. To explain this role, it is useful to discuss the model of scholarship promoted by the home economics tradition.

THE AMERICAN LAND-GRANT UNIVERSITY AND THE VISION OF HOME ECONOMICS

The contemporary mission of the American land-grant university is typically stated to be teaching, research, and service (with "service" often used interchangeably with the terms "extension" or "outreach"). The three components of this mission and the order that they are enunciated in have an important basis in the history of our nation (Enarson, 1989). It is useful to provide a brief recapitulation of this history.

As explained by the National Association of State Universities and Land-Grant Colleges (1989), the American land-grant university system was created through the first land-grant university act, the Morrill Act, which was signed into federal law by President Abraham Lincoln on July 2, 1862. This act provided 17.4 million acres of land to the states in order that each might have at least one college whose purpose was "to promote the liberal and practical education of the industrial classes in the several pursuits and professions of life" (NASULGC, 1989, p. 11). According to Bonnen (1993), the land-grant idea is democratic in a social sense, while elitist in an intellectual sense. It is committed to first class science and scholarship applied to the practical problems of society. This combination of both excellent scholarship and application to the needs of society is what represents the core of the land-grant idea. Chapter 2 in this volume further discusses the issue of land-grant universities.

A second Morrill Act was signed into law by President Benjamin Harrison on August 30, 1890, in order that the states provide a "just and equitable division of the fund to be received under this act between one college for white students and one institution for colored students." The enactment of this law was an impetus for the creation of 17 "historically black land-grant colleges" in Southern and border states (National Association of State Universities and Land-Grant Colleges, 1989, p. 14).

The Hatch Act was approved by Congress on March 2, 1887. It mandated the creation of agricultural experiment stations "to aid in acquiring and diffusing among the people of the United States useful and practical information on subjects connected with agriculture and to promote scientific investigation and experiment respecting the principles and applications of agricultural science." (NASULGC, 1989, p. 13).

The Smith-Lever Act was signed into law by President Woodrow Wilson in 1914. This law was intended to allow land-grant institutions to extend instruction beyond the boundaries of campuses. The purpose of this extension was:

> "aid in the diffusing among the people of the United States useful and practical information on subjects relating to agriculture and home economics, and

to encourage the applications of the same." The act further specified that the cooperative extension work of land-grant institutions "shall consist of the giving of instruction and practical demonstrations in agriculture and home economics to persons not attending or resident in said colleges in the several communities, and imparting to such persons information on said subjects through field demonstrations, publications, and otherwise."

(NASULGC, 1989, p. 15)

One way of representing the importance of the federal acts that created the combined teaching, research, and outreach mission of the land-grant system is to depict such an institution as the university *for* the people of the state: That is, the land-grant university's functions of knowledge generation (research), knowledge transmission (teaching), and knowledge utilization (outreach) exist to improve the lives of the people of its state as they live in their communities. This land-grant mission was refined through the vision of ecologically valid and useful scholarship articulated in the field of home economics (Lerner, 1993a, 1993b; Magrath, 1993; Miller & Lerner, 1994).

In 1892, Ellen Swallow Richards, the first woman faculty member in any science program in the United States (at the Massachusetts Institute of Technology), proposed a science of human ecology focused on the home and family, one labeled by her "home oekology" (Bubolz & Sontag, 1993). Since that time, the vision of the land-grant university, as the university for the people of its state, was operationalized in the field of home economics/human ecology as a university for the children, families, and communities of its state. Moreover, the human ecology vision of the tripartite, land-grant mission was that research, teaching, and outreach should be viewed as integrated, or synthetic, activities. Teaching about, or research conducted in the ecologically valid settings in which children and families live their lives (that is, in their homes and their communities), is predicated on an understanding of the needs, values, and interests of the specific people and particular community the land-grant institution is trying to serve. Accordingly, when knowledge generation or transmission occurs in a context that the community values and sees "practical" significance for these facets of knowledge, the application of this knowledge by the specific communities becomes more likely.

It is this vision of scholarship in the field of human development that is pursued by Michigan State University, through the programs of its Institute for Children, Youth, and Families (ICYF). The mission of the Institute for Children, Youth, and Families (ICYF) is to serve as:

> a university–wide, multidisciplinary unit integrating research, policy engagement, and outreach. Through human developmental and ecological models

and methods, the Institute promotes faculty–community collaborations involving the generation, transmission, application, and preservation of knowledge in order to: (a) promote the positive development of children, youth, and families; (b) respond effectively to contemporary problems; (c) acknowledge and celebrate the diversity and strengths of communities; and (d) create a new paradigm for professionals that merges research, outreach, and policy engagement.

As a consequence of its mission, ICYF sits at the interface of two cultures—the campus/faculty culture and the community culture. ICYF seeks legitimacy in both cultures. By creating this bridge, ICYF aspires to bring the campus and the community together in a productive, colearning collaboration embodying the land-grant tradition. The key product produced by this collaboration is termed "outreach scholarship."

OUTREACH SCHOLARSHIP

The Institute's model for integrating the faculty and the community cultures is depicted in Figure 1. At the core of our efforts lies a commitment to outreach scholarship. In a report by the Michigan State University Provost's Committee on University Outreach (1993, p. 2), outreach scholarship was defined as follows:

> the generation, transmission, application, and preservation of knowledge for the direct benefit of audiences to whom and for whom the university seeks to extend itself in ways that are consistent with university and unit missions.

In the context of the developmental approach fostered by ICYF, outreach scholarship is defined as the "systematic synthesis of research and application to describe, explain, and promote optimal developmental outcomes in individuals and families as they develop along the life cycle" (Fisher & Lerner, 1994, p. 4). To promote this form of scholarship requires input from both the faculty and community cultures, compelling collaboration, and leading to colearning.

From the perspective of the campus, ICYF is a different type of scholarly institute engaging in both research and outreach. Like other units, it is trying to be multidisciplinary. However, it is simultaneously and synthetically trying to be "multicultural" in several senses of the word. ICYF is attempting to link the cultures of different professions: the cultures of different disciplines, departments, and colleges; the cultures of the Cooperative Extension Service, termed MSU Extension, and of non-Extension colleagues; the cultures of the academy and the community; and the diverse

Training Applied Developmental Scientists for Community Outreach 171

FIGURE 1. Changes in the campus and community context promoted by the strategic actions of the Institute for Children, Youth, and Families.

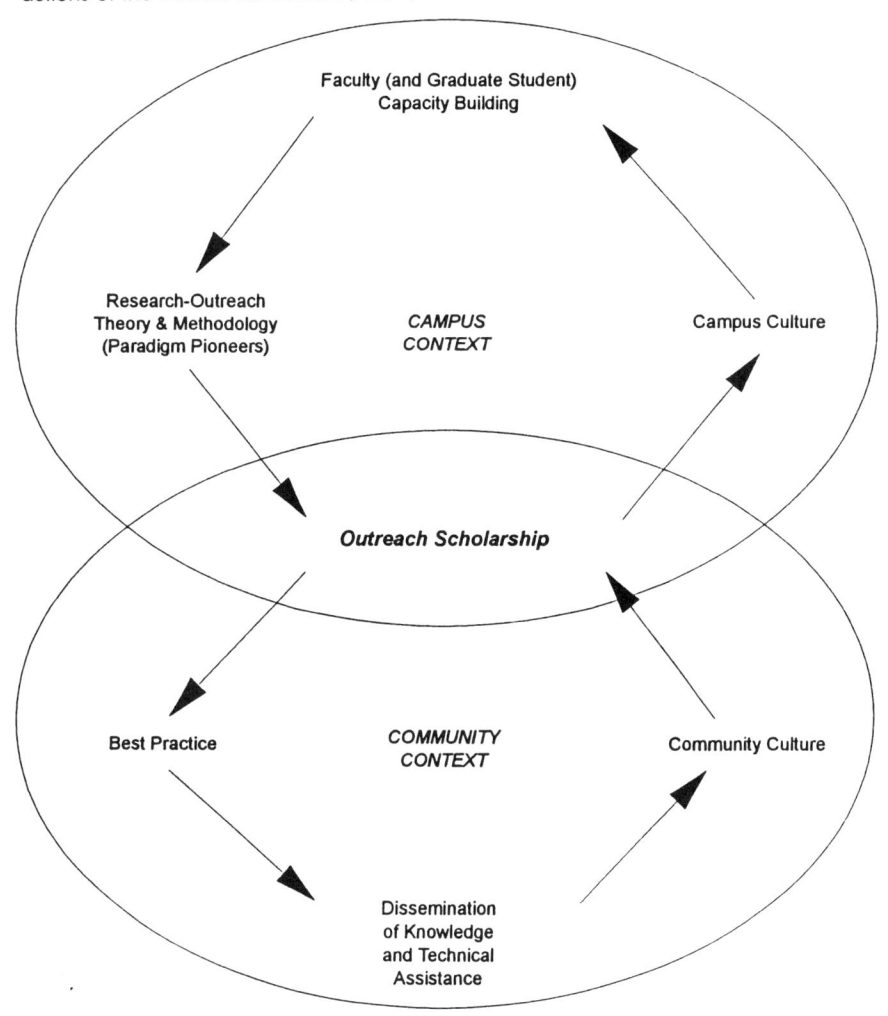

```
                    Faculty (and Graduate Student)
                         Capacity Building


  Research-Outreach
  Theory & Methodology        CAMPUS                    Campus Culture
  (Paradigm Pioneers)         CONTEXT



                         Outreach Scholarship



  Best Practice              COMMUNITY                  Community Culture
                             CONTEXT



                            Dissemination
                            of Knowledge
                            and Technical
                            Assistance
```

cultures within the spectrum of communities that are constituted by the children and families of Michigan. ICYF represents a new model of a scholarly institute, one that promises to embody the way in which a land-grant university can best position itself in the next century to respond to the multifaceted problems of the people it serves. To provide an overview of the new model, we now turn to a "tour" of Figure 1.

CAMPUS CONTEXT

As shown in the top half of Figure 1, outreach scholarship requires: (a) a change in campus culture; (b) faculty/graduate student capacity building; and (c) the development of research-outreach theory and methodology.

Campus Culture

Schein (1992) defines organizational culture as:

> a pattern of basic assumptions that a given group has invented, discovered or developed in learning to cope with its problems of external adaptation and internal integration, and that has worked well enough to be considered valid, and therefore, to be taught to new members as the correct way to perceive, think, and feel in relation to those problems. (p. 12)

The campus culture provides meaning and context for faculty. It holds people together and provides both an individual and collective sense of purpose. Perhaps most importantly, the campus culture defines the nature of reality for those who are part of the culture.

The current campus culture, with its overemphasis on research for the sake of research, has placed research universities in trouble. As noted by Hackney (1991):

> as the university has become more important to society, it is losing its special place it once held in the scheme of things. Knowledge has become much more central to society and to the economy, yet universities are increasingly pictured as just another snout at the public trough.

In this climate, Michigan State University has realized that it cannot take a "business as usual" approach. To this end, the University has undertaken a number of planning platforms. The key to the success of any of these approaches is to understand, and possibly change, the campus culture. Prior to discussing culture change, it is important to look at the two other components in the top half of Figure 1.

Faculty Capacity Building

We seek to build the capacity of faculty (and graduate students) to see the world as a "system." This may require helping faculty see beyond their disciplinary based perspectives and understand the changing interrelations among levels of organization that comprise human systems. One representation of this system, derived from the theory in developmental psychology labeled "developmental contextualism" (Lerner, 1986), is displayed in Figure 2. This figure illustrates the embeddedness of adolescent and parent in the complex and integrated ecology of human development. This illustra-

Training Applied Developmental Scientists for Community Outreach 173

tion of systems thinking has been useful to many scholars. In fact, it has provided one of the theoretical bases for the Applied Developmental Science (ADS) perspective supported by eight learned societies (Fisher, et al., 1993). However, we are not bound to any one specific instance of developmental systems theory (Ford and Lerner, 1992). Rather, we are open to any of the systems approaches comprising the "fifth discipline" (Senge, 1990; see also Levine & Fitzgerald, 1992).

Over the course of the past year, ICYF has been a collaborative partner in the formulation of a proposal for applied developmental science. Even though ICYF has no direct instructional role, the work of ICYF may be facilitated by a supporting educational program at the graduate level. The ADS program and ICYF will form a mutually reinforcing and beneficial partnership. Fisher and her colleagues (Fisher, et al., 1993) characterize the ADS approach in terms of the following five components:

1. The first component is the temporality of change; there is a temporal component to individuals, families, institutions, and community experi-

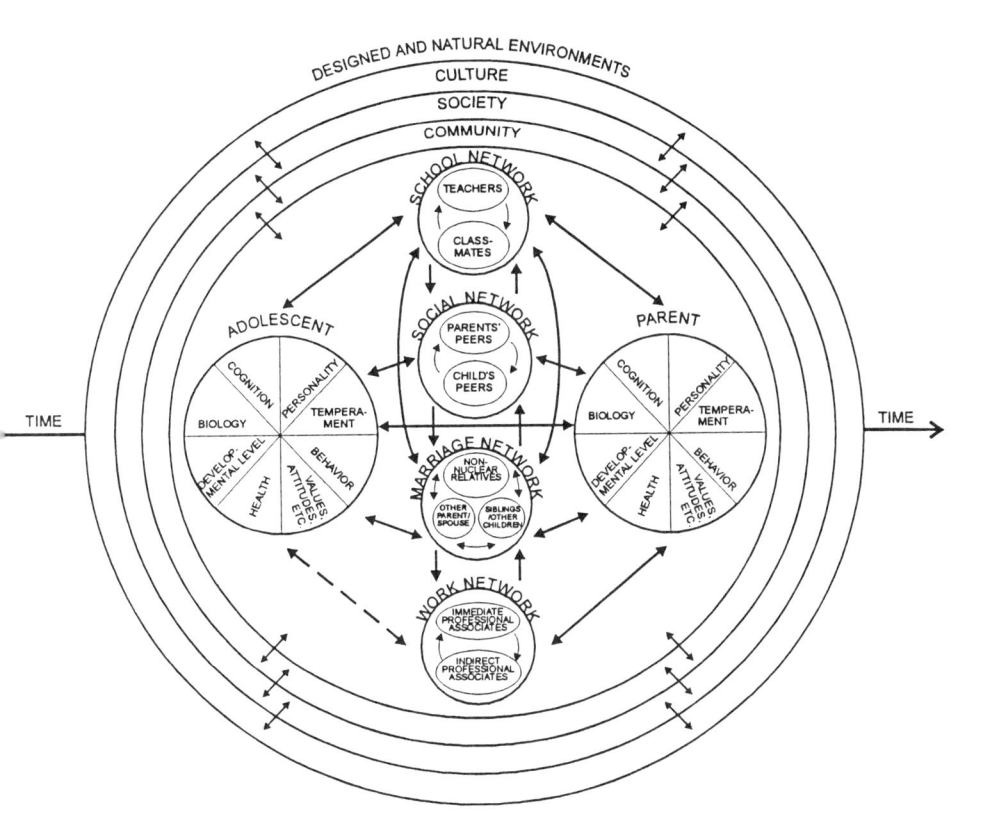

FIGURE 2. A developmental contextual model of adolescent-parent-context fusion.

ences. Some components remain stable over time; other components may change. The temporality of change has important implications for research design, service provision, and program evaluation.
2. The second component is sensitivity to individual differences and within-person change. What this means is that interventions must take into account individual differences, which means the diversity of racial, ethnic, social class, and gender groups.
3. The third component involves the centrality of context in terms of individual families and of family development. Context exists at all levels—biological, physical/ecological, sociocultural, political, economic, etc.—and invites systemic approaches to research and program design and implementation.
4. The fourth component is an emphasis on (descriptively) normative developmental processes, and on primary prevention and optimization, rather than on remediation.
5. The fifth component is respect for the bidirectional relationship between knowledge generation and knowledge application.

ICYF not only has a role to play in launching and sustaining such a program; it strives to provide a location for those trained in the program to organize the research and outreach portions of ADS activity. Examples of this include linking the Institute's outreach scholarship with: (a) graduate education in ADS (e.g., through graduate assistantships on ICYF-supported or related projects), and (b), undergraduate service learning experiences related to ADS that occur through undergraduates participating as program providers in the outreach scholarship conducted by faculty and graduate students.

Research-Outreach Theory and Methodology (Paradigm Pioneers)

The key feature of the model we are pursuing is the integration of theory and methodology. Accordingly, it is our view that in order to address adequately the serious problems faced by today's children, youth, and families, multidisciplinary research must involve more than just assembling researchers from different disciplines. Such an approach typically results in a simple layering of investigation and publication; project faculty from each discipline approach the topic with their own theory and method, and report their findings separately or in an edited collection of articles.

Pursuing this traditional paradigm has built the scholarly careers of numerous generations of faculty. However, this paradigm is not adequate for meeting the needs of the children and families of our communities. What is required is a pioneering effort to formulate a new paradigm promoting an integrative or, even better, "fused" and multicultural (in the earlier senses) approach to research.

The variables typically studied in various disciplines are all mingled in the day to day situations of real life. Only the building of integrated models, ones that focus on the combined interactions of systems studied by different disciplines, will allow the heretofore disconnected insights of those different disciplines to develop into a useful, synthetic theory guiding the development of policies and programs. The point is not simply the obvious one that the context is complex. Rather, it is that the fusing of distinct approaches requires building systemic, integrated, and dynamic models and methods.

To enable high quality outreach scholarship derived from this systems' perspective to be pursued productively requires innovative methodology. Such methods must be able to garner evidence that is both scientifically rigorous and persuasive to the faculty culture and relevant and compelling to the communities with whom we collaborate. As a consequence of our developmental systems perspective, the methodology that we pursue will be multivariate, longitudinal, and change-sensitive. The Research–Outreach Methodology (ROM) Program, developed in conjunction with Michigan State University's Institute for Public Policy and Social Research (IPPSR), will, in the coming year, begin to increase the capacity of MSU to bring the best developmental methodologies to bear on the issues of children, families, and communities.

There is one important implication that follows from our approach to methodology. Because of our methodological choices and, in particular, our commitment to the longitudinal approach, we must be involved in communities over a long period of time. This temporal commitment substantively means that activities associated with our outreach scholarship will avoid the "hit and run" character of many prior attempts at action research, applied research, and demonstration projects. We do not see as scientifically or ethically defensible, scholarship that "parachutes" into a community and fails to grapple with (a) the long term outcome of individual and family changes, (b) the status of the capacity of the community to sustain programmatic changes once the demonstration period has ended, or (c) the unintended consequences or new insights that arise during the period. Together, the shifts in theoretical and methodological foci that we pursue require "paradigm pioneers." We seek to facilitate the development of such colleagues and to be both the exemplar of, and the home for, the scholarship that they will pursue.

Campus Culture Change

To understand and effect these pioneering efforts requires a major qualitative change in the culture of our campus. We want to emphasize that the faculty's involvement in such cultural change is no small task. Indeed, because there are still relatively few faculty at MSU involved with the type of multicultural integration we have described, one of the major activities at ICYF has been the building of a team of colleagues that exemplify the integrations embodied in our concept of campus cultural change. The colleagues associated with or working at the Institute bring professional experience and expertise about: Human ecology and human development; community systems; federal, state, and local government; youth programming; organizational sociology; change methodology; political science; public policy; public and private foundations; education; the health professions; criminal justice, family development; family therapy; and home economics. It is this team that has created the quality, momentum, and accomplishments of ICYF.

With this team, we believe that we have a critical mass of leaders of outreach scholarship at ICYF. Furthermore, we have acted as a team to establish and maintain numerous faculty and community relationships with ICYF. What we have to do now is to institutionalize and extend the diffusion of these innovations on campus in the coming years. To this end, we believe that the cycle in the top part of Figure 1 is synthetically reinforcing; outreach scholarship will change the campus culture which, in turn, will lead to increases in the capacity of faculty and graduate students to conduct outreach scholarship which will lead to pioneering efforts to enhance theory and methodology.

Together, both the quality and quantity of outreach scholarship will increase as a consequence of these efforts. As well, our catalyzing of outreach scholarship will facilitate our efforts to collaborate within the communities with which we will interact. At this point, then, it is useful to review the bottom half of Figure 1.

COMMUNITY CONTEXT

As shown in the bottom half of Figure 1, outreach scholarship: (a) Generates a knowledge base about best practice; and (b) the knowledge base is disseminated through training and technical assistance. These activities (c) generate positive outcomes in the community, such that there is an increased likelihood that it will turn to the university for further collaborations involving outreach scholarship.

This process of community collaboration captures a sense of community that is at least as broad as the diverse settings and constituencies that influence the lives of children, youth, and families. Thus, included in our sense of community are geographical units (e.g., neighborhoods and municipalities), institutional units (e.g., school districts and service agencies), and governmental actors (e.g., elected and appointed officials). As well, this process of community collaboration rests on a colearning model. Members of the campus and the community contexts need to learn about each other's culture in order for productive and effective outreach scholarship to result.

There are several examples of such outreach scholarship currently underway at ICYF. For example, a set of ADS projects in Flint, Michigan are being coordinated by Professor Hiram Fitzgerald. Here, in collaboration with the Mott Children's Health Center (MCHC), MSU faculty and MCHC personnel are:

1. Evaluating a program aimed at families wherein one parent is incarcerated. The families have an infant or young child, and the goal of the program—"S.E.E.K.," or Services to Enable and Empower Kids—is to enhance parenting skills among the unincarcerated parent and, through such training, help promote positive developmental outcomes for the child;
2. Evaluating of adolescent developmental outcomes (e.g., related to self-esteem, engagement in safe sexual behaviors, and school achievements) associated with participation in two school based and multiservice "Teen Health Centers" administered by MCHC; and
3. Helping create, along with other citizen groups in Flint, a system of full service schools (Dryfoos, 1994, 1995). That is, we are working to help establish schools as: (a) The locus for the delivery of integrated and comprehensive social, health, family, and individual (e.g., mental health, career counseling) services; and (b) community resources that are open throughout the day, all year long, and focus primarily on developing in youth the skills for successful transitions to productive and healthy adult lives.

Other projects in Flint, led by Dr. Marvin H. McKinney, focus on the needs and personal and community assets of low income African American families with young children. In one component of this work, an assessment has been made of the early life development programs available to low-income families through the Flint public schools. Although eleven programs were identified, McKinney has found that personnel in any one program typically have little knowledge of the other programs. Even when such knowledge exists, there are few, if any, efforts to coordinate services. Rather, it appears that issues of "turf" (i.e., of protecting one's program as a secure, bounded entity, as well as protecting one's resources) are associated with the lack of service integration.

Many other ICYF projects have a locus in Lansing, Michigan—given both the propinquity of Lansing to the East Lansing MSU campus, and the fact that an important "member" of the Lansing community is state government, as Lansing is the capital of Michigan. Accordingly, there are several joint projects between ICYF and state government. For example, ICYF is collaborating with the Michigan Department of Public Health to help develop and evaluate a statewide program aimed at promoting healthy behaviors among nine to fourteen year-olds. Termed the "Michigan Abstinence Partnership" (MAP), the program is intended to prevent sexual activity and drug and alcohol use among children in this age group.

In addition, ICYF is helping evaluate the structure and outcomes for children and families of a statewide family preservation program—the Michigan Interagency Family Preservation Initiative. This program involves a collaboration across units of state government; the Departments of Mental Health, Social Services, Public Health, and Education are all involved. ICYF is helping ascertain how issues of "turf" can be overcome, and the impact of such interagency cooperation on the health and development of distressed families and their children.

Finally, several community-collaborative projects have been planned and will be initiated upon ICYF and its community partners securing necessary resources. For example, ICYF is working with the Black Child and Family Institute of Lansing to build a program enhancing foreign language, computer literacy, and multicultural competence among young African American children. We believe that participation in this program will enhance the perceived self-competence (Harter, 1982, 1986) in several domains (e.g., scholastic, social, and general self-worth) among these youth. By broadening the children's horizons beyond the Lansing area, we believe too that this program may also enhance the range of life choices pursued by the program participants.

In addition, ICYF is planning to initiate a longitudinal assessment of successful life transitions from adolescence to young adulthood among African American males. Working in Detroit, Lansing, and Flint, we seek to identify the people, programs, and agencies that help promote positive life developments among these youth. In working with MSU Extension, we plan to "replicate" these facilitative experiences among other youth within the communities with whom we are collaborating.

Thus, because of our commitment to scholarship predicated on a colearning model, ICYF is (from the perspective of the community) a different type of research institute. Whereas other research institutes see the community as a laboratory, we also see the community as a classroom in which both the university and community can learn. As such, our involvement with communities is one of mingled destinies. Each partner's success is interdependent with that of the other partner.

This mutuality means, then, that campus and community must become competent about the mores, values, and practices of each other's culture. Unless such cultural competence is developed, neither colearning nor effective scholarly and community outcomes can be achieved. ICYF is committed to bringing these cultures, and the other ones we have discussed, to bear on our pursuit of cutting edge outreach scholarship.

"Best Practice"

From the perspective of the community, the value of cutting edge scholarship is that it results in knowledge of the best practices available for policies, policy implementation, and program design and delivery. As noted by Washington (1992):

> Dozens of effective strategies have been used across the country to address the needs of youth and families. Yet, in all areas of social development there is the temptation to start over again, rather than build on efforts already underway and proven successful. . . . The time has come to focus on less glamorous, self-aggrandizing aspects of program development. Instead, professional communities need to cooperate more to leverage their collective investments and establish comprehensive, coordinated policies and practices that work efficiently and effectively.
>
> To avoid the temptation of starting over again, better systems for documenting what has been done and providing a clearinghouse for the information are needed. In addition, there is a need for development of a reporting and rating system for social development efforts that would help successful models that have been developed locally to be highlighted and shared nationally.
>
> University faculty, through their research and evaluation activities, can give important leadership to helping design appropriate techniques to learn and transfer information about "what works."

Colleagues associated with ICYF disseminate information about, and promote access to, the sort of information called for by Washington (1992), information that would include programs that have been developed, implemented, and evaluated all over the world. This information may allow public policymakers, community organizers, researchers, and others to better use their money and time developing or replicating successful programs. Many people in these groups know there are programs that succeed in improving the life chances of America's children, youth, and families. As emphasized eloquently and often by Edelman (1992, 1993) and by Little (1993), we possess a good deal of the knowledge and the skills needed to design and deliver programs that ameliorate undesirable behaviors, prevent the occurrence of problems, and enhance the abilities and life opportunities for the diverse children and families across our nation.

There are ways that we can construct the contexts of children that enhance their development across the lifespan, and do not squander their human capital. Indeed, many of these programs, and the policies and values that legitimate and promote them, have been identified by Hamburg (1992), and earlier by Schorr (1988) and Dryfoos (1990). However, despite the proven successes of selected programs—often documented through the results of rigorous evaluations—these programs are neither sufficiently sustained nor adequately replicated. We believe that a failure to replicate, or more primarily to disseminate, the details of successful programs so that replication can be attempted, means that practitioners in different communities must "reinvent the wheel." Best practice cannot be identified if replication does not exist. More primarily, however, even when a community finds that a program works, it is often not sustained because there is a lack of community based capacity to generate requisite leadership, infrastructure, and funds.

The needs exists, then, to catalog information about what works in specific communities in regard to preventive, enhancing, or ameliorative programs for children, youth, and families. We recognize, of course, that "best practice" is an ideal that can only be approached, especially given the fact that our developmental contextual model means that particular instances of individual and ecological relations may not generalize precisely to different person or context conditions (Lerner, 1986). Thus, our work here is more readily characterized as the pursuing of "better practice." Nevertheless, one way in which ICYF strives to approach this task is through helping to enhance the role of MSU Extension activities (e.g., the dissemination of rigorously evaluated practice procedures and the identification of community needs) in the ADS work of faculty and graduate students. Accordingly, we need also to disseminate best (or at least, better) practice information in order to inform communities and policy makers about the sorts of programs that may work and about how programs that have been sustained have managed to achieve this end. Moreover, dissemination is required to increase the capacity of the community to itself sustain activities beyond the period of university collaboration.

Dissemination of Knowledge and Technical Assistance

ICYF is proactive about disseminating knowledge and providing technical assistance. It takes this approach not only to help extend and sustain the best practices we identify, but also to assist in building the capacities of our community collaborators. In addition, as colearning members of a culturally competent community collaboration, ICYF initiates the delivery, to its community collaborators, of knowledge about and skills for enhancing the lives of children, youth, and families.

It is our conviction that the knowledge we value and seek must be usable and used. As a consequence, key facets of our approach to dissemination and technical assistance involve ascertaining the relevance of our knowledge and assuring accessibility to it. This view of knowledge utilization underscores the need for an abiding commitment to a campus–community partnership. Such partnerships build the understanding of ICYF as a potential part of a confederation of community members, a partnership that brings to the "collaborative table" knowledge based assets. In this way, the community can also be proactive in approaching ICYF. It can help further our attempts to learn with them the means to refine our outreach scholarship; to further the inculcation of best practices that meet their specific needs; and that, as a consequence, help merge the cultures of the campus and the community.

Community Culture

If our efforts at paradigm pioneering are effective in the community, then the community will alter the way it views its problems, the policy choices it pursues, the programs to which it subscribes, and, perhaps superordinately, the university based resources it perceives it can access for making these changes. In other words, if community culture change occurs, then the view of the role of the university will also change.

These alterations are what we hope to produce. We want legislative and community leaders to recognize that funds expended on the university–community relationship constitute a productive investment, one that has a tangible return in regard to the issues and problems they define as crucial. If ICYF's approach to developmental systems is useful in enhancing this role in the community context, then we will be able to contribute to the creation of economies of scale. Building better practices in one part of the system will enhance other parts. As a consequence, our model of colearning and community collaboration will help facilitate the development of systems thinking among policymakers, program professionals, volunteers, and the children and families with whom we collaborate.

To envision and enact plans to implement the goals embodied in Figure 1 is an admittedly ambitious agenda. At this writing, we know of few other institutes or universities challenging themselves in precisely this manner. Thus, the scope of the task we are undertaking requires us to be modest and deliberate in pursuing this agenda.

CONCLUSIONS

Michigan State has been a leader in articulating a vision of the land-grant mission that brings reality to the concept of the people's university, builds an ethos for multidimensional excellence, deeply commits itself to excellence through diversity, and that takes on, in a concerted and pronounced manner, the problems of Michigan (and of America) in the twenty-first century. As such, it is not surprising that Michigan State has initiated an experiment in regard to making an institutional commitment to bringing its knowledge resources to bear on the social issues facing our children, youth, and families. It may be that what we learn from our efforts to build this unit will tell us a great deal about the developmental changes institutions of higher education will have to experience in the next century.

The Institute belief is that, as a consequence of a long term commitment to partnership with communities, we will contribute to changing the life chances of the children, youth, and families of Michigan. That is, we will enhance the life trajectories of our children and families. We will not only help prevent undesirable problems from occurring but, in addition, we will help build models that will optimize the course of development of the individuals and families that live in our diverse communities.

This criterion of Institute success is certainly the most difficult one to attain. At the least, in order to provide evidence of success here, the outreach scholarship and community collaborations the Institute catalyzes will need to be focused and sustained for long periods of time. This is why longitudinal methodology is so central.

However, to be successful, we need to meet at least three challenges that now lie before us. First, we should focus our outreach scholarship on the diverse people and settings about that we must learn if we are to obtain an adequate understanding of the range of developmental patterns, and of the richness and potential, and of human life (Lerner, in press-a; McLoyd, 1994). Our research efforts should not only involve the implementation of a synthesis of ideas and methods from multiple disciplines—in addition, this integration should be employed in research with people of as wide a range of ethnic, racial, family, community, and sociocultural backgrounds as possible.

Second, it is clear that such research will not succeed unless the people from within these diverse settings are engaged cooperatively in the endeavor (Lerner, et al., 1994). As emphasized in developmental contextualism (Lerner, 1982, 1991, 1992), individuals are active producers of their own development. Thus, such outreach research must be seen as relevant and important by the individuals, families, and communities about whom we wish to learn. Such scholarship, then, should be seen as returning, or providing, something of value to these groups. Simply, the people we seek to understand and serve must become our collaborators in our research. As we seek to optimize their lives in the context of this collaboration, it is they who define what is of value and of importance to their lives. See Chapter 12 for a discussion of the challenges and rewards of building university–community human service agency collaborations.

Accordingly, techniques that give voice to the community need to be employed in order to activate this university–community collaboration. One example of how this interaction may occur exists in the sociological literature. Burton (1990) has used focus group methodology to elucidate the perspective of members of African American communities about parenting and intergenerational relations.

In offering such service, the policies implemented, and programs delivered by colleagues working in these settings become central. Accordingly, the knowledge and expertise of these professionals are necessary in many areas, not only for the critical conceptual reasons noted earlier. In addition, collaboration is vital in order to address the practical issues involved in doing research that advances knowledge of developmental diversity across life.

Finally, a third challenge, one that brings us full circle to the issues confronting higher education in the 1990s, is to provide an exciting and attractive basis for the reorientation of the work of established scholars (cf. Boyer, 1994; Magrath, 1993). In addition, educators in each of the disciplines involved in the study of human development should be presented with a vision for beginning to train their students differently (Birkel, Lerner, & Smyer, 1989; Fisher et al., 1993). An appreciation of systematic change, context, and human relationships should be the cornerstone of future graduate education. This is a central point stressed in the growing attention being paid among scholarly societies and universities to the importance of training in applied developmental science for future scholars and professionals in fields associated with human development and education (Fisher et al., 1993). We should instill in these future scholars and professionals a greater appreciation of the importance of interindividual differences in the timing of causal, dynamic interactions for the development of human diversity and for the contextual variation that is both a product and a producer of it (Lerner, 1982; Lerner & Busch-Rossnagel, 1981).

Furthermore, it is important to add that university tenure and promotion committees evaluating scientists studying development must be urged to begin to consider the relative value of multidisciplinary collaborative, and hence multiauthored publications in comparison to within-discipline, single-authored products. We must also consider the nature of the reception given by university review committees to the sort of contextual and collaborative research we are furthering. The issue to be debated here is whether we can train future cohorts of applied developmental scientists to engage productively in the multidisciplinary, multiprofessional, and community collaborations requisite for advancing understanding of the basic process of development and then not reward and value them for successfully doing so. In essence, we must engage in a debate about changing the reward system within our universities. If we follow a developmental contextual perspective that leads to the synthesis of science and service, then it would seem that we must devise means to assign value to, and reward, an array of collaborative, multidisciplinary, and multiprofessional activities (Boyer, 1994; Votruba, 1992). Similarly, if we are to take seriously the need for change oriented (and hence longitudinal), multilevel (and hence multivariate), and multidisciplinary research, we must recognize the need to educate government agencies and private foundations about the time and financial resources that should be given to such collaborative activities.

In sum, our challenge is to integrate multiple academic disciplines and multiple professional activities with the community. If we are to significantly advance science and service for the people of our nation, we must engage in such a new scholarly agenda. This is the challenge before us as we approach the next millennium, and the path upon which we, as scholars, educators, and, most basically, citizens, must embark. The stakes are high both for the university and for society—we have no time to lose.

REFERENCES

Anderson, E., & Hula, R.C. (Eds.). (1989). Symposium: Family policy. *Policy Studies Review, 8,* 573–736.

Baltes, P.B. (1968). Longitudinal and cross-sectional sequences in the study of age and generation effects. *Human Development, 11,* 145–171.

Baltes, P.B. (1979). Lifespan developmental psychology: Some converging observations on history and theory. In P.B. Baltes & O.G. Brim, Jr. (Eds.), *Lifespan development and behavior* (Vol. 2, pp. 255–279). New York: Academic Press.

Baltes, P.B. (1983). Lifespan developmental psychology. Observations on history and theory revisited. In R.M. Lerner (Ed.), *Developmental psychology: Historical and philosophical perspectives* (pp. 79–111). Hillsdale, NJ: Erlbaum.

Baltes, P.B. (1987). Theoretical propositions of lifespan developmental psychology: On the dynamics between growth and decline. *Developmental Psychology, 23,* 611–626.

Baltes, P.B., & Schaie, K.W. (1973). On lifespan developmental research paradigms. Retrospects and prospects. In P.B. Baltes & K.W. Schaie (Eds.), *Lifespan developmental psychology: Personality and socialization* (pp. 365–395). New York: Academic Press.

Birkel, R., Lerner, R.M., & Smyer, M.A. (1989). Applied developmental psychology as an implementation of a lifespan view of human development. *Journal of Applied Developmental Psychology, 10,* 425–445.

Bok, D. (1992). Reclaiming the public trust. *Change,* pp. 13–19.

Bonnen, J.T. (1993). Reflections on the land-grant idea. *Agriculture Staff Papers, 93–98.* East Lansing, MI: Michigan State University College of Agriculture.

Boyer, E.L. (1990). *Scholarship reconsidered: Priorities of the professoriate.* Princeton, NJ: The Carnegie Foundation for the Advancement of Teaching.

Boyer, E.L. (1994, March 9). Creating the new American college [Point of View column]. *The Chronicle of Higher Education*, p. A48.
Brim, O.G., & Kagan, J. (Eds.). (1980). *Constancy and change in human development*. Cambridge: Harvard University Press.
Bronfenbrenner, U. (1977). Toward an experimental ecology of human development. *American Psychologist, 32*, 513–531.
Bronfenbrenner, U. (1979). *The ecology of human development*. Cambridge, MA: Harvard University Press.
Bronfenbrenner, U., & Crouter, A.C. (1983). The evolution of environmental models in developmental research. In W. Kessen (Ed.), *Handbook of child psychology. Vol. 1: History, theories, and methods* (pp. 39–83). New York: Wiley.
Bubolz, M., & Sontag, M.S. (1993). Human ecology theory. In P. Boss, W. Doherty, R. LaRossa, W. Schumm, & S. Steinmetz (Eds.), *Sourcebook of family theories and methods: A contextual approach* (pp. 419–448). New York: Plenum.
Burton, L.M. (1990). Teenage childbearing as an alternative life course strategy in multigeneration black families. *Human Nature, 1*(2), 123–143.
Dryfoos, J.G. (1990). *Adolescents at risk: Prevalence and prevention*. New York: Oxford University.
Dryfoos, J.G. (1994). *Full service schools*. San Francisco: Jossey-Bass.
Dryfoos, J.G. (1995). Full service schools: Revolution or fad? *Journal of Research on Adolescence, 5*, 147–172.
Edelman, M.W. (1992). *The measure of our success: A letter to my children and yours*. Boston: Beacon Press.
Edelman, M.W. (1993). Awards Luncheon and Address by Children's Defense Fund President Marian Wright Edelman. Annual National Conference of the Children's Defense Fund. *Leave no child behind: Mobilizing Families and Communities for America's Children*. Children's Defense Fund: Washington, D.C.
Elder, G.H., Jr. (1979). Historical change in life patterns and personality. In P.B. Baltes & O.G. Brim, Jr. (Eds.), *Lifespan development and behavior* (Vol. 2, pp. 117–159). New York: Academic Press.
Elder, G.H., Jr. (1980). Adolescence in historical perspective. In J. Adelson (Ed.), *Handbook of adolescent psychology* (pp. 3–46). New York: Wiley.
Enarson, H.L. (1989). *Revitalizing the land-grant mission*. Blacksburg, VA: Virginia Polytechnic Institute and State University.
Featherman, D.L. (1983). Lifespan perspective in social science research. In P.B. Baltes & O.G. Brim, Jr. (Eds.), *Lifespan development and behavior* (Vol. 5, pp. 1–57). New York: Academic Press.
Featherman, D.L. (1985). Individual development and aging as a population process. In J.R. Nesselroade & A. von Eye (Eds.), *Individual development and social change: Explanatory analyses* (pp. 213–241). New York: Academic Press.
Featherman, D.L., & Lerner, R.M. (1985). Ontogenesis and sociogenesis: Problematics for theory about development across the lifespan. *American Sociological Review, 50*, 659–676.
Fisher, C.B., & Lerner, R.M. (1994). Foundations of applied developmental psychology. In C.B. Fisher & R.M. Lerner (Eds.), *Applied developmental psychology* (pp. 3–20). Cambridge, MA: McGraw-Hill.

Fisher, C.B., Murray, J.P., Dill, J.R., Hagen, J.W., Hogan, M.J., Lerner, R.M., Rebok, G.W., Sigel, I., Sostek, A.M., Smyer, M.A., Spencer, M.B., & Wilcox, B. (1993). The national conference on graduate education in the applications of developmental science across the lifespan. *Journal of Applied Developmental Psychology, 14*, 1–10.

Ford, D.H., & Lerner, R.M. (1992). *Developmental systems theory: An integrative approach.* Newbury Park, CA: Sage.

Hackney, S. (1991). *Commencement address.* Philadelphia, PA: University of Pennsylvania.

Hamburg, D.A. (1992). *Today's children: Creating a future for a generation in crisis.*

Harter, S. (1982). The perceived competence scale for children. *Child Development, 53*, 87–97.

Harter, S. (1986). Processes underlying the construction, maintenance, and enhancement of the self-concept in children. In J. Suls & A. Greenwald (Eds.), *Psychological perspectives on the self, 3*, (pp. 136–181). Hillsdale, NJ: Erlbaum.

Huston, A.C. (Ed.). (1992). *Children in poverty: Child development and public policy.* Cambridge, MA: Cambridge University Press.

Lerner, R.M. (1982). Children and adolescents as producers of their own development. *Developmental Review, 2*, 342–370.

Lerner, R.M. (1984). *On the nature of human plasticity.* New York: Cambridge University Press.

Lerner, R.M. (1986). *Concepts and theories of human development* (2nd ed.). New York: Random House.

Lerner, R.M. (1991). Changing organism–context relations as the basic process of development: A developmental contextual perspective. *Developmental Psychology, 27*, 27–32.

Lerner, R.M. (1992). *Final solutions: Biology, prejudice, and genocide.* University Park: Penn State Press.

Lerner, R.M. (Ed.). (1993a). *Early adolescence: Perspectives on research, policy, and intervention.* Hillsdale, NJ: Erlbaum.

Lerner, R.M. (1993b). Investment in youth: The role of home economics in enhancing the life chances of America's children. *AHEA Monograph Series, 1*, 5–34.

Lerner, R.M. (in press-a). Diversity and context in research, policy, and programs for children and adolescents: A developmental contextual perspective. In G.K. Brookins & M.B. Spencer (Eds.), *Ethnicity and diversity: Implications for research and policies.* Hillsdale, NJ: Erlbaum.

Lerner, R.M. (in press-b). The integration of levels and human development: A developmental contextual view of the synthesis of science and outreach in the enhancement of human lives. In K. Hood, G. Greenberg, & E. Tobach (Eds.), *Approach withdraw theory and behavioral development.* New York: Garland.

Lerner, R.M., & Busch-Rossnagel, N.A. (Eds.). (1981). *Individuals as producers of their development: A lifespan perspective.* New York: Academic Press.

Lerner, R.M., & Fisher, C.B. (1994). From applied developmental psychology to applied developmental science: Community coalitions and collaborative careers. In C.B. Fisher, & R.M. Lerner (Eds.), *Applied developmental psychology*, (pp. 505–522). New York: McGraw-Hill.

Lerner, R.M., & Kauffman, M.B. (1985). The concept of development in contextualism. *Developmental Review, 5*, 309–333.
Lerner, R.M., & Miller, J.R. (1993). Integrating human development research and intervention for America's children: The Michigan State University model. *Journal of Applied Developmental Psychology, 14*, 347–364.
Lerner, R.M., Miller, J.R., Knott, J.H., Corey, K.E., Bynum, T.S., Hoopfer, L.C., McKinney, M.H., Abrams, L.A., Hula, R.G., & Terry, P.A. (1994). Integrating scholarship and outreach in human development research, policy, and service: A developmental contextual perspective. In D.L. Featherman, R.M. Lerner, & M. Perlmutter (Eds.), *Lifespan Development and Behavior, 12*, 249–273. Hillsdale, NJ: Erlbaum.
Lerner, R.M., & Spanier, G.B. (Eds.). (1978). *Child influences on marital and family interaction: A lifespan perspective.* New York: Academic Press.
Lerner, R.M., & Spanier, G.B. (1980). *Adolescent development: A lifespan perspective.* New York: McGraw-Hill.
Lerner, R.M., Terry, P.A., McKinney, M.H., & Abrams, L.A. (1994). Addressing child poverty within the context of a community-collaborative university: Comments on Fabes, Martin, and Smith (1994) and McLoyd (1994). *Family and Consumer Sciences Research Journal, 23*, 67–75.
Lerner, R.M., & Tubman, J. (1989). Conceptual issues in studying continuity and discontinuity in personality development across life. *Journal of Personality, 57*, 343–373.
Levine, R.L., & Fitzgerald, H.E. (Eds.). (1992). *Analysis of dynamic psychological systems: Basic processes* (Vol. 1). New York: Plenum.
Levine, R.L., & Fitzgerald, H.E. (Eds.). (1992). *Analysis of dynamic psychological systems: Methods and applications* (Vol. 2). New York: Plenum.
Little, R.R. (1993). What's working for today's youth: The issues, the programs, and the learnings. *ICYF Fellows Colloquium.* East Lansing, MI: Michigan State University.
Lynton, E.A. & Elman, S.E. (1987). *New priorities for the university: Meeting society's needs for applied knowledge and competent individuals.* San Francisco: Jossey-Bass.
Magrath, C.P. (1993, November 12). Comments to the board on home economics. Unpublished presentation, Michigan State University Extension, East Lansing. (Transcript available from the National Association of State Universities and Land-Grant Colleges, One Dupont Circle NW, Suite 710, Washington, DC 20036-1191.)
McKinney, M.H., Abrams, L.A., Terry, P.A., & Lerner, R.M. (1994). Child development research and the poor children of America: A call for a developmental contextual approach to research and outreach. *Family and Consumer Sciences Research Journal, 23*, 26–42.
McLoyd, V.C. (1994). Research in the service of poor and ethnic/racial minority children: A moral imperative. *Family and Consumer Sciences Research Journal, 23*, 56–66.
Mead, M. (1930). *Growing up in New Guinea.* New York: Morrow.
Mead, M. (1935). *Sex and temperament in three primitive societies.* New York: Morrow.

Miller, J.R., & Lerner, R.M. (1994). Integrating research and outreach: Developmental contextualism and the human ecological perspective. *Home Economics Forum, 7,* 21-28.

National Association of State Universities and Land-grant Colleges. (1989). *State and land-grant universities: An American institution.* Washington, DC: Author.

Nesselroade, J.R., & Baltes, P.B. (Eds.). (1979). *Longitudinal research in the study of behavior and development.* New York: Academic Press.

Provost's Committee on University Outreach. (1993). *University outreach at Michigan State University: Extending knowledge to serve society: A report by the Provost's Committee on University Outreach* (Draft for review, July 1, 1993). Michigan State University, East Lansing.

Schaie, K.W. (1965). A general model for the study of developmental problems. *Psychological Bulletin, 64,* 92-107.

Schein, E.H. (1992). *Organizational culture and leadership.* San Francisco: Jossey-Bass.

Schorr, L.B. (1988). *Within our reach: Breaking the cycle of disadvantage.* New York: Doubleday.

Senge, P.M. (1990). *The fifth discipline: The art and practice of the learning organization.* New York: Doubleday.

von Eye, A. (1990a). *Statistical methods in longitudinal research,* Vol. 1: *Principles and structuring change.* New York: Academic Press.

von Eye, A. (1990b). *Statistical methods in longitudinal research,* Vol. 2. *Time series and categorical longitudinal data.* New York: Academic Press.

Votruba, J.C. (1992, Winter). Promoting the extension of knowledge in service to society. *Metropolitan Universities, 3*(3), 72-80.

Washington, V. (1992). Leadership for children in the 21st century: Professors, public policy, and philanthropy. *ICYF Fellows Colloquium,* September 24, 1992, Michigan State University, East Lansing.

PART IV
SPECIAL ISSUES IN APPLIED DEVELOPMENTAL SCIENCE EDUCATION

10

Applied Developmental Psychology Graduate Training Should Be Grounded in a Social–Cultural Framework[1]

Irving E. Sigel
Educational Testing Service
Princeton, NJ

The purpose of this chapter is to justify and advocate a social–cultural model as a framework for a graduate training program in applied developmental science. The rationale for such a proposal is based on the funda-

---

[1] I use the term "social–cultural," borrowed from James Wertsch, as a way to designate the framework within which to study human development. Others have used the terms, cultural psychology, ethnopsychology, and cultural anthropology to denote the integration of the psyche with the environment. Although there are points of disagreement too numerous to discuss in the context of this chapter, I feel that the social–cultural label joins the cultural concept with enactment in the social and physical environment. For those interested in a discussion of the differences in conception, I recommend the Shweder article referred to above (Shweder, 1990). For the purposes of this chapter, the differences in conception will not change the nature of my presentation.

mental principle that humans are embedded in a culture which is a requisite for physical, social, and psychological survival. Every culture has a profound influence on the development of its members. Although cultures vary in their mores, customs, language, and geographical locale, these variations do not negate the universal principle—individuals cannot survive without the group. The few isolated examples of children surviving in nonhuman cultures show that these children did not develop language nor ways of relating to other humans (Eibl-Eibesfeldt, 1988). In spite of considerable evidence from a host of studies by anthropologists and some educators over the years, developmental psychologists have not integrated such knowledge into their theorizing about human development.

I believe that every graduate student in psychology should integrate a social–cultural perspective to maximize his or her understanding of human development and any of its related human oriented sciences. This perspective is essential for the ADS professional because of its mission of carrying out intervention programs in service, education, prevention, or remediation.

It follows, then, that graduate training should provide a program that will create opportunities for the student to achieve the following goals: internalizing a social–cultural determinist stance through self-exploration; knowledge of the research literature in psychology and related disciplines in the social sciences and humanities; and experience in application of developmental principles in individual and program assessment, evaluations, and consultations. The rationale for such recommendations is that there is a need to ground the program in a social–cultural framework in order to fulfill the mission of ADS practice: the application of developmental principles for purposes of intervention in, and prevention of, psychological dysfunction in children, families, and institutions. Engaging effectively with diverse populations requires an awareness that everyone, including trainees and faculty, is an exemplar of a cultural heritage which may be different from our clients. This is a determinant of how each of us interprets the actions, values, attitudes, and beliefs of others. The centrality of social–cultural influences in much of our actions is undisputed. This chapter sets out to demonstrate the logic in, and psychologic and sociologic merits of, this assertion. Dewey (1916) put it so well when he wrote:

> The living creature is a part of the world, sharing its vicissitudes and fortunes, and making itself secure in its precarious dependence only as it intellectually identifies itself with things about it, and, forecasting the future consequences of what is going on, shapes its own activities accordingly. If the living, experiencing being is an intimate participant in the activities of the world to which it belongs, then knowledge is a mode of participation, valuable in the degree in which it is effective. It cannot be the idle view of an unconcerned spectator (p. 393)

Additionally, a prototypic program sequence will show how the creation of a social–cultural program can achieve its mission.

Goals of the Chapter

The following issues will be addressed: a. the rationale for advocating a social–cultural model; b. the lack of cultural integration in the applied developmental sciences; c. the meaning of culture for the ADS training program; d. the definition of the concept of culture for practice use; and, e. prototypic graduate training program

Rationale for advocating a social–cultural perspective

It is obvious that serious attention should be given to a social–cultural perspective when applying the principles of developmental psychology to practical social and personal problems. The significance of culture as a source of influence on human development has been well documented for decades (including, among others, Boas, 1928; Eibl-Eibesfeldt, 1989; Erikson, 1950; Mead, 1949; Whiting, 1963). A number of modern investigators have been strong advocates of incorporating social–cultural material into developmental psychology because they are convinced that culture is the warp and woof of human development. Bornstein and Bruner (1989); Cole, Gay, Glick, and Sharp (1971); Goodnow (1988); Greenfield and Cocking (1994); Kluckhohn and Murray (1949); Shweder, (1990); and Whiting and Child (1953)[2] have documented the cultural experiences that have had a profound influence in directing the course of human development from different theoretical models. Each of these investigators has conclusively shown that from the moment of birth, the individual becomes part of a cultural system which defines his or her place in the society. The socialization experiences of children, for example, comprise a continuous process of indoctrination that enables them to find their niche in the society. The socialized individuals share common cultural manners used to interact with family and group members, to communicate (common language), think, believe, trust, and express feelings.

Although every society exerts demands on its members to comply with the mores and customs of the culture, variations do exist, in that cultures allow group members to deviate without punishment or exclusion. For example, Muslims in Iran or Saudi Arabia have explicit rules which allow virtually no deviation for a wide array of behaviors such as religion, dress,

---

[2]There are other approaches to the issue of what culture is—for example, those who work with folk models or cultural models (see Quinn & Holland, 1993). At this stage of our discussion, it matters little which definition or conceptualization is chosen: the implications of any one are similar.

family organizations, or freedom of movement for women. On the other hand, Muslims living in the United States have considerable latitude in self-determination in how they will practice their religion because of the separation of church and state. In effect, cultural norms and boundaries help to set the degrees of freedom that individual group members have to express their personal values and beliefs. Although psychologists acknowledge the basic principle that humans are not only embedded in a culture, but are also a part of it, they have not assimilated such knowledge into their theorizing. Acknowledgement of cultural impact is obviously not powerful enough to change the way people think, talk, and conduct research in the developmental sciences. The most blatant example of the separation of the person from the culture is expressed in many titles of books and journals. Note how often the word "and" is used in scientific psychological literature to denote relationships, for example *The language and thought of the child* (Piaget, 1952). The reader is encouraged to peruse any table of contents in psychology journals to check this point. The word "and" connotes additions, not integration or assimilation. It accentuates the separation between entities such as person and society, nature and nurture, and language and its acquisition. As much as we use such terminology to show a relationship, we are actually engaging in a discourse of separation, in spite of the fact that the parts we label are part of a larger whole. I do not believe that the use of conjunctive "and" statements is accidental; rather, these statements signify the reunification of the separations. Of course, this may be a constraint of the English language, since such separations are evident in our everyday language, as well as in our scientific language. However, since language reflects thought, it may well be the case that we think in such separateness.

In spite of such overwhelming evidence that the individual and his or her culture evolve in a reciprocal relationship, developmental theories rarely integrate cultural constructs into their conceptualization of human development, other than to acknowledge that environments and cultures do influence the course of development.

Why has culture not been integrated into the applied developmental sciences?

This glaring omission, characteristic of academic programs in developmental sciences in general, is also true of applied programs in professional psychology (Persico, 1990). The resistance to change is, in part, due to the commitment to the traditional scientific paradigm, with emphasis on experimental control, standardization of procedures, and a presumption of objectivity. In the experimental approach, the assumption is that the individual enters the situation as a naive subject, a blank slate, as far as the particulars in the experiment are concerned. The individual is viewed in a decontextualized fashion, just as a representative of the population sampled. The data obtained with such a research paradigm are dealt with as aggregates, with minimal attention paid to the variability within the group. The data gathered is usually limited to a small number of variables, each of which is treated in a decontextualized fashion. The experimental situation which, in fact, is a source of influence, is not a part of the data analysis. These research strategies are presumed to yield generalizations which are usually the focus of the study. Statistics are used to solve some of the variance problems by procedures such as compressing scores when the variance is too high or using nonparametric techniques that, in reality, may mask individual variations. For many investigators this state of affairs is not a problem since the intent is to seek generalizations, not sources of individual differences. The fact that the individual and the environment are inexorably bound is of little interest to many experimenters. The oneness of the individual with his environment is the reality. Every separation of person and environment into discrete variables denies the wholeness of the person. The separation of person and environment is a metaphor revealing the guiding ideology of the scientist's view of the world (Pepper, 1970).

Decontextualization characterizes most psychological research, and it is this fact that compromises the empirical research for application to real-world settings. The paradigm used in most research studies in developmental psychology overlooks, denies, or deliberately discounts a social–cultural analysis in setting up research projects or defining a problems for study.[3]

If we accept the proposition that elements of the human condition can be separated into components, we can come to understand why the person denies the fact that human characteristics are not additive. Knowledge of development needs to be built hierarchically with interdependent components. If, in fact, it is necessary to select variables by focusing on a select few, care must be taken to develop some theoretical statements attesting to the fact that separation is, in fact, meant for the convenience of the investigator. By working within a broader framework, social–cultural factors, such as language comprehension and attitudes toward strange adults, should be

---

[3]In a recent survey of research publications in two major journals, *Child Development* and *Developmental Psychology*, we found very few groups of subjects defined in terms of religious or ethnic status, unless the particular group was singled out for study, e.g., African Americans or Chicanos. Yet, religious affiliation and beliefs or ethnic membership does influence a host of intellectual and social-emotional characteristics. The assumption may be that these differences are distributed among the samples and therefore are not significant. My argument is that these differences in ethnicity and religious orientation may influence performance. Hence variation in assessment measures, for example, may well be due to so called sampling error which is, in this case, a sampling error due to ignoring what may, in fact, be an error in variable designation and not a psychometric error.

considered when planning studies. This is one way in which the separateness belief can be counteracted. Otherwise, we continue with the belief that the person can be psychologically dissected—a belief so deeply rooted in our approach to the behavioral sciences, that we lose sight of the connectedness of the parts. We create artificial distinctions, and, in so doing, accept the artificial separation of psychological components of the person as a reality. Whether the logical positive paradigm that is used is a reality based belief that componential analysis of the human psyche is rational, or because there is no other methodology which meets the specification required for good science, that is, obtaining valid and reliable data, is unclear.

Academic researchers working in the paradigm of the logical positive model have not attempted to develop methodologies which meet holistic requirements. Thus, while most investigators may, in principle, agree on the unified nature of human reality, they cannot find the acceptable scientific methods by which to undertake empirical studies.

Wertsch (1991) argues that this task is not possible within the current approach to research in human development. Although he emphasizes mental functioning in his discussion, the tenor of his remarks has a familiar ring of generalization. He writes:

> Much contemporary research in psychology does not, in fact, have the practical implications so often claimed for it. In my view, a major reason is the tendency of psychological research, especially in the United States, to examine human mental functioning as if it exists in a cultural, institutional, and historical vacuum. Research is often based on the assumption that it is possible, even desirable, to study the individual, or specific areas of mental functioning in the individual, in isolation. In some cases, its proponents justify this approach by claiming that we must simplify the problems we address if we are to get concrete research underway. Only then, it is argued, can we go on to understand how cultural, historical, or institutional "variables" enter into the picture. (p. 2)

In spite of the fact that we live in a pluralistic society, these cultural differences are not used to explain individual differences. Note how infrequently religion or ethnic identity is presented as a sample attribute. Yet if investigators would think in terms of social–cultural variables, they would need to alter their way of doing research with diverse populations on the basis of religion and ethnic identity (meaning "ethnic" in terms of the family's identity with it's country of origin).

It is ironic that, in spite of the uniqueness of the American scene, where many cultural groups coexist in spite of their diversity, that these are differences which are ignored. At the same time, all of these groups are living in a society referred to as "American," with a presumed set of values, beliefs, and attitudes. It is the case that there is an American value system as embodied in our laws and customs. However, these "American values" are not necessarily shared by all members of the society. There is the obvious cultural diversity, as evidenced in the array of groups which have, as their cultural identity, something quite different from the politically organized society.

The easiest way to signify this state of affairs is to note the preferred designations used to identify American groups: African American, Italian American, American Hispanics, Native Americans, etc. Each of these designations signifies a different cultural group. The students of human development, then, need to come to realize that this is a complex world. Children and their parents must cope with a diverse social scene that can create conflicts among the citizens due to their dual loyalties to both their nation and to their culture. Examples of this occurred during World War II, when a number of German Americans were in conflict over a war with their culture of origin. As obvious as this observation is, it does not influence the scientific academic research in human development, yet there is academic research literature that ADS trainees will, in all likelihood, study to get the principles of developmental psychology.

The point that this chapter is making is really quite simple—most of our research does not reflect the social reality depicting the lives of those individuals who are the likely clients for ADS training. Ethnic and cultural diversity also have profound moral implications for every applied professional in the social and behavioral sciences. Is it not a moral responsibility of the professional worker to respect the integrity and the identity of individuals, especially when working with developmental principles to influence behaviors in the service of intervention and prevention of difficulties in their lives (Fisher & Tryon, 1990)?

What does culture mean for the ADS training program?

There is no question of our agreement that cultural forces are fundamental; they play an important role in our development. This agreement is, however, at an abstract level. Cultural influences and personal characteristics that are culturally determined are expressed in language use, social interactions, and personal values, as well as in the more obvious style of dress and eating habits. The challenge is to discern the cultural elements and distinguish them from some more personal deviation from cultural norms. This is the challenge.

How is the concept of culture defined for practical use?

Cultures differ in the demands they make on their members to enable them to become participants in that culture. It is these differences, in the ways of socialization of all its members, that account for the diversity among these groups. Also, groups differ in the degree that they provide a coherent lifestyle or allow their members to accept the ways of other cultures. For example, the Old Amish are very strict as to the lifestyle of their members and allow little leeway for change. In contrast, most Italian Americans participate in both their Italian culture and the mainstream American society (probably with few restrictions), enabling their members to function in a bicultural fashion. This is probably the case for the bulk of Americans who are descended from recent immigrant groups. Nevertheless, remnants of their socializing in the culture of immigrant families has created a society which functions on many cultural levels. In recent years however, attention has been directed not at these model groups which have assimilated successfully into the mainstream, but at many groups that have not attained this acculturated status. These are some of the most recent immigrant arrivals from South and Central America, South East Asia, and Eastern Europe. These new immigrant arrivals have added to the obvious diversity. Perhaps, more importantly, has been the emerging awareness to the plight of the indigenous American populations that have been referred to as the "underclass." These are the poverty level African Americans, Native Americans, and Latinos from Mexico and Puerto Rico. However, it has also been the case that there have been limited opportunities available to members of these groups due to racial, cultural, and social discrimination. This state of affairs creates a cauldron of social dislocations and stress. It forces professionals who wish to contribute active social interventions, to develop new paradigms for the social and behavioral sciences in order to come to grips with these problems.

Conceptions of Culture

Let us move from the simplistic marker characteristics of cultural groups, such as race and social status, to more generic considerations such as beliefs, values, and day to day living, for example, the roles of family members and ways in which each interacts with other family members or with nonrelatives. It is from such a broad, yet deep, perspective that we can discover how culture is reflected in virtually every part of everyone's lives. The focus is now on role of culture:

> A cultural model is a cognitive schema that is intersubjectively shared by a social group. Such models typically consist of a small number of conceptual objects and their relations to each other. (D'Andrade, 1987, p. 112)
>
> By culture we mean those historically created definitions of the situation which individuals acquire by virtue of participation in or contact with groups. (Gergen, 1990, p. 571)

The term *culture* is utilized here to mean an organized body of rules concerning the ways in which individuals in a population should communicate with one another, think about themselves and their environments, and behave toward one another and objects in their environments. The rules are not universally obeyed, but are recognized by all; they ordinarily operate to limit the range of variation in patterns of communication, belief, value, and social behavior in that population. (Le Vine, 1973, p. 4)

It is assumed that culture consists of learned and shared systems of meaning and understanding, communicated primarily by means of natural language. These meanings and understandings are not just representations about what is in the world, they are also directive, evocative, and reality constructing in character. Through these systems of meanings and understandings, individuals adapt to their physical environment, structure interpersonal relationships, and adjust psychologically to problems and conflicts (D'Andrade, 1985). These systems of meanings and understandings are only one set of variables that influence human behavior; social and environmental conditions, the distribution of power, economic opportunity, personality characteristics, genetic constitution, and other classes of variables also influence what people do and think.

The abstract definition of culture first given fails to indicate the pervasiveness and importance of culture in normal human life. If we try to enumerate the actions that a normal person carries out in an average day, we quickly discover that a great deal of what people do is culturally shaped—culturally shaped in the sense that both the goal and the means to the goal are part of a learned and shared system of understandings about the appropriate thing to do (Swartz & Jordan, 1976). For example, an average American male, on waking does things like shaving, showering, dressing, eating breakfast, and reading the morning newspaper. These conventional actions, evaluated by conventional standards, are replicated daily by millions of other Americans, but not performed at all by millions of non-Americans. (D'Andrade, 1990)

These definitions serve as illustrative of the problem of cultural definition and the implications of it. The culture in which one is reared permeates the individual and defines her social behaviors, attitudes, beliefs, values, and language. One's cultural identity defines who one is. One's name often reveal a person's cultural membership.

In addition to family names, other cultural artifacts contribute to one's cultural place, for example: family or group rituals, myths, narratives, art, literature, and family and group histories. These are the artifacts found among all cultures. However, it is very important to understand that the categories of cultural artifacts may be similar among groups, but the content and importance of each artifact may be strikingly different. For example, virtually every culture has a type of religious belief, however these range from the monotheistic religions of the Western world, to the pantheistic types among African groups. Language is used in all human groups, but the diversity in linguistic content is tremendous. By examining cultural categories such as language or myths, a comparative approach is possible. This will be discussed later in the section on program.

Heretofore, culture has been discussed as a transcendent construct, as though every culture is homogeneous. This is not the case as many culture's subgroups exist that, while related to the transcendent culture, have unique characteristics that can even produce differences within the culture.

The term *ethnic* is a concept used to differentiate the subgroups within a culture. The position taken is that culture and ethnicity are not interchangeable; while there is cultural commonality, ethnic differences may play a more important role. Think, for a moment, of Italy. The Italians in the north are different from the Italians in Sicily. The common language, the common nation state, and a common religion are not enough to transcend these regional and ethnic differences. So how does one distinguish the culture and ethnicity? For example, if a language is spoken by different language groups (say, Chinese), is the difference an ethnic or a cultural difference? If it is only an ethnic difference (say, the Mandarin as compared to Cantonese), the culture similarities may override the significance of the ethnic differences. Do some cultures have an ethnic component and others do not? Among Jews, one finds different religious practices and different dietary patterns in the different sects of the religion, for example, the differences between Jews from a Sephardic tradition contrasts those from an Ashkenazi tradition. There are traditions that differentiate these groups, as well as some common features. However, people of the Jewish faith do share some religious traditions, yet have different values and practices. To demonstrate the confusions in these concepts, one can present a concept of ethnic and ethnicity:

> Patterned differences . . . [are] based on the national, cultural, religious, racial identification, and membership of groups of people who do not set the dominant style of life or control the privileges and power in any given society. These differences are embedded in what generally are known as "ethnic groups." Ethnicity usually is displayed in the values, attitudes, lifestyles, customs, rituals, and personality types of individuals who identify with particular ethnic groups. (Mindel, Habenstein, & Wright, 1988, p. 1)

An ethnic group has been defined as "those who conceive of themselves as alike by virtue of their common ancestry, real or fictitious, and who are so regarded by others." (Shibutani & Kwan, 1965, p. 23). Ethnicity describes a sense of commonality transmitted over generations by the family and reinforced by the surrounding community. It is more than race, religion, or national, and geographic origin (this is not meant to minimize the significance of race, or the special problems of racism). It involves conscious and unconscious processes that fulfill a deep psychological need for identity and historical continuity. Ethnicity patterns one's thinking, feeling, and behavior in both obvious and subtle ways. It plays a major role in determining what one eats, how one works, how one relaxes, how one celebrates holidays and rituals, and how one feels about life, death, and illness:

> Our cultural values and assumptions are generally outside of our awareness. We see the world through our own "cultural filters," often persisting in established views despite even clear evidence to the contrary.... (McGoldrick, 1982, p. 4)

Cole and Scribner (1974) have frame the issue well:

> If investigators have difficulty with the psychological concept of cognition, there is unhappily little less confusion over the anthropological concept of culture.
> It might appear, at first blush, that there should be no problem in knowing that the people you are studying are members of a different culture, and in most cases, this has been true. When Margaret Mead went off to live with the Manus people of New Guinea, she knew that she was observing Manus culture. The definitional problem arises when you ask: What features of Manus life make us aware that there is such a thing as Manus culture? Some seem obvious at first: the people all speak a particular language called Manus; they dress in a noticeably different way from Americans; they build their houses in a common and (to us) unusual way; they share common beliefs about the world and treat their children in a distinctive fashion. There is simply no question about it—they are Manus!
> But which of these things are necessary to define *culture*? For example, we can speak of both a Spanish culture and a Peruvian culture even though a vast majority of people in both groups speak the same language. We can speak of European culture in spite of large variations in dress, language, child rearing practices, and religious beliefs among the people on the continent. (pp. 5-6)

The distinctions between "culture" and "ethnicity" have a heuristic value for the practitioner because the construct will enable the practitioner to be sensitive to group differences within the larger cultural context. An example of this might help to clarify the issue. For example, a Spanish speaking group invited an APS consultant to come to address the group on the question of child rearing. In graduate school, Spanish speakers were considered to be Hispanic or Latinos. The consultant proceeded, assuming that Hispanics share a common culture. On the basis of generic language they do, but their group identity may not be the language, that was a designation not of their own choosing, but rather an ethnic criteria, for example, Puerto Rican, Spanish, or Mexican American. Each of these groups has different histories, traditions, and, possibly, religious orientation. The overlap between the larger cultural characteristics and ethnic divergences may be obvious in some ways, but the differences may be more subtle, or vice versa. In either event, for all practical purposes, the safest course for a practitioner would be to use the clients as informants to get a sense of their cultural beliefs, values, practices, and traditions, rather than to proceed on the basis of preconceived notions. However, if the APS trainees are not oriented to these distinctions, there is a good chance that there will be miscommunication and even program failure.

One of the major types of activities that APS graduates will be involved in will be educational, for example, early education (daycare), and parent education. Here again, cultural sensitivity and respect for ethnic orientation are required, even in those difficult situations where the parent and child refuse to cooperate any time there is a discrepancy between program objectives and ethnic values. This may be especially the case in educational intervention where the values, attitudes, and language of instruction may be in conflict, including tension between the school and the family or community.

Care must be taken that the program's objectives are not incompatible with the cultural values of the participants. For example, some educational intervention curricula specify the importance of encouraging the children toward psychological autonomy and questioning (Copple, Sigel, & Saunders, 1979, 1984). Yet, for some cultures, children are discouraged from displaying autonomous behaviors and initiating dialogue with adults (Ramírez & Castañeda, 1974).

Before presuming what is a universal educational goal, the ADS worker will have to do a cultural values assessment, focusing on the particular compatibility between the program and the population to be served. The dilemma here is whether an effective change is compatible with cultural values or antagonism.

Such cultural differences pose a challenge to the intervention programmer. How one deals with these cultural differences can be viewed as an effort by mainstream culture representatives to destroy the indigenous culture of the group. Since this type of situation is predictable from the history of acculturation of minorities, it would behoove graduate training programs to prepare students to deal with such controversial and potentially explosive issues.[4]

---

[4]In so brief an article as this, all that can be done is to raise the issue and hope that training programs will incorporate appropriate problem-solving strategies to deal with such situations, thereby preparing the students to cope with cultural conflicts.

Applied Developmental Psychology

In presenting this case example, it should be pointed out that it has inadvertently been assumed that the practitioner is someone other than a member of the cultural group to be studied. If that is the case, the illustration sets up a "me"/"not me" situation, where the "me" is the member of the out group. But what if the "me" is a member of the cultural group that is being observed in the daycare center? Does that mean that the cultural issues are no longer relevant? The answer to that question is "no," since each and every member of a cultural group, while sharing some common characteristics with the group, may be from a subgroup of that culture. These differences develop from idiosyncratic experiences in a cultural context that shares some features with every other culture. For example, African American teachers may often reflect establishment values, as far as education for their low-income African American pupils. These teachers' perspectives are often in sharp contrast to some of the lifestyles of their students, who come from a poverty level, single-parent family on welfare. In fact, it is highly probable that teachers at any grade level would reflect the values of the established culture, in addition to their own African American cultural identity. The teachers still have to consider the children as African Americans. The difference between the teacher and the student in this case is also based on socioeconomic class differences. The teacher will have his or her own "cultural filters" that differ from the students'. Thus, although teachers and students share in the African American category, they are culturally different. Awareness of our own "cultural filters" is crucial, particularly the awareness that all cultures are complex. Judging them as monolithic, or defined by singular attributes, will usually lead to misjudgment or cause one to overlook the multiple variants in a culture. This is particularly the case when individuals from different racial or ethnic groups are involved. For example, if one looks at an African American from the single attribute of complexion alone, it is impossible to define the individual's status. Nevertheless, such judgments are often made, usually to the detriment of the minority member. A good example of such a poignant experience is cited by Cornell West (1993) when he writes:

Years ago, while driving from New York to teach at Williams College, I was stopped on fake charges of trafficking cocaine. When I told the police officer I was a professor of religion, he replied, "Yeah, and I'm the 'Flying Nun.' Let's go nigger!" I was stopped three times in my first ten days in Princeton for driving too slowly on a residential street with a speed limit of twenty-five miles per hour. (p. x)

West was judged solely on the basis of his color that, for the police officer, signalled a bias denying West's individuality.

The term "minority" is also a euphemism for race or ethnic identity of the powerless of the underclass. It is not based on numbers, or gender, or sexual orientation. If numbers were the criterion for minority status, why are albino males, or hermaphrodites, or children born with cleft palates, not considered to be members of a minority group? Why are some ethnic groups such as Jews, Croatians, Ukrainians, Estonians, Lithuanians, and Jehovah's Witnesses not classified as "minorities" when, in fact, they are minorities in terms of numbers or percentage of the total United States population? The fact is that the label "minority" is a code word for the powerless and the oppressed—not a statement of the size of one's group. Such labelling is probably the outcome of attempts to mute the underclass status or powerlessness. If, on the other hand, the label "minority" were eliminated and groups designated by their cultural identity, then particular populations would be identified on their own terms instead of by the mainstream political decision. Would this approach not show some respect for the group's unique identity? This has been done in some cases, for example in the use of the term Inuit or Aleut instead of Eskimo. However, as indicated earlier, the current practice is inconsistent, for example, the use of the term "Asian" includes Chinese, Japanese, and Korean. Can this not be offensive to Koreans who do not want to be identified along with the Japanese? Another example is the term, "Native American" instead of "Indian." Why not Iroquois or Sioux, or whatever the appropriate term would be? Use of the new politically correct labels masks cultural identity and denigrates the individual by using stereotypic thinking. Whether the overall term that is used is culturally appropriate or not, each is a generalization which still has limited use because some individuals wish to be treated as a person, not as a member of a group. While sharing the common rubric designated by the majority culture, they may define themselves in an idiosyncratic way.

Trainees should be helped in this arena, even when reading the research literature dealing with minorities. Our social science research literature, whether it is anthropology, psychology, or sociology, often works with aggregated data, with statistics that use such terms as "means," lead to generalizations about cultural groups.[5] For example, we often read about "inner city" children, children from middle-income homes, Asian children, or American children. These statements imply that every individual so designated is like every other individual so labelled. In other words, the individuals identified as members of a class or group are interchangeable. This assumption is exemplified by the selection of participants in a research

---

[5]Over the past 25 years or so, the label for the poor and underclass has shifted from culturally deprived to culturally disadvantaged to minorities—each change attempting to eliminate the use of the terms deemed to be derogatory. However, to my knowledge, none of these labels has come from the groups themselves, but rather are a reaction to the White establishment's designations.

project. Participants are selected at random; this implies that any member of a class is equivalent to every other member. While such sampling procedures and research methodologies are appropriate for some types of activities, the conclusions from such studies have to be tempered by many cautions when efforts are made to apply research findings to intervention programs. It can be argued that it is obvious that one cannot apply generalizations to the individual case. Although this is an often repeated statement, its verity is not salient in recommendations given by psychologists to educators, parents, and policymakers.

The reason for focusing on these issues at the outset, is to acknowledge that most of us have developed lenses through which we filter our judgments of others. The essential task for the professional engaging in applied developmental activities is to come to acknowledge his or her own attitudes, feelings, and beliefs about members of other groups, be they racial, ethnic, social class, religious, handicapped, mentally deficient, or members of any other social group that does not fit into the practitioner's concept of social acceptability. Facing up to one's own cultural orientations or biases is no easy matter and requires considerable psychological effort.

Another principle one must work with, states that language of social discourse in any context is influenced by the demands of that setting. Discourse in the school, the clinic, the market place, and the church differ in profound ways. In each of these settings, the language used reflects the values and the beliefs of the significant individuals. For example, when the teacher tells the student about the importance of studying, or of doing homework, these terms have particular referents. Homework is not helping in the home. Homework is doing schoolwork and schoolwork is different from any other kind of work. So studying is similar to a task-specific activity. Studying is not reflecting on the state of the world. Studying in the context of school has specific goals and criteria for academic achievement.

Cultural meanings must be understood from the perspective of the member of that group. For example, to read the history of African Americans from the point of view of white historians can be far different for African American historians. This is best exemplified in the discussions of slavery. White historians will use such terms as "benign masters," those who treated their slaves in a humane manner. For African American writers the notion of "benign masters" is an oxymoron—anyone holding someone in bondage as property with the right of sale as any other object, and not even allowing them a surname—can in no way be benign. Rather, these so called benign slave holders were protecting their property. A farmer would not be cruel to his horse or cow if he wanted them to produce. If one is, therefore, reading about slavery and the individual differences among slave owners, the fact that they share a common acceptance of slavery in itself is an indication of their participation in an abominable institution that each participant shares responsibility in. This is a good example where the issues discussed earlier, in terms of generalizations, have to be qualified. In the earlier discussion, it was emphasized that distinctions should be made between the individual and the group in order to avoid stereotyping. In the case of the slave holder, the very fact that he owns slaves indicates that he acts like every other slave holder participating in common practice, even though he might be different in some ways from his peers. The distinguishing characteristic is the salience of the attribute used to define a class. So, for the individual slave holder, the central attribute of owning slaves is a marker of his group status. That marker is an evil one, outweighing all of the other benign attributes.

Markers of distinction are important to applied developmentalists because in intervention programs they have to evaluate the salience of each characteristic of a population in order to be effective in working with them. For example, if one is working with a gang of teenagers from a particular ethnic group, can one criticize one of the members without fear of being called prejudiced? Is it not demeaning to treat every member as every other member in spite of an individual's action? Cornell West (1993) offers a most poignant discussion of this principle in discussing the appointment of Clarence Thomas to the Supreme Court. Liberals among African American and White groups were reluctant to speak out against Thomas, even though they reported privately that he was not the best choice of an African American candidate. Why? The liberal Whites did not wish to be judged as racist and the African Americans were reluctant to criticize publicly one of their own. The issue is accentuated in the gang example. Does one assume common values and practices are interchangeable, that is, individual differences are ignored? Thus, the answer would be "yes," and what they share is what makes them potentially antisocial. Of course there are individual differences among specific members as to their responsibilities, their reasons for being in the gang, and their degree of acceptance of their role of being coerced. Nevertheless their active participation makes them equally responsible for the actions of the group.

What this analysis leads one to, is the need to make a distinction between being a member of a cultural group that is due to circumstances that the person, the individual self, could not control as compared to voluntary membership. Of course, one does not choose the family one is born into, or even into which family one is adopted into. These are the nonvoluntary givens (see Ogbu, 1994, for a discussion of this issue). However then there are a number of choice points in the course of development that the child, or his or her family, elects to share, group values or not, for example, church, neighborhood, or schools. If the notion of cultural sensitivity is to be examined in depth and acknowledged, the fact that each of us, by being embedded in a culture, has "cultural filters." Training for cultural sensitivity requires some reflective thought as to just how to explicate such an attitude in our teaching, practice, and writing.

How do we effectively integrate a social–cultural perspective into practical educational terms?

Three areas need to be addressed to create a culturally sensitive environment in which the professional developmental scientist will be educated. The three areas of concern are the faculty, formal course structure and content, and field placements. At first blush, these topics are no different from any other program requirement—a competent faculty, a well informed student body, good practical experience, and supervision. Where is the difference? The difference rests with the attitudinal aspects inherent in engaging in reflective activity with cultural self-analysis as a constant. It is this task which is the most challenging and of the utmost importance if the developmental science practitioner will provide the kind of service that will maximize his or her contribution.

PROTOTYPIC GRADUATE TRAINING PROGRAM

Role of Faculty

Faculties and trainees in ADS programs will have to commit themselves to more than superficial acknowledgment of the place of cultural determinants in all aspects of living among their prospective clients.

An important caveat for those seriously entering into this arena of social–cultural thinking, as applied to ADS graduate training, is that cultures, at least in the United States, are not monolithic, but subject to extra cultural influences. As mentioned earlier, the cultural boundaries can vary in permeability. Some are more open than others. Individual difference will occur as a function of the permeability of the culture's rules and enforcement. The importance of this point will become clear as the chapter proceeds, but for now let it suffice that practitioners working with members of different cultural groups should be observing at two levels—the norm and the individual interpretation of that norm from his or her cultural perspective. To judge otherwise would be to engage in stereotypical thinking. Human beings, while sharing some common characteristics, are highly differentiated in terms of their life experiences, that, as indicated earlier, are largely shaped by the culture in which they develop. Recognizing the powerful impact of cultural diversity in all phases of one's life is a necessary requisite for coming to understand and render service sensitively to people of different cultures. However, the resistance to change one's perspective is considerable in the academic realm of psychology and in the applied field where resistance to change is common among faculty, administrators, and students (Troy, 1990).

Let us begin with the faculty who are the key players in this enterprise. Remember that we wish to move away from lip service, from academic rhetoric, and come face to face with our own attitudes, feelings, anxieties, and concerns related to cultural analysis. But where is one to begin? The chapter has already discussed the various definitions of "culture." Given those definitions, now is the time to concertize the abstractions by examining overt and covert cultural artifacts such as: the language spoken, style of dress, church attended, social manners, and the like. One must also examine covert cultural features such as: expressiveness, values, trust, and attitude toward nongroup members. These are cultural artifacts that are built into our institutions, schools, and families; they are deeply embedded in each of our psyches. Usually, we do not look inward at our own cultural baggage as we work with other groups. We might recognize and identify the various cultural characteristics, believing that we are objectively evaluating them as culturally appropriate to that group. Are we perhaps judging in an ethnocentric way, thereby coloring (no pun intended) our judgment? It seems that the first thing anyone who intends to work with clearly different cultural groups does, is to spend considerable time engaging in self-analysis—brutal as it may be—regarding feelings, attitudes, and beliefs about that group. For example, one could ask oneself: If I (a White senior citizen) was walking down the street at night and a well dressed African American were to approach me, would I be frightened? If an African American teenager was walking down the street in the evening and saw a policeman approaching, would he or she be anxious about being stopped just because he or she is there?

These examples reflect real life experiences of African American youth, as well as White senior citizens. They demonstrate the situation in which our antennae are raised, usually without actual provocation.

This phenomenon is characteristically human. There is considerable research evidence to support the fact that bias exists in reasoning, judgments, and decision making. Categories are developed that serve as bases for responding to virtually every encounter in everyday living. Ironically, these categorical judgments are so deeply ingrained that we are not aware of the implications of these perceptions. Therefore, it is critical that issues relating to these phenomena be addressed. I believe that such consciousness raising is a requisite to enhance the quality of professional work for the ADS professional. I am not referring to being politically correct, but rather to being culturally sensitive.

Faculty members have to be particularly sensitive to these issues, because as role models and instructors, and often as supervisors, they bear an inordinate ethical and professional responsibility to represent an awareness of cultural issues.

Discussion of these issues should be dealt with in private faculty meetings since they require quasi-public soul searching to acknowledge individual cultural biases. Cornell West (1993) faces this issue when he writes:

> We confine discussions about race in America to the "problems" black people pose for whites, rather than consider what this way of viewing black people reveals about us as a nation.
> This paralyzing framework encourages liberals to relieve their guilty consciences by supporting public funds directed at "the problems"; at the same time, reluctant to exercise principled criticism of black people, liberals deny them the freedom to err. Similarly conservatives blame the "problems" on black people themselves—and thereby render black social misery invisible or unworthy of public attention.
> Hence, for liberals, black people are to be "included" and "integrated" into "our" society and culture, while for the conservatives they are to be "well behaved" and "worthy of acceptance" by "our" way of life. Both fail to see that the presence and predicaments of black people are neither additions to nor defections from American life, but rather constitutive elements of that life. (pp. 2–3)

These comments of West's are not limited to matters of race; they also apply to matters dealing with the underclass and the poor, as well as individuals culturally different from the mainstream culture. His is indeed a perspective that transcends cultural differences and leads directly to the heart of the social scene where discrimination and harm are done on the basis of these cultural and social markers.

Why bring this matter up in terms of faculty first? The reason rests on the simple belief that the faculties in these programs are in positions of power. It is they who define the quality of a student's performance, provide the opportunities for professional careers, supervise his or her work, and, in effect, have an important role to play in the student's developing a sense of professional competence and self-esteem. Unless faculty members come to terms with their own feelings about cultural diversity and develop a culturally sensitive and respectful posture, they will not provide the kind of training required for applied developmental science.

A second and related concern to be addressed in the context of faculty attitudes, is the acceptance of an interdisciplinary (not a multidisciplinary) approach to the problems under discussion. The difference is that a multidisciplinary approach is the use of a number of disciplines combining to bear on a problem with no requirement to integration. An interdisciplinary approach asks for an integration of relevant disciplines to create a holistic approach. An interdisciplinary construct is, by definition, social–cultural because it brings together social and cultural bodies of knowledge under a single rubric. So the challenge is to integrate readings from different content areas. Why? Because we work from the basic principle that the types of challenges faced in applied developmental science are multidetermined and cannot be understood from a single disciplinary perspective. For example, I have heard colleagues adamantly oppose certain kinds of psychometric assessments of children because the tests are biased. This outright rejection negates the possible value of the data if the examiner interprets it, not as a fixed unchangeable index of the child's performance, but rather as an index of how the child can cope with the particular type of tasks representing the culture. The test is a reflection of experience, not of one's biological character. So, if a child who speaks Spanish is given a vocabulary test from the Binet and he or she has difficulty taking the test, it may well be an index of his or her limited understanding of English, not of his or her native intelligence. I am aware that some school systems have administered intelligence tests in the English language to non-English speakers, thereby determining that the children were retarded and in need of special education. Imagine giving the examiner the same text in Chinese and expecting him or her to pass it. This reflects incompetence.

The issues discussed to this point refer to the quality and the sensitivity of faculty. The points I have made are proper guidelines for enlisting faculty in such graduate programs and the converse criteria for exclusion.

Course Work

The formal part of the program deals with course work. To accomplish conceptual restructuring involves more than just adding a course to the program. It necessitates incorporating the cultural orientation in all aspects of the program. The seminar is a place for students to explore and share their understanding of, and knowledge about, their own culture. Since it agreed that everyone, irrespective of race, social status, and all of the other markers attributed to groups, has a culture; it is evident in family myths, rituals, and daily living arrangements. Identification of these cultural markers, through examining family scripts, can sensitize the students to their own cultural experience. Sharing these with fellow classmates will enable students to observe similarities and differences in their cultural experiences. Sameroff and Fiese (1992) discuss this question in the context of the family, and provide a way of thinking about the issue where they write:

> Developmental regulations . . . are carried within codes: the cultural code, the family code, and the individual code of the parent. These codes regulate cognitive and socioemotional development so that the child ultimately will be able to fill a role defined by society. They are hierarchically related in their evolution and in their current influence on the child. The experience of the developing child is partially determined by the beliefs, values, and person-

alities of the parents, partially by the family's interaction patterns and transgenerational history, and partially by the socialization beliefs, controls, and supports of the culture. (p. 353)

Cocking (1994) has articulated the general principles that should guide the assimilation of such thinking in a developmental model, which can be interpreted as a social cultural model:[6]

(A) Articulating the processes and levels of variable functioning in ways that cut across cultures and subcultures and in a language of science that has common meaning, (b) accounting for inconsistent findings within a framework of developmental continuities and discontinuities, (c) going beyond how variables function, toward a model of how they influence one another in predicting developmental trajectories, (d) accounting for normative trends and their variations in cultural and individual differences parameters, (e) separating enduring from transitory effects and accounting for transitory behaviors as part of the developmental cycle, (f) specifying patterns of relationships in cognitive and social influences on development, and (g) specifying the vulnerabilities and resiliencies so that the models can account for cultural and contextual features that protect children or put them at risk. (p. 402)

Working with the principles formulated by Cocking, a curriculum can be developed that pays attention to developmental theory and research literature. Amplifying Cocking's discussion with the following comments of Robert Le Vine (1973), will generate a workable framework for organizing the literature the students should read. Although Le Vine begins with an anthropological frame of reference, he moves quickly into a discussion of personality as a psychological construct, then engages in an analysis of the development of the individual in the social–cultural context. He addresses theoretical issues, such as an evolutionary framework and methods of research, as one proceeds to do comparative work between cultures and in pluralistic societies in the United States. In doing this, Le Vine provides the student with a comprehensive way to embed the individual in a social–cultural milieu, which is, of course, a foundation for an appreciation of a multicultural perspective when applying developmental principles.

This not the place to create a syllabus for that seminar, but some of the reading materials are suggested in the bibliography (e.g., Cole & Scribner,

---

[6]I do not intend to elaborate the argument as to why I made this appropriation of Cocking's model in this chapter because it takes us too far afield. However, I do maintain that his claim of being "less ethnocentric" is an understatement, and his model accomplishes just the type of program which I am advocating. Further, it counteracts the pessimism of Wertch regarding the applicability of developmental research for practical intervention programs.

1976; Edwards, 1986; Fisher & Lerner, 1994; Le Vine, 1973; Rogoff, 1990; Stigler, Shweder, & Herdt, 1990; Wertsch, 1985, 1991).

Field Work

This brings us to the next topic—the field experiences that create the opportunities to observe cultural differences in action. Preparation for such experiences, of course, requires some familiarity with the institutions, language, beliefs, and values of the particular group. If a student is going to work with any ethnic or cultural group in the United States, he or she needs to acquire some familiarity with whatever groups they will be working with. While general histories of these groups will help, there is no substitute for hand-on experience and participation. To be sure, the usual guidelines for field work should be created for all to follow when entering into any service setting, especially when it is culturally novel for the student. The greater the cultural difference between the trainee and the population of the programs, the greater the need for careful preparation. The next step beyond the general understanding of the group is a reintegration of what cultural markers should be the center of attention. Here we return to our basic definition of culture. Cultural artifacts are critical of attention. These are central ingredients: the discourse patterns, that is, the method of communication; methods of social interaction; customs; and rituals of engagement. Each of these is a critical prerequisite to maximize the potential for developing trusting relationships.

Discourse of "Multiculturalism"

Students and faculty develop ways to deal with cultural diversity. Discourse analysis from a social–cultural perspective becomes one of the central concerns. All discussions of culture, and its details, are couched in linguistic terms which often need clarification. The use of the term "Asian," as referring to the Japanese, might be viewed as a negative term. If used in discussions of cultural differences, does that term not preclude an open discussion? Certain words are not acceptable to some groups, such as explicit sexual terms, while that is not the case for others. The entire process of linguistic communication can lead to quagmires, miscommunication, and subsequent distance between groups. Intervention programs focusing on social problems can often exacerbate cultural conflict, dissemble intentions, generate distrust, and preclude mutual understanding. Sometimes the language intended to illuminate actually obfuscates and obscures meaning.

Language is the powerful medium that arouses conscious and unconscious feelings, perceptions, and misunderstandings among individuals as they strive to enhance communication and get a better understanding of themselves and others in the course of social engagement. To understand how effective communication can be carried out, "one needs to invoke the notion of intersubjectivity. Intersubjectivity exists when interlocutors share some aspect of their situation definitions. Typically this overlap may occur at several levels, and hence several levels of intersubjectivity may exist" (Wertsch, 1985, p. 159).

According to Rommetveit's approach to the study of human communication, "Communications aims at transcendence of the 'private' worlds of the participants. It sets up what we might call 'states of intersubjectivity'" (Rommetveit, 1979, p. 159). One can refer to this phenomenon as *shared meaning* (Sigel, 1993).

Since the students and faculty in any ADS program are concerned about how to establish cultural contacts (especially for interviews), interviews used as either research tools, or just for information gathering in preparing programs, require special care since it is in this context of probing and asking questions where resistance and conflict may occur. Much preplanning needs to be done.

Which particular aspects of a culture should be singled out as potentially important from a causal point of view? Some guiding hypotheses are clearly essential if investigations are not to proceed on a hit and miss basis. But, as yet, there is no general theory or conceptual framework in psychology that would generate specific hypotheses how about cultural patterned experiences influence the development of cognitive processes in the individual. (Cole & Scribner, 1974, p. 6–7)

Let me give an example from my own experience as director of an early education program, that I established while at the State University of New York at Buffalo. The program objective was to test an intervention model beginning with two year olds in a half day program. The program was funded by a federal grant, based on the argument that the earlier the intervention began, the more likely the children would profit from subsequent educational experiences in kindergarten. The first problem was selecting a population. Since this was an experiment, the population was to be made up of African American children from a housing project, so that there would be proper matching of children. Social class and race were central characteristics. This population represented children from the most disorganized homes. This led to the first criticism—that I was racist—from both Black and White psychologists. The Black psychologists objected that a White professor was using Black children as guinea pigs for his own advancement. My White liberal colleagues objected to the segregation aspects, in spite of the fact that they also acknowledged comments about research designs and the usual scientific concerns of sample bias. The fact that I was a professor with an established reputation did not seem to quell the criticism. The real-world problem of recruitment was not part of their world view.

Science and politics were mixed at the expense of testing a model that could be of use for children from a variety of backgrounds. The model of preschool education was an inquiry based model in that children were encouraged to problem solve and the teachers were encouraged to ask questions and interact with the children through coconstruction of activities. For a detailed description of the program see Copple, Sigel, & Saunders (1979, 1984).

The recruitment of teachers posed another set of problems. Some of the African American colleagues I spoke with were not supportive of the program, as they believed that the goals of the educational program were inappropriate for the type of children who would be enrolled because those children would be expected to develop middle-class verbal skills. The program emphasized communication skills, an area that covers more than oral language skills. We are not instructing them in Standard English. Some White professional colleagues were also not supportive because they believed that the children's attention span was so limited that they would not be able to profit from this type of inquiry dialogue. Teachers needed to be convinced that the program could work, but it was found that once they were engaged in teaching, they had to be carefully monitored to follow some program directives, for example, listen to children's conversations, allow them opportunities to explore, encourage interaction without interference, and not to correct their language. This was especially the case for the White teachers. They also had to avoid making comments about the parents. For example, one day a child came in and said to a White teacher, "My mother and father just got married." The teacher's comment was: "It's about time." I felt that she was not the appropriate person for the job. Another White teacher said to the children, "I will bring in some bananas for you little monkeys." This also created a crisis. Finally, a White research assistant said to the children (who were lining up to go outside), "If you kids don't line up, I will have to put a ball and chain on your legs." The African American secretary stormed out of her office and berated the assistant for his insensitivity by using a threat reminiscent of slavery (a topic these children may never have known, nor thought about, especially in that context). On the other hand, one grandmother withdrew her grandchild because she felt that the teachers allowed the children too much freedom. Each of these incidents is an example of a cultural perspective. What appears to be trivial and innocent to some may be insulting to others.

The most dramatic incident occurred at the parent meetings, that were held once a month. Each meeting usually opened in a very formal and staid manner, irrespective of attempts made by the teachers and me to create an informal environment. The parents sat in a large circle and raised only a few questions, but supposedly listened to the discussion of experts on various relevant topics of child health and development. I always made it a policy to be there at the opening of the meeting and stayed for any questions, but thereafter left soon after refreshments were served. The nature of the meeting changed once I left. The parents had a party and left after a few hours of dancing and sharing food. Had I stayed, the meeting would have continued in a formal and stiff manner.

The final event (which clearly reveals a shift in cultural values) was when the children were leaving the program to go on to kindergarten. The parents wanted to have a graduation ceremony and invite the local television station to come to videotape the event. If that is what they wanted, so be it! Who was I to negate their sense of pride in the achievement of their children, and, of course, themselves? I was criticized for enabling this middle-class achievement value to permeate the final event and found this criticism to be very arrogant and demeaning. I felt that the message that many of my colleagues were sending out was that the parents were not able to decide what they wanted for themselves and for their children. In fact, I would venture to guess that my professional colleagues were, perhaps, out of touch with the values of the parents who were achievement oriented. After all, that is why they participated in the program. The graduation was a huge success, having been planned by the parents with some help from the teachers. Camera flashed, people were dressed in their Sunday best, and the food was plentiful. I discouraged the television videotaping because of the way in which the media would present the children—"Poverty children profit from SUNY Buffalo professor's program." I did not want to join this type of exploitation of the children.

Throughout the days of this program, graduate students from SUNY Buffalo worked as research assistants or researchers. Their participation required long term supervision and sensitivity training. First, the students had to learn how to avoid condescending and patronizing behavior. Their expectations of children's play and conversation were different from what they observed. The discourse they used also had to be monitored. I did not want them to mimic the children, but to use standard English. If the student was African American, then the use of Black English was authentic for him or her. It would not, however, be authentic for Whites. Even children as young as those in this group are aware of the difference. For example, when some of the children were being interviewed by a White interviewer they were able to code switch and speak standard English.

The experience of working in this group revealed that the students, the teachers, and the parents had to learn to communicate in a discourse pattern that was understandable, while avoiding the creation of self-consciousness. This issue of discourse pattern, by the way, is a constant issue in programs comprised of different cultural groups. This will be discussed later in the course of supervision.

In sum, students entering field settings with different cultural groups need to be oriented to interact and communicate in ways that are culturally appropriate. This concept of authentic discourse and cultural sensitivity should not be confused with political correctness, as the former deals with the reality of communication based on understanding and efforts at shared meaning, while the latter is rhetorical and avoids honest engagement.

What are the initial tasks for entering a field setting with a culturally different population? First, the student is to bring into awareness the principles learned in the formal seminar, especially the important notion that she or he has culturally filtered vision.

Second, the student should listen carefully to the dialogues that go on among participants and acknowledge, when appropriate, that they have a different background and this is a new experience. They should feel free to ask for help, but avoid being intrusive. In some groups, asking direct questions about personal matters, such as views on children or family, might be considered impertinent. Observation and listening are important first steps. Students should tread sensitively and acknowledge any misunderstanding on his or her part, but at the same time they should not necessarily believe that they are the source of misunderstanding where the participants may be attempting to exploit them. For example, in working with prisoners in detention centers of prisons, care has to be taken not to be seduced into the belief that the criminal justice system is all wrong and the prisoner is just being oppressed because of his or her race. Any prisoner, irrespective of race or gender, may be guilty of the crime, not because of race or creed, but because of the act itself. It is very easy for the novice to be sympathetic to the client because of his or her own feelings about the society and the system.

Finally, we come to the supervision of students working with different cultural groups. Here, it seems reasonable to suggest two types of supervisory experiences. One is in a group context, which would allow trainees to compare experiences in different settings, and the other, perhaps a more personal one, is where the individual may share some personal concerns about dealing with the setting in which he or she is working. I can well imagine the difficulty some students may have in facing situations in hospitals or other settings where individuals are ill or disturbed. The focus of the supervisory situation could also involve textual materials, be they observations, audio recordings, or some materials which can be shared. Working from memories in this area is fraught with possible misunderstandings and misinterpretations.

Some Final Words

In this final section, it should be pointed out what this program is not: It is not only focused solely on the acquisition of social knowledge, but is also aimed at cognitive restructuring of one's point of view to assimilate a social–cultural perspective. For example, I examined the recent recommendations of the National Conference on Graduate Education in the Application of Developmental Science Across the Lifespan (Fisher et al., 1993). This final report contains a comprehensive outline of the program objectives for adequate training in the field of applied developmental science. The report describes an array of courses students should have in a number of academic disciplines, for example, biology and sociology. The report additionally discusses field experiences that involve interaction with various types of populations representing different racial, ethnic, religious, and age groups. The populations can be found in different types of field settings such as schools, medical and psychological clinics, prisons, juvenile detention centers, courts, educational institutions, and family and child care, among other service oriented facilities. These experiences should be shared in a seminar setting where the students will be expected to come to terms with their own beliefs and values in order to engage the clients in ways that they can relate to where the other person is coming from. This recommendation is based on research from two perspectives: one from ethnomethodology such as Garfinkel (1967), and the other from the empirical work of anthropologists and psychologists (D'Andrade, 1987, 1990; Schank & Abelson, 1977).

Glick (1978) writes:

Ethnomethodologists, such as Garfinkel (1967), have adopted specialized classes of inquiry procedures to make visible some of the invisible structures underlying social cognition. They have found that our sense of social reality is, in fact, based on an elaborate structure of presuppositions which are sometimes elaborately maintained in action, but normally escape explicit formulation in social–psychological and developmental accounts of social life. (p. 6)

D'Andrade (1987, 1990) has concluded from his own research, that those who use the social domain paradigm tend to operate with stored belief systems which may, in fact, override presently available information.

Findings such as these make the same point, namely, that preexisting belief systems can influence observations, interactions, and recording of experiences in settings divergent from one's own. Herein lies the greatest challenge to the graduate student faculty because these beliefs may be deep seated and held with considerable conviction. To change one's point of view requires considerable understanding of cognitive restructuring—a difficult task to say the least.

This is not the place to discuss all of the potential sources of conflicts that will inevitably arise when a diverse student body reflects its beliefs, not only about their experiences and their clients, but about each other.

Graduate training in ADS is going to pose many challenges to faculty and students because it requires entering into an arena fraught with interracial, interethnic, and interreligious conflict. This is a particularly difficult task in ADS programs, in that applied programs are essentially interventions in various essential and intimate phases of individuals and families. In contrast to other educational endeavors such as schooling, and career educations, once we embark on a interventionist route there is no turning back because, simply put, we already entered the fray as social change agents. We create perturbations no matter how insignificant the beginnings are. Failure at the inception of a program might preclude success at a later time. Progress will inevitably be slow and painstaking, but there is no alternative but to go on, as we have a moral obligation to follow through once we have assumed the responsibility of engagement. To do otherwise would be unprofessional and irresponsible. It seems ADS is facing a challenge greater than any other branch of the psychological sciences because the need is great and the rewards are slow in coming.

Urgency for Program Change Now

The current social and political scene, fraught as it is with cultural conflicts, necessitates instantiating the APS's mission statement as a guide for preparing ADS practitioners as soon as possible. The synthesis of current social and behavioral science knowledge as preparation for undertaking the activities MUST be couched in social–cultural terms in order to be effective. There is enough evidence to support the argument that failures in the intervention and prevention fields have been of limited value because of the inability to carry programs out, as they were not instituted in the context of cultural sensitivity of the populations served. Appropriating a cultural awareness orientation will meet the challenge for creating and implementing successful intervention and prevention programs. The challenge, then, is to develop intervention and prevention programs which will have a better chance of being effective if, and when, the students will be educated to understand the dynamics of cultures, their potency as sources of generating political conflicts, and develop activities and strategies for dealing with them.

REFERENCES

Boas, F. (1928). *Anthropology and modern life*. New York: N.W. Norton.
Bornstein, M.H., & Bruner, J.S. (Eds.). (1989). *Interaction in human development*. Hillsdale, NJ: Erlbaum.
Cocking, R.R. (1994). Ecologically valid frameworks of development: Accounting for continuities and discontinuities across contexts. In P.M. Greenfield &

R.R. Cocking (Eds.), *Cross-cultural roots of minority child development* (pp. 393–409). Hillsdale, NJ: Erlbaum.

Cole, M., Gay, J., Glick, J., & Sharp, D.W. (1971). *The cultural context of learning and thinking*. New York: Basic Books.

Cole, M., & Scribner, S. (1974). *Culture and thought: A psychological introduction*. New York: Wiley.

Copple, C., Sigel, I.E., & Saunders, R. (1984). *Educating the young thinker: Classroom strategies for cognitive growth*. Hillsdale, NJ: Erlbaum.

D'Andrade, R. (1985). Character terms and cultural models. In J. Dougherty (Ed.). *Directions is cognitive anthropology* (pp. 88–119). New York: Cambridge University Press.

D'Andrade, R. (1987). A folk model of the mind. In D. Holland & N. Quinn (Eds.), *Cultural models in language and thought* (pp. 112–148). New York: Cambridge University Press.

D'Andrade, R. (1990). Some propositions about the relations between culture and human cognition. In J.W. Stigler, R.A. Shweder, & G. Herdt (Eds.). *Cultural psychology: Essays on comparative human development* (pp. 65–129). New York: Cambridge University Press.

Dewey, J. (1916). *Democracy and education: An introduction to the philosophy of education*. New York: Macmillan.

Edwards, C.P. (1986). *Promoting social and moral development in young children: Creative approaches for the classroom*. New York: Teachers College Press.

Eibl-Eibesfeldt, I. (1989). *Human Ethology*. New York: Aldine de Gruyter.

Erikson, E.H. (1950). *Childhood and society*. New York: N.W. Norton.

Fisher, C.B., & Lerner, R.M. (Eds.). (1994). *Applied developmental psychology*. New York: McGraw-Hill.

Fisher, C.B., Murray, J.P., Dill, J.R., Hagen, J.W., Hogan, M.J., Lerner, R.M., Rebok, G.W., Sigel, I., Sostek, A.M., Smyer, M.A., Spencer, M.B., & Wilcox, B. (1993). The National Conference on Graduate Education in the Applications of Developmental Science Across the Lifespan. *Journal of Applied Developmental Psychology, 14,* 1–10.

Fisher, C.B., & Tryon, W.W. (Eds.). (1990). *Ethics in applied developmental psychology: Emerging issues in an emerging field*. Norwood, NJ: Ablex.

Garfinkel, H. (1967). *Studies in ethnomethodology*. Englewood Cliffs, NJ: Prentice Hall.

Gergen, K.J. (1990). Social understanding and the inscription of self. In J.W. Stigler, R.A. Shweder, & G. Herdt (Eds.). *Cultural psychology: Essays on comparative human development* (pp. 569–606). New York: Cambridge University Press.

Glick, J. (1978). Cognition and social cognition: An introduction. In J. Glick & K.A. Clarke-Stewart (Eds.). *The development of social understanding* (pp. 1–9). New York: Gardner Press.

Goodnow, J.J. (1988). Parents' ideas, actions, and feelings: Models and methods from developmental and social psychology. *Child Development, 59,* 289–320.

Greenfield, P.M., & Cocking, R.R. (Eds.). (1994). *Cross-cultural roots of minority child development*. Hillsdale, NJ: Erlbaum.

Kluckhohn, C., & Murray, H.A. (Eds.). (1949). *Personality in nature, society, and culture*. New York: Alfred A. Knopf.
Le Vine, R.A. (1973). *Culture, behavior, and personality*. Chicago: Aldine.
McGoldrick, M. (1982). Ethnicity and family therapy: An overview. In M. McGoldrick, J.K. Pearce, & J. Giordano (Eds.). *Ethnicity and family therapy* (pp. 3–30). New York: Guilford Press.
Mead, M. (1949). *Male and female*. New York: William Morrow.
Mindel, C.H., Habenstein, R.W., & Wright, R., Jr. (1988). Family lifestyles of America's ethnic minorities: An introduction. In C.H. Mindel, R.W. Habenstein, & R. Wright, Jr. (Eds.). *Ethnic families in American: Patterns and variations* (3rd ed., pp. 1–14). New York: Elsevier.
Ogbu, J.U. (1994). From cultural differences to differences in cultural frame of reference. In P.M. Greenfield & R.R. Cocking (Eds.), *Cross-cultural roots of minority child development* (pp. 365–391). Hillsdale, NJ: Erlbaum.
Pepper, S.C. (1970). *World hypotheses: A study in evidence*. Berkeley, CA: University of California Press.
Persico, C.F. (1990). Creating an institutional climate that honors diversity. In G. Stricker, E. Davis-Russell, E. Bourg, E. Duran, W.R. Hammond, J. McHolland, K. Polite, & B.E. Vaughn (Eds.), *Toward ethnic diversification in psychology education and training* (pp. 55–63). Washington, DC: American Psychological Association.
Piaget, J. (1952). *The language and thought of the child*. Routledge & Kegan Paul.
Quinn, N., & Holland, D. (1993). Culture and cognition. In D. Holland & N. Quinn (Eds.). *Cultural models in language and thought* (pp. 3–40). New York: Cambridge University Press.
Ramírez, M., III., & Castañeda, A. (1974). *Cultural democracy, bicognitive development, and education*. New York: Academic Press.
Rogoff, B. (1990). *Apprenticeship in thinking*. New York: Oxford University Press.
Rommetveit, R. (1979). On the architecture of intersubjectivity. In R. Rommetveit, & R.M. Blaker (Eds.). *Studies in language, thought, and verbal communication*. London: Academic Press.
Sameroff, A.J., & Fiese, B.H. (1992). Family representations of development. In I.E. Sigel, A.V. McGillicuddy-DeLisi, & J.J. Goodnow (Eds.) *Parental belief systems: The psychological consequences for children* (2nd ed., pp. 347–369). Hillsdale, NJ: Erlbaum.
Schank, R.C., & Abelson, R.P. (1977). *Scripts, plans, goals, and understanding: An inquiry into human knowledge structures*. Hillsdale, NJ: Erlbaum.
Shweder, R.A. (1990). Cultural psychology—What is it? In J.W. Stigler, R.A. Shweder, & G. Herdt, (Eds.). *Cultural psychology: Essays on comparative human development* (pp. 1–43). New York: Cambridge University Press.
Shibutani, T., & Kwan, K.M. (1965). *Ethnic stratification*. New York: Macmillan.
Sigel, I.E. (1993). The Centrality of a distancing model for the development of representational competence. In R.R. Cocking & K.A. Renninger (Eds.), *The development and meaning of psychological distance* (pp. 141–158). Hillsdale, NJ: Erlbaum.

Stigler, J.W., Shweder, R.A., & Herdt, G. (Eds.). (1990). *Cultural psychology: Essays on comparative human development.* New York: Cambridge University Press.
Swartz, M.J., & Jordan, D.K. (1976). *Anthropology: Perspective on humanity.* New York: Wiley.
Troy, W.G. (1990). Ethnic and cultural diversity and the professional psychology training curriculum. In G. Stricker, E. Davis-Russell, E. Bourg, E. Duran, W.R. Hammond, J. McHolland, K. Polite, & B.E. Vaughn (Eds.), *Toward ethnic diversification in psychology education and training* (pp. 179–187). Washington, DC: American Psychological Association.
Wertsch, J.V. (1985). *Vygotsky and the social formation of mind.* Cambridge, MA: Harvard University Press.
Wertsch, J.V. (1991). *Voices of the mind: A sociocultural approach to mediated action.* Cambridge, MA: Harvard University Press.
West, C. (1993). *Race matters.* Boston, MA: Beacon Press.
Whiting, H.W.M. (Ed.). (1963). *Six cultures: Studies of child rearing.* New York: Wiley.
Whiting, H.W.M., & Child, J.L. (1953). *Child training and personality.* New Haven, CT: Yale University Press.

ACKNOWLEDGMENT

Thanks to Rodney R. Cocking, Celia B. Fisher, Jacqueline Jones, Claire Kopp, and Brian Smedley for their challenging comments, some of which I could deal with and others that still remain controversial. Of course, the final decisions and responsibility for the views expressed are mine. My gratitude to Linda Kozelski for her careful work in preparing this manuscript.

11
Field Experiences in Applied Developmental Science

George W. Rebok
The Johns Hopkins University

Anita Miller Sostek
National Institutes of Health

Field experiences are among the core areas of education training in the conceptual model recommended for graduate programs in applied developmental science (ADS). As reported in the Conference Proceedings of the National Conference on Graduate Education in the Applications of Developmental Science Across the Lifespan (Fisher et al., 1993), the goals of the field experience component of applied developmental graduate education are threefold: (a) to extend students' skills and understanding of development in context; (b) to address issues of societal import; and (c) to focus on the application of developmental science in a broad variety of community settings. Although more traditional (i.e., less applied) developmental graduate programs occasionally offer field experience credit, the presence of a formal field component is the central feature that distinguishes applied developmental graduate programs from those offering more traditional developmental graduate training.

This chapter focuses on the major goals of the field experiential component in applied developmental science graduate training programs and the specific ways in which field experiences can be structured to achieve those goals. Examples of the types and ranges of field experiences available to applied developmental graduate students and how those experiences are monitored and evaluated by faculty members and on-site field supervisors are discussed. We also consider issues raised by the integration of the academic components of applied developmental science training programs with applied practice in the field. These include discussion of the similarities and differences between applied developmental field experiences and traditional clinical psychology placements, the roles of research and evaluation as core components of the field experience, and the specific types of expertise required for faculty and on-site supervisors of students in the field.

The more we thought about applied developmental science graduate training, the more we realized that we, in fact, did not know what is currently offered to students or what is expected of them. To gain a reasonably informed idea, we conducted a survey at the National Conference on Graduate Education in the Applications of Developmental Science Across the Lifespan (Fisher et al., 1993). The conference was organized by the National Task Force on Applied Developmental Science, and included representatives from several professional organizations whose members work in applied developmental science. These organizations ranged in interest from the International Society for Infant Studies to the Gerontological Society of America. The delegates came from universities, research institutes, the Educational Testing Service, the National Institutes of Health, the Red Cross, municipal governments, and the American Psychological Association. Survey data from applied developmental science graduate training programs within different developmental disciplines are presented in this chapter to illustrate key points.

TYPES AND RANGES OF FIELD EXPERIENCES IN APPLIED DEVELOPMENTAL SCIENCE

Prerequisite preparation for field experience work consists of: specialized didactic training in applied developmental science (Fisher et al., 1993; Fisher, Rau, & Colapietro, 1993; Chapters 4–9, this volume); knowledge of the populations, settings, and activities that will be encountered during the field experience; and a clear commitment to the professional, ethical, and legal principles of one's discipline. Field experiences in applied developmental science encompass a diverse array of neighborhood and community settings, such as:

Field Experiences in Applied Developmental Science 223

- families (e.g., home visits for assessment and parent education)
- schools and other educational institutions
- child development centers (e.g., daycare centers, developmental disability centers)
- departments of human service (e.g., child protection agencies)
- social welfare agencies (e.g., homeless shelters)
- correctional facilities (e.g., juvenile detention centers)
- senior centers and nursing homes (including adult care services)
- group homes for the developmentally disabled
- health facilities (e.g., intensive care nursing, pediatric units, chronic care)
- marriage and family therapy clinics
- policymaking units
- governmental agencies
- private corporations

These sites should provide ample opportunity for applied developmental students to participate in research, evaluation, assessment, service delivery, and policy development. Such participation includes experience with translating research knowledge and methodologies into practical application and application into research. An important area for students to pursue in this regard involves the relationship between evolving developmental processes and intervention efforts (Cicchetti & Toth, 1992; Kellam & Rebok, 1992). In particular, developmentally guided preventive interventions, when done in clearly defined community populations, may serve as means for testing developmental theory (Kellam & Rebok, 1992). Conversely, the design of intervention efforts can be based on our knowledge of normative and atypical developmental processes. Students working in the field should have the opportunity to help develop and conduct interventions based on relevant research findings, to apply the results to devise new interventions, and to study the policy implications of implementing the interventions in various community contexts. For example, students may draw on the developmental research literature on normal and atypical cognitive changes in later life to devise an intervention program for improving the mental health of elderly adults, and, if successful, explore the feasibility of implementing the program at a local retirement community.

Field placement sites also should provide a context in which applied developmental students can obtain intracultural, cross-cultural, cross-language, and intergenerational experiences. These experiences might include working with ethnic minority children in an urban school setting, minority teens or adults in an ethnic community center, frail elderly in multigenerational families, or impoverished migrant farmers in a rural environment. Such experiences should involve not only the technical application of developmental knowledge but also the development of competencies to work with diverse groups of community agencies, organizations, and individuals to design alternative developmental services and interventions for children and adults with very different needs, and families with different orientations, expectations, and interests. Such competence requires knowledge of the local community and the needs of the residents of that community, as well as agencies that provide these services.

Encouraging sensitivity to multicultural diversity is reflected in many of the National Conference recommendations, including those dealing with field placements (Fisher et al., 1993, Chapter 11). Cultural diversity is recognized as an important aspect of applied developmental science graduate education in a multicultural world. Diversity here is not limited to ethnic diversity, but also includes religious orientation, age, gender, sexual preference, and lifestyle. Applied developmental science graduate programs are encouraged to emphasize cultural diversity in formal courses and field work. Such an emphasis is a key aspect of applied developmental training since one cannot assume that the general rules of development and human behavior apply in the same way to all individuals and families (Lerner & Fisher, 1994). Diagnosis and treatment intervention information that is acceptable to one group may not be acceptable to another. In some cultures, for example, an overweight baby is considered healthy and strong, while other cultures may see the baby as at risk for health problems, obesity, and slow motor development. Clearly, the acceptability of diet recommendations would vary between such cultures. Similarly, cultural expectations differ regarding activity level, verbal facility, gross versus fine motor skills, etc., and these expectations are often influenced, to varying degrees, by the sex of the child.

Field placements can offer an opportunity to expose applied developmental students to budgetary and management decision making in relation to research and applied practice. For example, policy choices regarding interventions in the field are made from a variety of perspectives, one of which is economics (Barnett & Escobar, 1990; Vinokur, van Ryn, Gramlich, & Price, 1991). Knowledge of the principles of cost analysis, the costs of different intervention programs, and the ways that cost-benefit ratios affect public policy are important aspects of applied developmental training.

Out of the field experience, applied developmental students can obtain a breadth of practical experience that complements the substantive and scientific research expertise they gain through formal didactic instruction. From the field experience, students should develop an understanding of, and an appreciation for, individual, familial, and cultural differences in human development across the lifespan. They also should gain a broader perspective on the budgetary and managerial decisions that affect the implementation of programs and policy in the real world environment.

Multidisciplinary Collaborative Field Experience

Applied developmental scientists frequently work with professionals from other scientific fields who may have different disciplinary orientations. The range of other disciplines varies by different field placement sites and may include, among others, medical, educational, developmental, social work, correctional, anthropological, and/or counseling professionals. The provision of field experiences involving functioning as a member of a multidisciplinary collaborative team is considered an essential component of applied developmental graduate training for a number of reasons (Fisher et al., 1993). First, working with professionals from other disciplines helps one appreciate the limitations of any discipline's theory and methods. Only by viewing one's own disciplinary perspective in the context of a multidisciplinary knowledge base, will the applied developmental scientist be able to successfully address issues of societal import (Lerner & Fisher, 1994). Unidisciplinary approaches to complex societal problems such as AIDS, poverty, teen pregnancy, homelessness, health care delivery, and aging are unlikely to be effective.

Second, multidisciplinary involvement with other professionals helps promote integrations in the developmental science knowledge base that are not possible in the confines of one's own discipline (Baltes, 1987). This involvement goes beyond a mere recognition of the limitations of one's own discipline and the strengths of other disciplines. Rather, the emphasis is on how knowledge from diverse disciplines can be integrated to produce a richer, more differentiated view of the continually changing person–context interactions that form the base of human development across the lifespan.

There is another aspect of multidisciplinary collaboration that needs to be emphasized in regard to applied developmental field experiences. Just as it has become clear that no single discipline can provide all the answers to complex social problems, it is equally clear that the problems addressed by applied developmental scientists do not cluster neatly across cultures, communities, and neighborhoods (Lerner & Fisher, 1994). Rather, as mentioned above, the problems tend to vary, quantitatively and qualitatively, by specific geographical locale, socioeconomic stratum, age level, and religious and ethnic background. In order to attain expertise to address these nested problems, applied developmental scientists must be able to collaborate as members of community teams to address issues of mutual interest (Lerner & Fisher, 1994; Rebok et al., 1991). For example, in a series of classroom based preventive intervention trials in Baltimore, it has been possible to develop and implement multiple methods of developmental assessment and randomly assign children to intervention and control classrooms by building strong collaborative partnerships with public school administrators, principals, teachers, and parents (Rebok et al., 1991).

Survey of Applied Developmental Programs

The exact nature, duration, and sequencing of developmental field experiences will vary by the background, interests, and level of the student, type of graduate education program, and needs of the field. An informal survey conducted prior to the National Conference revealed a diversity of settings and formats for developmental field experiences. The survey (see Appendix) was administered to the approximately 50 participants of the conference, and 33 responded (no information was available to compare the participants who did not respond because identification of the respondent was optional). Nine conferees found it not applicable because they were in administrative positions or nontraining settings. Of the remaining 24, half of the respondents were in applied developmental programs that required field experiences and half were in programs that did not. Of those that did not require placements, seven "encouraged" field experiences, one left it up to the advisor, and one did not offer placements. The departments that were represented are listed in Table 11-1. Most programs found that 75 to 80 percent of the trainees took advantage of field experiences. The duration of the field placements varied, and programs offered one to three placements for each student. Typical durations were one to three semesters, eight to ten hours per week, or "enough for research." In nine cases, the field experience was research based, and in seven it was not. For the remaining programs, some trainees have research experiences while some do not.

According to the survey, academic prerequisites for field placements are the standard, with one year of coursework being typical. The nature and duration of the field experience may vary with the educational background and career goals of the trainee. For example, masters level students typ-

TABLE 11.1
Program Affiliation of Participants at the National Conference on Applied Developmental Science (ADS) Responding to a Survey on Field Experience in ADS

Department	Number*
Human development or family studies	12
Psychology	8
School psychology or education	4
Psychiatry/mental health	2
Mental retardation center	1
Pediatrics	1

*The total is greater than the number of respondents (N = 24) because some are in joint departments.

ically have brief, less specialized practical experiences lasting for a single semester. Doctoral level experiences are typically more focused and may involve placement at one or more agencies for a minimum of two semesters, with some didactic or discussion group held at the university.

Typical field placements involve developing, implementing, and evaluating programs in a wide range of settings, populations, and developmental activities. In addition to the more common placements in developmental disability or child care centers, schools, nursing homes, etc., student field experiences included parent education programs for teenage mothers, conducting psychoeducational assessments and tutoring of institutionalized children awaiting placement, conducting infant/child sexual abuse assessment, and working in a weight control and eating disorders clinic. Other placements involved working with a congressional staff person on policy issues related to aging, working in a migrant worker health clinic, providing services in a children of Vietnam veterans counseling center, and providing financial counseling for welfare families.

Some applied developmental science training programs use a rotational model to maximize exposure to different experiences and contexts, whereas others favor an in depth, long-term model to provide greater specialization. Choice of model depends, in part, on the student's prior experience in developmental science. Students with greater knowledge of the theory, content, and methods of developmental science may benefit from a long-term model, whereas those with less experience may benefit from an appropriately sequenced, rotational exposure.

EVALUATION AND QUALITY CONTROL

Each graduate program offering applied developmental science training needs to ensure that students receive an appropriate, supervised field experience. The quality of the field experience demands that each placement agency demonstrate a clear commitment to providing appropriate on-site supervision that supports the academic and applied goals of the training and an awareness of the legal, political, and ethical issues that arise in the field setting. The survey data cited above indicated that supervision was provided by both the academic and on-site advisor in three quarters of the programs, and by the academic or on-site advisors only in three cases each.

Criteria for Field Placement Supervisors

There is a need to be creative with students and field sites in establishing criteria for field placement supervisors. On-site supervisors should have an appropriate educational background, administrative skills, and sensitivity to the special purposes and demands of applied developmental science. Questions that need to be considered include: Do on-site supervisors need to hold a doctoral degree or have a certain administrative status? Do they need to be trained as professional psychologists? How much developmental training or science-service background are required to supervise an applied developmental field experience? Because of the nature of the applied developmental field experience, there may need to be greater interaction between day to day supervisors and academic advisors than is traditional in clinical psychology and counseling education.

In many cases in applied developmental field experiences, the on-site staff member may not be a science-based professional (e.g., social worker, nonsocial science administrator). This raises many challenges for the student and faculty member, in that administrators at a social agency may not view program evaluation in the same way an applied developmental scientist would. Some administrators might be threatened by formal evaluation, that, if negative, might have implications for funding. If academic faculty provide the "scientific" component of the field experience in many social service agencies, what does the on-site supervisor provide? It has been our experience that the administrator or supervisor's contribution can often best be understood and utilized in terms of exposing students to institutional, administrative, and policy issues, as well as to the problems practitioners and the population they serve face in real-world settings.

Although the day to day supervision of the field experience is more likely be carried out by professionals at the training site, final evaluation of the experience is usually carried out by the student's academic advisor. Thus, the qualifications of the academic advisor also are an important consideration. All faculty who supervise a field experience in applied developmental science or who teach developmental courses specific to the application of developmental knowledge in the field, should have completed appropriate training in their discipline and be actively engaged in, and knowledgeable about, developmental research. They should also be knowledgeable about the ethical, institutional, and policy issues that arise in applied developmental work.

Formulating a Field Experience Work Plan

Field experience supervisors are expected to work with applied developmental trainees in formulating a clearly defined work plan with explicit goals and action steps. Although the specific details of individual work plans may vary, most should include a statement of how developmental theory and application are to be integrated, a description of the setting(s) and population(s) in which the field activity will be carried out, and a description of the research methods and approaches that will be applied to study normative and atypical developmental changes. The plan also should specify the time configuration for the experience and the evaluation procedures that will be followed.

Developmental field placements are arranged in a variety of ways. Most are designed around the student's interests and needs. In some programs, lists of possible field experiences are available and the field sites are often prescreened. It is typical for field placements to be negotiated on an ad hoc basis, and they are often based on faculty connections with other programs and professionals in the field. Specific curricula are most likely to be developed jointly by the academic as well as the field advisor, although in some cases the curriculum may be developed by one or the other alone. However, it is generally agreed that the responsibility for specifying the content of the curriculum rests with the faculty advisor, not any external body (Bickman, 1987). Again, our survey data revealed a variety of different practices. Some programs attempt to integrate the content with a research experience, and some have particular coursework specified for the field placement. Multicultural exposure is considered by two-thirds of the programs we surveyed. Exposure to different cultures prepares the trainee for working in a variety of settings, developing sensitivity to different cultural issues, and dealing with issues around the use of assessment and treatment procedures that may be primarily designed for the dominant culture. Often, future opportunities for employment and research support depend on the ability to function in multicultural settings.

Types of Evaluation Procedures

Our survey results revealed that evaluation of the field experience can take different forms as well. A joint evaluation by both the academic and on-site supervisor is most common. In a few cases, only one or the other advisor does the evaluation. Our survey indicated that on-site supervisors only evaluate field placements in a minority of cases. Often a paper with or without field notes is required to describe the experience. Some programs have specific evaluation forms, some are quite informal in their evaluation, and a few perform no evaluation at all.

There was great concern among participants at the National Conference about the quality of the field experience in applied developmental science programs and the need for formal evaluation. According to their recommendations, evaluation should include ongoing, final, and follow-up assessments. On-going evaluations monitor the implementation of the field experience work plan. Such evaluations may involve a reciprocal and ongoing evaluation process that includes evaluation of trainees by an academic advisor and/or a field supervisor as well as an evaluation of the field experience site by all parties. Final evaluations consider the extent to which students have achieved the overall goals of the work plan, including the implementation of specific knowledge domains in applied developmental science and the exposure to broader issues germane to the application of developmental theory in context. Follow-up evaluations rest on a retrospective evaluation of the extent to which the field experience contributed to career development. Of particular interest here is the extent that the field experience imparted competencies and skills leading to a professional position in the applied developmental field.

INTEGRATING APPLIED EXPERIENCES WITH ACADEMIC TRAINING

There was a strong consensus at the National Conference that supported the integration of the applied developmental science field experience with academic training. It was not as clear whether a standard core curriculum for the field experience should exist or whether each program should formulate its own core content and goals. As discussed in Chapter 1, applied developmental science has a shared content and curriculum, but the non-shared elements of each program also must be respected.

The integration of the academic components of graduate education in developmental science with applied experiences in the field raises several important questions for discussion. Each of these is discussed in detail below.

How are Applied Developmental Field Experiences Similar to and Different from Traditional Clinical Placements?

Similar to applied developmental field placements, clinical practicum/externship placements: encompass a diverse array of settings; emphasize the need for ongoing liaison with placement agencies for monitoring student progress; insure the placement agencies' ability to participate meaningfully in the educational process; and stress the integration of theory and practice (Report of the Joint Council on Professional Education in Psychology, 1990).

A major difference between the two placements is that clinical field placements are more intensive and more highly structured. The practicum/externship experience includes a minimum number of 600 hours of supervised practice (including supervision and didactic experience), extends over at least two academic years, provides students stipends and professional liability insurance coverage (where feasible), and includes an on-campus seminar where students learn from each other by sharing and discussing field experience (Report of the Joint Council on Professional Education in Psychology, 1990).

To what extent applied developmental field placements should adopt such standards is an open question (Fisher et al., 1993). As indicated by our survey of Conference participants, most developmental field placements last less than one year and involve far fewer than the 600 hours recommended for clinical practica/externships. It also seems the case that much of developmental field work is unpaid and liability insurance is not provided. Some applied developmental programs do offer on-campus seminars for field placement students (see Chapter 4 for an example of an applied developmental psychology program offering both formal seminars and liability insurance). We strongly encourage all programs to develop such seminars as a means of students exchanging field experiences and learning from other students in the program.

Can Applied Developmental Students do an APA-Accredited Internship?

Prerequisite preparation for the internship consists of the didactic, practicum/externship, and research based experiences obtained in a doctoral program that trains professional psychologists (Report of the Joint Council on Professional Education in Psychology, 1990). Internship training is viewed as a necessary part of professional education for psychologists. In addition to psychologists who provide direct services, those who administer, supervise, teach, or carry out research related to practice should have completed an internship (Report of the Joint Council on Professional Education in Psychology, 1990). By these criteria students in applied developmental psychology programs may need an internship.

The question then becomes—Do applied developmental students need the same type of internship as clinical psychology students? Internships consist of one year full-time experience or two years of half-time experience (Report of the Joint Council on Professional Education in Psychology, 1990), and are usually situated in medical or health care settings that can fund students through third-party payments and government support (Fisher & Koocher, 1990). For applied developmental students, there is less need to serve an internship in a setting where professional psychological services are offered. A more appropriate internship might involve learning developmental assessment, program design and evaluation, and public policy application in community based settings such as schools, daycare programs, or senior citizens centers (Fisher & Koocher, 1990, Chapter 4). It has been recommended that clinical internship programs have at least three internship positions available and provide opportunities for interaction among interns to facilitate professional socialization (Report of the Joint Council on

Professional Education in Psychology, 1990). Because this recommendation is meant to ensure a more formalized training experience, it is applicable to applied developmental programs as well.

In evaluating the quality of applied developmental internship experiences, there is a need to go beyond the current level of American Psychological Association (APA) accreditation (see Fisher & Koocher, 1990; Fisher, Rau, & Colapietro, 1993; Chapter 4, for a fuller discussion of accreditation and credentialing in applied developmental science education). There appears to be a need to support the development of new evaluation procedures since the mechanisms for ensuring quality are different in applied developmental programs. It is important to emphasize that accreditation is just one type of quality measure.

Should the Field Experience Entail a Research/Evaluative Component?

A research/evaluative component in field experiences is a defining element of applied developmental science, distinguishing it from practice. As discussed earlier, only about half of the applied developmental programs we surveyed had a research/evaluative requirement as part of the field experience. Although it is unlikely that every field placement will emphasize research to the same extent, graduate education and training in applied developmental science should provide opportunities for research in the area of applied emphasis. This could take the form of applying theory and research findings on early cognitive development to assessments of children with learning disabilities, developing evaluation and feedback procedures for a communication skills program in a nursing home, or conducting formal statistical analyses of the impact of a family education program on parent–child interactions.

Is There a Need in the Field for Uniformity in Applied Developmental Field Experiences?

Applied developmental graduate students should be provided choices of the types of field experiences available. Although this range may be limited by particular program goals or emphases, the range should be broad enough to encompass diverse student interests and goals. Having students doing several different types of field placements and sharing common experience in a seminar is one way to provide breadth while allowing diversity. Another way is to permit two or more students to do a field placement together at the same site. This may or may not be feasible depending on the availability of placement opportunities and how receptive the particular field site is to the idea. Shared experience is seen as valuable from a training standpoint because it fosters professional socialization and provides an interpersonal support structure. It is recommended that students in applied developmental programs be allowed to share a field placement where feasible. The emphases of each student may differ within the field placement, and opportunities to discuss the experience from different perspectives could be valuable.

SUMMARY

The task force working on the field experience component of the recommendations (Task Force III) realized early in its discussions that the National Conference was not the final step in answering questions about the nature of field work, but rather was one of the first steps. Answering the questions discussed earlier will be an important next step in the evolution of the recommendations made at the National Conference and in structuring applied developmental science graduate education and training. To that end, dissemination of the Conference recommendations to various sources should stimulate debate and provide feedback for further discussion. Systematic national surveys of applied developmental science graduate programs also should provide us with better information on how field experiences are planned and implemented across diverse educational settings.

In summary, the National Conference on Graduate Education in the Applications of Developmental Science Across the Lifespan strongly supported the integration of the academic components of graduate education in applied developmental science with the field experience (Fisher et al., 1993). Each field experience should provide exposure to a broad range of real-world issues and institutions that builds on the applied developmental science curriculum. The overall goal is to have a breadth in practical experience that is matched by a depth in scientific knowledge and expertise. This combination will provide students with the practical and scientific experience necessary to study development in context and to scientifically address issues of societal import.

REFERENCES

Baltes, P.B. (1987). Theoretical propositions of lifespan developmental psychology: On the dynamics between growth and decline. *Developmental Psychology, 23*, 611–626.

Barnett, W.S., & Escobar, C.M. (1990). Economic costs and benefits of early intervention. In S.J. Meisels & J.P. Shonkoff (Eds.), *Handbook of early childhood intervention* (pp. 560–582). New York: Cambridge University Press.

Bickman, L. (1987). Graduate education in psychology. *American Psychologist, 42,* 1041–1047.
Cicchetti, D., & Toth, S.L. (1992). The role of developmental theory in prevention and intervention. *Development and Psychopathology, 4,* 489–493.
Fisher, C.B., & Koocher, G.P. (1990). To be or not to be? Accreditation, credentialing, and applied developmental psychology. *Journal of Applied Developmental Psychology, 11,* 381–394.
Fisher, C.B., Murray, J.P., Dill, J.R., Hagen, J.W., Hogan, M.J., Lerner, R.M., Rebok, G.W., Sigel, I., Sostek, A.M., Smyer, M.A., Spencer, M.B., & Wilcox, B. (1993). The National Conference on Graduate Education in the Applications of Developmental Science Across the Lifespan. *Journal of Applied Developmental Psychology, 14,* 1–10.
Fisher, C.B., Rau, J.B., & Colapietro, E. (1993). The Fordham University doctoral specialization in applied developmental psychology. *Journal of Applied Developmental Psychology, 14,* 289–302.
Kellam, S.G., & Rebok, G.W. (1992). Building developmental and etiological theory through epidemiologically based preventive intervention trials. In J. McCord & R.E. Tremblay (Eds.), *Preventing antisocial behavior: Interventions from birth through adolescence* (pp. 162–195). New York: Guilford Press.
Lerner, R.M., & Fisher, C.B. (1994). From applied developmental psychology to applied developmental science: Community coalitions and collaborative careers. In C.B. Fisher & R.M. Lerner (Eds.), *Applied developmental psychology* (pp. 505–522). New York: McGraw-Hill, Inc.
Rebok, G.W., Kellam, S.G., Dolan, L.J., Werthamer-Larsson, L., Edwards, E.J., Mayer, L.S., & Brown, C.H. (1991). The Johns Hopkins Prevention Center on early risk behaviors: Process issues and problem areas in prevention research. *Community Psychologist, 24,* 18–21.
Report of the Joint Council on Professional Education in Psychology (1990). The Joint Council on Professional Education in Psychology: Baton Rouge: Land and Land Printers, Inc.
Vinokur, A.D., van Ryn, M., Gramlich, E.M., & Price, R.H. (1991). Long-term follow-up and benefit–cost analysis of the Jobs Program: A preventive intervention for the unemployed. *Journal of Applied Psychology, 76,* 213–219.

ACKNOWLEDGEMENTS

We would like to thank Dr. Lynn R. Offermann for her helpful comments on an earlier version of this chapter.

Appendix

APPLIED DEVELOPMENTAL TRAINING SURVEY

This survey concerns how field experience is offered and handled at various institutions. The information will be compiled and used to organize Task Force III's discussion at the Applied Developmental Science meetings in New York on October 10–12, 1991. We appreciate your cooperation in filling it out and returning it promptly.

1. Does your program offer field experience credit?
    yes _____ no _____
If field experience is not part of your current professional situation, please check here and return _____.

2. Describe typical field placements in your program. For each, please outline the populations served, the type of activities and settings, for example, developing intervention programs for the elderly in nursing homes. _____
_____
_____

3. Are field experiences required? yes _____ no _____
If not, what percentage of the trainees elect to participate in them? _____
If required, what number of experiences or what duration of field placements is expected? _____
_____
_____

4. Who supervises the field experiences? Is supervision off the field site, on-site, or both? _____

5. a. What education background is required prior to beginning field experiences, for example, so many graduate credits, a master's degree, etc.? _____

b. What is the average duration of field experiences at different educational levels?
_____

6. Are the field experiences research based? yes _____ no _____

7. How are field placements arranged? Are placements prescreened by your program or arranged by the trainee? Is a list of approved placements available? ____
_____

8. Is cross-cultural or multicultural exposure considered in the field placements? yes _____ no _____

9. Are curricula developed on-site or by the academic advisor? How are field curricula integrated with academic work? _____
_____

10. How are field experiences evaluated? _____
_____

11. Your name (optional) _____
12. Type of department, for example, psychology, human development, family relations, etc. _____

12

Building Successful University–Community Human Service Agency Collaborations

Christina J. Groark
Robert B. McCall[1]

University of Pittsburgh

Applied developmental scholars are very likely to need to collaborate with community agencies "to understand and promote development in individuals and families" and "to evaluate the human and economic cost and benefits of intervention programs designed to optimize development . . ." (Fisher et al., 1993, p. 1). Such study and education must be conducted, in part, in real-world contexts, such as "families, schools, child development centers, departments of human service, social welfare agencies, correctional facilities, senior centers, health facilities, the media, policymaking units, governmental agencies, and private corporations" (Fisher et al., 1993, p. 7). Activities might include research, program evaluation, and field place-

---

[1]This paper supported in part by a grant from The Howard Heinz Endowment to the University of Pittsburgh Office of Child Development and by Grant No. 252A20082 to the junior author from the U.S. Department of Education's Urban Communities Services Program.

ments, as well as serving as consultants and on advisory boards. The need for scientists and students to collaborate with such service agencies is especially acute for scholars who are trained in disciplines, departments, or programs that emphasize research skills and basic scientific knowledge at the relative exclusion of applied content and settings, particularly human service agencies.

Such university–community collaborations not only help to provide an important context for applied developmental training and research, they also can contribute directly to the welfare of children, youth, and families. The total of federal and state dollars for services to children and families is far greater than the amount available for research. Currently, at least two themes dominate requests for funding of demonstration service programs: a) *Comprehensiveness,* that usually means case-managed collaboration among agencies providing services for different needs and problems; b) *Accountability,* which usually means program evaluation. For example, several federally funded, multisited, comprehensive intervention projects with substantial evaluations have recently been implemented, including the Comprehensive Child Development Program of the Administration for Children, Youth, and Families and the Infant Health and Development Program of the Center for Disease Control. These, and countless other smaller programs, require collaboration among academics and service professionals for the purpose of developing, assessing, and improving preventive and remedial services for children, youth, and families. Therefore, much is to be gained if these university–community collaborations operate smoothly and productively.

But such a smoothly operating and productive collaboration is by no means assured, especially when it involves professionals trained in different disciplines with different methods and values and who have different professional purposes and standards of performance. Collaborations require talented and competent contributors who work together with mutual trust and respect toward a common goal (Friend & Cook, 1992; Vandercook, York, & Sullivan, 1993), sacrificing, in the process, considerable independence, personal control, and personal recognition. These requirements are often antithetical to the way we train researchers, for example, who typically are taught to work independently, to maintain control over every aspect of the research enterprise, and to achieve within a profession that rewards individual productivity and contribution. The service professions are often not ideally suited for collaborations either, especially collaborations with researchers, because the primary responsibility of a service provider is to provide services, not to generate data for a researcher. If the research consists of a program evaluation, the outcome of the research may constitute the financial life or death of the program or agency and the job of the service professional, not simply a publication on a vita.

What follows, then, is an outline of the typical barriers to successful university–community human service agency collaborations and some guidelines on how to overcome them. This is primarily aimed at students and academics about to embark on a university–community collaboration (see also Friend & Cook, 1992; Mattessich & Monsey, 1992; Vandercook et al., 1993). For convenience, we have lumped researchers together on the one hand and service professionals on the other. We acknowledge that our generalities about these two groups are overdrawn, and notable exceptions exist within each. As Mordock (1993) has cogently pointed out, for example, some service professionals have a better grasp of research literatures and relevant methodologies than many researchers, especially those service professionals likely to be reading this chapter. Also, these thoughts derive from our experience as an administrator of professional service (CJG) and as a researcher (RBM), not from objectively collected data on representative samples, and we ask the reader to share our recognition of the limitations of this approach.

Barriers to Successful Collaborations

Attitudes

One of the biggest problems in this type of collaboration can be the attitudes about each other that the two parties bring to the joint enterprise. For example, some researchers view themselves as being substantially more knowledgeable than service providers about the problem and its treatment, and this attitude may be perceived as arrogance by service professionals.

Actually, researchers and service professionals are often knowledgeable about different things. While the researcher may have broad-based research knowledge about a problem in general (e.g., drug addiction, intelligence), the service professional is likely to know more about the particular problems of the clients served by that agency, types of services and approaches that are feasible and those that are not, and ways of dealing with the legal, policy, and political constraints of the "system" (Groark & McCall, 1993). Of course, both types of knowledge are likely needed for a successful project.

For their part, service professionals may display an attitude of distrust toward researchers. Some believe, for example, that researchers are exceedingly self-centered, interested in a collaboration almost exclusively for their personal professional gain (e.g., publications), not very knowledgeable about applied issues and applied research, and likely to give the agency little in return for its cooperation (e.g., Mordock, 1993). Sometimes these attitudes are based on actual experience or the experience of a colleague, but these views can also be rooted in stereotype and rank prejudice. Ironically, a few service professionals can be just as self-centered, but in other ways. Some, for example, simply want to maintain rigid personal control over the activities of the agency, the staff, and the clients, even at the expense of best practices and innovations.

Groark and McCall (1993) have written about the problems created by these attitudes of superiority and distrust (see also Mordock, 1993), that can be especially acute when the researcher's purpose is to evaluate the process and outcome of the agency's service program. Most professionals of any type would prefer not to be evaluated, directly or indirectly, by others, especially those they do not trust. The tension is exacerbated if the evaluation is imposed on the service agency by a funder, especially if the evaluation is initiated long after the program is up and running, which establishes a "we/they," rather than an "us," type of relationship. Also, some funders and program evaluators display an attitude that reveals that the evaluation constitutes a "report card" on the program, rather than adopting the more cooperative purpose of contributing to program development and improvement.

Typically, these divergent attitudes reflect different values, purposes, and reward structures for these two professional groups. Substantial progress can be made if both parties view themselves as bringing complementary and necessary knowledge and skills to a partnership that is a sincere collaboration with mutual responsibilities, benefits, and respect aimed at a common goal of improving the services. The purpose of program evaluation, for example, is not to produce a report card on the services delivered, but to contribute to program development and more effective services. Ideally, both parties should have their interests served by the collaboration.

Purposes

The purpose of most agencies is to improve the welfare of a client group by delivering certain services and obtaining and maintaining the funding necessary to do so. This is a serious business, sometimes literally life and death for both clients and agency. The case loads and psychological demand on personnel are often high, and the salaries and gratitude of clients and society are typically low. In contrast, a few service professionals perceive most research to be irrelevant and self-serving (Mordock, 1993), the researcher is not likely to lose his or her job if the project does not go well, and the academic is probably better paid but with less apparent social responsibility. Occasionally, these allegations are accurate, especially if the researcher is studying a basic process, the conclusions of the research have little implication or value for the agency's program, and the primary purpose of the "collaboration" is for the agency to provide subjects for the scientist's research.

Successful collaborative projects are ones that do not interfere with the primary purpose and procedures of a service agency, but instead hold the promise of contributing in a meaningful way to improving the services and the outcome for clients. At the same time, the results must satisfy the researcher's need to publish and contribute to general knowledge. It is not easy to satisfy both criteria.

Stakeholders

What an agency can and cannot do in a project often depends not only on its primary purpose but on its stakeholders—individuals or institutions to whom the administration and staff of the agency are responsible (Groark & McCall, 1993). Other than themselves and funders, academics have few stakeholders, and their relationship with funders is often formal, distant, and impersonal. It's likely to be much different in most agencies; there are many more stakeholders of several different types and the agency has a much more personal or political relationship with them.

One type of agency stakeholder, for example, is *funders.* Many agencies, even specific programs, are funded by several sources, and large agencies with several programs may have literally dozens of funders, typically city or county agencies and local foundations. This means that funding is based not only on the quality of the program but on the values and interpersonal relationships of agency and funding administrators. These uncertain personal factors can be crucial to the existence of an agency, most of which are financially fragile, live year-to-year if not month-to-month (i.e., county and state funding may be year-by-year), and constantly need to recruit funds for survival.

Most agencies have *boards of directors,* stakeholders who are often influential in the agencies' financial and political well being. They may be staunch advocates for the agency or people of power and influence who are not necessarily thoroughly committed to the agency. While some boards are merely advisory, others have legal responsibility and authority over the agency and its staff. These individuals may be even further removed from the agency's program, but nevertheless very powerful on stage and behind the scenes.

Other stakeholders may include *policymakers and the media,* both groups being capable of influencing the operations and funding of the agency and the public perception of it. Policymakers (and funders) may dictate the types of programs they will fund, sometimes having sociopolitical ideals and cost savings as criteria. An agency may implement a program to serve these goals even if the program is not very effective. Mordock (1993), for example, has pointed out that a variety of programs for handicapped children have been adopted primarily because they save costs, appeal to democratic ideals, or are considered to be the legal rights of such clients. Similarly, some home-based crisis intervention programs designed to prevent foster care placements are implemented, not because of their effectiveness (some types of children do better in foster care), but because they save money and appeal to the noble ideology of saving the family (Mordock, 1993).

Collectively, these stakeholders may wield substantial public and private, dependable and capricious, valid and invalid, knowledgeable and naive influence, and the agency must accommodate and contend with it. Researchers accustomed to justifying projects and procedures only in terms of their scientific merit will find the personal preferences and biases of stakeholders, some of whom display a "don't-confuse-me-with-the-fact" attitude, an alien criterion at best. For example, an agency director may insist that particular questions cannot be asked or options discussed with clients because a board member or funder would find it objectionable, regardless of the validity or reasonableness of that viewpoint. For example, abortion may not be an option that can be presented to pregnant teenagers served by a private agency who happens to have one or more staunch right-to-lifers on their board of directors. Alternatively, questions about depression and suicide cannot be assessed in an evaluation of a program for teenage mothers, even though minimizing depression is a major program goal, because a lawyer on the board fears that such questions could be alleged to contribute to an actual suicide and constitute the basis of a law suit against the agency. No evidence may exist that such questioning could have this effect, but courts decide such matters in the absence of such evidence, and the lawyer is appropriately performing his or her duty as a board member.

Regulations

Agencies must comply with a variety of legal and policy standards, regulations, licensing requirements, guidelines, directives, and "best practices," that may limit the agency's ability to alter the nature of services, staff–client ratios, staff qualifications, labor practices (e.g., breaks, lunch hours), certain features of the physical environment, space allocations, safety provisions, client rights, and other procedures to accommodate to an experimental project, a new program, or even the evaluation of an existing program (Groark & McCall, 1993).

In addition to formal regulations, agencies are often ethically bound to serve all eligible clients with their best practices and "best practice" may be based on the belief and conviction of the agency administrator, the service professionals, or the funder, not on what has been empirically documented in the research literature to be effective. Therefore, it may be very difficult for an agency to create comparison groups; omit or decrease services, even untested or innovative services, to some individuals; or randomly assign individuals to one or another approach, especially when they intuitively believe (but have no evidence) that one method is better than the other. It is not just a question of professional ethics, because the agency's reputation of implementing best practices is critical to their future funding. Also, agencies are often visited by regulators and required to submit reports documenting services, clients, and procedures. It may be hard to justify certain experimental practices to such regulators.

For example, in the process of planning a program evaluation of a home-visiting service to severely financially and emotionally stressed parents of infants at extreme medical and psychological risk, the researcher wanted case workers to make a few global ratings of the mothers' coping ability and mental stability. The agency director refused because she feared that the court system could subpoena such evaluations and use them as a basis for removing the child from the mother's care. She had witnessed such proceedings on several occasions and found the court's decision frequently to be at odds with her judgments as a mental health professional. As a result, she lacked confidence that the court system would use such ratings wisely—it was her professional judgment that many families who were having difficulty coping and wherein the parent was mentally unstable, did not deserve to have their child removed. While the researcher may have felt this was unreasonable on the part of the director, that it was unlikely that the courts would attempt to subpoena the records, and that it might be impossible for the court to obtain them under a doctor–patient privacy argument, the agency director perceived herself to be doing her job as a mental health professional and as a support and protective service for these families.

Resources

In addition to scarce financial resources, the greatest asset of an agency is its personnel. Good people are difficult to find and to hold, given the salaries, case loads, psychological demands, and working conditions of many agencies. To ask service providers to spend five additional minutes with each client (i.e., 5 min. × 30 clients equals 2.5 extra hours per week) to ask a few extra questions may appear a trivial request to the scientist, but unreasonably burdensome to an overloaded service provider. Furthermore, a major task of the provider is to keep the client in the service, and probing questions about depression, alcohol and drug use, family violence, and other problem or illegal behavior necessary for research and even program evaluation may alienate the client and defeat the provider's first goal.

Also, the backgrounds of service providers may vary substantially. Many staff are extensively trained and experienced in the services they provide, but human service agencies also employ college graduates without special training in human services, as well as professionals from other disciplines (e.g., law, business, education) who have been disillusioned with their chosen careers. These people are likely to be the academic's "research assistants," and unlike homogeneously trained graduate students, they bring different perspectives, values, and skills to the enterprise.

Service professionals and their staff members tend to rely on a different knowledge base than do researchers. Veteran service professionals often speak and act on the basis of their experience with clients, whereas the academic may be rooted in knowledge from a research literature. The conclusions from these two knowledge bases may be, or appear to be, very different. Teachers, for example, may readily attribute hyperactivity, attention deficit disorders, and behavioral control problems to prenatal cocaine exposure, whereas scientists find only inclusive and contradictory evidence that prenatal drug exposure, per se, produces these consequences. Many service programs claim to improve parent–child relations, mental health, and intellectual development, while the scientist may observe that no evidence exists to support claims that such interventions are likely to be effective in this way.

A classic, but extreme, example propagated by Glen Doman (1964, 1979) was that exposure to flashcards containing words or numbers could create genius level reading and math ability in young children. More commonly and subtly, researchers may find service provider claims—for example, that experience with arts and crafts produces better problem-solving skills in children or that free play alone will improve the intelligence of low-income children—to be unsupported by, or at odds with, the research literature. The service professional argues that he or she "sees it in the clinic or center every day," while the researcher counters that no serious scientific evidence exists that such interventions have, or are likely to have, such effects.

The imperfect laboratory

Not surprisingly, these and other factors make a service agency a very imperfect laboratory relative to the textbook ideal. Treatments may not be rigidly applied in the same way to each client, assessments may be casually administered in nonstandard ways or omitted entirely by caseworkers, whole treatment programs and practices may change in midstudy, personnel may turnover, regulations may be revised, and discipline-wide innovations may be implemented in the middle of a project. Moreover, comparison groups are difficult to create, clients are often unpredictable and irresponsible, and research protocol can be abandoned in the face of client, agency, or staff crises or episodic time constraints.

Such circumstances are simply the facts of professional life when conducting research in ecologically valid contexts and not necessarily the result of poor professionalism or irresponsible service administrators and staff. Researchers working in applied contexts simply must accommodate to most of these circumstances and accept the best obtainable, rather than an ideal standard for their work. A failure to appreciate these limitations is often expressed by lab researchers who criticize their colleagues who work in applied settings (e.g., educational or social work researchers) because they do not follow ideal research practices. Actually, applied research often requires *more* creativity, intellectual resourcefulness, and skill—not less— and it is irresponsible for scientists accustomed to total control in the lab to disparage those who must work in circumstances in which most of the control resides with others.

Guidelines for Successful Collaborations

Successful collaborations are possible in this environment, but they take work and must be true collaborations. While some collaborations are between a single researcher and a single agency, a recent major theme in services is an emphasis on comprehensive case managed services and their evaluation, which may require dozens of academics, administrators, and human service agencies.

Attitudes

It helps if researchers come to the enterprise with respect for the agency and its personnel as well as for its purpose and procedures (Friend & Cook, 1992). Similarly, it helps if the agency values and appreciates the skills that the researcher brings to the collaboration and desires the information that might be generated from the collaborative project. Of course, such respect must be merited by both parties, but each party should come to the collaboration with an attitude and an expectancy that this will be fulfilled.

This attitude can be expressed in several ways. For example, the researcher might come to the agency expecting to develop a project collaboratively, rather than simply looking for an agency and clients (i.e., subjects) for a predetermined research project. To illustrate, one program evaluator assigned by the funding agency to evaluate the process and outcome of three community collaborations, attended as an observer more than 30 meetings of these collaboratives before proposing specific assessments and procedures. He then gave the collaboratives a right-of-refusal on all assessment instruments and specific items on questionnaires, including their wording. Although this ran the risk of extreme censorship or disparities between the three collaboratives in what they would permit, the researcher felt that without their involvement, cooperation, and endorsement, the entire evaluation would be impossible to implement or of dubious validity. As a result of having spent substantial time with each collaborative before this review process, the collaboratives had come to trust the researcher and substantially fewer changes in the assessment instruments were requested than might have been the case.

Project selection

Specific projects should be selected for possible collaborative activities only if they have the potential of providing the agency with valuable information. The project must be mutually beneficial for agency and researcher. Simple access to client subjects for research is not mutually beneficial.

Sometimes it helps for the researcher to approach an agency indicating the desire to study a broad general topic, and then to explore with agency administrators their interest in specific questions that a collaborative project might address. Mutual benefit and collaboration are more likely to be achieved if the agency is, from the beginning, a contributing partner to the purpose and procedures of a project.

In the case of program evaluation, the project is typically preselected, with the program evaluator sometimes arriving on the scene after the intervention is established and, perhaps, in progress. While the design of the evaluation is primarily the responsibility of the researcher, a great many decisions must be made about the nature and procedure of the evaluation, and these should be done cooperatively with the agency (and perhaps the funder). Specifically, the first step is typically to listen to the agency describe the nature of the program and the behavioral outcomes the agency thinks the program can achieve. Some goals are more necessary or likely to be achieved than other goals, and the level of effort (e.g., need for periodic assessments, comparison groups) and intrusiveness of the procedures (e.g., assessments) required to answer some questions is much greater than to answer other questions. Structuring these choices for the agency and working together to select options is one way to demonstrate a cooperative style and to build trust and confidence. Another major decision that should be made cooperatively is to determine the nature, extent, and precision of the information to be obtained relative to the cost in terms of finance, personnel time, and intrusiveness. Psychologists, for example, prefer to observe actual behavior, distrust personal reports, devise large batteries of assessments for a great many different behavioral dimensions, and insist on one or more comparison groups. While this may be the ideal, at least from a psychological perspective, it may constitute much more precision and detail than can be afforded or needed. Some veteran program evaluators believe that consumer satisfaction surveys composed of both specific ratings and open-ended comments provide 90% of what the agency and funder need to know, albeit with somewhat less precision, detail, and certainty. Again, such decisions should be made cooperatively.

A liaison person

Cooperation is often facilitated if the researcher employs a project director or liaison person who is familiar with the service agency, its practices, and the constraints under which it operates. A former social worker, nurse, or educator, depending upon the agency, might be hired as the project director or coordinator responsible for developing the cooperative linkages and implementing the project. Such individuals may be more readily trusted by service agencies, and their knowledge may help avoid proposing procedures that would be difficult or unreasonable. Such a liaison person can also help researchers and service professionals speak a common language. The words "research," "evaluation," "data," and "control group" can mean very different things to a service provider than to a researcher.

Partners

Some projects require the expertise of many research and service partners, not just one of each. Who is selected to participate in such a large collaborative team is crucial to the smoothness of how the team functions and the quality of its products. The team, and therefore the collaborative project, will be only as strong and successful as each individual partner. A good team needs a balance of expertise (Mattessich & Monsey, 1992), perhaps including people with research knowledge, content knowledge, service techniques, administrative and management experience, and influence with funders and gatekeepers. However, they must also have several personal characteristics, including loyalty and commitment to the common goal, and a willingness to compromise and share control, responsibility, and credit. Ideally, each of the partners should be selected because they have these attributes, but typically not all the people who have the necessary expertise will have the desired personal characteristics.

Even if the team is excellent going into the collaboration, a team spirit of mutual respect, responsibility, ownership, and belonging must be developed (Abrams & Frantz, 1991). This may take some educating of individual players of what each member of the team can and will contribute. Also, the more each member actually works and contributes to the project, the more ownership, investment, and responsibility that individual will feel, and the more dependent the other individuals will be on that person's participation. This mutual dependency results in team spirit, belongingness, loyalty, and shared responsibilities for the successes and failures of the program. Further, each member is likely to become an ambassador for the program, advertising its virtues and contributing to its visibility, fundability, expansion, influence, and contribution. Researchers must remember that service programs are successful as much because of their public relations and personal relationships with funders and policymakers, than as a result of scientifically documented behavioral benefits.

Common mission

There must be a common mission and purpose (Friend & Cook, 1992). The team players should meet regularly and frequently as a group to develop the mission of the research as a group with complete participation and agreement. Developing a solid mission includes discussions about group values and vision. The process alone provides for a better awareness of the issues and the direction of the collaboration, and in large collaborative projects it may help to have a written mission statement. In the future, this mission statement should be used as a touchstone to guide the team back on track.

Communication

Communication is critical, especially in large projects. All activities should be communicated to all players, and communication should be regularly scheduled, accurate, cordial, and professional. The process of communication must give participants a signal that it's okay to disagree and to use the resolution of conflicts as a means of moving forward (Groark & McCall, 1993). While academics are accustomed to open, piercing, and public disagreement and criticism, service professionals typically are not. Criticism is often best voiced as questions, suggestions, or alternatives, and in private. But if disagreements are not immediately faced head on, problems will not be solved and may fester, jeopardizing the collaboration.

Proactive nature

Collaborations work better if they are proactive, that is, deliberate attempts to work together toward a common outcome that is selected by the group, rather than if they are reactive, that is, are created to solve a crisis. To many researchers, all research is proactive, in the sense that it is investigator initiated and created, it is funded predominantly by grant programs that operate continuously through the year, and it is conducted without the need to cooperate with other people or agencies. In contrast, much of a service professional's life may be crisis oriented. Funding mechanisms are often one-shot offerings that typically allow very little time to prepare an application (e.g., as little as two to three weeks is not uncommon). And funding mechanisms are often very short term, for example, year-to-year, so that it is not uncommon to be notified that a source of current funding will be drastically cut or eliminated in a few weeks. Also, much public policy is generated in response to a crisis, and policymakers call for immediate action—this often must be implemented by service professionals who may or may not be prepared to do so.

Proactive collaborations work better because the partners have voluntarily agreed to participate, and they are freer to craft the project according to their own desires. As in any collaboration, partners should frequently discuss how the work is progressing and trust each other enough to be open and honest about the process. They should agree on what decisions will be made by the group, subgroups, and by individuals, and the group cannot be dominated by one sector (i.e., researchers, service professionals, policymakers) or a few individuals. Rights and responsibilities of partners should be clearly defined and agreed on. The critical characteristic of partners is that they be effective liaisons to their organizations and to the other collaborators.

A potential liability of proactive collaborations is that they can become mere discussion groups characterized by contemplation and mutual education, rather than action (assuming action is their primary purpose). Academics are especially prone to want to discuss, debate, and quibble rather than act, especially if no deadline exists for some product. Occasionally, service professionals can also fail to act, especially if the partners who volunteered for the collaborative do not have the authority, clout, resources, or skills to move ideas into practice.

Leadership

The quality of leadership is often determined by style, experience, and competence. It is the combination of these characteristics that grants a leader legitimacy from other partners (Mattessich & Monsey, 1992). Good leaders of collaborations are able to motivate players while they manage. They perceive and make sure the group sees all sides of an issue, and they help identify common ground and alternative solutions.

A good leader must be fair. A leader may have a strong commitment to a certain goal or approach, but this must not be imposed overtly or covertly on the group. Even if the lack of neutrality is only perceived and not based in reality, it may be just as damaging to the collaboration. This is one reason why it may be preferable to have a neutral leader whose only role is to support the collaboration and not be a vested partner, because he or she is more likely to be perceived as unbiased with respect to the demands of participating collaborators.

Another way to avoid the perception of conflict of interest is to establish co-leaders who complement the assets and interests of each other. For example, one leader who is an academic and a conceptualizer may complement the skills of a program professional who is goal and task oriented. Either one alone may not be totally effective, but working together they might make a powerful leadership team. In a sense, they must perform and model as leaders the same collaboration they seek to promote in the partners.

Carried to the extreme, all team members might share leadership responsibilities. Through formal assignment of responsibilities or rotation of typical responsibilities, a more solid sense of ownership of the collaboration and its effort can be developed. This approach requires and promotes group problem solving and communication among members. Shared leadership comes about naturally in a collaborative that has co-chairs, competent staff support, and active members who are asked to be responsible for certain agenda items.

Monitoring progress

The collaborative process must go smoothly if there is to be a successful product. Therefore, the process needs to be monitored continuously. Are all the partners satisfied with their roles, the performance of others, and progress toward short- and long-term goals? Have relationships in the collaboration developed and matured so that compromise, give and take, openness, assertiveness and deference, trust, respect, and cooperation come easily? Does the group readily tackle new issues, tasks, and even new projects? Is the collaboration attaining the milestones and outcomes for which it was established?

CONCLUSION

Collaborations are useful and sometimes necessary when the required expertise for a project is so diverse and demanding that it outstrips the ability of a single person or agency to perform, and when resources, authority, and responsibility needed to conduct the project are disbursed among individuals or groups. As knowledge, research and professional skills, and services become more specialized, the need for collaborations will increase. Collaborations work best when the partners can achieve something together that they could not attain alone, whether it is financial resources, access to client groups, expertise, the opportunity to be involved in a project, or make a contribution to society. When those circumstances are present, the collaboration is most likely to be successful and to contribute to the welfare of children, youth, and families.

REFERENCES

Abrams, P., & Frantz, C. (1991, November 11). Best practices of interagency collaboration and implications for training. Presented at the meetings of the Council for Exceptional Children, New Orleans, LA.

Doman, G. (1964). *How to teach your baby to read.* New York: Random House.

Doman, G. (1979). *Teach your baby math.* New York: Simon & Schuster.

Fisher, C.B., Murray, J.P., Dill, J.R., Hagen, J.W., Hogan, M.J., Lerner, R.M., Rebok, G.W., Sigel, I.E., Sostek, A.M., Smyer, M.A., Spencer, M.B., & Wilcox, B. (1993). The National Conference on Graduate Education in the Applications of Developmental Sciences Across the Lifespan. *Journal of Applied Developmental Psychology, 14,* 1–10.

Friend, M., & Cook, L. (1992). *Interactions: Collaboration skills for school professionals.* White Plains, NY: Longman Publishing Group.

Groark, C.J., & McCall, R.B. (1993, Spring). Building mutually beneficial collaborations between researchers and community service professionals. *SRCD Newsletter, 6,* 14.

Mattessich, P.W., & Monsey, B.R. (1992). *Collaboration: What makes it work? A review of research literature on factors influencing successful collaboration.* St. Paul, MN: Amherst H. Wilder Foundation.

Mordock, J.B. (1993, Fall). Diversity: More on collaboration. *SRCD Newsletter,* 1, 12.

Vandercook, T., York, J., & Sullivan, B. (1993, Winter). TRUE OR FALSE? Truly collaborative relationships can exist between university and public school personnel. *OSERS News in Print,* 31–37.

13

Birds of a Feather:
Administrative Choices and Issues in Creating a Specialized Applied, Multidisciplinary, Developmental Unit

Robert B. McCall
University of Pittsburgh

Academics, like birds of a feather, tend to flock together, first into traditional academic departments and, occasionally, into other units, typically called institutes, centers, and offices. These units serve special purposes—for example, they may consist of a collection of scholars and, sometimes, students who are concerned with a narrower or broader focus than typical departments, an interdisciplinary set of individuals interested in a common problem that cuts across traditional academic disciplines, or a few administrators and staff who provide research and demonstration program support services to faculty and, perhaps, professionals in the community.

Such units vary in nature as a function of their mission. Some are private while others are university based; some are residential (i.e., professionals perform their primary work in the unit's building) while others are facilitative (e.g., they promote activities among a great diversity of faculty); some emphasize basic research while others focus on applied, demonstration, and policy studies; and some are unidisciplinary while others are multi- or interdisciplinary.

Over the years, several general changes in such units in the field of child development have taken place. First, many private research institutes have disappeared; most current units are university based. Second, years ago, most were residential, but now some are purely facilitative and a few even reach beyond a single university setting.

Third, although traditional units tended to focus solely on basic research, more modern centers may also embrace applied research, program evaluation, service demonstration programs, and policy studies.

Fourth, there is greater contemporary interest in promoting serious *inter*disciplinary activities wherein professionals from different disciplines contribute necessary skills to the execution of a joint project, rather than simply *multi*disciplinary activities, wherein professionals from different disciplines reside, but do not necessarily work, together.

Fifth, many traditional units in the field of child development conducted major, typically longitudinal, institutional studies; now, more secondary analyses of major databases collected elsewhere are being conducted, and much more data sharing transpires within and between units.

The movement toward applied developmental research and educational activities represented in this volume captures many of these contemporary themes. For one thing, applied developmental is a focus within the broader sphere of developmental studies, and such foci have often been the stimuli for the creation of specialized units. Second, applied developmental activities are more likely to be multidisciplinary. While the impetus for the applied developmental movement may have come from psychologists, if the approach is to be integrated with traditional mainstream applied work pertaining to children, youth, and families, applied developmental psychologists must join scholars from those disciplines (in addition to clinical child psychology) that have traditionally conducted applied work in this field—namely, social work, public health, education, medicine and nursing, government and public affairs. Third, a major aspect of applied developmental work involves the delivery of services to children, youth, and families. Since the delivery of services is almost exclusively performed by institutions other than universities, a university based unit, focusing on applied work, is likely to collaborate with nonuniversity agencies in the pursuit of their activities (e.g., conducting service demonstration and evaluation projects, contributing to the policy process). Fourth, because of these thrusts, an applied developmental unit is more likely to be facilitative of existing units and promote and orchestrate collaborations among individuals and agencies within the university and between the university and the community, than it is to be a residential unit wherein a small group of faculty conduct their own projects in relative independence from each other and those outside the unit. Consequently, it is likely that applied developmentalists will consider forming a specialized unit within or outside of the university to support their activities. This may be a new unit, or it may be a resurrection and/or modification of an existing unit that is redirected toward an applied developmental purpose. In either case, a variety of choices are available for the administrative structure and operation of such a unit. It is necessary to make some fundamental decisions about certain issues that will be faced in the course of creating such a unit. This paper provides some structure to this decision process by outlining several administrative dimensions along which specialized units vary and suggesting the pros and cons of the poles of such dimensions. The purpose is to provide administrators and those wishing to create an applied developmental unit with a structured set of choices about which deliberate decisions may be made.

A substantial portion of the material presented below is based on an informal meeting of directors[1] of institutes, centers, offices, and task forces

---

[1]This paper is based, in part, on discussion sessions that took place at a 1991 meeting of directors of specialized child development units. The discussion sessions included "Operating Within a University" led by Andrew Collins (Director, Intercollege Center for Research on Interpersonal Relations, University of Minnesota), "Membership Alternatives" led by Joseph Campos (Director, Institute of Human Development, University of California at Berkeley), "Promoting Interdisciplinary Projects" led by Richard Weinberg (Director, Institute of Child Development and Center for Early Education and Development, University of Minnesota), "Collaborative Databases" led by Anne Colby (Director, Murray Research Center, Radcliffe College), and "Policy Studies" led by Sharon Lynn Kagan (Associate Director, Bush Center, Yale University). Other contributors to the discussions and their affiliations at the time included Mary Andrews (then Acting Director, Institute for Children, Youth, and Families, Michigan State University), Judith Dunn (then Director, Center for the Study of Child and Adolescent Development, Pennsylvania State University), Dorothy Eichorn (then President, Federation of Behavioral, Psychological, and Cognitive Sciences, University of California at Berkeley), Celia Fisher (Director, Graduate Program in Developmental Psychology, Fordham University; Co-Chair, National Task Force on Applied Developmental Science), John Hagen (Executive Director of the Society for Research in Child Development and Director, Center for Human Growth and Development, University of Michigan), Rosanne Kermoian (Assistant Director, Institute of Human Development, University of California at Berkeley), Harry McGurk (then Director, Thomas Coram Research Unit of the Institute of Education, University of London), Gary Melton (then Director, Center on Children, Families, and the Law, University of Nebraska), Kimbrough Oller (Co-Director, Hearing and Language Programs at the Mailman Center for Child Development, University of Miami), Chaya Piotrkowski (Director, Center for the Child, National Council of Jewish Women), Craig and Sharon Landesman Ramey (Co-Directors, Civitan International Research Center, University of Alabama at Birmingham), Lonnie Sherrod (Vice-President for Program, William T. Grant Foundation), Tricia Summers and Abe Wandersman (then Program Developers, Center for Family in Society, University of South Carolina), and Donald Wertlieb (Chairperson, Eliot-Pearson Department of Child Study, Tufts

pertaining to children, youth, and families who characterized the nature of their units, shared information about their administrative and programming procedures, and discussed the advantages and disadvantages of different structures, program features, and approaches.[1] Most of these directors were relatively new to their administrative assignments, many reported that the missions of their units had changed recently, and they desired to learn alternative approaches to deal with common administrative issues. The units represented by these directors were not limited to those having an applied focus, and therefore the thoughts offered here span the entire range of the dimensions and issues of specialized units.

DIMENSIONS OF PURPOSE AND STRUCTURE

Specialized units vary along several dimensions of structure and purpose. What follows is an outline of the dimensions of such administrative structures as discussed by the group[1], plus the implications of each dimension for units specializing in applied activities as perceived by the author.

University Based vs. Independent Units

Whereas many prominent units in years past were freestanding (e.g., Fels Research Institute, Yellow Springs, Ohio; Merrill-Palmer Institute, Detroit, Michigan), most units today are based in universities.

Independent units value their relative freedom from university bureaucracies (e.g., administrative restrictions on hiring procedures, salaries, purchasing, budget lines), from the narrow academic value for basic research along unidisciplinary lines, and from the demand for spending time on activities tangential to the main purpose of the unit (e.g., teaching, advising, departmental and committee affairs). Establishing a freestanding unit independent of the university may be particularly attractive to applied developmentalists who find their universities resistant to applied work and plan to devote major energies to working with community groups and agencies.

But independence comes at a cost. Although they are proud of their efficiency and flexibility, independent units sometimes lament the time and expense required to create their own bureaucratic and administrative poli-

---

University). The informal conference was held in Birmingham, AL, in 1991 and was supported, in part, by the William T. Grant Foundation of New York, the Civitan International Research Center at the University of Alabama at Birmingham, and the University of Pittsburgh Office of Child Development, with funds from the Howard Heinz Endowment and the University.

cies that are necessary to satisfy governmental regulations, the cost of establishing and maintaining the units, being without certain support services (e.g., substantial library and accounting personnel knowledgeable about the myriad federal grant policies), and the financial uncertainty produced by not having stable core funding in the face of the vicissitudes of grant and contract funding. Even those units that want to relate strongly to community groups may find a university affiliation useful, because the university is an intellectually and financial credible institution that may be favored by granting agencies for financial and legal reasons. Also, it is independent and less likely to be perceived as a rival to local service agencies.

Most specialized applied developmental units will be located within universities, and such units vary along several dimensions that have major implications for how they operate.

Reporting line

In contrast to freestanding units that typically report to a funding source or board of directors, university units report to a university administrator. The particular administrator may vary from unit to unit and university to university, and it may be a department chair, a graduate dean, the provost, a vice president, or a vice chancellor. Where in the university system one reports to is not just an administrative detail; it often influences directly the purpose and mission of the unit and how it is evaluated. For example, department chairs and deans may be concerned primarily with student hours taught, publications, and grant support for academic products and training programs, whereas university administrators may place more importance on indirect costs and/or the university's image in the eyes of the local community, citizens of the state, other universities, and state legislators.

Interdisciplinary units that cut across different departments and schools tend to report to university administrators who are above the department or dean level. This has the advantages of keeping the interdisciplinary unit independent of any one of its collaborating partners and having an administrator who presumably shares a multidisciplinary, if not interdisciplinary, perspective. It has the potential disadvantages that the administrator has less understanding of, and value for, the program or function of the unit. Another disadvantage is that the unit appears too small or insignificant relative to departments, schools, or even colleges to command the attention of and resources dispensed by that administrator.

An alternative is to have a council of the deans or department chairs, who form the constituency of the unit, to oversee its operation. This has the potential advantages of mutual support between the unit and its university constituencies, and it promotes visibility for the unit among university administrators. However, it can have the disadvantage of having the unit governed, or heavily influenced, by people who understandably have the interest of their own schools, not the unit, foremost in mind. Also, someone once said "for God so loved the world, He did not send a committee," so a higher administrator with some power may be needed to oversee such a governing body. Alternatively, the administrator oversees the unit with the council as a board of advisors.

Some units report to administrators in a medical school. This may have both advantages and disadvantages. Medical schools often are more accustomed to collaborations, which is useful if the unit is interdisciplinary, although they also may have a more rigid status hierarchy that can impede certain collaborations, for example, between medical and nonmedical faculty. Medical schools also are thought to have more money, and are useful in gaining access to clinical populations as research subjects. Finally, medical schools are accustomed to and value applied activities, even policy studies, more than do many traditional colleges of arts and sciences.

A special problem for some interdisciplinary units is that their universities lack an administrative structure and reporting line especially designed for interdisciplinary units. For example, many universities are strongly organized around traditional departments and schools (e.g., "strong dean model"), with no single administrator specifically designated to oversee interdisciplinary institutes or centers. Resources, as well as a variety of administrative and bureaucratic policies, may be tightly organized around department and school lines. This may inhibit, or at least make difficult, serious interdisciplinary programming. This can be a special problem if some schools within the university (e.g., arts and sciences, professional schools, medical school) have very different administrative policies (e.g., salaries, returns of indirect costs, hiring procedures, criteria for promotion of faculty, funds for students and projects). In most cases, interdisciplinary units are forced to fit into the traditional administrative structure of the university, rather than the university creating an administrative structure especially for one or two new units. Presumably, the best solution is to have one university administrator (e.g., vice chancellor or dean of research, graduate studies, and/or public service) who is designated to oversee all interdisciplinary institutes and centers. He or she would be charged with fitting them into the university administrative and financial system and solving the unique administrative problems they can encounter.

Applied developmental units, especially those that are interdisciplinary and relate intensively to community agencies, would probably be best finding an administrator who also has a value, if not designated responsibility, for promoting the university as a resource to the local community and for improving the image of the university among the citizenry. Ideally, this is a high-level administrator formally designated to have such responsibilities (e.g., vice chancellor for research, graduate studies, and public service). If such a position does not exist, then another administrative arrangement must be made. It helps if the chosen administrator is close to power and policies if the specialized unit is likely to break new administrative ground (e.g., creating interdisciplinary programs in a strong dean university, or relating to community agencies in a university that has traditionally operated in isolation).

Criteria and evaluation

Some units have well defined and traditional academic missions and functions. They may operate like a department—faculty have their primary appointments in the unit and the unit has its own university approved training program (e.g., University of Minnesota's Institute of Child Development). Other units may be research centers that, as one director put it, have three purposes—research, research, and research (e.g., University of Michigan's Center for Human Growth and Development). Other units may have less clearly defined missions and purposes, they may be less traditional, and they may be deliberately experimental and changing (e.g., University of Pittsburgh's Office of Child Development). In all cases, especially in the latter, the mission and purpose of the unit, as well as the criteria by which it is to be evaluated, should be clearly stated, understood, and agreed upon by the unit and its oversight administrator and funding agencies. For example, it might have a written mission statement with goals and operational policies, and it helps if the oversight administrator, collaborating administrators in the university, in relevant community agencies, and representatives of the unit's constituency (e.g., faculty, service agency directors, policymakers) have some say in the creation of such a statement. For existing units, a strategic planning process, with the goal of developing such a statement or revising an existing one, might be conducted. This can include informal or formal surveys of constituencies, focus groups, and constituency reviews of drafts of the mission statement.

Having clear purposes and policies seems like obvious advice, but it is not always followed. Oversight administrators may change, and a new administrator may not understand or value the purpose of a particular unit; directors, especially those newly appointed, may shift the mission or program of a unit; or the unit's purpose may be evolving, or even be required to change, by an external funder who needs to have innovation on each renewal application to avoid the impression of funding a "continuing operation." Whatever the circumstance, it is crucial that the unit, its administrator, and its constituency see eye to eye on purpose and criteria. These issues should be clearly stated, and a process for evaluation be established, especially if quantifiable measures (e.g., amount of grant money, number of publications) are not appropriate criteria.

To help in this process, most units have an advisory board of relevant local or national professionals. Typically, they are composed of leaders representing the unit's constituency, people whose support is needed, and professionals in the topical areas represented by the unit. Such a board meets regularly and provides guidance and informal evaluation to the unit's director and oversight administrator. A board of visitors, or similar group composed of professionals from outside the university, may be assembled periodically at the behest of the university to conduct process and outcome evaluations to determine if the unit has performed adequately with respect to its mission. It is advisable to have regular meetings and, in some cases, a schedule for rotating memberships on such boards.

Applied units may have advisory boards composed of both university faculty and administrators and representatives of community agencies, including agency directors, program officers of local foundations, and policymakers. Bringing such an advisory board together may itself represent a purpose of the unit, given that many university and community leaders rarely talk to one another. But community and university people may be accustomed to playing different roles when serving on advisory boards. Faculty, for example, readily criticize policies and procedures, even individual projects—it is part of the academic value for public criticism of scholarly work. Community professionals, however, may be unaccustomed to, or even shocked or disturbed by, such open criticism, preferring a public posture of support and endorsement and proffering suggestions in more private forums. Also, university boards tend to be advisory, have almost no direct power or responsibility, and do little more than review, criticize, and offer a few suggestions. Community boards, on the other hand, may have legal responsibility for their units, have the power to hire and fire unit administrators, and are often key links to financial resources and political power. Consequently, if an applied unit has a mixed university–community board, its functions and responsibilities should be clearly stated, and some sensitivity displayed to the different contexts from which its members derive (perhaps by having university and community co-chairs of the board). Also, boards may be more supportive and useful if they are given some real responsibility and are asked to work on behalf of the unit.

Some units have more difficulty than others defining, documenting, and evaluating their processes and outcomes; this may be a special problem for some applied units. For example, if the unit is largely facilitative of other people's research, training, and service activities, it may be difficult to determine in an objective way whether the unit contributes to facilitating a particular research project, since the grant for that project may go to the researcher's unit rather than to the facilitating unit. Specifically, a unit may regularly send out notices of requests for proposals, but never know how many of those notices actually stimulate a faculty member or agency director to submit a grant application or whether funds are received. In such cases, it is important for the unit to list its activities (e.g., notices distributed, colloquia sponsored, support services rendered) to document its activities, even if the outcomes cannot be determined.

Nontraditional and evolving units and their university administrators should meet periodically to ensure that all parties understand and agree on the purpose and criteria of the unit. A retreat for self-examination is sometimes useful to consider several questions: what have we tried to do, where have we been successful and where have we failed, what alternative procedures or structures might we consider, and what is the best direction for the future? Periodic strategic planning activities may also help keep a unit fresh and in step with its administrators and constituencies.

The role of students

Some units operate complete educational programs in the same way as do departments, and some operate training programs that are taken as supplements by students primarily allied with traditional academic departments. Additionally, some only employ students as research assistants or in other capacities, and other units are primarily facilitative or administrative and do not train or employ students directly.

Students may be integral to the primary purpose of an applied developmental unit. The unit may be established, for example, for the primary purpose of administering an applied, interdisciplinary training program. Even if it is not the major purpose, most faculty value what they do and want students to follow in their footsteps. A secondary purpose might be to encourage students who come from disciplines that train them well in research methodology to be more interested in focusing those skills on applied issues. In addition, the involvement of students in the unit's activities may be valued by university administrators because they perceive the unit as contributing directly to traditional university functions. Moreover, the unit may see students as a more affordable source of labor (especially undergraduates and work–study students), and the students may perceive the unit as a potential source of funding. While psychology graduate students are accustomed to being fully funded, graduate students in social work, education, and other applied professions often have very limited financial support and must work outside the university to put themselves through graduate school.

University funding

Units also differ in the extent to which they receive hard money funding from the university. Not surprisingly, the more a unit's mission conforms to that of traditional academic departments, the more likely it is to receive university funding, which is often divided between faculty salaries and operating expenses. Some units receive modest amounts of funds from the university but have commitments of faculty time from major departments or schools involved in its programs. A few units receive direct lines from the state, within or outside of the university's budget, while other units receive relatively little money or in-kind support from the university and rely almost entirely on "soft money" to operate their programs. The dependability of university funding is highly valued relative to "soft money," but several directors have learned, during recent budget crunches, that the dependability of university funds has its limits and even written commitments may not be honored fully under tight financial circumstances.

Applied developmental units may need to be more creative about funding themselves than basic research centers. They may get less direct university support, because their purpose is less traditional. Moreover, faculty are accustomed to seeking research funding from federal agencies and national foundations, but applied activities typically are funded by different federal agencies and, more likely, by local sources, including local government, foundations, and even private individuals. Such local monies are obtained in much different ways than applying for federal research grants, relying more heavily on personal relationships, endorsements, and politics than solely on a good detailed proposal.

Residential vs. Facilitative Units

Residential units

The traditional model of an institute or center located within or outside of a university consists of a building or floors that house researchers whose activities often are subsumed under a common theme (e.g., child development, or child abuse). Such "residential" units provide office and research space, some facilities and finances, clerical and administrative support services, and, perhaps, salary support. In the extreme, these units may operate very similarly to a department, with faculty having their primary appointments in the unit and the unit offering an educational program or even a major. Often, however, such residential research centers in universities are adjuncts to departments, sometimes representing the research facility of a department or several departments.

Facilitative units

In contrast, recent emphasis has been placed on facilitative units, ones that do not house faculty or research, but attempt to promote basic and/or applied projects of a collaborative and interdisciplinary character that will be conducted in other, existing facilities at the university or in the community. They have appeal during financially austere times because they require substantially less space than residential units, do not need new faculty appointments or faculty salary support, and attempt to promote new collaborative projects using existing personnel and facilities. These benefits, however, may have a cost. Such units may be less traditional in structure and function, for example, and as a result they can have more administrative and financial problems in their relationship to the university, (see following section).

Combinations

The demarcation between residential and facilitative units may blur in the future. In the current climate of university budget cuts, it is expensive for universities to build buildings and hire faculty exclusively to do research in new residential institutes or centers without substantial federal support, that may be lacking. Existing residential units are likely to be pressured to offer their support services to a greater number and diversity of faculty members. Finally, public and private funding of scholarly activities has become more problem focused, such problems tend to be interdisciplinary and more applied, and the major participants in such collaborative programs are likely to be different from problem to problem. Accommodating to these trends requires blending facilitative functions with some residential support services.

For example, the University of Pittsburgh Office of Child Development began as a purely facilitative administrative unit. In the process of putting together interdisciplinary and university–community collaborative groups, these groups requested that the office continue to fill the role of convener, manager, or project administrator once funding was obtained. Thus, the office began to house the administrative portion of some collaborative projects. Later, when the federal Department of Education initiated the Urban Community Services Program of funding, the office became the residence of program evaluation and policy professionals and their projects, while still maintaining its facilitative functions.

Selective vs. Open Membership

Some units have selective memberships, wherein only a small number of members have permanent or temporary appointments of a faculty, nonfaculty, or honorary nature. Others, especially facilitative units, have an open membership, or no membership system at all.

Selective memberships

Membership in selective units tends to be of three broad types.

In the most traditional university or nonuniversity units, faculty have their *primary appointments* in the unit. While the criteria for appointment varies with the purpose of the unit, they tend to be similar to the usual criteria for faculty appointments in departments—research quality and productivity, teaching quality (if part of the unit's purpose), etc. Titles may be traditional academic titles or some variant (e.g., Senior Scientist, Fellow). The benefits of such membership may include all, or a portion, of one's salary—possibly including summer salary, teaching buy outs, "tide" or "bridge" money in the event of loss of research support, "seed" or "start up" funds, research funds, research support services (e.g., grant preparation, administrative, accounting, statistical, computer, graphics), space, travel money, and participation in the unit's program. The program may consist of weekly or biweekly faculty or faculty–student seminars on topics of mutual interest; colloquia or brown bag presentations; study groups; luncheon discussion groups; RFP notification service. There could also be periodic informal social gatherings, including monthly TGIF gatherings, weekly sherry hours, daily coffee and donut hours, afternoon tea, and wine and cheese receptions. Problems may include how to handle nonfaculty appointments for individuals who might be worthy of faculty status and terminating appointments. Also, changes in the direction of such units are often difficult when staff are permanent and accustomed to functioning with academic freedom.

Other units award *adjunct appointments* to faculty and others who have their primary appointments in traditional departments. They may be called "Fellows," "Scientists," "Associates," or "Affiliates." Such appointments may be indefinite, have renewable or nonrenewable fixed terms, or be determined by certain criteria (e.g., has a funded project relevant to the unit's mission).

If appointments are for a short duration, some representative process is recommended for selecting members, and some clearly defined method of terminating members (e.g., fixed terms, routine changes in theme, lack of project support over a specified time period) is necessary to avoid animosity and conflict and to maintain a membership with contemporary vitality.

The benefits to members may include the same range of benefits just listed for those having primary appointments, but, more likely, the benefits will be less extensive, especially in facilitative units that may not be able to offer salary, research support, or space. The value and status of membership depends on whether the benefits and services are needed and appreciated by the members. Value can be increased by having members contribute to the selection of such services. If the benefits are not sufficiently valuable, faculty participation wanes, and the survival of the unit may be threatened.

Essentially all units have a third category that might be called *staff*. In addition to secretaries, administrators, and research assistants, staff also includes doctoral level persons who initially may be hired to work on funded projects and whose continuing status is dependent on the availability of outside funds—sometimes their own grants. These appointments often pose a special problem when such individuals develop superb research credentials, perhaps better than many faculty members, but do not have faculty status and lack the prestige and job security of faculty appointees. On occasion, their lower and ambiguous status may become associated with concerns about racial or sexual discrimination if such persons are disproportionately of one sex or race that is different from the majority of faculty, and they may feel they are passed over for new faculty appointments because they are already employed at the university. At the same time, a "support yourself" arrangement may be all that is available, regardless of the person's credentials, and some job may be better than no job. Again, clear policies, sometimes in writing, for appointments within the unit, faculty appointments in academic departments, and term and termination criteria are desirable.

Special issues for all membership categories arise when the purpose of the unit changes. This may be occasioned by a new director, changes in the nature of the membership, a new charge by central administration, or by an evolution of the function of the unit (e.g., from residential to more facilitative activities, or from basic to applied projects). It is helpful if structural changes that have implications for membership are implemented in conjunction with a committee representing the new constituencies of the unit, and are backed by the firmness and support of the university administrator overseeing the unit. Grievance procedures, which should exist routinely if membership is selective, are especially important when such changes in purpose are contemplated or implemented.

Open membership

Some units, especially facilitative ones, have no formal membership but serve one or more large constituencies (e.g., all faculty with interests in children, youth, and families; all faculty in specified departments or schools; all agencies in the county providing services to families; local or state legislators). Although such an approach seems to avoid the problems of selecting and terminating members, the same issues actually arise in more subtle forms: Who shall receive the services of the unit, who shall be invited to participate in specific collaborations, and who shall be awarded certain benefits (e.g., seed grants, invitations to special events)? In circumstances wherein such benefits cannot be accorded to everyone, some policies and criteria should be established that designate who can and cannot be served or participate, how benefits shall be shared equitably across departments and faculty, and how potential collaborators shall be selected (e.g., "We advertise to everyone but we help those who help themselves"). These policies are helpful, but they are not always sufficient to avoid occasional antagonisms and irritations (e.g., "Why were no members of my school included in that collaboration?").

Interdisciplinary Character

As indicated above, applied developmental units are likely to be interdisciplinary in character; this raises special issues of concern.

Multi- vs. inter- vs. transdisciplinary units

Although some units primarily operate within a single discipline, others are created with the express purpose of bringing together professionals from different disciplines around a common theme or problem. In actuality, most such units have been primarily *multidisciplinary,* wherein different disciplines are represented within the unit, but actually do not work together on common projects, rather than *interdisciplinary,* wherein individuals from different disciplines make necessary and valuable contributions to the same projects. *Transdisciplinary* projects are even rarer. They involve the creation of new methods, approaches, or products that are unique combinations of different disciplines, rather than projects that are simply the sum of their disciplinary parts.

Horizontal and vertical

Interdisciplinary projects may be both horizontal and vertical in character. Horizontal refers to contributions made by different disciplines that operate at roughly the same level on the basic research/application/policy dimension. For example, three faculty—a developmental psychologist, a survey researcher, and an educator—may collaborate to conduct research on underachieving high school students. Vertical refers to a collaboration involving professionals varying in their loci on the basic research/application/policy dimension. For example, a child welfare training program may involve faculty from the School of Social Work, community service agency directors, practicing judges, and the police. Projects can be both horizontally and vertically interdisciplinary, such as when pediatricians and developmental psychologists join with home visiting nurses and early childhood agency directors to create a comprehensive child and family services demonstration program and evaluate its process and outcome. Applied developmental programs are likely to be both horizontally and vertically interdisciplinary.

Promoting interdisciplinary projects

A major issue is how one promotes true interdisciplinary or transdisciplinary collaborations, especially in view of the historical lack of such projects on the one hand and the current demand of funding agencies for such broad based approaches to research and demonstration programs on the other.

First, the goal is not to be interdisciplinary for its own sake, but, to create the best approach to achieving the purpose of a specific project. Second, participation must be "marketed" rather than "sold," so that participation provides each collaborator with something that he or she wants and could not otherwise obtain. Such benefits may include getting research funds, access to certain populations of subjects, involvement in a project of importance that requires more or different expertise than any participant possesses alone, a chance for a basic researcher to contribute more directly to solving a real-world problem, and an opportunity for applied professionals to conduct basic or publishable research.

But collaborations can cost their participants as well as bring them such benefits. They often require compromises, accommodations, group decisions, and more time and effort than it first appears (see Groark & McCall, 1994). Each member needs to know and accept as valuable the contributions of the others to the project. Sometimes this can be accomplished by selecting collaborators who are really interdisciplinary in their personal behavior and style. At other times, an independent project manager who does not necessarily direct the program operations is necessary to hold the group together. Facilitating units often play this vital role of independent manager.

Promoting interdisciplinary training programs presents its own problems. For example, professional credentialing systems (e.g., clinical psychology, social work, education) frequently make substantial demands on students, leaving little time in their elective schedules to take courses in an interdisciplinary training program (e.g., in child abuse and neglect, early childhood education, child and family welfare). One solution is to offer breadth and specialized material in a new proseminar format rather than in a set of whole courses. Alternatively, the content of existing required courses can be broadened to include interdisciplinary perspectives.

Academic reward system

A major barrier to interdisciplinary projects is that the academic reward system is organized strictly along disciplinary lines and may not be responsive to interdisciplinary or applied activities, regardless of quality. Few journals (or journal reviewers) are interdisciplinary, even journals published by interdisciplinary societies. Theoretical—but not applied—justification for an article is often required, so it may be especially difficult to publish truly interdisciplinary applied research. Even if published, articles authored by a collaborative group dilute or cloud the contributions made by individuals, so it may be very difficult for a young investigator to gain tenure in a particular department if most of his or her scholarly activities have been jointly published projects. Indeed, departmental tenure review committees may be even more disciplinarily narrow than granting agencies or journal editors, and young faculty who have joint appointments are really in "double jeopardy" when it comes to promotions. Such faculty may need to be "switch hitters" and function academically in both disciplines separately, in addition to their collaborative activities. Under the current system, interdisciplinary work often is the luxury of a tenured professor.

These issues are exacerbated when the interdisciplinary activity is vertical, not just horizontal, that is, when the project is also applied in nature. Working collaboratively on research and demonstration programs in the community may be part of the normal activity of faculty in some professional schools (e.g., social work, education), but it may not be valued by departments and deans in colleges of arts and sciences. Contributing to the policy process may be valued even less (see following section). Such activities may be considered public service, which may carry some weight in promotional reviews in certain professional schools and in land-grant universities (e.g., Cooperative Extension Services), but less in colleges of arts and sciences or in private universities that are not concerned with serving the citizenry. Factors in the successful promotion of vertical collaborations have been discussed by McCall (1990) and Weinberg, Fishhaut, Moore, and Plaisance (1990).

Policy studies

Policy studies, which are increasing recently (see Gallagher, 1990), perhaps as a consequence of the financial death threat to whole disciplines made by recent federal administrations, present the same issues plus some unique ones. Policy studies may consist of debate and advocacy on legislation or policy issues; research on the policy process or its consequence; policy relevant research including needs assessment and program evaluation; policy analysis in which potential or actual benefits and liabilities of a certain policy are assessed; and background reports of literature (e.g., "white papers") pertinent to a policy issue. Further, policy does not necessarily need to be governmental; social policy may be made by corporations, nonprofits, the media, and other bodies.

A first issue is to decide which of these activities will be part of the unit's agenda. Some years ago, behavioral scientists became interested in writing or directly influencing legislation, especially national legislation, but the likelihood of actually doing so appears to be quite small. Instead, some have decided to focus on what academics do best—research, evaluation, program design, and the generation and communication of broad based information about a problem, all of which policymakers in turn may use to create policies, especially local policies.

Second, policy studies are a specific, perhaps extreme, form of interdisciplinary applied activity. Policy issues are rarely the province solely of one academic discipline, and often involve extremely different professionals and values that inevitably must be accommodated or compromised in the final result, sometimes to the dissatisfaction of all of the collaborators. Also, professionals have limited control or influence over the policy process—things can go wrong, legislation is passed that a collaborator disagrees with, and results of academic research can be ridiculed, exaggerated, or misinterpreted by legislators and the press to suit their own needs. Finally, policy studies are often more difficult to publish than traditional or interdisciplinary academic work, and such activity is valued less by tenure review committees and by some university administrations.

Applied developmental units that emphasize service demonstration, program evaluation, and policy studies on the local level can encounter unique problems associated with the fact that such projects must be done collaboratively, or at least with the agreement and support of policymakers, funders, and service agencies. These groups have different values and operate in different ways. Funders and policymakers may have marked preferences based on personal or political considerations that dictate what individuals and agencies will be involved, what conclusions will be drawn, and who will talk to the press.

Shared Databases

Historically, many specialized developmental units were created for, or at least featured, the collection of a large database, typically a longitudinal study. When longitudinal research temporarily fell from favor, so did a central institutional project as a cornerstone of the specialized unit. Now, however, longitudinal research is recognized as the lifeblood of developmental studies despite its limitations, and data collection is becoming more difficult to fund, especially massive data collection. Moreover, in applied circles, collaborative enterprises are being emphasized, and service demonstrations are increasingly being required to have management information systems, client tracking systems, and program evaluation. Consequently, it is likely that many applied developmental units will have a large collaborative database that numerous professionals, both faculty and service providers, may have or will desire access to.

Such databases may be of three general kinds. First, historically, some units were founded to conduct a large institutional research project, typically a longitudinal study that often was multidisciplinary, if not interdisciplinary in character. Different members of the unit have access and use of the data, and sometimes data are shared with nonmembers of the unit, even those located at other universities. Second, individual scholars may conduct secondary analyses of existing databases, which are often longitudinal, multidisciplinary, and massive in scope. Third, funders of major demonstration and evaluation projects are increasingly supporting multisited projects in which the same or similar programs are implemented in different locations around the country, but which collectively produce a common database.

The sharing of data in these ways produces special issues. A major concern is who owns the data and who has access to the data for the purpose of analysis and publication. Generally, any data collected with federal funds, at least after a period of time, is considered to be in the public domain and therefore available to anyone. In practice, however, insistence on making data publicly available and encouraging their use typically occurs only for large, often nationally representative, samples or multisited projects. Individual investigators are often reluctant to make data available to others even after the initial use of the data is completed, primarily because a) they have invested a great deal in the collection of the data, b) they want to have maximum opportunity to use the data themselves to conduct secondary analyses, c) they are concerned about being embarrassed by the subsequent publication of studies that may attack or contradict their own previous reports, and d) they are worried that the subsequent work may be inferior in academic quality, which may retroactively stain by association their own reputation.

Shared databases from applied projects may have additional issues. Competing hospitals that have joined in a collaborative project may regard information on their patients and programs as proprietary, and different human service agencies may be very uneasy about the prospect of being compared with one another in terms of program effectiveness. Projects with policy implications may be prevented from releasing information about program effectiveness until certain policy considerations (e.g., funding of the next round of demonstration programs) have been accomplished.

Units possessing a shared database have several options depending on the circumstance. First, if the data were collected with private funds, they may not be made accessible to individuals other than the data collector. Second, the unit may set up criteria and a process for approving requests made by members or nonmembers of the unit to use the data for specific purposes. For example, applicants may be required to describe the particular variables and sample requested, the research question to be addressed, and methods of analysis to be used—much like in a grant request. In addition, the unit may specify the right to review and to deny publication of the study, it may require data be returned or destroyed after use, and it may demand a new application to use the data to address other questions. A major consideration in deciding whether a request by a scholar outside the unit will be approved is the likelihood that a member of the unit wants to analyze the data for a similar purpose now or in the foreseeable future.

If data are collected by teams of collaborators at the same or several sites, special problems arise, mainly concerning who has what rights and privileges to analyze and publish papers from the data and whose names shall appear on those papers and in what sequence. Various possibilities exist. Some individuals may have free access, while others have limited access or access only by petition. Individual sites may have access to the data from their site, but not the data from other sites, and certain time delays may be instituted (e.g., no site-specific data can be published until N years after completion of the data collection or until the aggregate results are published). Certain investigators in a single-site collaboration may have free access to the data they collect (e.g., behavioral data), but not to data collected by others (e.g., medical). Authorships may depend on which parts of the data are used. For example, analyses of data collected by an individual may be published under that individual's name, all data collectors may be included as authors, or no authors may be listed for reports from the total data set of a multisited project (roles of contributors may be described in a footnote).

It is strongly suggested that policies and procedures pertaining to these issues be stipulated in advance and in writing, and that criteria and/or committees be established to make decisions on individual cases or to resolve disputes.

CONCLUSIONS

Special units have performed a valuable function in the history of most disciplines. In child development, for example, such units (e.g., Fels Research Institute, Merrill-Palmer Institute, Institute of Human Development) contributed many of the milestone longitudinal studies to the intellectual history of this discipline, and many institutes and centers are synonymous with contemporary concentrations of excellence in the field.

Special units are likely to continue to make valuable and unique contributions. Increasingly, it appears, funding in the behavioral sciences is aimed at specific problems (e.g., family violence, substance abuse), rather than at disciplines, or sets of disciplines (e.g., mental health, behavioral sciences). Further, many new funding priorities are interdisciplinary and applied (e.g., comprehensive services for at-risk families). Universities, especially those that are very traditionally structured, will need special units and administrative structures and policies that promote and facilitate research and education that concentrates on such problems and cuts across academic disciplines and the frequent psychological barriers between faculty and service professionals to conduct such projects. Such specialized, applied, multidisciplinary units, especially those that relate to community service providers and policymakers, have a chance to demonstrate in a new way how universities can contribute the skills of their faculty to creating a better life for children, youth, and families in the community where those universities reside.

REFERENCES

Gallagher, J.J. (1990). Emergence of policy studies and policy institutes. *American Psychologist, 45,* 1316–1318.

Groark, C., & McCall, R.B. (1994). Building successful university–community collaborations. In J. Murray and C.B. Fisher (Eds.), *Applied developmental science for graduate programs in education and the human science professions.* Washington, DC: APA Books.

McCall, R.B. (1990). Promoting interdisciplinary and faculty–service provider relations. *American Psychologist, 45,* 1319–1324.

Weinberg, R.A., Fishhaut, E.H., Moore, S.G., & Plaisance, C. (1990). The Center for Early Education and Development: "Giving away" child psychology. *American Psychologist, 45,* 1325–1328.

Author Index

A
Abelson, R.P., 215, *218*
Abramovitch, R., 110, *116*
Abrams, L.A., 164, 165, 166, 167, 182, *187*
Abrams, P., 247, *251*
Achenbach, T.M., 101, *116*, *117*, 156
Achenbaum, W.A., *158*
Ahlborn, H.H., 101, *118*
Allison, K.W., 33, *35*
Alluisi, E.A., 4, *20*
Alpert, R., 92, *119*
Anderson, E., 164, *184*
Andrews, M., 255n
Arnold, K.D., 101, *118*
Asarnow, J.R., 132, *139*, 153, *158*

B
Baltes, M.M., 144, 148, 156, *158*
Baltes, P.B., 4, 5, *18*, *19*, *20*, 56, 57, *72*, *73*, 94, *117*, 144, 147, 148, 156, *158*, 166, *184*, *188*, 225, *233*
Barnett, W.S., 224, *233*
Basinger, K.S., 105, *118*
Beeghly, M., 109, *117*
Belanger, S., 56, 59, 61, *72*
Belar, C.D., 156, *159*
Benjamin, L.T., *19*, 121, 134, *139*
Bergemann, C.S., 148, 150, *159*
Bergman, L.R., 58, *72*
Bevan, W., 4, *19*, 47
Bickman, L., 229, *234*
Bieliauskas, L.A., 156, *159*
Birkel, R.C., 147, *158*, 183, *184*
Birren, J.E., 147, *158*
Boas, F., 191, *216*
Bok, D., 18, *19*, 32, *35*, 164, *184*

Boll, T.J., 4, *19*
Bonnen, J.T., 168, *184*
Bornstein, M.H., *21*, 191, *216*
Bowen, W.G., 41, *50*
Boyer, E.L., 10, 18, *19*, 33, 34, *35*, 157, *158*, 164, 166, 183, *184*, *185*
Brach, 134
Brannon, D., 145, 152, *160*
Brassard, M.M., 115, *117*
Bremner, R.H., 42, *50*
Brennan, M., 4, 12, 13, *19*, 54, 56, *72*, 114, *118*, 134
Brim, O.G., Jr., *20*, 73, *117*, 166, *185*
Brim, P.B., *117*
Bronfenbrenner, U., 4, 12, *19*, 54, 57, 58, *72*, 94, *117*, 121, 122, *139*, 147, 148, *158*, 166, *185*
Brown, A., 69, *72*
Brown, C.H., 225, *234*
Bruck, M., 111, *117*
Bruner, J.S., 191, *216*
Bubolz, M., 169, *185*
Burton, L.M., 183, *185*
Busch-Rossnagel, N.A., 166, 183, *186*
Butler, R.N., 147, *158*
Bynum, T.S., 165, 166, *187*

C
Cahan, E.D., 44, 45, *50*, 123, *139*
Callan, J.E., 80, *89*
Campbell, F.B., 105, 110, *120*, 153
Campbell, R.T., *160*
Campos, J., 255n
Carey, J.C., 25, *35*
Cass, L.K., 94, 107, *117*
Cassel, C.K., 156, *158*
Castañeda, A., 200, *218*

274 Author Index

Cavanaugh, J.C., 156, *158*
Ceci, S.J., 111, *117*, 147, 148, *158*
Chambers, C.M., 65, *74*
Chandler, M.J., 101, 105, *117*
Cheesman, F.L., 101, *118*
Chen, 134
Chesildine, H.C., 25
Child, J.L., 191, *219*
Cicchetti, D., 4, *19*, 58, *72*, 94, 95, 96, 109, *117*, *119*, *120*, 223, 234
Clemmens, R.L., 77, *89*
Coben, S., 42, *50*
Cocking, R.R., 2, 4, *21*, 191, 209, 209n, *216*, *217*
Coffman, H.C., 42, *50*
Cohen, G.D., 147, 148, *158*
Cohen, R.D., 121, *139*
Cohler, B.J., 148, 156, *158*
Cohn, M.D., 145, 152, *160*
Coie, J.D., 132, *139*, 153, *158*
Colapietro, E., 11, 12, 13, 14, 15, 16, *20*, 48, *50*, 54, 55, 56, 57, 59, 70, *73*, 79, *89*, 109, *118*, 138, *140*, 222, 232, *234*
Colby, A., 255n
Cole, M., 191, 199, 209, 211, *217*
Cole, T.R., 156, *158*
Collins, A., 255n
Cook, L., 238, 239, 245, 248, *251*
Cook, W.A., 4, *20*
Copple, C., 200, 212, *217*
Corey, K.E., 165, 166, *187*
Craighead, W.E., 4, *20*
Cravens, H., 121, *139*
Crawford, I., 33, *35*
Crouter, A.C., 166, *185*

D

D'Andrade, R., 196, 197, 215, *217*
Dann, S., 101, *118*
Davidson, E.S., 121, *139*
Davies, M., 125, *140*
DeLeon, P., 137, *140*
Dewey, J., 123, *139*, 190, *217*
Diamond, M.C., 144, 147, *158*

Dill, J.R., 2, 6n, *20*, 23, *35*, 54, 55, 56, 60, 62, 67, 68, 71, *73*, 79, 81, 88, *89*, 95, 112, *118*, 125, 127, 128, 130, 135, *139*, 144, 145, 147, 153, *158*, 166, 173, 183, *186*, 215, *217*, 221, 222, 224, 225, 231, 233, *234*, 237, *251*
Dobb, L.W., 92, *117*
Dolan, L.J., 225, *234*
Dollard, J., 92, *117*, *119*
Doman, G., 244, *251*
Donnerstein, E., 34, *35*
Dryfoos, J.G., 167, 177, 180, *185*
Dunn, J., 255n

E

Echemendia, R., 33, *35*
Edelbrock, C.S., 101, *116*, *117*
Edelman, M.W., 179, *185*
Edwards, C.P., 210, *217*
Edwards, E.J., 225, *234*
Eibl-Eibesfeldt, I., 190, 191, *217*
Eichorn, D., 255n
Elder, G.H., Jr., 166, *185*
Eliot, A.A., 122, 123
Elkind, D., 122, *139*
Elman, S.E., 164, *187*
Ely, 134
Enarson, H.L., 167, 168, *185*
Erickson, M.T., 130, *140*
Erikson, E.H., 191, *217*
Escobar, C.M., 224, *233*

F

Fagan, T.K., *19*, 121, 124, 128, *139*
Fairchild, H., 34, *35*
Fantz, R.L., 5, *19*
Featherman, D.L., 166, *185*
Feinburg, S., 135, *139*
Feldman, D.H., 121, 124, *139*
Fernberger, S.W., 91, *117*
Feshbach, N.D., 34, *35*
Fiese, B.H., 208, *218*
Finn-Stevenson, M., *21*, 132, *141*
Fisher, C.B., 2, 4, 5, 6n, 9, 11, 12, 13,

Author Index 275

14, 15, 16, *19, 20,* 23, *35,* 48, 50, 54, 55, 56, 57, 58, 59, 60, 61, 62, 65, 66, 67, 68, 69, 70, 71, *72, 73, 74,* 78, 79, 81, 88, *89,* 94, 95, 99, 107, 109, 111, 112, 114, *118,* 125, 127, 128, 130, 132, 135, 138, *139, 140,* 144, 145, 147, 153, *158,* 165, 166, 167, 170, 173, 183, 185, 186, 195, 210, 215, *217,* 221, 222, 224, 225, 231, 232, 233, *234,* 237, *251,* 255n
Fishhaut, E.H., 268, *272*
Fitzgerald, H.E., 173, 177, *187*
Ford, D.H., 166, 173, *186*
Forehand, G.A., 4, *20*
Fosdick, R.B., 42, *50*
Fox, R.E., 121, *140*
Frank, L.K., 42, 43, *50*
Frantz, C., 247, *251*
Freedman, J.L., 110, *116*
Freud, A., 101, *118*
Friend, M., 238, 239, 245, 248, *251*
Fuller, D., 105, *118*
Fyrberg, D., 56, *72*

G
Gallagher, J.J., 268, *272*
Garfinkel, H., 215, *217*
Garmezy, N., 95, 97, *118, 119*
Gatz, M., 147, 156, *159, 160*
Gay, J., 191, *217*
Gergen, K.J., 196, *217*
Germain, R.B., 115, *117*
Gerstein, A.I., 65, 69, 70, 71, *73*
Gessell, A., 122
Gibbs, J.C., 101, 105, 109, *118*
Glick, J., 191, 215, *217*
Glidden, R., 68, *73*
Goldstein, D., 65, 69, 70, 71, *73*
Goodnow, J.J., 191, *217*
Gramlich, E.M., 224, *234*
Grant, W.T., 44, 45, 77, 255n, 256n
Greenfield, P.M., 191, *217*
Groark, C.J., 239, 240, 241, 242, 248, *251,* 267, *272*

Grualnik, J.M., 156, *160*
Gudas, 134

H
Habenstein, R.W., 198, *218*
Hackney, S., 172, *186*
Hagen, J.W., 2, 6n, *20, 21,* 35, 42, 43, *51,* 54, 55, 56, 60, 62, 67, 68, 71, *73,* 79, 81, 88, *89,* 95, 112, *118,* 125, 127, 128, 130, 135, *139,* 144, 145, 147, 153, *158,* 166, 173, 183, *186,* 215, *217,* 221, 224, 225, 231, 233, *234,* 237, *251,* 255n
Hall, G. S., 42, 50, 123, 128
Hamburg, D.A., 18, *20,* 180, *186*
Hanson, M.J., 58, *73*
Hardison, O.B., 33, *35*
Harris, D., 45
Harrison, B. (President), 168
Hart, S.N., 115, *117*
Harter, S., 101, *118,* 178, *186*
Hartup, W., 47
Hawkins, J.D., 132, *139,* 153, *158*
Hayes, S.C., 70, *74*
Herdt, G., 210, *219*
Hertzog, C.K., 150, *159, 160*
Hetherington, E.M., *73,* 147, *159*
Higgins, A., 56, 59, 61, *72*
Hoagwood, K., *19, 72*
Hoch, E.L., 98, *119*
Hoeflin, R., 25, 26, *35*
Hogan, M.J., 2, 6n, *20,* 23, *35,* 54, 55, 56, 60, 62, 67, 68, 71, *73,* 79, 81, 88, *89,* 95, 112, *118,* 125, 127, 128, 130, 135, *139,* 144, 145, 147, 153, *158,* 166, 173, 183, *186, 217,* 221, 222, 224, 225, 231, 233, *234,* 237, *251*
Holland, D., 191n, *218*
Hoopfer, L.C., 164, 165, 166, 167, 182, *187*
Howell, W.G., 4, *20*
Hudson, R.B., 156, *159*
Hula, R.C., 164, *184*
Hula, R.G., 165, 166, *187*

Author Index

Hunt, J.McV., 93, *119*
Huston, A.C., 34, *35*, 164, 166, *186*

J
Jacobs, F., 125, *140*
Jakobi, P.L., 156, *158*
Jensen, P., *19*, 72
Jones, H., 42
Jordan, D.K., 197, *219*

K
Kagan, J., 166, *185*
Kagan, S.L., 255n
Kahn, R.L., 148, 156, *159*
Kanfer, F.H., 127, 128, *140*
Kanner, L., 101, *119*
Kastenbaum, R., 156, *158*
Katz, P.A., 34, *35*
Kauffman, M.B., 166, *187*
Kazdin, A.E., 95, *119*
Keating, D.P., 2, 4, 12, 13, *20*, 46, 47, 50
Kellam, S.G., 33, *35*, 223, 225, *234*
Keller, 33
Kells, H.R., 65, *74*
Kendall, P.C., 4, *20*
Kennedy, D., 126, *140*
Kenny, T.J., 77, 79, *89*
Kermoian, R., 255n
Kessel, F., 47, *50*, 121, *139*
Kessen, W., 121, *139*
Kiesler, S.B., 4, *20*
King, N.J., 93, *119*
Kivnick, H.Q., 148, *159*
Klatsky, R.L., 4, *20*
Klepac, R.K., 156, *159*
Kluckhohn, C., 191, *218*
Knepp, D., 33, *35*
Knott, J.H., 165, 166, *187*
Koch, D.A., 105, *117*
Koocher, G.P., 4, 14, 15, 16, *19*, *20*, 48, *50*, 65, 66, 68, 69, 70, 72, 73, 107, *118*, 138, *139*, 231, 232
Koretz, D.S., 153, *159*
Kuther, T.L., 56, 59, 61, *72*, 73
Kwan, K.M., 198, *218*

L
La Greca, A.M., 95, *119*
Lamb, M.E., *21*
Larsen, K.G., 156, *159*
Lenzenweger, M.F., 147, 148, *158*
Lerner, R.M., 2, 4, 6n, 9, *19*, *20*, 23, 35, 54, 55, 56, 57, 58, 60, 62, 66, 67, 68, 71, *72*, *73*, 78, 79, 81, 88, *89*, 94, 95, 99, 111, 112, *118*, *119*, 125, 127, 128, 130, 132, 135, *139*, 144, 145, 147, 153, *158*, *159*, 164, 165, 166, 167, 169, 170, 172, 173, 180, 182, 183, *185*, *186*, *187*, 210, 215, *217*, 221, 222, 224, 225, 231, 233, *234*, 237, *251*
Levin, H., 92, *119*
Le Vine, R.A., 197, 209, 210, *218*
Levine, R.L., 173, *187*
Levine, S.Z., 77, *89*
Levy, L.H., 122, *140*
Lewis, M.I., 58, *73*, 109, *119*, 147, *158*
Lincoln, A. (President), 17, 24, 168
Lipsitt, L.P., 4–5, *19*, 56, *72*
Litmer, 128
Little, R.R., 179, *187*
Long, B., 132, *139*, 153, *158*
Lonnborg, B., 34, *36*
Lord, C., 2, 4, 12, 13, 46, 47, *50*
Lynch, E.W., 58, *73*
Lynton, E.A., 164, *187*

M
Maccoby, E.E., 92, *119*
Maddux, J.E., 4, *20*
Magnussen, D., 58, *72*
Magrath, C.P., 167, 169, 183, *187*
Manning, M., 123, *140*
Markman, H.J., 132, *139*, 153, *158*
Masten, A.S., 95, 97, 109, *118*, *119*
Masterpasqua, F., 132, *140*
Mattessich, P.W., 239, 247, 249, *251*
Mayer, L.S., 225, *234*
McCall, R.B., 239, 240, 241, 242, 248, *251*
McClearn, G.E., 147, 150, *159*

McGoldrick, M., 199, *218*
McGurk, H., 255n
McKinney, M.H., 164, 165, 166, 167, 177, 182, *187*
McLoyd, V.C., 182, *187*
Mead, M., *187*, 191, 199, *218*
Melton, G., 255n
Meredith, W., 153, *160*
Miller, E., 92, *119*
Miller, J.R., 164, 165, 166, 167, 169, 182, *186*, *187*
Miller, N.E., 82, *89*, 92, *117*
Miller, S.M., 58, *73*, 109, *119*
Mindel, C.H., 198, *218*
Monsey, B.R., 239, 247, 249, *251*
Montada, L., 4, *20*, 54, *73*, 132, 133, *140*
Moore, S.G., 268, *272*
Mordock, J.B., 239, 240, 241, 242, *251*
Morrison, F.J., 2, 4, 12, 13, *20*, 46, 47, *50*
Mowrer, O., 92, *117*
Mozdzierz, G., 137, *140*
Muehrer, P., 153, *159*
Murray, H.A., 191, *218*
Murray, J.P., 2, 3, 4, 5, 6n, *20*, 23, 34, 35, *36*, 54, 55, 56, 60, 62, 67, 68, 71, *73*, 79, 81, 88, *89*, 95, 112, *118*, 125, 127, 128, 130, 135, *139*, 144, 145, 147, 153, *158*, 166, 173, 183, *186*, 215, *217*, 221, 222, 224, 225, 231, 233, *234*, 237, *251*
Musil, C.M., 148, 150, *161*
Myers, H.F., 80, *89*

N
Nasulgc, 168, 169
Nesselroade, J.R., 148, 150, *159*, 166, *188*
Nikolich, C.C., 110, *116*
Nuechterlein, K.H., 109, *119*

O
Ogbu, J.U., 204, *218*
Ollendick, T.H., 93, *119*

Oller, K., 255n
Olshansky, S.J., 156, *158*

P
Paget, K.F., 105, *117*
Park, D.C., 156, *158*
Parke, R.D., 124, *140*
Pearson, Mrs. H.G., 122
Pedersen, N.L., 148, 150, *159*
Pepper, S.C., 193, *218*
Perlmutter, M., *19*, 72, *118*, 147, *159*
Perry, N.W., Jr., 128, *140*
Persico, C.F., 191, *218*
Peterson, D.R., 122, *140*
Philibert, M., 143, 156, 157, *159*
Piaget, J., 116, *119*, 192, *218*
Piotrkowski, C., 255n
Pitcher, E., 122, 129
Place, 134
Plaisance, C., 268, *272*
Platt, 3, 17, *20*
Plomin, R., 147, 148, 150, *159*
Poon, L., 150, *159*
Price, R.H., 224, *234*
Procidano, M.E., 58, *73*

Q
Qualls, S.H., 150, *160*
Quinn, N., 191n, *218*

R
Ramey, C., 255n
Ramey, S.L., 132, *139*, 153, *158*, 255n
Ramírez, M., III, 200, *218*
Rasmussen, W.D., 17, *20*, 24, *36*
Rau, J.B., 11, 12, 13, 14, 15, 16, *20*, 48, *50*, 54–57, 59, 61, 70, 72–73, 79, 89, 109, 118, 138, 140, 222, 232, 234
Rau, L., 92, 119
Rawlings, S.C., 153, 160
Read, P.B., 33, 36
Rebok, G.W., 2, 6n, 20, 23, 33, 35, 54, 55, 56, 57, 60, 62, 67, 68, 71, *73*, 79, 81, 88, *89*, 95, 112, *118*, 125, 127, 128, 130, 135,

278 Author Index

139, 144, 145, 147, 153, *158,* 166, 173, 183, *186,* 215, *217,* 221, 222, 223, 224, 225, 231, 233, *234, 251*
Redl, F., 101, *119*
Reese, H.W., 4, 5, *19, 21,* 56, *72, 74*
Reid, J.D., 150, *161*
Resnick, L.B., 132, 134, *140*
Rheingold, H.L., 3, *20,* 45, *51,* 54, *73*
Richards, E.S., 16, 25, 169
Rie, H.E., 97, *119*
Roberts, M.C., 4, 130, *140*
Robins, L., 109, *119*
Robinson, L., 33, *35*
Rockefeller, J.D., 42
Roditi, 134
Rogoff, B., 47, *51,* 210, 218
Rolf, J., 33, 36, 109, 119
Rommetveit, R., 211, *218*
Rosovsky, H., 33, *36*
Ross, A.O., 91, 94, 98, 107, *119*
Ross, D.F., 111, *117*
Routh, D.K., 78, *89*
Rovine, M.J., 153, *159*
Rowe, J.N., 148, 156, *159*
Rubinstein, E.A., 34, *35*
Rudberg, M.A., 156, *158*
Rudenstine, N.L., 41, *50*
Rutter, M., 94, 97, 109, *119, 120*

S
Sameroff, A.J., 208, *218*
Saunders, R., 200, 212, *217*
Scarr, S., 15, *21,* 70, *73,* 147, 148, *159*
Schaie, K.W., 5, *19,* 144, 150, 153, *159, 160, 161,* 166, *184, 188*
Schank, R.C., 215, *218*
Schein, E.H., 172, *187*
Schmitt, M., 4, *20,* 54, *73*
Schneider, E.L., 156, *160*
Scholnick, E.K., 4, *21*
Schooler, C., 148, *160*

Schorr, L.B., 49, *51,* 180, *188*
Schultz, L.H., 109, 111, *119*
Scribner, S., 199, 209, 211, *217*
Sears, R.R., 3, *21,* 54, *73,* 92, *117, 119*
Selman, R.L., 109, 111, *119*
Senge, P.M., 173, *188*
Senn, 43, *51*
Serafica, F.C., 91n
Shaefer, A.B., 78, *89*
Shakow, D., 134, *140*
Shantz, C., 4, 5, *21,* 54, *73*
Sharp, D.W., 191, *217*
Shea, D.G., 144, *160*
Sherrod, L.R., 147, *160,* 255n
Shibutani, T., 198, *218*
Shure, M.B., 132, *139,* 153, *158*
Shweder, R.A., 189n, 191, 210, *218, 219*
Siegel, A.W., 2, 3, *21,* 54, *74,* 121, 135, *140*
Sigel, I.E., 2, 4, 6n, 11, *19, 20, 21, 23, 35, 54,* 55, 56, 60, 62, 67, 68, 71, *73,* 79, 81, 88, *89,* 95, 112, *118,* 125, 127, 128, 130, *139,* 144, 145, 147, 153, *158,* 166, 173, 183, *186,* 200, 211, 212, 215, *217, 218,* 222, 224, 225, 231, 233, *234,* 237, *251*
Sledden, E.A., 4, *20*
Sloane, R.B., 147, *158*
Smith, A.D., 156, *158*
Smuts, A.B., 3, *20, 21,* 42, 43, 44, *51,* 54, *74*
Smyer, M.A., 2, 6n, *20,* 23, *35,* 54, 55, 56, 60, 62, 67, 68, 71, *73,* 79, 81, 88, *89,* 95, 112, *118,* 125, 127, 128, 130, 135, *139,* 144, 145, 147, 148, 150, 152, 153, 156, *158, 159, 160,* 166, 173, 183, *184, 186,* 215, *217,* 221, 222, 224, 225, 231, 233, *234,* 237, *251*
Snodgrass, R., 137, *140*
Solomons, G., 78, *89*
Sontag, M.S., 169, *185*

Sorenson, B., 147, *160*
Sostek, A.M., 2, 6n, *20*, 23, *35*, 54, 55, 56, 60, 62, 67, 68, 71, *73*, 79, 81, 88, *89*, 95, 112, *118*, 125, 127, 128, 130, 135, *139*, 144, 145, 147, 153, *158*, 166, 173, 183, *186*, 215, *217*, 221, 222, 224, 231, 233, *234*, *251*
Spanier, G.B., 166, *187*
Spencer, M.B., 2, 6n, *20*, 23, *35*, 54, 55, 56, 60, 62, 67, 68, 71, *73*, 79, 81, 88, *89*, 95, 112, *118*, 125, 127, 128, 130, 135, *139*, 144, 145, 147, 153, *158*, 166, 173, 183, *186*, 215, *217*, 221, 222, 224, 225, 231, 233, *234*, 237, *251*
Sroufe, L.A., *20*, 94
Stigall, T.T., 156, *159*
Stigler, J.W., 210, *219*
Storandt, M., 156, *160*
Streit, A., 144, *160*
Stricker, G., 156, *160*
Strzok, 134
Sullivan, B., 238–239, *251*
Summers, T., 255n
Sundberg, 92
Sunderland, T., 147, *158*
Swartz, M.J., 197, *219*

T
Tellegen, A., 95, *118*
Teri, L., 150, 156, *160*, *161*
Terry, P.A., 164, 165, 166, 167, 182, *187*
Thoden, K., 110, *116*
Thomas, C., 204
Toglia, M.P., 11, *117*
Tornstam, L., 156, *160*
Toth, S.L., 96, *117*, *120*, 223, *234*
Troy, W.G., 205, *219*
Tryon, W.W., 2, 4, 12, 13, *20*, *21*, 54, 56, 57, 66, 71, *73*, *74*, 99, *118*, *119*, 195, *217*
Tubman, J., *187*

Tuma, J.M., 78, *89*, 91n, 130, *140*, *141*
Tyler, 92

V
Valentine, J., 93, *120*
Vandercook, T., 238, 239, *251*
Van Ryn, M., 224, 234
Vinokur, A.D., 224, *234*
Von Eye, A., 153, *159*, 166, *188*
Votruba, J.C., 164, 184, *188*

W
Walls, C.T., 145, *160*
Wandersman, A., 255n
Washburn, A., 45
Washington, V., 179, *188*
Watt, N.F., 132, *139*, 153, *158*
Weinberg, R.A., 255n, 268, *272*
Weinert, E., 147, *160*
Weintraub, S., 109, *119*
Weithorn, L.A., 105, 110, *120*
Wenar, C., 91n, 94, 95, 96, *120*
Werthamer-Larsson, L., 225, *234*
Wertlieb, D., 4, *21*, 134, 138, *141*, 255n
Wertsch, J.V., 189n, 194, 209, 210, 211, *219*
West, C., 201, 204, 207, *219*
West, S.G., 132, *139*, 153, *158*
White, S., 121, *139*
White, S.H., 3, *21*, 48, 54, *74*, 121, *140*
Whiting, H.W.M., 191, *219*
Wilcox, B.L., 2, 6n, *20*, 23, 34, *35*, 54, 55, 56, 60, 62, 65, 67, 68, 71, *73*, 79, 81, 88, *89*, 95, 112, *118*, 125, 127, 128, 130, 135, *139*, 144, 145, 147, 153, *158*, 166, 173, 183, *186*, 215, *217*, 221, 225, 231, 233, *234*, 237, *251*
Willis, S.L., 144, *160*, *161*
Wilson, K., 70, *74*
Wilson, R.J., 69, 70, 71, *73*
Wilson, W. (President), 168

Winder, C.L., 98, *119*
Wineman, D., 101, *119*
Witmer, L., 92, 95, 107, *120*, 124
Wohlford, P., 80, *89*, 92, *120*
Woodworth, R.S., 43, 44, 45, 47, *50*
Wright, L., 4, *20*, 75, 78, *89*
Wright, R., Jr., 198, *218*
Wykle, M.L., 148, 150, *161*

Y

Yeates, K.O., 109, 111, *119*
York, J., 238, 239, *251*

Young, K.E., 65, 68, *74*
Youniss, J., 3, 12, *21*, 54, *74*, 121, *141*

Z

Zarit, S.H., 147, 150, 152, *160*, *161*
Zigler, E., 2, *21*, 93, *120*, 132, *141*
Zimet, C.M., 156, *159*
Zimiles, H., 48
Zuckerman, D.M., 34, *35*

Subject Index

A
Academics, see Universities
Accreditation
  advantages and disadvantages of, for applied developmental psychology programs, 65–66, 68–69
  American Psychological Association guidelines
    description, 65
    proposed criteria, 66–68
  effect on internships, 68–69
  professional psychology programs
    characteristics of, 65
    definition of, 66
    description of, 65
ADP, see Applied developmental psychology
Adult development, programs for, see Human Development and Family Studies
Aging, graduate education programs for
  Human Development and Family Studies Department, at Penn State University
    curriculum
      adult development and aging requirements, 153
      degree requirements, 152–153
      intervention research requirements, 153–154
      postgraduate requirements, 154
    description of, 144
    faculty of, 144
    field experiences
      function of, 154
      internships, 155
  future progress, 157–158
  planning procedures
    individual, 151–152
    institutional, 149–150
  premises of
    regarding adult development and aging, 147–148
    regarding graduate education, 146–147
American Psychological Association, accreditation guidelines of
  description, 65
  proposed criteria, 66–68
APA, see American Psychological Association
Applied child development
  description of, 124
  graduate education in, Eliot-Pearson Department of Child Study
    accreditation, 138
    curriculum
      doctoral student requirements, 131
      masters degree requirements, 131
      multidisciplinary approach, 132–133
      stages of, 133–134
      theoretical coursework, 130–131
    dissertation preparation and completion, 134
    establishment of, 122–123
    faculty of, 123–125, 128–130
    field experiences
      goals of, 135
      internships, 135–136
    goals of, 127–128

281

282 Subject Index

multidisciplinary approach of, 123–125
philosophy of, 123–124
principles of, 125
structure of, 126–127
Applied developmental psychology
and clinical child psychology, 97
integration of curriculum during graduate education, 105–106, 109–111
similarities and differences, 112–114
and clinical psychology, comparison, 13–16, 48, 62, 78
definition of, 47, 55
description of, 12
goals of, 66
graduate education programs, 13, 15
accreditation of, 67, 69
challenges for, 48–49
development of, 46
Fordham University
accreditation, 69–70
application strategies, 60
curriculum, 57–58
ethics and conduct training, 60–61
field experience
assistantships and internships, 63–64
practicum, 62–63
licensure, 69–70
overview of, 55–56
program development, 56–57
research methodology training, 58–59
student participation rates, 57
historical origins, 46
multidisciplinary approach, 56
recommendations for reforming, 48–49
research and application utilization, methods to determine, 71
licensuring and, 15–16
objectives of, 14

populations targeted by, 115–116
psychotherapy and, 71
Applied developmental science
applicability of, to human science, 32–34, 79
applied child development, see Applied child development
applied developmental psychology, see Applied developmental psychology
areas of study, 3–4, 78
basic developmental science and, transition from, 4
and clinical child psychology, similarities and differences between, 112–114
community collaborations
advantages of, 238
barriers to
attitudes of the involved parties, 239–240
purpose, 240–241
regulations, 242–243
resources, 243–244
stakeholders, 241–242
description of, 237–238
guidelines for success
attitudes of the involved parties, 245–246
common mission, 248
communication, 248
defining partnerships, 247–248
leadership, 249–250
liaison participation, 247
proactive interaction, 248–249
progress monitoring, 250
project selection, 246–247
requirements of, 238
contributions of, 2–3
definition of, 124
evolution of, 78
graduate education for
disciplinary and multidisciplinary emphases of, 11–12
field experiences
budgetary and management decisions regarding, 225

Subject Index   283

evaluation methods of, 229-230
goals of, 221
integration with academic training
overview, 230
questions regarding
APA-accredited internships, 231-232
clinical placement vs. field experiences, 230-231
research/evaluative components, 232
uniformity among field experiences, 232-233
intervention efforts, 223
multicultural diversity of, 224
multidisciplinary collaborative nature of, 225-226
practicum experience and, comparison, 230-231
quality control of
devising a work plan, 228-229
overview, 227
survey of, 226-227
types of, 222-223, 227
funding of, 42
growth of, 42
Institute for Children, Youth, and Families, at Michigan State University
campus context of
changes in campus culture, 172, 175-176
multidisciplinary emphasis of faculty, 172-174
research-outreach theory and methodology, 174-175
community involvement
beneficial effects, 179-180
collaborative projects, 177-178
description of, 176
mission statement of, 169-170
outreach scholarship, 170-171

integrative approaches, 33-34, 164-166
methods to enhance, 32-34
multicultural training, 10-11
past and current trends in, 3-4
recommendations for reforming, 47-48
reorganization of training, 164-165
socio-cultural approach
advantages of, 190
conceptions of culture, 196-198
cultural labeling, 201-202
cultural meanings, 203-204
culture and ethnicity, relationship between, 197-198
diversity, 194-195
importance of, 195
integration of, into educational program, 205
minorities, 201-202
objectives of, 200-201
practical definition of, 195-196
preconceptions, 203
prototypic program
coursework, 208-209
field work, 210
importance of intervention, 216
multicultural discourse, 210-214, 213
role of faculty, 205-208
supervisory experiences, 214
teacher recruitment, 212-213
rationale for, 191-192
reasons for omission, 193-194
historical origins of, 3-4
Institute for Children, Youth, and Families, at Michigan State University
campus context of, integration of applied developmental science, 173-174
community involvement, knowledge and technical assistance dissemination, 180-181

multidisciplinary emphasis of, 16–17
National Conference on Graduate Education in the Applications of Developmental Science Across the Lifespan, conference proceedings
  curriculum development, 7–8, 54, 215
  determining framework, 6–7
  field experiences, 8, 135, 215, 221, 229–230
  and pediatric psychology
    community systems model, 86–88
    description of, 75–76
    field experience, 82–84
    research experience, 84–86
    training programs
      models, 80–81
      practicum experience, 82
      preparation, 81–82
  populations targeted by, 115–116
  principles of, 95, 124
  and psychology departments
    overview, 12
    traditional developmental psychology, 12–14
  recent changes in, 254
  transition to, from basic developmental science, 4
  unit creation, criteria for
    interdisciplinary nature
      academic reward system, 267–268
      horizontal and vertical contributions, 266
      multi- vs. inter- vs. transdisciplinary units, 266
      policy studies, 268–269
      projection promotion concerns, 266–267
      residential vs. facilitative, 262–263
    selective vs. open membership
      open, 265–266
      selective, 263–265
    shared databases, 269–271

university-based vs. independent advisory boards, 260
chain of authority, 257–258
criteria and evaluation, 259–260
funding, 261–262
overview, 256–257
role of students, 261
Assessment training, for pediatric psychology, 83
Assistantships, see Internships
Association of American Universities, 41

B
Behavior therapy, 93

C
Campus culture, 173
CCD, see Committee on Child Development
Child development
  applied, see Applied child development
  components of, 124
  laboratory research, 46
  programs
    Head Start, 93
    historical origins of, 42–44, 93
    objectives of, 43–44
Child psychology, see also Pediatric psychology
  applied developmental science studies of, 3–4
  clinical, see Clinical child psychology
Child study movement
  early financings of, 3
  social history of, 3–4
Clinical child psychology
  American Psychiatric Association view of, 108
  and child psychology, similarities between, 91–92, 95
  and developmental psychology, 94–95, 104–105, 107–108
  curriculum content, 109

Subject Index 285

integration of research, 109–110
similarities and differences, 112–113
and developmental science, similarities and differences between, 112–114
effect of psychological theories on, 92–93
nonpsychopathologic populations of, 115
objectives of, 97–98
Ohio State University program
curriculum
didactic courses, 99–102, 100t
integration of developmental psychology, 109–111
professional socialization, 103
research training, 102–103
establishment of, 96
field experience
accreditation, 106–107
internships, 103–106
practicum experience, 103–106
goals of, 98
philosophy of, 96–98
planning procedures and structures, 98–99
origins of, 91–92
Clinical psychology
and applied developmental psychology, comparison between, 62
child, see Clinical child psychology
child-oriented vs. adult-oriented, 91–92
historical origins of, 91–92
internship programs of, 231–232
training programs, 77–78
Colleges of Human Ecology
compared to other universities, 31
School of Family Studies and Human Services, at Kansas State University
disciplines studied at, 30
founding of, 26
objectives of, 27–28

Committee on Child Development
description of, 42
purpose of, 43
Community
and applied developmental science, collaborative relationship
advantages of, 238
barriers to
attitudes of the involved parties, 239–240
purpose, 240–241
regulations, 242–243
resources, 243–244
stakeholders, 241–242
description of, 237–238
guidelines for success
attitudes of the involved parties, 245–246
common mission, 248
communication, 248
defining partnerships, 247–248
leadership, 249–250
liaison participation, 247
proactive interaction, 248–249
progress monitoring, 250
project selection, 246–247
requirements of, 238
and pediatric psychology training programs, 86–88
Community mental health
development of, 93
principles of, 93
Community outreach, see also Outreach scholarship
and applied development science programs
integration into university graduate education programs, 167–168
overview, 165–166
Community psychology, 87
Community systems model, for pediatric psychology training, 86–88
Cooperative Extension Services, publications of, 34
Coursework, see Curriculum

286   Subject Index

Culture
  components of, 197
  effect on human development, 191–192, 197–198
  ethnicity and, relationship between, 198–200
  field experiences and, 224
  lack of, in developmental psychology training, 192–194
  practical use of, 195–196
Curriculum, program
  for adult development and aging program, at Human Development and Family Studies Department of Penn State University
    adult development and aging requirements, 153
    degree requirements, 152–153
    intervention research requirements, 153–154
    postgraduate requirements, 154
  for applied child development program, at Eliot-Pearson Department of Child Study, 130–134
  for applied developmental psychology program, at Fordham University, 57–58
  for clinical child psychology program, at Ohio State University
    didactic courses, 99–102, 100t
    professional socialization, 103
    research training, 102–103
    National Conference on Graduate Education recommendations, 7–8
  for socio-cultural emphasis, 208–209
  theoretical studies, 130–131

D
Developmental contextualism, 166, 172–173
Developmental processes, study of, by developmental scientists, 2
Developmental psychology, applied, see Applied developmental psychology

Developmental psychopathology
  advent of, 94
  principles of, 94
Developmental science
  applied, see Applied developmental science
  basic, 4
Developmental scientists
  developmental process studies by, 2
  function of, 1
Doctoral programs, see Graduate education

E
Education, graduate
  for applied child development, graduate education programs, see Eliot-Pearson Department of Child Study
  for applied developmental psychology, 13, 15
    accreditation of, 67, 69
    challenges for, 48–49
    development of, 46
    Fordham University
      accreditation, 69–70
      application strategies, 60
      curriculum, 57–58
      ethics and conduct training, 60–61
      field experience
        assistantships and internships, 63–64
        practicum, 62–63
      licensure, 69–70
      overview of, 55–56
      program development, 56–57
      research methodology training, 58–59
      student participation rates, 57
    historical origins, 46
    multidisciplinary approach, 56
    recommendations for reforming, 48–49
    research and application utilization, methods to determine, 71

Subject Index 287

for applied developmental science
field experiences. see Field experiences
funding of, 42
growth of, 42
Institute for Children, Youth, and Families, at Michigan State University
campus context of
changes in campus culture, 172, 175-176
integration of applied developmental science, 173-174
multidisciplinary emphasis of faculty, 172-174
research-outreach theory and methodology, 174-175
community involvement
beneficial effects, 179-180
collaborative projects, 177-178
description of, 176
knowledge and technical assistance dissemination, 180-181
mission statement of, 169-170
outreach scholarship, 170-171
integrative approaches, 33-34, 164-166
methods to enhance, 32-34
National Conference on Graduate Education, conference proceedings
curriculum development, 7-8
determining framework, 6-7
field experiences, 8
training goals, 7
recommendations for reforming, 47-48
reorganization of training, 164-165
socio-cultural approach
advantages of, 190
conceptions of culture, 196-198
cultural labeling, 201-202
cultural meanings, 203-204
culture and ethnicity, relationship between, 197-198
diversity, 194-195
importance of, 195
integration of, into educational program, 205
minorities, 201-202
objectives of, 200-201
practical definition of, 195-196
preconceptions, 203
prototypic program
curriculum, 208-209
field experiences, 210
importance of intervention, 216
multicultural discourse, 210-214, 213
role of faculty, 205-208
supervisory experiences, 214
teacher recruitment, 212-213
rationale for, 191-192
reasons for omission, 193-194
historical origins of, 41-42
Eliot-Pearson Department of Child Study, for graduate education in applied child development
accreditation, 138
curriculum
doctoral student requirements, 131
masters degree requirements, 131
multidisciplinary approach, 132-133
stages of, 133-134
theoretical coursework, 130-131
dissertation preparation and completion, 134
establishment of, 122-123
faculty of, 123-125, 128-130
field experiences
goals of, 135
internships, 135-136
goals of, 127-128
multidisciplinary approach of, 123-125
philosophy of, 123-124
principles of, 125
structure of, 126-127

288 Subject Index

Ethics, 61
Ethnicity
  culture and, relationship between, 198–200
  definition of, 198
  effect on human development, 191–192
Experiences, field, see Field experiences

F

Faculty, of applied developmental science programs
  at Eliot-Pearson Department of Child Study, 123–125, 128–130
  at Human Development and Family Studies Department, at Penn State University, 146–147, 149–150
  at Institute for Children, Youth, and Families, multidisciplinary reorientation, 183
  with socio-cultural emphasis, 205–208
Field experiences, see also Internships; Research programs
  for applied child development program, at Eliot-Pearson Department of Child Study
    goals of, 135
    internships, 135–136
  for applied developmental psychology program, at Fordham University
    assistantships and internships, 63–64
    practicum, 62–63
  for applied developmental science
    budgetary and management decisions regarding, 225
    evaluation methods of, 229–230
    goals of, 221
    integration with academic training overview, 230
    questions regarding APA-accredited internships, 231–232
    clinical placement vs. field experiences, 230–231
    research/evaluative components, 232
    uniformity among field experiences, 232–233
    intervention efforts, 223
    multicultural diversity of, 224
    multidisciplinary collaborative nature of, 225–226
    practicum experience and, comparison, 230–231
    quality control of
      devising a work plan, 228–229
      overview, 227
    survey of, 226–227
    types of, 222–223, 227
  for clinical child psychology program
    applied developmental science and, comparisons, 114
    at Ohio State University
      infant stimulation program, 106
      internships, 103–106
      practicum experience, 103–106
    function of, 8–9
    National Conference on Graduate Education in the Applications of Developmental Science Across the Lifespan recommendations, 8–9
  for socio-cultural approach to applied development science, 210–214
  training survey, 235–236
Field regulation, see Accreditation
Field work, see Field experiences
Fordham University, applied developmental psychology program
  accreditation, 69–70
  application strategies, 60
  community collaborations, 64
  curriculum, 57–58
  ethics and conduct training, 60–61
  field experience
    assistantships and internships, 63–64
    practicum, 62–63

Subject Index

licensure, 69-70
lifespan approach, 56
multidisciplinary emphasis, 56
overview of, 55-56
program development, 56-57
research methodology training, 58-59
student participation rates, 57
Freudian theory, child psychology and, 92

G

Gerontology, applied
 definition of, 144
 graduate education programs, see Human Development and Family Studies
Graduate education
 accreditation criteria, 66-68
 for adult development and aging program, Human Development and Family Studies Department, at Penn State University
  curriculum
   adult development and aging requirements, 153
   degree requirements, 152-153
   intervention research requirements, 153-154
   postgraduate requirements, 154
  description of, 144
  faculty of, 144
  field experiences
   function of, 154
   internships, 155
  future progress, 157-158
  planning procedures
   individual, 151-152
   institutional, 149-150
  premises of
   regarding adult development and aging, 147-148
   regarding graduate education, 146-147
  research programs, 144-145
  structure and goals of, 148-149
 for applied child development, Eliot-Pearson Department of Child Study
  accreditation, 138
  curriculum
   doctoral student requirements, 131
   masters degree requirements, 131
   multidisciplinary approach, 132-133
   stages of, 133-134
   theoretical coursework, 130-131
  dissertation preparation and completion, 134
  establishment of, 122-123
  faculty of, 123-125, 128-130
  field experiences
   goals of, 135
   internships, 135-136
  multidisciplinary approach of, 123-125
  philosophy of, 123-124
  principles of, 125
  program goals, 127-128
  program structure, 126-127
 for applied developmental psychology, 13, 15
  accreditation of, 67, 69
  challenges for, 48-49
  development of, 46
  Fordham University
   accreditation, 69-70
   application strategies, 60
   curriculum, 57-58
   ethics and conduct training, 60-61
   field experience
    assistantships and internships, 63-64
    practicum, 62-63
   licensure, 69-70
   overview of, 55-56
   program development, 56-57
   research methodology training, 58-59
   student participation rates, 57

290 Subject Index

historical origins, 46
multidisciplinary approach, 56
recommendations for reforming,
  48–49
research and application utilization, methods to determine,
  71
for applied developmental science field experiences, see Field experiences
funding of, 42
growth of, 42
Institute for Children, Youth, and Families, at Michigan State University
  campus context of
    changes in campus culture,
      172, 175–176
    integration of applied developmental science, 173–174
    multidisciplinary emphasis of faculty, 172–174
    research-outreach theory and methodology, 174–175
  community involvement
    beneficial effects, 179–180
    collaborative projects, 177–178
    description of, 176
    knowledge and technical assistance dissemination,
      180–181
  mission statement of, 169–170
  outreach scholarship, 170–171
integrative approaches, 33–34, 164–166
methods to enhance, 32–34
National Conference on Graduate Education, conference proceedings
  curriculum development, 7–8
  determining framework, 6–7
  field experiences, 8
  training goals, 7
  recommendations for reforming,
    47–48

reorganization of training, 164–165
socio-cultural approach
  advantages of, 190
  conceptions of culture, 196–198
  cultural labeling, 201–202
  cultural meanings, 203–204
  culture and ethnicity, relationship between, 197–198
  diversity, 194–195
  importance of, 195
  integration of, into educational program, 205
  minorities, 201–202
  objectives of, 200–201
  practical definition of, 195–196
  preconceptions, 203
  prototypic program
    coursework, 208–209
    field work, 210
    importance of intervention,
      216
    multicultural discourse, 210–214, 213
    role of faculty, 205–208
    supervisory experiences, 214
    teacher recruitment, 212–213
  rationale for, 191–192
  reasons for omission, 193–194
historical origins of, 41–42
Grant foundation, see William T. Grant Foundation

H

Hatch Experiment Station Act, 25, 168
HDFS, see Human Development and Family Studies
Hispanic Research Center, utilization of, for applied developmental psychology field training, 64
Home economics, historical origins of,
  16–17, 25–26, 169
HRC, see Hispanic Research Center
HSI, see Human Sciences Institute
Human development
  effect of culture on, 191–192, 197–198
  lifespan approach, 5, 56, 166

Subject Index   291

Human Development and Family Studies, at Penn State University, applied developmental program for adult development and aging
 curriculum
  adult development and aging requirements, 153
  degree requirements, 152–153
  intervention research requirements, 153–154
  postgraduate requirements, 154
 description of, 144
 faculty of, 144
 field experiences
  function of, 154
  internships, 155
 future progress, 157–158
 planning procedures
  individual, 151–152
  institutional, 149–150
 premises of
  regarding adult development and aging, 147–148
  regarding graduate education, 146–147
Human ecology programs
 and applied developmental science, 33
 colleges of, see Colleges of Human Ecology
 development of, 26, 169
Human sciences
 applied developmental psychology, see Applied developmental psychology
 applied developmental science, see Applied developmental science
Human Sciences Institute
 characteristics of, 38
 funding of, 39
 implementation of, 39
 strengths of, 37–38
 structure of, 38

I

ICYF, see Institute for Children, Youth, and Families

Institute for Children, Youth, and Families, at Michigan State University
 campus context of
  changes in campus culture, 172, 175–176
  integration of applied developmental science, 173–174
  multidisciplinary emphasis of faculty, 172–174
  research-outreach theory and methodology, 174–175
 community involvement
  beneficial effects, 179–180
  collaborative projects, 177–178
  description of, 176
  knowledge and technical assistance dissemination, 180–181
 mission statement of, 169–170
 outreach scholarship, 170–171
Interdisciplinary emphasis, for unit creation, in applied developmental science programs
 academic reward system, 267–268
 advantages and disadvantages, 257–258
 chain of authority, 258
 criteria and evaluation, 259–260
 definition, 254
 horizontal and vertical contributions, 266
 multi- vs. inter- vs. transdisciplinary units, 266
 policy studies, 268–269
 projection promotion concerns, 266–267
Internships, see also Field experiences
 for applied child development program, at Eliot-Pearson Department of Child Study, 135–136
 for applied developmental psychology programs, 63–64, 69
 for clinical child psychology and applied developmental science, comparisons, 114
 effect of accreditation on, 68–69

292 Subject Index

Ohio State University clinical child psychology program, 103–106
for pediatric psychology training, 82–84
questions regarding necessity of, 231–232
Iowa Child Welfare Research Station, 42–43

K
Kansas State University
founding of, 24–25
School of Family Studies and Human Services
disciplines studied at, 30
founding of, 26
objectives of, 27–28

L
Lake Placid Conferences
description of, 16
principles of, 26
topics discussed at, 29–30
Land-grant universities
federal acts, 168–169
Morrill Act, 24, 168
historical origins of, 17, 168
mandated teachings of, 17
principles of, 168
Language comprehension, 193–194
Laura Spelman Rockefeller Memorial Fund
dissolution of, 44
establishment of, 42
purpose of, 42
Leadership, role in university–agency collaboration, 249–250
Learning theory, child psychology and, 92
Licensure
advantages of, 69–70
in applied developmental psychology programs, 15–16
description of, 69–70
Lifespan approach, to applied developmental science, 5, 56, 146

LSRM, see Laura Spelman Rockefeller Memorial Fund

M
Michigan State University, Institute for Children, Youth, and Families
campus context of
changes in campus culture, 172, 175–176
integration of applied developmental science, 173–174
multidisciplinary emphasis of faculty, 172–174
research-outreach theory and methodology, 174–175
community involvement
beneficial effects, 179–180
collaborative projects, 177–178
description of, 176
knowledge and technical assistance dissemination, 180–181
mission statement of, 169–170
outreach scholarship, 170–171
Morrill Act, provisions of, 24–25, 168
Multidisciplinary emphasis
in applied child development, 132–133
in applied developmental psychology graduate programs, 60
at Eliot-Pearson Department of Child Study, 123–125, 132–133
of faculty, at Institute for Children, Youth, and Families, 172–174, 183
of field experiences, 225–226

N
National Conference on Graduate Education in the Applications of Developmental Science Across the Lifespan, conference proceedings
curriculum development, 7–8, 54, 215
determining framework, 6–7

Subject Index 293

field experiences, 8, 135, 215, 221, 229-230
objectives of, 54
training goals, 7
National Institute of Mental Health, 46

O

Ohio State University, clinical child psychology program
accreditation, 106-107
curriculum
didactic courses, 99-102, 100t
professional socialization, 103
research training, 102-103
establishment of, 96
field experience
infant stimulation program, 106
internships, 103-106
practicum experience, 103-106
goals of, 98
philosophy of, 96-98
planning procedures and structures, 98-99
Outreach, community. see Community outreach
Outreach scholarship, at Institute for Children, Youth, and Families
campus context of
changes in campus culture, 172, 175-176
integration of applied developmental science, 173-174
multidisciplinary emphasis of faculty, 172-174
research-outreach theory and methodology, 174-175
community involvement
beneficial effects, 179-180
collaborative projects, 177-178
description of, 176
goals of, 182-183
knowledge and technical assistance dissemination, 180-181
definition of, 170
development, 169-170
integration of research theory and methodology, 174-175
multidisciplinary approach, 170-171

P

Pediatric psychology
and applied development science
community systems model, 86-88
description of, 75-76
field experience, 82-84
research experience, 84-86
training programs
models, 80-81
practicum experience, 82
preparation, 81-82
description of, 75
impediments to, 79
origins of, 76-77
research increases in, 78
Pediatrics
origins of, 76-77
training programs, 77-78
Penn State University, Human Development and Family Studies Department, gerontology program
curriculum
adult development and aging requirements, 153
degree requirements, 152-153
intervention research requirements, 153-154
postgraduate requirements, 154
description of, 144
faculty of, 144
field experiences
function of, 154
internships, 155
planning procedures
doctoral and postdoctoral requirements, 151-152
individual, 151-152
institutional, 149-150
premises of
regarding adult development and aging, 147-148
regarding graduate education, 146-147

research programs, 144–145
structure and goals of, 148–149
Practicum experience
for applied developmental psychology program, at Fordham University
components of, 63–64
description of, 63
field experiences and, comparison, 230–231
and integration of developmental science and child psychology, 108–109
for pediatric psychology training programs, 82
at Ohio State University, 103–106
Psychology
applied developmental, see Applied developmental psychology
clinical child, see Clinical child psychology
professional, accreditation of, 65–66
Psychopathology, developmental
establishment of, 94
and normal development, comparison, 97
origins of, 97
Psychotherapy, applied developmental psychology and, 71

R
Religious beliefs, effect on human development, 191–192
Research–Outreach Methodology Program, 175
Research programs, see also Field experiences
community and, collaborations between
advantages of, 238
barriers to
attitudes of the involved parties, 239–240
purpose, 240–241
regulations, 242–243

resources, 243–244
stakeholders, 241–242
description of, 237–238
guidelines for success
attitudes of the involved parties, 245–246
common mission, 248
communication, 248
defining partnerships, 247–248
leadership, 249–250
liaison participation, 247
proactive interaction, 248–249
progress monitoring, 250
project selection, 246–247
requirements of, 238
field experiences and, relationship between, 43–44, 232
methodology
for applied developmental psychology, 58–59
for faculty, at Eliot-Pearson Department of Child Study, 129
for pediatric psychology training, 84–86
at Ohio State University, 102–103
and theory, integration of, 174–175
socio-cultural effects on, 194–195
Rockefeller, Laura Spelman Memorial Fund, see Laura Spelman Rockefeller Memorial Fund
ROM Program, see Research–Outreach Methodology Program

S
Scholarship of integration, 33
Scholarship of teaching, 33
School of Family Studies and Human Services, at Kansas State University
disciplines studied at, 30
faculty organization, 30–31
founding of, 26
objectives of, 27–28

Subject Index   295

Schools, see Universities
Seminar training, for pediatric psychology, 84
Shared meaning, 211
Smith-Lever Act, 168–169
Society for Research in Child Development
  founding of, 44
  principles of, 44
  research goals, 45
Socio-cultural approach, to applied development science education program
  advantages of, 190
  conceptions of culture, 196–198
  cultural labeling, 201–202
  cultural meanings, 203–204
  culture and ethnicity, relationship between, 197–198
  diversity, 194–195
  importance of, 195
  integration of, into educational program, 205
  minorities, 201–202
  objectives of, 200–201
  practical definition of, 195–196
  preconceptions, 203
  prototypic program
    coursework, 208–209
    field work, 210
    importance of intervention, 216
    multicultural discourse, 210–214, 213
    role of faculty, 205–208
    supervisory experiences, 214
    teacher recruitment, 212–213
  rationale for, 191–192
  reasons for omission, 193–194
SRCD. see Society for Research in Child Development

T
Teachers, see Faculty
Training, see Education, graduate
Tufts University, Eliot-Pearson Department of Child Study, see Eliot-

Pearson Department of Child Study

U
Universities, see also Graduate education; specific university
  community and, collaboration between, 9–10
  advantages of, 238
  barriers to
    attitudes of the involved parties, 239–240
    purpose, 240–241
    regulations, 242–243
    resources, 243–244
    stakeholders, 241–242
  description of, 237–238
  guidelines for success
    attitudes of the involved parties, 245–246
    common mission, 248
    communication, 248
    defining partnerships, 247–248
    leadership, 249–250
    liaison participation, 247
    proactive interaction, 248–249
    progress monitoring, 250
    project selection, 246–247
  requirements of, 238
  land-grant
    federal acts, 168–169
    Morrill Act, 24, 168
    historical origins of, 17, 168
    mandated teachings of, 17
    principles of, 168
  vs. independent agencies, for unit creation in applied developmental science
    advisory boards, 260
    chain of authority, 257–258
    criteria and evaluation, 259–260
    funding, 261–262
    overview, 256–257
    role of students, 261

W

Westchester Institute of Human Development, utilization of, for applied developmental psychology field training, 63–64
WIHD, see Westchester Institute of Human Development

William T. Grant Foundation
 founding of, 45
 objectives of, 45
 purpose of, 44
"Woman's Course," 25